Understanding Web

Sam Whimster

Routledge
Taylor & Francis Group

LONDON AND NEW YORK

First published 2007
by Routledge
2 Park Square, Milton Park, Abingdon, Oxon OX14 4RN

Simultaneously published in the USA and Canada
by Routledge
270 Madison Avenue, New York, NY 10016

*Routledge is an imprint of the Taylor & Francis Group,
an informa business*

© 2007 Sam Whimster

Typeset in Sabon by
Prepress Projects Ltd
Printed and bound in Great Britain by
The Cromwell Press, Trowbridge, Wiltshire

British Library Cataloguing in Publication Data
A catalogue record for this book is available from the British Library

Library of Congress Cataloging in Publication Data
A catalog record for this book has been requested

ISBN10: 0-415-37076-0 (pbk)
ISBN10: 0-415-37075-2 (hbk)
ISBN10: 0-203-03056-7 (ebk)

ISBN13: 978-0-415-37076-9 (pbk)
ISBN13: 978-0-415-37075-2 (hbk)
ISBN13: 978-0-203-03056-1 (ebk)

[T]he rational world can be considered as a great, immortal individual which ceaselessly produces that which is necessary and thereby comes to control the accidental.

Goethe (letter from Dornburg, July 1828)

Isn't that splendid, such a historical chain of arguments in which each part is remorselessly pieced together without any gaps, where, as in this case, 'the writer' makes himself totally invisible but nevertheless everything that is there is involuntarily animated by the heartbeat of a grand personality.

Mina Tobler on reading *The Protestant Ethic*
(letter to her mother, October 1912)

Contents

Figures

Acknowledgements

As in the *Essential Weber*, much of the scholarship and debate in this book draws on the lively state of the international network of Weber studies. Earlier versions of Chapters 2 and 6 have appeared, respectively, in *Max Webers 'Grundbegriffe'*, edited by Klaus Lichtblau, and *Das Faszinosum Max Weber*, edited by Karl-Ludwig Ay and Knut Borchardt; my thanks to the editors of these collections for inviting me to their conferences – in Bielefeld and Munich – and for permission to use the chapters in this book. A number of people have been especially helpful in reading and discussing parts of the manuscript, suggesting approaches, offering information and guiding me away from error. The failings that remain are, of course, of my own making. My thanks are due to Robert Bellah, John Breuilly, Hinnerk Bruhns, Hans Henrik Bruun, Brian Hall, Edith Hanke, Austin Harrington, Scott Lash, Raymond Lee, Hartmut Lehmann, Mohammad Nafissi, Kari Palonen, Guenther Roth, Yolanda Ruano, Keith Tribe and Stephen Turner. I must thank Gerhard Boomgaarden and his team at Routledge for their understanding and nudging me, and the book, towards successful completion.

Abbreviations

Archiv   *Archiv für Sozialwissenschaft und Sozialpolitik.*
AS   *Agrarian Sociology of Ancient Civilisations*, edited and trans-
            lated by R.I. Franks, London, New Left Books, 1976.
Cat   'Some Categories of Interpretive Sociology', translated by
            E. Graber, *The Sociological Quarterly*, 22, pp. 151–80, 1981.
EEWR   Economic Ethics of the World Religions.
EOPS   Economy and the Orders and Powers of Society. This was the
            title in the Outline Plan of 1914 for the first draft of what even-
            tually was published as Part Two of *Economy and Society*.
ES   *Economy and Society: An Outline of Interpretive Sociology*,
            edited by G. Roth and C. Wittich, New York, Bedminster Press,
            1968.
EW   *Essential Weber*, edited by Sam Whimster, London, Routledge,
            2004.
FMW   *From Max Weber*, edited and translated by H.H. Gerth and
            C.W. Mills, London, Routledge & Kegan Paul, 1947.
GARS   *Gesammelte Aufsätze zur Religionssoziologie*, 3 vols, Tübin-
            gen, J.C.B. Mohr (Paul Siebeck), 1920–1.
GAWL   *Gesammelte Aufsätze zur Wissenschaftslehre*, 4th edn, edited by
            J. Winckelmann, Tübingen: J.C.B. Mohr (Paul Siebeck), 1973.
MWG   Max Weber Gesamtausgabe, edited by H. Baier, M.R. Lepsius,
            W.J. Mommsen and J. Winckelmann, Tübingen: J.C.B. Mohr
            (Paul Siebeck), 1984–.
PE Debate   *The Protestant Ethic Debate*, edited by D. Chalcraft and A.
            Harrington, translated by A. Harrington and M. Shields, Liv-
            erpool, Liverpool University Press, 2001.
PESC   *The Protestant Ethic and the Spirit of Capitalism*, translated by
            T. Parsons, London, Allen & Unwin, 1930.
SocRel   *The Sociology of Religion*, translated by E. Fischoff, London,
            Methuen, 1965.

Introduction

In an article published in 1974, the scholar Benjamin Nelson asked some very direct and simple questions of Max Weber's work. He called for an adequate appreciation of Weber's central intentions and horizons over the years of his life. He noted that, as yet, there was no critical edition of the Protestant ethic essays that would allow us 'to see how the horizons of Weber's thinking shifted with the shifts of contexts demanded of him by his various sorts of critics'. There was no hope, he said, of a convincing and comprehensive interpretation of his life's work 'without a synoptical and synchronic reading of his *Economy and Society*, his *Collected Essays in the Sociology of Religion* and the stratum of discussions illustrated in the "Author's Introduction"'. Nelson correctly perceived that the last named article was a dense sedimentation of a lifetime's knowledge and could provide 'a master clue' to Weber's aims.[1]

What excited Nelson in such an inquiry was the uncovering of the full measure of what he called a 'differential historical sociology of sociocultural process' that would clarify civilizational configurations. Nelson observed that complex societies in the world were undergoing extraordinary change in respect of their central institutions, schemes of orientation and technologies and that Weber's lead had to be followed.

He called attention to 'the different variable mixes of "religions" and "worlds", organizational and regulative juridical structures, communal as well as associational living patterns, collective as well as individual identifications and identities'. This was the agenda of a future sociology and one that would 'contribute to the necessary progress towards our common goals'.[2]

He speculated that there 'is strong reason to believe that if Weber had lived beyond 1920, he would very probably have gone forward to recast the argument and emphasis of *The Protestant Ethic*'. He would have given greater prominence 'to the distinctive origins and features of the modern "rational" Occidental science and technology'. There could be no understanding of 'the most fateful force of our Western modern life, *capitalism*, without seeing it against the background of the historical rationalizations of science and sensibility in all the spheres of thought and action'.

Culture, religion, capitalism and power are the grand themes of Weber's writings. Nelson flags their importance yet registers the need for a more exact location of these themes within the overall body of his work. Writing in 2006 and commenting on the renewed interest in Weberian sociology in France, Catherine Colliot-Thélène notes 'the gap left in the theoretical field by the retreat of Marxism and evaporation ("essoufflement") of the structuralist paradigm' and, accompanying this, a turn to policy expertise in place of critical reflection. This vacuum has occurred, she writes, at a time when the social and political effects of religion are meeting a renewed interest.[3] This reinforces Benjamin Nelson's earlier demand for a sociology that can analyse the civilizational dynamics of modernity in their interrelated complexity.

This book argues that the confidence in Weber is well placed but can only be justified by a far closer engagement in the full dimensionality of Weber's disciplinary range and how his ideas and interests developed over time. Nelson was correct in his speculation that the 'Author's Introduction' of 1920 placed a different emphasis – on science and technology in the west – as a wider basis for explaining the emergence of modern capitalism, compared with the more restricted arguments put forward in *The Protestant Ethic and the 'Spirit' of Capitalism* (PESC). The stark importance of this issue can easily be demonstrated. The 'Author's Introduction' highlighted the pervasive importance of rationalism *throughout* occidental history. The Protestant ethic studies of 1904–5 laid great stress on a form of rationalism (ascetic life conduct) that was part of and followed on from the European Reformation of western Christianity. How do we weigh the larger narrative in relation to the 'case study' of Puritanism? A great deal turns on the kinds of answer that are given to the question. Puritanism is fairly restricted in its scope as a form of rationalism, for it is built on a blinkered view of the world in search of divine assurance. Western rationalism, and especially the emphasis Nelson placed on science, can with greater justification claim wider validity.

There is not much evidence that Weber would have recast his argument in relation to the Protestant ethic study, although equally there is considerable scholarly evidence that the original thesis had drifted far from its original moorings – even if Weber was not prepared to admit this. This indicates that a close engagement with Weber's writings will have to be a critical one: one that does not accept his own estimates and defences, and one prepared to advance the issues beyond where he left them.

Looking at modern scholarship, do we have the synoptic and synchronic account of Weber's writings that Nelson called for? Not quite. The Max Weber Gesamtausgabe have published two-thirds of Weber's writings in a critical historical edition. Under its rules, the dating, origins and contextual background of each of the texts has to be made known. But some important texts have no clear origination or dating. For example, the so-called 'older part' of *Economy and Society* consists of texts found in unmarked brown envelopes after Weber died. He probably had no intention of publishing them in the state they were left. Do we have a synoptic, that is an overall, view of the texts? My own view is that we do not, and this relates only in part to the difficulty in dating the texts. Commentators on Max Weber have usually tried to come up with an overall interpretation of Weber's many and varied writings; rationalization has often been chosen as *the* integrating theme. Wolfgang Schluchter has done more than anyone to show how Weber's ideas developed, how they reoccur in more than one project and how they form a more or less systematic unity.[4] In *The Essential Weber*, I argued that my selection had a degree of coherence, not least because Weber can be seen to cross-reference the various departments of his work. *Economy and Society* and the 'Economic Ethics of the World Religions' (which forms the major part of the Collected Essays in the Sociology of Religion) pursue different but complementary paths.

But a selection of the most important academic texts is not the same as a synoptic and synchronic account, of Nelson's bidding. PESC had always struck me as a work of eruptive genius, difficult entirely to coordinate within the rest of Weber's writings. In *The Essential Weber*, I selected only part of its final chapter, and I preferred to rely in my commentary on a later formulation (from 1915) in which Weber integrates the Protestant ethic thesis into a comparison with Confucianism. My selection also avoided the problem of what Lawrence Scaff has termed 'Weber before Weberian sociology', by which he meant the writings of the 1890s prior to PESC.[5] Weber wrote a small mountain of studies in the 1890s, and mainstream social science has more or less ignored it. This situation has been partly rectified by recent scholarship, not least the publication of most of his works from the 1890s by the Max Weber Gesamtausgabe. But in many ways, the output of the 1890s, mostly in national-economy, raises the question of why he switched to studying Protestantism. Contrary to some commentators, Weber did not move into this field in order to develop the sociology of religion. He disliked sociology in its then current form, and he only developed his own version of it around 1910 to handle issues in comparative studies of religion and economy. Nor is it wholly convincing to argue that PESC was a response to the Marxist, materialist philosophy of history. The situation in national-economy, a broad-ranging discipline at the time, was more complex than this.

We now know far more about Max Weber's life. A number of scholars have gained access to the archives and read large chunks of his correspondence, and the Max Weber Gesamtausgabe have published his letters for the period 1906–14.[6] The picture that is emerging is of a very complex and contradictory personality. He had some sort of affectual disorder in which periods of high productivity were followed by actual depression or exhaustion. He tried to compensate for these affectual disorders through medication, using quite large amounts of opiate-based drugs to calm his excitability. He developed a pattern of working hard through the autumn and winter and then convalescing at Easter and during the summer months. He was a strongly reactive person, easily provoked by a keen sense of competition as to what fellow academics were producing. He was part of a golden era in the social, cultural and historical sciences, feeding off and closely connected with major figures such as Werner Sombart, Ernst Troeltsch, Georg Simmel, Alfred Weber, Ferdinand Tönnies, the Austrian economists, as well as the leading historians in ancient, medieval and modern history. He had a large and sensitive ego, and this impacted upon his work in ways that have proved quite tricky for subsequent interpreters of his work. Although he was hugely original, he tended not to indicate how his work related to previous work in the field, and it is only by paying close attention to his footnotes and sources that a picture of the ongoing debates can be reached. He never admitted to weaknesses in what were, after all, very bold hypotheses and theory construction, and he would often accuse his critics, somewhat pettily, of misunderstanding what he had written. How works originated in his mind, and what he thought might be their potential weak points, can only be surmised.

We know from the memoirs of contemporaries that Weber had a terrifying ability to talk *ex tempore* on seemingly any subject with great authority and knowledge.[7] He was not a superman. He did take notes, and he was dependent, like any student, on libraries and interlibrary loan. But the first drafts of *Economy and Society* were written straight out at high speed, so fired was Weber at the time by his new ideas and project. It is not unreasonable to see him as a virtuoso who could devise an original theme and then play with it at will. PESC appeared in journal form in 1904–5. It reappeared threaded into his comparative sociology of religion sometime around 1912. Also at that time, it was merged into a more conventional account of religious and political history in a large chapter on political and hierocratic rule. It resurfaced again in an almost symmetrical comparison (of differences) with Confucianism in 1915. And, as Nelson notes, it was overlaid in the 'Author's Introduction' of 1920 by the larger theme of rationalism.

We have to consider the possibility that the sort of careful synoptic and synchronic picture that Nelson was calling for is ruled out by the nature of Weber's intellectual personality. Ernst Troeltsch, who knew Weber as well as anybody, was asked in October 1917 to provide a report on Weber for the University of Bonn – with a view to a possible appointment there. He said Weber was presently concentrating on sociology but could with great ease pick up again as a professor in national-economy. He also said that Weber had two minds: one absolutist that always stood up for justice and fairness on an almost instinctual basis; the other was relativist, able to reduce any action, thought or decision to its sociological reality and underlying interest. The latter aspect was highly sharp and cynical. 'To me, by the way,' Troeltsch wrote, 'he is in many ways deeply problematic and hard to fathom. I don't know what his ultimate intellectual motives are.'[8] Hence, Weber cannot be pinned down with complete precision. He could pursue two projects at the same time, and he was not beyond telling his publisher that his latest interest would not be a distraction from some other previously agreed contract and deadline. At the least, we need a certain wariness in forming our view of Weber's output and should not impose on it a too schoolmasterly order. He was a virtuoso with his materials and ideas: he could state a theme, invert it, introduce another tune alongside it and perhaps even become bored with it. Rainer Lepsius has noted that, in the last months of his life (before he was struck down by pneumonia), Weber was going to write on culture, Tolstoy and music – a switch of mind and of focus – after he had completed *Economy and Society* and the studies of the economic ethics of the world religions.[9]

I have taken some care in this book to register the particular characteristics of the format in which Weber wrote. He used a variety of formats – the essay, the research survey and research report, encyclopaedia entries, scholarly dissertation, the journal article and the academic public lecture. Weber rarely used the book form – only his doctoral and habilitation theses and one agrarian survey appeared as books. He preferred the long essay to the book form, and it needs to be noted that many of Weber's 'books' are in fact collections of his essays. Some of the essays were intended by Weber to form a collective entity, for example 'The Economic Ethics of the World Religions'; other collections of his writings were put together after his death by Marianne Weber. Just to emphasize this point: only one English translation of a Weber text can be taken to be the equivalent of a book published by Weber in his lifetime – his doctoral thesis.[10] *The Protestant Ethic and the 'Spirit' of Capitalism* is an essay; *Economy and Society* is a collection of manuscripts and corrected proofs brought together after his death.

Unities, complementarities and sequencing can be drawn, but I have not tried to force these upon his writings. To take the largest of his questions: what were the causal origins of modern occidental capitalism? His career can be seen as continuously developing the question and creating new methodologies and new studies to answer it. We may have to accept that the question is unanswerable in a way that would meet agreed academic criteria of causal proof. At this point, the question becomes *how* does modernity develop in the west and *how* have similar religious-based trajectories of life conduct developed in other civilizations. The 'how' question is just as significant and valid as the exact specification of causal origins. My sense of Weber's career is that he started out with a unique explanation (in Puritan asceticism) for the origins of modern capitalism, but this modulated into how occidental modernity was distinctive from other civilizations. Weber found this as intensely interesting and absorbing as his original starting point. This sense provides a trajectory to this book, but one that is not adhered to strictly. It is not assumed that Weber planned his scholarly career according to such a trajectory – quite the contrary. It is always a puzzle to figure out how Weber proceeded from one project to another. But now that there is sufficient information available about the dating and origins of these projects, it is possible to chart his movements along, around and across the line of this trajectory.

Chapter 1 examines Weber's career in national-economy in the 1890s.

Weber cannot be termed a sociologist in this period, but he was undertaking social survey research on contemporary agrarian conditions, which had a sociological dimension. There is a debate as to whether in this period Weber was more structuralist in his account of the determination of market forces and political power over the lives of individuals and social groups. Weber is shown to express quite forcibly the role of ideas and psychological motivation in the behaviour of people in the face of determining forces of social and economic structure. Even though Weber has yet to develop an explicit sociology, the distinctive Weberian approach to structure and action is already evident. Weber's lecture course in theoretical national-economy from 1898 is outlined. It can be established that he had both a good grasp of the historical development of capitalism as well as a theoretical understanding of capitalist exchange economies in terms of marginal utility. Also evident is a predilection to insert a cultural interface into the analysis of economic activity.

Chapter 2 locates some of the major debates over capitalism that were being conducted in national-economy. Particular attention is given to Werner Sombart's and Georg Simmel's analysis of the origins of modern capitalism as the antecedents to Weber's own Protestant ethic studies. Weber provided a culturally specific explanation of one section of the historical argument on the origins of modern capitalism. The wider argument was laid out in Sombart's very large book *Der moderne Kapitalismus*. This in its turn was, in part, a response to Simmel's *Philosophy of Money*, which treated the question of origins in a philosophical mode. First Sombart and then Weber supplied causal explanations for a phenomenon that remained speculative in Simmel's treatment. Weber's Protestant ethic 'essay' was a limited intervention in a wider debate but, ever since its publication, it has been regarded as constitutive of the debate on the origins of modern capitalism. PESC provided an inspired interpretation of psychological motivation of an economically significant religious group. How economically significant that group was is not exactly specified by Weber, but the success of the essay made it a continuous topic of debate, for both Weber and his critics. Simmel's contributions to a psychological theory of action are discussed, as is Sombart's use of something very similar in his theorization of economic activity. Weber's PESC remains within the same psychological framework. It would be some years before a version of social action was put forward by Weber (in 1913) – and then as a solution to issues raised by his comparative studies in religion and economic action.

Chapter 3 offers a commentary on PESC, which concentrates on what Weber was actually doing in that study rather than what Weber says he was doing. Although it was a study that is formulated with regard to debates in national-economy over the origins of modern capitalism, it is written in a literary mode. It is not only a work of original scholarship and genius, but it also has imaginative and literary properties that lift it entirely out of the mode of social science. Weber employed not only historical and philological

scholarship; he used literary techniques, rhetoric and – above all – hermeneutics to make the essay such a success. It is against these last standards that
it needs to be assessed.

Chapter 4 notes what is effectively his retreat to methodology in the
face of his own creativity. The scholasticism of Rickert's methodology is
favoured over the expansiveness of Dilthey's project for the human sciences.
I argue that PESC is more compatible with Dilthey's ambitions than with
Rickert's prescriptive methodology. Nevertheless, Weber fashions his own
methodological solutions for the cultural and human sciences in his 1904 essay on 'Objectivity'. This essay served as a way forward in the methodological battles of the day for the relaunched *Archiv für Sozialwissenschaft und
Sozialpolitik*. It also acted as a methodological supplement to PESC, but in a
number of respects that work had outstripped all methodological protocols.
It attracted criticism from the outset, as it has done throughout the twentieth
century. In his replies to his critics, the issue of multiple causation proved
especially difficult, with Weber being heavily reliant on the 'elective affinity'
between ideal and material causes.

Chapters 5 and 6 examine the huge expansion of Weber's writings into
comparative and systematic work on the economy in relation to the special
sociologies of religion, law, power, the formation of communal groups and
the formation of associative groups. Weber took on the editorial responsibility for the encyclopaedic and multivolume *Outline of Social Economics* (*Grundriss der Sozialökonomik*). And in the same period, broadly dated
1910 to August 1914, Weber completed the first drafts of economic ethics
influenced by Confucianism, Taoism, Hinduism, Buddhism and Judaism. To
date, nine separate volumes of the Max Weber Gesamtausgabe cover this
period and, in addition, the letter volumes (*Briefe*) chart Weber's volumi-
nous and intricate correspondence with his publisher and fellow academics.
The painstaking and detailed scholarship of the Gesamtausgabe editors has
revealed the precise contours of Weber's manifold studies. Chapters 5 and
6 undertake a mapping of those contours and suggest that more than one
map is required. Multiple causation in relation to developmental history is a
continuous concern, addressed by more than one strategy. Weber's own interpretative sociology makes its first appearance in this period, and its terminology feeds into the substantive studies and provides Weber with a reliable
method when working with such a broad range of materials. The move into
sociology was not wholly successful, and its role is a topic of a significant
scholarly dispute. Weber's sociology of religion stands at the centre of this
period. Hans Kippenberg's scholarship and editing of the relevant MWG
volume (*Religiöse Gemeinschaften*) demonstrates just how immersed Weber
was in the scientific study of religion, including the latest ethnographic field
studies. I express the view that Weber's sociology of religion is both brilliant and hesitant. Even now, the problems Weber was addressing remain
unresolved.

Chapter 7 goes outside Weber in order to revisit the issues of multiple causation that are inherent in any account that seeks to explain developmental sequences at the level of society and civilization. I reformulate the Protestant ethic thesis in terms of Harold Innis' work on the modalities of communication and their impact on rulership and control. I also consider recent work by S.N. Eisenstadt and others on multiple modernities. I contrast this with Weber's work as construed as an argument of the singularity of modernity. The sobering conclusion to be drawn from this is that, even though Weber had widened the terms of his argument on the origins of western (or as he called it, occidental) modernity, the research framework can be further enlarged. The hopes for a complete multifactorial analysis of the rise of the west appear unlikely to succeed.

Chapter 8 takes up Weber's special sociology of power and rulership. Weber's general theory of power is three-dimensional (economic, political and social status), and I compare this with recent treatments by Gianfranco Poggi and Michael Mann. Using the informative scholarship provided by Edith Hanke in the Max Weber Gesamtausgabe volume (*Herrschaftssoziologie*), I track the changes from the first draft of Weber's political sociology to its final formulation in *Economy and Society*. This allows the emergent pattern of Weber's sociology to be followed, and his choking back of developmental history in favour of classificatory types. In the final section, I ask whether political scientists should be taking more note of Weber's analysis of leadership democracy ('Führer-Demokratie') in a contemporary world where presidents and prime ministers use the skills of rhetoric and demagoguery, aided by press offices and the media, to extend their power over the thick structures of democratic culture. Weber had already noted this tendency, and he took power and its control to be a constant in all rulerships, including constitutional democracies.

Chapter 9 examines Weber's long second chapter of *Economy and Society*, 'The Basic Sociological Types of Economising'. This represents the turning of the full circle of Weber's ambitions, first as a national-economist in the 1890s and, finally, as a sociologist driving forwards the project of social economics. Significantly, in 1920, his contract at the University in Munich made mention of him as a sociologist as well as a national-economist.[11] The function of sociology, whose operation is laid out in great clarity in Chapter 1 of *Economy and Society*, is to underwrite all the special fields of interest that had occupied his intellectual career: the economy, culture and religion, power and rulership, law, the orders of society, the formation of communal groups and associative groups and, alongside these, the developmental dynamics of societies and civilizations.

A coda to Chapter 9 asks whether there is a Weber paradigm. As a sociologist, probably not, because Weber's overall approach sought a multidisciplinarity in trying to formulate the grand themes of historical development. In terms of his approach to academic knowledge in the social sciences, there is something very distinctive to Weber. He insisted, with the suitable humility of a genius, on the transience of social scientific knowledge, where fifty years counts as a long time. There was, for Weber, no march of history, only the endless flux and flow of social reality that could never be comprehended in its entirety. Time and viewpoints move on; knowledge immediately starts to date and its relevance fades. Weber, as Leo Strauss observed,[12] thought harder and deeper about modernity than anyone ever had before. Nobody in the future is likely to achieve such stature, for modernity is now practically taken for granted despite its manifest conflicts and problems. The Weber paradigm obligates us to intervene in the flux of social reality. By making a value connection of relevance, social scientists may effect that flux of which they are a part, even though they should work under the pitiless demands of 'objectivity'.

Is Weber still relevant, then, after a hundred years, as we pass the centenary of the publication of PESC? Are his concerns still our concerns? Modernity, sometimes referred to as progress, is on the way to becoming a global destiny. Its grand themes of rationalization, disenchantment, fragmentation of value spheres, life conduct, bureaucracy, power and legitimacy, stratification, charisma and the interplay of value and instrumental rationality still remain central stage – and in ways Weber would probably not have imagined. Benjamin Nelson was prescient in calling for a Weberian sociology capable of analysing the different mixes of 'worlds' and 'religion', changing forms of power and organisation, and new patterns of living and identity formation.

My approach in this book is not so much to pursue the grand themes, which have been well handled by other distinguished and eloquent interpretators – Karl Löwith, Reinhard Bendix, Guenther Roth, Julien Freund, Wolfgang Schluchter, Wilhelm Hennis, and Wolfgang J. Mommsen – as rather a close examination of the texts and their interrelation. In this, I sometimes fail to provide the synoptic, or characterizing, account, and I also resist the temptation to finish or round off Weber's theories for him. Imposing a systematic account on Weber's writings misses I think the very real difficulties he faced, difficulties inherent in his understanding of the project of social science. Likewise it can be a mistake to assume that Weber solved all the theoretical and methodological issues he posed in the pursuit of his grand, as well as his smaller scale, research problems. Weber was very proficient in analysing the claims of warring schools – of historicism, marginalism, materialism, monism, psychologism, the place of free will – and this is where we take our cues from him as a classic thinker. But he rarely saw the need to spell out his treatments of complex problems as a set of explicit methods. This applies both to his survey work and his 'Verstehende' work. Weber drew no great distinction between those two modes of doing social research, and he certainly would not have designated one as quantitative and the other as qualitative – each with their own battery of methods and issues.

Hence I am prepared to accept that Weber came up with brilliant solutions to research problems but without any fanfare of methodological reflection; likewise that there were difficulties he did not solve, or which he moved around trying different solutions. Also a close examination underlines the sheer diversity and range of social science problems and issues he engaged with. Interpretators quite rightly gloss the grand Weberian themes that are common to his various research issues, but Weber's involvement in the specifics of evidence, sources, theories, presentation of findings, and their implications should also be accorded its very large due. The world is complex and we aspire to conceptual order – these are two sides of the Weberian coin.

1 Weber before Weberian sociology, revisited

Lawrence Scaff, in a path-breaking article some twenty years ago, asked how Weber's works prior to the Protestant ethic studies of 1904–5 were to be classified.[1] The Protestant ethic studies belonged to an interpretative sociological approach; the works before that, from the 1890s, had the character of a *marxisant* political economy, dealing as they did with issues of class, power, and societal and economic change. I revisit this argument, bringing in more information about the decade of the 1890s, about which we now know far more. I shall also alter the terms of the argument. Weber was a national-economist in the 1890s, and this has to be investigated in some detail to find out what was distinctively Weberian in his approach, which was not a form of Marxist sociology by another name. I do not follow the usual consensus of opinion that the Protestant ethic studies belonged to sociology. The best description of them is descriptive psychology being applied to national-economy. And, finally, Weber did not become a sociologist until around 1910. Prior to that, he regarded sociology as suspect, whose overall approach was either positivist or organicist – both completely untenable positions for Weber. He fashioned a sociology to his own needs in pursuit of his universal historical comparative studies. Across all these phases of activity, there is a constant concern with the meanings, values and culture, an area that is one of the hardest parts of the social, historical and cultural sciences to handle proficiently.

At the start of the article, Scaff broaches a subject that goes to the heart of sociological theory, especially today. There appear to be two sociologies in Weber's work. One is structuralist and determinist and is often referred to as belonging to Weber's 'substantive' work: 'one in which status groups, social classes, patterns of domination, and material interests define the analytic core'.[2] Bryan Turner has portrayed this side of Weber's sociology as Marxist:

> ... that Weber's sociology anticipates much that has been central to
> the empirical and theoretical focus of modern Marxism. The analysis
> of the state, legal fetishism, the separation of ownership and control,

bureaucratic management, de-skilling, ethnic identity, professions and secularisations as crucial concerns of neo-Marxism are all pre-figured in Weber's analysis of rational capitalism.[3]

One initial comment on this is that these were straightforwardly Weberian themes rather than neo-Marxist ones. But Turner also makes for him the central point that Weber's sociology is deterministic in the sense that the individual's fate or destiny is decided irrespective of his or her intentions and ambitions. 'The social contexts which Weber studies have a logic or fate undermining the meaningful actions of individuals.'[4]

The 'other' sociology in Weber is the methodology of 'Verstehen', that sociologists have to understand the motivations and values and the context of meaning in which the individual is placed. Bryan Turner was writing at a time when a younger generation of sociologists interpreted social action theory as the theoretical underpinning of the emancipatory attempt to gain control of the world and one's own destiny. The cue to this was Alan Dawe's essay 'The Two Sociologies', which argued that the theme of control in sociology should not be seen as a thing external to the individual, belonging to an ideology of order and pertaining to the structures of economic and political power. Instead, control should belong to the autonomous, acting individual who was the real 'unit' around which sociology should be framed.[5] The high point of this movement was that part of Anthony Giddens' sociology which framed the semi-autonomous individual within the social world as a reflexive subject capable of understanding the world and contributing to the social world and, accordingly, being empowered.[6] Neo-Marxism registered the solidity of structures of power and saw Giddens' insistence on the plasticity of the social world as naïve. In respect of Weber, Turner objected to what he took to be the contradiction of a 'verstehende' sociology that privileged the social actor as autonomous and the doom-laden stress Weber also placed on the giganticism of modern, high capitalism (which was reaching its zenith in Weber's day). In France, as Catherine Colliot-Thélène notes, Raymond Aron and Julien Freund advanced Weber as a theorist of social action in opposition to the Marxist sociology of structures.[7] This was, and still is, a classic debate. Something of the same tensions, we will shortly see, entered into the young Weber, who belonged to an academic generation who pushed hard against the authoritarian political and social order imposed by an older generation of nation builders.

Turner's objections can also be framed in purely Weberian terminology without drawing on the language of neo-Marxism. In his book, *Max Weber and the Sociology of Culture*, Ralph Schroeder places the analysis of culture at the centre of Weber's concerns. Culture belongs to a macro level of analysis, and the individual faces culture as 'an inescapable fate', as the expression of ideas in religious beliefs or in western rationalism. Weber's analysis of culture is built around the concept of worldviews that have an inner logic and consistency of their own. Belief systems have a logic of change through differentiation, from the relative simplicity of magic to the complexity of religion. At the religious stage, the individual is subdivided into autonomous life orders (politics, religion, economy, art), and this differentiation into orders and value spheres continues into modernity where science, knowledge and technology form another autonomous realm. Each of these life orders, having their own system of values, contributes to the fragmentary nature of modernity. Ideas can change the course of history, but only as a force as a collective entity. Human beings may be cultural beings, but culture exists as a force beyond and outside the individual. Hence, what is required in its analysis is not Weber's methodological advice on interpretative sociology, but the use of his substantive high-level concepts such as worldviews, life spheres, ideas as switchmen, routinization, rationalization. Schroeder writes, 'although is has been suggested that Weber should be seen as a theorist of social action (Kalberg, 1985a: 895), Weber rarely uses these concepts or an action-oriented approach in his substantive writings'.[8]

There is an obvious problem here. It is not sociologists who might have 'suggested' the theory of social action, it was Weber who *insisted* upon it. He developed it as a methodology as he moved away from case study historically specific subjects into universal history. I see the chronology of the development of sociology by Weber somewhat differently from Scaff, but agree with his statement affirming the integral role of sociology with the 'substantive' studies. 'Far from establishing the "autonomy" of sociology, Weber's approach seems to be self-consciously embedded within a set of assumptions about the nature of history, society, and human understanding.'[9] Turning to Weber's writings in the 1890s, we encounter a national-economist dealing with issues of economic transformation (the industrialization of German society, the flight from the land into the cities and the decline of artisanal craft enterprises in favour of the large factory and mass production), of a changing distribution of power and social stratification, and Germany's claim to be a great power within the international order. These were real and pressing issues, and they could be treated through a 'realist' analysis of power and interests. Weber did not shy away from these issues; indeed, he had a rather uncontrolled tendency to spell out the issues, vociferously and uncompromisingly, to his readers and audiences. But at the same time, he stressed the role of values and ideas in the mighty processes under way, and it is in the writings of the 1890s that we see him grappling with causation as capable of handling both material and ideal causes. I provide methodological detail of these studies, because Weber's views on causation are still very much open to debate, as indeed is the issue itself. His activities as an academic researcher and as engaged social policy activist form an important strand in the prehistory of the Protestant ethic studies of 1904–5.

The agrarian question

The agrarian question was a massive social policy and political issue in Germany in the 1890s. German unification had been achieved in 1871, and it kick-started a process of rapid industrialization and urbanization – at a rate of change not dissimilar to that being experienced by China today. The young Weber (he was 28 at the time) was commissioned to conduct a study of a facet of this enormous transformation. In many provinces of the German Reich,[10] farm labourers were deserting the farms and their villages either to look for work in the new factories and towns or to emigrate to North America. The profitability of domestic farming had declined with the rise of Germany as an industrial, trading nation able to afford the import of cheaper foreign food, in particular wheat and cereals. Production of those staples had become far more economic in North America and Russia, and grain could be bought more cheaply on world markets than domestically. With the sharp drop in the price of grain (in Prussia, a ton of wheat priced at 232 marks and had fallen to 174 marks in 1890), farmers experienced a loss of profitability, and farmworkers saw a reduction in their living standards and wages.[11]

Weber was approached by Germany's leading social policy organization, the *Verein für Sozialpolitik*, to conduct a study of farming in the regions east of the Elbe (which have now become the territory of Poland and Russia). The *Verein für Sozialpolitik* was set up by Gustav Schmoller in the 1870s in order to monitor and investigate the social consequences of rapid industrialization and urbanization. German business, as well as the political class, was pretty much indifferent to the forces of dislocation unleashed by Germany's economic transformation. But early in the 1880s, the political class signalled their concerns, not least in face of the growth of a radical working-class political party, the Social Democrats. Schmoller was a leading national-economist and economic historian at the University of Berlin, and he was successful in forming links between policy scientists and economists and government on questions of social and economic policy. His policy association – he was its founder and leader – stood out against classical British political economy and its belief in the free market. The *Verein* was very much a 'third way' organization. It was against unregulated competition in the domestic and world economy, and it was against working-class movements that sought a socialist transformation in the conditions of their existence. Government in the German Reich was strong, conservative and not unafraid of regulating many aspects of society and its development from above.[12] Schmoller positioned the *Verein* as a source of evidence-based policy advice but with a bias towards paternalism. A conservative state would legislate for small improvements in living, social and legal conditions for the mass of the population.

The *Verein* itself was something of a top-down organization. In September 1890, its working committee under Schmoller had decided that three issues would be investigated: the condition of the agricultural worker in the German Empire; the question of migration from the countryside; and trade policy. Weber was allocated the provinces east of the Elbe for study – East and West Prussia, Pomerania, Posnia, Silesia, Brandenburg, Mecklenburg and the duchy of Lauenburg. A subcommittee of the *Verein* had designed two questionnaires. The aims of the survey ('Enquete') were to gather exact data on the forms of payment relationships and the developments in the social and cultural conditions of the agricultural worker. Over and beyond these goals there was a concern about the consequences of the loss of profitability of farming, debt and the shortage of farmworkers. The first questionnaire, which gathered quantitative data on prices, wages, crop areas, etc., was sent out in December 1891 to 3,180 landowners/farmers. The second, which asked for more descriptive reports, was sent out in February 1892 to 562 'key informants' ('Generalberichterstatter'). Weber started work on the analysis of the questionnaires in the middle of February 1892, and he was given six months to complete his report, ready in time for a debate at the general meeting of the *Verein für Sozialpolitik* that was to take place that same autumn.[13]

This was a massive empirical undertaking on Weber's part, and it resulted in an 800-page report. Weber received back 650 completed questionnaires from the farmowners in his regions. From these, he tabulated the data for each area within each region. More specifically, to give an idea just how detailed the research was, he carried out the following cross-tabulations: length of the working day for each season for male workers, their wives, the children and servants tabulated against each county ('Kreis') in a region; wages and payment in kind for each type of farm work (and the extent of each sort of farm work, e.g. wheat, root crops, cows, etc.) tabulated against county; income and yield for each sort of farm work against county; the proportionality of wages to payment in kind for each type of farmworker; annualized wages for farmworkers and their wives against county. Weber then had to collect data on seasonal migratory labour. Here, he tabulated the duration of seasonal work, its purpose on the farm, place of origin of the seasonal workers, their wages and costs, the daily wages of domestic workers and their destination as migrants off the land – all this tabulated against county. Finally, he provided a table of the annual costs of the independent farmworker (the 'Instmann') – cost of seed, housing, fuel, rent, consumption, payments to farmworkers, fodder for livestock, wages for domestic maids. Weber repeated the same tabulations for each of the eight provinces and their dozen or so counties, providing descriptive material for each category of data. Summaries were given for each province, and an overall summary was provided in the final chapter.

The *Verein für Sozialpolitik* would collect the reports from the other German provinces. The reports would be debated at the *Verein*'s annual meeting, and a series of conclusions and recommendations would be made and publicized, not least to the government.[14] From the standpoint of national-economy as a policy science, the *Verein* tended towards an inductive empiricism whereby the data would speak for itself.[15] Wages, prices, migration and emigration, types of agricultural production – all of this would tell its own story. But as any competent methods student will point out, data have to be interpreted, and it is through the process of interpretation that the policy recommendations are arrived at. What was happening to Prussia farming was the same fraught transformation that affects so much of agriculture in the developing world today. And it becomes a highly political question: what to do about the 'facts' when they become known. Should governments put in place measures to support the small farmer in order to keep him, his family and village community on the land, should governments place import duties on cheap food imported from the world market, should governments allow the 'natural and inevitable' forces of global markets to work their way through their society? These are not either/or choices, for different social groups will take opposed positions on the question.

Germany was an industrializing country, and cheap imported food materials were clearly to the benefit of the industrial sector. Industry also benefited greatly from the flow of migrants into the towns from the land as a source of cheap labour.[16] The landowners agitated successfully for import duties on foreign grain and cereal, in order to prop up the failing profitability of their farms (that agriculturally were no match for the grain from the prairies of North America and the Ukraine). In Weber's areas, the landowners (the so-called 'Junkers') formed the bedrock of the Prussian kingdom and, because of peculiarities in the German imperial constitution (of 1871), they were the predominant elite in the political system. The German Chancellor at that time, Caprivi, maintained import duties, although he did reduce them somewhat from the level at which his more conservative predecessor, Bismarck, had fixed them.

Leaving aside the linkage between the local and the national, which greatly interested him, Weber's interpretation and description of his data shows him to be an intuitive sociologist. There are a number of oppositions he draws in making the data 'come alive', sociologically speaking. Conditions and behaviour, objective and subjective factors, the situation of individuals and groups and their psychology together form two axes of what could be termed his 'immanent' sociology. These axes may be labelled 'exterior' and 'interior' factors or causes.

In his opening remarks to the report ('The position of the farm worker in Germany East of the Elbe'), Weber states that nothing less than a revolution in social structure is involved in transformations which have been going on for decades and that his report will shed light on the 'stage of development' reached so far. What has to be grasped, says Weber, is the direction these changes are moving towards.[17] The old traditional ways of farming and the organization of labour are being replaced by a new 'employment regime' based on capitalistic wage labour. While the material, or objective, circumstances of the farmworker can be represented by the survey data, Weber also argues that it is crucial to include the subjective factors at work – how the various categories of farmworkers view their prospects. Data on fluctuations in the price of corn or cattle are insufficient to explain the interests of the workforce.

It is impermissible to leave out of consideration the *subjective* dimension and this is very much the case when one attempts to investigate the consequences which follow or are produced by the visible transformation of the social class structure, the reciprocal relationship between the landowner and workforce and for the position of the latter in the social body of the nation. It does not so much concern the actual level of the worker's income as whether it is possible to pursue an ordered economic way of life ('geordnete Wirtschaftsführung'), whether the worker and employer *subjectively* regard each other – justifiably or not – in a favourable light or not, and so which tendencies inhere in the *subjective* wishes or interests of both parties, since it is on these that the further line of development in the future depends.[18]

In the next section of his report, Weber demonstrates how subjective factors are implicated in the structural conditions of what he terms the employment regime ('Arbeitsverfassung').[19] Farm labour in the Prussian regions had yet to move over to unregulated 'free' wage labour, where the price of labour was dictated by market conditions. Peasant serfdom had only been abolished as late as 1807 in Germany, and there were still semi-servile survivals, especially in Prussia. The main categories of farmworkers were in fact, as well as in law, employed as servants. Weber's report starts by describing the somewhat peculiar arrangements that landowners were using, even in the 1890s. Unmarried workers, male as well as female, were placed on a fixed wage contract for the year and, in addition, they were given fixed shares in the cultivation of agricultural produce. Above them was another class of servants who were married, employed their family on the farms and hired casual labourers. They were also on a yearly contract, but both the money component and their right to share in the produce were variable not fixed. These servants were termed 'Instleute'. They were given housing, land, livestock, grazing rights in addition to a share in the main crop (usually corn). Seen from the economic point of view, they were part of a cooperative venture, but one in which the landowner had the largest share. A good harvest, good weather, high prices for agricultural produce were in the joint interest of owner and 'Instleute'. Effectively, the landowners had subcontracted a large part of the farming to the 'Instleute' on a cooperative basis. But on the legal, social and status level, the 'Instleute' were very much inferior to the Junker landowner.

In his report, and in subsequent follow-up studies, Weber defended this paternalist set-up. Whether he should have defended the situation, as a good bourgeois, is another matter. But he goes out of his way, one might say sociologically, to underline what gave stability to an employment regime that was beginning to dissolve. 'The estate owner ('Gutsherr') was not a normal employer, but a political autocrat who ruled over the worker.'[20] The strong patriarchal leadership is tolerated because it corresponds to the economic basis of relationships.[21] The old patriarchalism provided a form of security and limited independence for the settled farm tenant. '. . . the continuity of the patriarchal organisation and the greater flexibility of the opposed relations between employer and employee preserve quite effectively the living standards of the worker and the community of interest'.[22]

In order to explain his position, Weber reaches deep into the psychological underpinnings of what he sees as a shared community, where he gives an explanatory role to the motivation of the farmworker. Under the old patriarchal estate system, the estate owner could claim a conservative legitimacy by being seen 'as a born representative of the interests of his people'.[23] Paternalism worked as a managerial ideology and as a form of cooperative enterprise. The breakdown of this system came with the move to a fully capitalistic employment regime. The basic problem with year-long contractual labour was the unevenness of the need for labour power ('Arbeitskraft'). The seasonal high points of demand were planting and harvesting but, prior to the introduction of steam threshing machines, the corn was threshed by hand over the long winter months. In addition, sugar beet and root crops were introduced on the best, most fertile land as a new cash crop, i.e. they were grown so that it could all be sold on the market by the landowning farmer alone. Root crops required intensive labour but only at two points in the year (planting and harvesting).[24] A capitalistic employment regime that used wages alone was far more favourable to the economic interests of the Junkers. If they ended their servant labour contracts with the 'Instleute', the Junker landowners could then concentrate on the more profitable root crops and employ seasonal casual labour at low prices. The casual workers came across the border from Poland and the Ukraine.

But with the move to a fully waged system of labour, the tenants lost their security and the community of interest was broken. Weber comments that 'the patriarchal system is completely hopeless in terms of popular psychology'. There was no incentive, psychologically or economically, to remain on the old estates. Motivation also operated as a pull factor, drawing the farmworkers into the towns. Weber, in the conclusion of his study, observed that it was not the issue of wage levels alone that drove the farmworker off the land (although this was a factor as seasonal labour had undercut the previous standard of living of the German farmworker). In the town, the farm 'servant' would be free from the everyday paternal authority of the estate owner, he and she would have their own independence as a free wage labourer. Weber is quite expressive about this. He calls it 'the pure psychological magic of "freedom"'.[25]

Summarizing this section, then, Weber is receptive to different levels of explanation. As a national-economist, he analyses the movement in food prices and its effects on the income of farm labourers. His depiction of the situation of the labourer involves the sociological analysis of cooperative interest and patriarchal authority, and the dissolution of those social and economic bonds by new labour market practices. And, if prices and markets represent objective factors, for Weber, the subjective, motivational or psychological factors have to be given equal attention if one is to assess the future direction of developments.

Weber's report was immediately recognized as authoritative and insightful as well as breaking new ground in research on the agrarian question. Weber used his empirical study and analysis to great effect in the political and policy debates which followed on the publication of the report at the end of 1892. Weber's own political position, which has been expounded in detail elsewhere,[26] argued for maintaining a German agricultural workforce on the grounds that the eastern borders would only be secure with a settled German workforce and not a Polish migratory one. Given that the psychological and motivational grounds for the joint community of 'Instleute' and Junker were no longer viable, farmland should be made available by the government for small German farmers. For a bourgeois academic, Weber's political position was somewhat eccentric and hardly progressive. In terms of agrarian development, sounder arguments could have been made to allow the inevitable migration to the west – both of German farmers to the towns and of farmworkers from central Europe to Prussia. This would have optimized the development of central Europe, which was then very backward, and have been in the interests of both landowners and dissatisfied German farmworkers.

The national-economist

It is still not generally understood just how immersed Weber was in national-economy. Overall, there has been a tendency to regard the Weber of the 1890s as an emergent sociologist who was informed about economics rather than an economist in his own right who later developed sociological interests. His professorial post was in national-economy, first at Freiburg and then at Heidelberg, and that is what he principally lectured on. His work on the agrarian conditions in the east of Germany was done as an economist, even though we can see the signs of social researcher in those studies. In addition, he became an expert on the stock exchanges, or bourses as they were called. An impression has been formed that, because Weber trained as a legal historian, his 'switch' into national-economy, when he took up a chair in that subject at Freiburg in 1894 at the age of 30, was artificial. Also, his immense reputation as a sociologist has provided the lazy assumption that he was never properly an economist.

But even in his postdoctoral work at Berlin, prior to his appointment at Freiburg, law, economy and capitalism in the ancient world had become the focus of his interests. His habilitation thesis, published in 1891, was entitled 'Roman Agrarian History and its Significance for Public and Private Law'.[27] Wolfgang Mommsen comments that, while the thesis was intended as an analysis of the Roman legal system and its impact upon the agrarian economy, it soon escaped this narrow framework. What Weber discovered in his research was that 'aided by the legal system there had emerged a full-fledged system of agrarian capitalism'. Mommsen describes Weber's turn towards the analysis of capitalism as follows:

> Against the backcloth of a traditional economy, Weber described the emergence, the dominance and, eventually, the decline of what he described as a fully developed agrarian capitalism. The progressive spread of the principle of unconditional 'freedom of disposal of land ownership and its total economic mobilisation'[28] was, in Weber's view, the key factor that more than anything had made possible the rise of a large-scale agrarian capitalism. Indeed, by abolishing all restrictions on the acquisition and the marketing of land, there occurred, as Weber put it, 'the most unlimited capitalism in land property that the world ever has seen'.[29] The gradual implementation of the principle of unrestricted ownership of land during the Roman Republic was the backbone of a market economy which had made possible the rise of Rome to a huge political and commercial empire. According to Weber, the traditional communal structures as well as the relatively independent position of the smaller farmers were totally destroyed in favour of an agrarian economy dominated by large-scale estates.[30]

It would be wrong to extend the concept of the market economy beyond the market for land. That market arose from the specific circumstances of a militarized empire, expanding its borders through conquest. With conquest came a large supply of slaves whose labour was used by the estate owners. This slave labour displaced the small independent farmer who had previously been the key social stratum in the rise of Rome as a Mediterranean great power. Changes in law not only permitted the rise of agrarian capitalism, they also dispossessed an economic class of farmers. This transformation was followed by slow decline as the supply of slaves ceased, as the empire reached the limits of its military capability.

> the system of agrarian capitalism gradually withered away and eventually the free market economy was supplanted by the 'Kolonat'. This was a system of huge landed estates that became self-sufficient economic units and no longer produced for the market. This eventually led to the destruction of the essential preconditions for dynamic economic growth and free market exchange. In the end agrarian capitalism gave way to a stagnant economic order that foreshadowed the economic conditions during the early Middle Ages.[31]

While it is reasonable to see Weber's expertise as lying in the field of legal history, it was an approach sensitive to the forms of capitalism. He asked the question, notes Mommsen: 'what consequences do legal regulations have on the economy? In the background of this work we discover the contours of a specific concept of world history, namely the recurrent rise and fall of world civilisations respectively caused by specific economic and/or cultural conditions.'

Weber's move to Freiburg as a professor of national-economy should therefore be seen as justified by his expertise in agrarian economics, first those of the ancient world and, second, the contemporary crisis in agriculture east of the Elbe. It should also be added that Weber had expertise in the medieval economy, again approaching the subject from the discipline of legal history. His doctoral dissertation and research was published in 1891 and entitled 'The History of Commercial Partnerships in the Middle Ages'. Its subject matter was the development of medieval trading partnerships in northern Italy. Weber's research problem was to explain how investment for overseas trading expeditions could be mustered and how the risks and returns of these expeditions were to be shared. Modern company law, which was created in the nineteenth century, solved this problem through the legal device of the limited liability company. This separated the risk of bankruptcy from the individual investors who were no longer made personally liable, to the complete extent of their wealth, for the debts of a failed company. It then became more attractive for investors to risk their money by investing in such legally constituted companies. What Weber was seeking to explain was how, in the context of the medieval economy, investment funds could be assembled in the first place for an overseas venture when there were few laws to regulate such transactions. Using the records of trading partnerships and analysing the laws and regulations available and specially developed, Weber explained the rules according to which such partnerships operated. Lutz Kaelber, who has recently translated Weber's dissertation publication into English, argues that this research fed into PESC, *Economy and Society* and the *General Economic History*.[32]

As a national-economist, Weber developed specialist expertise on the stock exchanges during the mid-1890s. He lectured publicly on the subject, he wrote pamphlets, he served on a government commission on the workings of the stock exchange, and he wrote several long academic treatises on the subject. It was a very technical and very controversial area. Public concern centred on the speculative opportunities of the exchanges. Knut Borchardt writes, 'Particularly intensive was discussion relating to the casino-like qualities of the bourse (*Börsenspiel*). This was principally related to the question of whether obligations arising from trades which did not conclude with the delivery of and payment for securities or commodities, but simply balanced the difference between an agreed future price and the price actually prevailing in the exchange on the delivery date . . .'. This was seen as gambling on the difference in prices. Borchardt makes the point that Weber was relatively well equipped to write on the subject because of his legal training. The stock exchange had not yet become a topic within economics. Instead, it was lawyers who contributed to the growing literature 'concerning inadequate regulation of brokers (*Makler*), the numerous abuses of business on account (*Kommissionsgeschäft*), and the problems relating to those investing in securities'.[33]

Reactionary agrarian interests objected to the development of futures in grains being traded on the stock exchanges. They thought this contributed to the lowering of cereal prices through opening the market to international trade. Their views were successful when the German parliament ('Reichstag') passed a new Bourse Law in June 1896 forbidding the trading in futures. The new law undermined the work of the Bourse Commission on which Weber was sitting. Weber was bitter about this result, for he had consistently argued that Germany could not afford to turn its back on world markets in favour of agricultural protectionism. 'The representatives of the agrarian interest needed the decision for their masses of thickheaded votes, "ut aliquid factum videatur" ("in order to show something was being done"). A few of them even believed in the particularly detrimental character of futures trading itself . . .'.[34]

Borchardt queries whether Weber should be seen in this period exclusively as an economist, which is a viewpoint he attributes to Wilhelm Hennis, Keith Tribe and Heino Nau. He observes that, while Weber's appointment in Freiburg was Professor of Economics and Public Finance, he also offered classes in commercial law and lectures in the history of German law. Borchardt's point is well made and needs to be retained. Today, we would say that Weber was interdisciplinary, but this is only because of the differentiation of the specialist academic knowledge into the separate disciplines of law, economics, philosophy, sociology, politics and so on. Weber's appointment in Freiburg was in the Faculty of Philosophy, as was his appointment in Heidelberg in 1898. But it would not have seemed too strange – perhaps maybe energetic – to offer a course in the Faculty of Law. In the historical approach to both law and economics, which was then dominant, the interface of law and economy received considerable attention, not least by Weber's own teacher in Berlin, Levin Goldschmidt. The ability to trade is dependent on laws and conventions. Who then decides on those laws and regulations? In *The History of Commercial Partnerships in the Middle Ages*, Weber said, in respect of the trading societies, it was not clear 'how in each case the law had been formed – whether it involved entirely new legal thinking springing from the burgeoning needs of the day, finding general acceptance through transformation onto mercantile usage, and from thence into mercantile customary law'.[35] Whether laws are created by merchants for their own use, or law and regulation are created autonomously of economic interest groups remains a central issue, both historically and today. The economic historian Hinnerk Bruhns has recently argued that this forms the basis of a theory of regulation in Weber's writings and is to be found in *Economy and Society*.[36]

In addition, Weber gave a lecture course on national-economy from 1894 to 1898, and his reading list and exposition of one section of the course have been published. The full course is to be published shortly by the Max Weber Gesamtausgabe, so what we can say about the bits published so far should probably be placed in the provisional category awaiting fuller confirmation.[37] Weber provided his students with a structured reading list. Removing the references from this produces the following syllabus outline.

Title: Outline of lectures on general ('theoretical') economics

Introduction

§1.   Problems and methods of theoretical national-economy.

Book 1. The conceptual foundations of economic theory ('Volkswirtschaftslehre')

§2.   The economy ('Wirtschaft') and its elementary forms ('Erscheinungen').
§3.   The national-economy ('Volkswirtschaft') and its elementary forms.

Book 2. The natural foundations of the economy

§4.   The natural determinants of the economy.
§5.   Population ('Bevölkerung').
§6.   The biological and anthropological foundations of society.
§7.   The economy in its relation to other cultural forms in particular law and state.

Book 3. The historical foundations of the national-economy

§8.   The typical prestages of the national-economy.
§9.   The economic development of the coastal civilization of antiquity.
§10. The agrarian foundations of the medieval inland civilization.
§11. The urban economy and the origin of modern forms of enterprise.
§12. The origination of the national-economy ('Volkswirtschaft')

Book 4. The stages of development of economic theory

§13. Economic science until the creation of liberal economic theory.
§14. The economic theory of the so-called classical national-economy ('Nationalökonomie').
§15. The theoretical bases of scientific socialism.

Book 5. The theoretical analysis of the modern exchange economy

§16. Production and its theoretical problems.
§17. Exchange and its theoretical problems.
§18. Distribution and consumption and their theoretical problems.

§19. The regulating principles and forms of organization of want satisfaction ('Bedarfsdeckung') in terms of trade and enterprise and their functions and developmental tendencies.

Book 6. *The development and analysis of economic and social ideals*

§20. (No rubric provided, only three references.)

Going through Weber's 'Books', we can allocate them – but only approximately – to today's subject areas. Book 1 is about economic theory. Weber outlines the main tenets of Austrian marginalism and gives a detailed account of the rationale behind opposed economic actors conducting a market exchange. Each party will buy and sell a commodity only when its marginal utility is positive. Weber extends his treatment of marginalism into price theory and money. He also shows that the use of labour and capital by owners follows marginalist principles. Weber had read and understood the three leading Austrian economists – Carl Menger, Bohm-Bäwerk and von Wieser. Weber was practically the only German economist to accept and teach the new Austrian marginalist economics, which, it should be pointed out, underpins the whole of modern neo-classical theory. But, as we shall see, he does insert at the start his own distinctive set of definitions of economic action.

Book 2 is a combination of economic geography, population studies and the ethnographic foundations of the economy. §7 outlined the relation of the economy to other cultural forms, including law and the state. Book 3 is economic history and presents a clear periodization of economic eras: the early or primitive stages, the coastal civilization of antiquity, the agrarian foundations of the Middle Ages, the city economy and the origins of modern entrepreneurship, and the arrival of the modern national-economy.

Book 4 treats the development of economics as a science, and competing versions of economics as a science, and could stand as a miniature version of Schumpeter's later book *Economic Doctrine and Method. An Historical Sketch*.[38] Book 5 concerns the operation and formation of markets and trade, money, credit and finance, the firm, industry and the rural economy, production and consumption and the distribution of income sources, and the regulation of the economy – all these in the modern era, i.e. it is a complete applied economics. Book 6 is concerned with policy and with reform and social ideals.

I have given a somewhat schematic summary, whereas the great range and number of topics listed indicate that Weber was not following any programmatic syllabus (as in a modern economics textbook today) but felt free to follow his own intellectual interests. The lecture course does not allow Weber to be placed firmly within any one school or tradition. For this reason, it is quite hard to translate what he lectured in, which was then called 'Nationalökonomie'. His exposition of marginalism in Section Three (see more on this in my footnote) shows he had read Carl Menger's *Principles of Economics*, which was published in 1871, and then elaborated by von Wieser and Bohm-Bäwerk.[39] All these three economists were Viennese, hence the name 'the Austrian School'. To the extent that Weber had embraced marginalism, he could be called simply an economist. His pronounced interest in history, politics and culture make him more than an economic historian. His concern with the interaction of economic interests and politics and issues of income distribution (rent, interest and wages) point to the English tradition of classical political economy. Against this, though, he knew that Bohm-Bäwerk had destroyed the economic theoretical grounds for attributing the distribution of income to the three main classes of modern society (landowners, capitalists and wage labourers).[40] In the modern era, Weber's point of reference is the economy of a country or nation ('Volkswirtschaft'). These considerations give no firm guidance, so it is probably best to keep with the term then current: a national-economist. This is a 'satisficing' solution and by no means perfect. It contains an important ambiguity. Weber, in his personal political views, was highly national in his economic policy recommendations, yet the study of national-economy was rather the study of the economy as it had developed within the boundaries of the modern nation state, i.e. the national-economy could be studied in a value-free way.[41]

Weber prepared and printed lecture notes of §2 and §3 of his lectures, and I will outline the first four subsections of §2 to show the basis of how he thought about the economy in relation to history, society and culture. (These passages are not yet translated and my own translation here is slightly paraphrased.)

§2 The conceptual foundations of modern economic doctrine ('Volkswirtschaftslehre')

1   Concept of the 'Wirtschaft'. This is a specific form of striving for an external goal, that is consciously planned behaviour in relation to nature and to man ('Mensch') that is occasioned through those needs that require external means for their satisfaction, whether they are of a 'material' or 'ideal' nature, and includes provision for the future. 'Wirtschaft' is the complex of measures that is occasioned by the economic activity of the individual ('Wirtschaften eines Individuums') or of the human community.

2   Presuppositions of the abstract theory of the economy. Economic activity ('Das Wirtschaften') is instilled into man through a thousand-year process of adaptation. The bulk of the planned economic activity in the modern sense was and is very differently developed (and then not completely) according to race and (within the modern occidental culture) according to occupation ('Beruf'), education, intellect and character of individuals; correspondingly, the scope that is given for purely economic motives within the determining drives of the action of individuals is historically

and individually extremely changeable. Abstract theory originates in the modern occidental type of person and his economic activity. It seeks first of all to investigate the most elementary living phenomena ('Lebensphänomene') of the fully educated ('erzogenen') human being.

To this end, economics establishes a constructed 'economic subject' in relation to the contrasting state of empirical human beings.

a   All not specifically economic motives, which do exert pressure on empirical persons, are ignored.

b   It defines (i) perfect insight into the actual situation – economic omniscience, (ii) full commitment of most appropriate means to the actual goal without exception – absolute 'Wirtschaftlichkeit', (iii) complete application of own forces in the service of economic meeting of needs – 'weightless acquisitive drive' ('trägheitslosen Erwerbstrieb').

Therefore, economics uses in its argument an unrealistic human being analogous to a mathematical ideal figure.

3   Economic needs. The only needs that come into consideration are economic needs. Insofar as they are satisfied, this necessitates disposal over the forces of nature and human beings.

3.1 Decisive for the theory are the facts of the actual subjective perception by the economic subject. Economic theory is ethically indifferent to the subjective feelings and perceptions ('Empfundenwerden') of the economic subject. These subjective states of what counts as an economic need are highly variable over history. The whole economic history of the west is the history of the qualitative expansion of the state of need.

3.2 The perception of need will vary with how pressing the need remains in relation to its fulfilment/satiation and the fulfilment of other economic needs. The reduction in the urgency of one need is accompanied by an increase in the sense of urgency of other needs. Future needs are perceived as less pressing than present ones; their urgency increases with the satiation of present needs and with a rising level of awareness of economic need, i.e. raised cultural expectations.

4   Goods ('Güter')

4.1 'Goods' in the sense of theory are the utility satisfactions ('Nutzleistungen') performed by human beings and material objects, as follows:

a the usable output ('Leistung') of mental and physical labour power ('Arbeitskraft') for human purposes;

b the usable power of nature (living or dead) for human purposes, either as found in nature as 'natural goods' or as fabricated by man as 'products'.

4.2 What is decisive for the quality of goods is their usefulness ('Brauchbarkeit'). This is not objective but simply means the actual or intended means of satisfaction of perceived human needs. These therefore are subjective and vary and (i) the need has to be perceived, and (ii) the usefulness has to be recognized and believed in.

What is decisive is the standpoint of human beings. 'National-economy is a science not of nature and its properties but of human beings ('Menschen') and their needs'.

Weber's opening definition reflects the emphasis placed on subjective utility by the science of economics at the time. Economics is an activity of purposeful activity directed to the satisfaction of subjectively perceived needs. But Weber immediately flags up that those needs can be material, as in commodities, or they can be ideal. In his own lecture notes, Weber indicates just what can count as ideal needs. The building of pyramids is a spectacular example of an economy organized around the politico-religious significance of the preservation of corpses. 'The organisation of the satisfaction of human needs is influenced by the totality of cultural phenomena and conditions, by climate, race, law, other material needs, religious needs, too: pyramids. Here religious creeds are more important than anything else it breeds entirely different human beings, money economy, capitalism, slave labour.'[42] In his commentary on this, Wolfgang Mommsen notes: 'This passage indicates that Weber saw economics as part of a cultural science, or, as he puts it occasionally, a science about the living-together of human beings – social science (eine "W[issenschaft] vom *Zusammenleben* der Menschen – Sozialwissenschaft") . . .'.[43]

The subjectively perceived needs are bracketed by the type of society in which an individual or community lives. People make economic choices and plans, and estimate their own advantage, but they do this within a framework of cultural values, which to a large extent are pregiven – individuals are born into a particular society and culture. While economic activity is mostly concerned with the meeting of present and future material needs, these needs turn out to be qualitatively limitless, depending on what a culture can conceive of consuming. Economics, says Weber, is not a science of nature but of the needs of human beings, although as a science it has as its object a constructed 'ideal figure' – an entity not to be confused with actual human beings ('Menschen') with culturally determined material needs.

Weber's thinking as a national-economist, therefore, can be seen as forming a framework for a religion-based explanation of the rise of modern capitalism, of most of whose aspects – in theory and in history – he already had a sophisticated knowledge. As §2 shows, he was also already thinking about the role of modern occidental culture in the determination of economic needs. In addition, as the layout of §2 demonstrates, Weber was quite able to deal with the subject of economics (not yet a discipline) in a systematic manner. His lecture notes are set out like a legal treatise with main headings, main sections and with three or more descending subsections.

This is the basis for asserting a continuity between Weber's work as a national-economist in the 1890s and the Protestant ethic studies of 1904–5. The latter did not come out of thin air, even though its highly original arguments and format might suggest that. In particular, it would be wrong to suggest, as many commentators do, that, because Weber had a nervous collapse and gave up his chair in national-economy at Heidelberg (in 1903), he had in some way turned his back on his former studies and knowledge. Weber's prodigious output during the 1890s may well have contributed to his collapse in 1899, but I would propose that his work on national-economy forms the platform for his later work in what he was to call social economics; also that his lecture programme of 1898 reveals his academic footprint that provided the conceptual breadth and depth for his later studies in comparative historical sociology. For these reasons, I will in later chapters refer back to the lecture outline presented in this chapter.

My conclusion on sociology is that national-economy could accommodate without much difficulty the sociological themes that Weber raised, especially in his empirical and policy studies on agriculture in eastern Germany. He was able and prepared to think in terms of economic classes, interest groups and social strata, and to counterpose to this a descriptive psychology of attitudes. At the same time, there is no evidence that Weber identified himself with sociology, or a sociological theory that provided a framework of integrating structure and action. Section 7 of his lecture outline ('The economy in its relation to other cultural forms in particular law and state') did contain a list of sociologists, but mostly of the 'wrong' sort. If one takes out the evolutionary theorists, the positivists and the organicists, who most probably would have been critiqued in his lectures, practically only Simmel (*Über soziale Differenzierung*, 1890) and Tönnies (*Gemeinschaft und Gesellschaft*, 1887) remain.

2 Capitalism in contemporary debates

Sombart, Weber and Simmel

This chapter argues that capitalism was an object of wide-ranging debate in Weber's generation of national-economists, and that *The Protestant Ethic and the Spirit of Capitalism* was an intervention in those debates. It was an intervention at once highly specific – the cultural aetiology and cultural significance of modern capitalism – but also a more general contribution to the wider debates in national-economy. PESC's part in the general debates on national-economy remain virtually unseen when the essay is read today. The chapter starts by outlining some of the main contours of the debate over capitalism. It expounds the major stances towards it taken by Werner Sombart and Georg Simmel, into which Weber's own PESC fits. The chapter highlights the role given to the psychology of motives, by Weber in particular.

Hartmut Lehmann has recently published an exchange of letters between Max Weber with Lujo Brentano.[1] Lehmann argues that Weber was keen to commission an intelligent and judicious review of Sombart's newly published book, *Der moderne Kapitalismus* (1902) and, for this, he turned to one of the foremost economic historians of the day, Lujo Brentano, professor at the Karl Maximilian University in Munich. Weber wrote to Brentano in October 1903, '. . . I consider it absolutely essential that one of the leading scholars in our field should write this review'.[2] Weber added that he himself would address the methodological issues in the book. Brentano only partly committed to the commission, and Weber in reply sent him some references on English Puritanism, which Brentano might well have asked for, or Weber thought relevant.[3] Weber, in his second letter, says that he would himself look again at the source material on English Puritanism because, as Lehmann paraphrases, he intended 'to write an essay on the matter for the *Archiv*'.[4] Lehmann concludes, 'What we have in front of us, therefore, looks like a division of labour: While Brentano was supposed to look at the relevance of Calvinism and Puritanism for the genesis of modern capitalism, it was, supposedly, Weber's task to discuss the methodological implications.'[5] 'Concludes' probably puts it too strongly, but it is a very interesting inference: PESC started life as a book review, which grew into a freestanding essay. In a third letter to Brentano (9 March 1904), Weber again pressed Brentano for a proper scholarly review, which, unlike some other 'limited minds', Brentano could deliver. Brentano wrote back to say he 'most certainly'[6] would try to point out the positive aspects in Sombart's book. No review was written by Brentano, but Weber, like a good journal editor, kept on pushing. In May, Weber wrote to Brentano that he hoped he would address the 'considerable issue of the genesis of the modern economic spirit'. By this time, Weber had already started writing PESC, and it seems reasonable to suppose that one early stimulus for this was the appearance of Sombart's *moderne Kapitalismus*.

It is quite clear from the above exchanges that Weber was well disposed to Sombart's enterprise. Weber's goodwill extended beyond the book itself, as Sombart was a fellow editor (along with Edgar Jaffé) of the *Archiv für Sozialwissenschaft und Sozialpolitik*, and Weber and Sombart were leading figures in Germany's premier policy research association, the *Verein für Sozialpolitik*. Weber's relationship with Sombart could not be described as one of close personal friendship – actually more of sibling rivalry – but, in many ways, Sombart had an academic and political profile closely resembling that of Weber's. They were born within a year of each other, both brought up in Prussia, both studied at the University of Berlin and were connected to Gustav Schmoller who was the senior and controlling academic influence in their field of study. And in Germany, Weber and Sombart were marked out as the rising stars within national-economy.

Their joint editorship of the *Archiv für Sozialwissenschaft und Sozialpolitik* (hereafter abbreviated to *Archiv*) points to their substantive academic links and association. Edgar Jaffé, the third editor, who received his doctorate at Heidelberg in 1902, was previously a banker and financial expert. It was his money that founded and helped to run the *Archiv*. Jaffé bought the *Archiv für soziale Gesetzgebung und Statistik* from its previous editor Heinrich Braun, and it was relaunched under its new title in 1904. The old title concerned social legislation and statistics and was a very fact-based journal reporting on new social legislation and collecting evidence on the social and health conditions of working people in the new industrial capitalism. The old journal followed a revisionist social agenda, i.e. non-Marxist, and Sombart was one of its leading writers and supporters – providing financial help. The relaunched new journal undertook to maintain the reform agenda, as the 'Sozialpolitik' in its title indicates, but it moved its emphasis away from factual reporting and descriptive statistics to a more theoretically oriented investigation of social and policy issues.

Under the new editors, the labour question was to be widened and deepened to consider the origins and consequences of the revolutionary process of capitalism on economic life and to consider this in the interaction of the social with the economic. The journal would be international and non-partisan, and value judgements about social reform would be derived not from personal opinion and political affiliation but would be informed by insights into the historical and sociopolitical situation. The editors accept that capitalism was now irreversible – there can be no anti-modernity movement, which many in Germany did espouse. The existence of a proletariat was a fact of political life, and the working classes had a consciousness of their own history and condition. A reform agenda should be adopted, backed by social scientific knowledge, and the politics of social reform had to be treated in a realistic way, i.e. neither revolutionary Marxism nor authoritarian and patriarchal government. The editors wrote as economists ('Nationalökonomen') but, in the pursuit of the study of the 'general cultural significance of capitalist development', the journal would include work from political science ('Staatslehre'), legal philosophy, social ethics, social psychology and what went under the name of sociology.[7]

Capitalism was a new word and, for Sombart and Weber, is a carefully formulated concept. Other academics and commentators simply did not have the word in their vocabulary, and they thought about the transformational process in Germany (and Europe) from an agricultural and artisanal society to factory production and urbanization in more descriptive terms. This was in part a generational divide and can be seen in the highly influential reform group, the *Verein für Sozialpolitik*. This was founded in 1872 by the national-economists Gustav Schmoller, Lujo Brentano and Adolf Wagner. Gustav Schmoller remained the leading force in the association for the next three decades. He and his co-founders belonged to the 'founder generation' of the German Empire. This generation was active in the political, legislative, educational and cultural construction of a new united Germany (1871). Germany's economic development would be a continuation of a previous north German free trade area and would be liberal in character: removal of restrictions on trade and a move away from state mercantilist policies of steering the economy according to the interests of the government. By the late 1870s, Schmoller had become alarmed at the unrestricted growth of industries and their social consequences and the alarming cyclical turns from boom to depression in the economy. In his mind, what was needed was some return to state intervention in the economy to protect it from its worse excesses and to place the interests of society as a whole as the goal of state policy. For him, the founding of the Reich was always a political and constitutional exercise, and the more dynamic features of the new society had to be guided by judicious state policies.

The sons of the founding generation, who came to maturity in the 1890s, men such as Werner Sombart, Max Weber, Alfred Weber, Schulze-Gaevernitz and Ferdinand Tönnies, argued for a more radical programme of reforms based on a more radical analysis of social and economic problems. They argued that a new type of society had come into being. This was modern capitalism. It was simply inadequate for Schmoller and his colleagues, such as Adolf Wagner, to argue that the contemporary conditions were a continuation of the old. Above all, the new generation was acquainted with the writings of Marx and Engels, which held that capitalism was a revolutionary development in the course of world history. Schmoller dismissed Marx's economics as 'speculative conclusions drawn from the writings of Ricardo and previous socialists, and modified by German philosophy and the ideas of political radicalism of the 1830s and 40s'.[8]

The younger generation paid attention to the Marxist analysis and realized its disruptive if not revolutionary potential. The younger generation belonged to the academic middle class ('Bildungsbürgertum') and were committed to social and political reform – what today would be called the establishment of a viable civil society in the face of Prussian authoritarianism. The context of their reading and understanding of Marxism was edgily informed by the possibility of a mass revolutionary uprising led by the German Social Democratic Party (SPD). In 1891, the SPD had committed to Marx's analysis of the need for revolution as the only way to improve the position of the working class. In this analysis, propagated by the SPD leader Karl Kautsky, the economics of capitalism pointed to the growing immiseration of the working class, as wages were driven down by capitalist competition and capitalist exploitation. This would lead to a crisis of profitability as consumption was depressed in the name of profit. The only way out of this pathological dynamic was for the organized working class to seize control of the means of production and institute social production for the needs of the people. The SPD also adhered to the tenets of world revolution (rather than local or national class struggle), as laid down by Marx himself in 1864 at the First International of Working Men's Associations. Kautsky's line became the orthodox position of the SPD in Weber's lifetime, although Eduard Bernstein led a revisionist position within the party that argued that wages were in fact rising and that crisis was by no means inevitable. Bernstein recommended a political route for the democratization of politics and the amelioration of the position of the working class through radical reform. Both options were very much on the table during this period. The early 1890s had seen an economic depression with 30% either unemployed or earning less than subsistence, and price deflation. In Berlin, there were 400,000 homeless. Weber's bride, Marianne, was amazed to see so many people sleeping rough in the 'Tiergarten' when she first came to Berlin in 1892.

For the younger generation of national-economists, the dynamics of capitalism had to be understood as a series of causal relationships. These would define the possibilities of profit, growth, economic strength and 'national destiny' (to use Friedrich Naumann's phrase); they would also define politics, either in the direction of revolution or in a reform direction. Naumann was himself a leading politician in the camp of those who wanted to see far-ranging social reform. He wrote an article in 1911 saying that, while the big question in France was the great revolution, in Germany, national destiny was concerned with 'what is capitalism?'.[9] He looked back to the analysis of capitalism by the younger generation, naming in particular the work of Sombart, Max Weber, Troeltsch, Schulze-Gaevernitz, Tönnies and Simmel among others (and he pointedly excluded the work of the older generation

– Schmoller, Adolf Wagner and Lujo Brentano). The overall thrust of this generation 'was to reveal the nature of that huge general change which has emerged from the middle ages up to the present day'. He continued that the work of Sombart and Max Weber had taken up anew the Marxist problematic ('Fragestellung') 'with new means on the basis of a new half century'. Marxism provided the 'explanatory principle of the present', as Dieter Lindenlaub comments.[10]

Hence, the historical question of how the capitalist process had started and what were the exact dynamics of its development was not a mere academic question – it went to the heart of contemporary debates and fears. It was Karl Marx who had dated the start of modern capitalism at the transition point of the late Middle Ages, as the towns developed independently and unfettered by the old feudal lordship. Marx periodized this transition as the dialectical move from a class society based on peasant serfs and feudal rulers to one based on the rising bourgeoisie who were constituting the new capitalist society and were becoming the new ruling class, exploiting the landless peasant as wage labourers.

The younger generation accepted Marx's terminology but rejected his dialectical account of historical change. They accepted there were classes; there were those who owned property and those who owned nothing but the ability to sell their labour; also the accumulation process, the means of production and social and political structures of inequality; above all, the idea that there were causal linkages between these various terms. While they did not adopt the crude determination of a material base controlling political, economic and cultural actions, they did accept that capitalism was an entity with interlinked parts and that it had its own historical dynamic of development. So facts, trends and developments had in some way to be causally modelled and thought about; they had to be fitted into some sort of pattern – but not into a schematic pattern as Marx and Engels had argued.

Werner Sombart and the origins of modern capitalism

Of the younger generation, Sombart had by far the closest engagement with Marxism. He had written critical expositions of Marxism, he himself belonged to the SPD, and he was a political activist in Breslau where he was assistant professor. (He remained stuck at assistant professor level, despite his outstanding academic reputation, because no ministry of education would accept a member of the SPD as a full professor.)

My argument in this section is that Sombart's *moderne Kapitalismus* represents a theoretical reorientation around the issue of capitalism within the field of German national-economy and, in this sense, Sombart became the leading intellectual influence among the younger generation of the *Verein*. *Der moderne Kapitalismus* (1902) offered, in its opening chapters, a methodological way of integrating the motives of people and groups in pursuit of economic goals with resultant economic organization and institutions created for those purposes.[11] In this respect, it went further than the very suggestive ideas in Weber's own lecture outline in national-economy. Sombart provided some key concepts for the analysis of the emergence of modern capitalism: economic rationalism, acquisitive behaviour and the profit motive, and 'high capitalism' – a very far-reaching concept whose subsequent influence can be seen, for example, in Habermas' theory of the colonization of the life world. He also demanded that history had to be investigated through the aid of clearly defined concepts and theories, and he stood out against the assumption that the historical facts alone would provide their own explanation of events. In my view, Sombart's subsequent publications, which were extremely numerous and not least a much enlarged second edition of *moderne Kapitalismus* (1916 onwards), detract from and disguise the originality and sheer achievement of the first edition of the book. (I make this point because Sombart is often portrayed retrospectively through his later publications, many of which command little or negative credibility today.[12])

If we confine our attention just to titles for a moment, we can see the sequencing of ideas and their standpoints as so many stepping stones. Marx wrote *Das Kapital*, Sombart *Der moderne Kapitalismus* and Weber *Die protestantische Ethik und der 'Geist' des Kapitalismus*. The semantic shift from 'Das Kapital' to 'der Kapitalismus' is enormous. Marx's capital is neuter in gender – impersonal, brutish – and it outlines the laws of accumulation of an object whose dynamics demand the crude servitude of all social classes caught in its embrace. Sombart made the accumulation of capital the result of individuals behaving according to an array of economic motives. While these motives, psychological in origin, could be crudely acquisitive, Sombart had humanized capital accumulation to the extent that he made it the outcome of individuals and groups and their self-organization, and not the impenetrable dialectic of impersonal forces. Capita*lism* was a matter of the motives of individuals and social and economic relationships. For Sombart, the outcomes of high capitalism were unacceptable and unwanted, and he still remained the socialist critic of certain forms of capitalism. But he argued that there were individual and institutional factors in play that produced a particular outcome and, equally, the socialization of the means of production was still possible in terms of the logic of capitalistic development and the reinsertion of cooperative ideas and institutions. Weber's title signals his acceptance of the shift to capitalism as the object of study, and 'Geist' – as is probably not realized by most Anglophone readers – was Sombart's term. To see this, *Der moderne Kapitalismus* (hereafter *mK*) has to be looked at in closer detail and, in particular, Weber's somewhat devious way of relating to Sombart's *mK*.

In the second and revised edition of PESC, Weber dropped the quotation marks around 'spirit' ('Geist') in the title. No doubt he felt he had made the term his own, not least through a sixteen-year intellectual tussle played out by both men, Sombart and Weber.[13] But in 1904, 'Geist' appeared in quotation marks, partly as an acknowledgement of Sombart's prior use of the term and that he, Weber, was going to use it in another way. (And both men had to be definitionally careful in using 'Geist' because, for most readers, it would have signalled Hegel's big idea of Reason as the progressive supra-individual force within the dialectic of history. 'Geist' in German and, to a lesser extent, 'spirit' in English also have plainer and far more everyday meanings. There is also a suggestion by both men that they chose, or at least did not dislike, the term because it was a play on the word 'Geist' at Hegel's expense. Both Weber and Sombart were resolutely against Hegel, and Sombart saw part of his role as taking Hegel out of Marx – and this meant removing a dialectical philosophy of history.)

There is a series of corrective passages and footnotes in Weber's PESC to Sombart's *mK*. They refer to Sombart's dismissal of religion as a factor in western economic development and to Weber's highlighting of the role of religious ethics in economic behaviour. Weber's references to Sombart, while aiming to be corrective are also slightly belittling, and they give the effect that Sombart's thesis can be disregarded. The relationship of book to essay surfaces here. Weber's PESC could adopt an essayistic form as a critique of what was a very large and quite systematic book. *mK* appeared in two volumes, it had an elaborate set of divisions into books, sections and chapters, and totalled 28 chapters and 656 pages. *mK* is now virtually unread, whereas in its day, it was a considerable academic publishing sensation. It needs, therefore, to be seen as a situating reference point in the debate on capitalism. Weber's PESC is of course freestanding in its own right; indeed, its self-containedness is one of its remarkable features. But some part of its ability to assume the form of an essay was the opportunity to offer a critical perspective on one aspect of a larger thesis and enterprise.

mK outlined a whole programme for national-economy that offered a way of integrating economic history with economic and sociological theory. It opens with several methodological chapters that assert the need to distinguish between phenomenal facts presented by historians and the mediation of those facts by the concepts of national-economy. Historians tend to miss the economic significance of facts because they lack a theory of economic activity. The major distinction Sombart wanted to introduce was between an enterprise ('Betrieb') and the wider economy ('Wirtschaft'). Sombart argued that one could find similar enterprises, such as the industrial workshop, throughout history. The point, however, was to situate the enterprise within the dominant principles of an economy. The industrial workshop could be found in ancient Greece, in the medieval guilds and in modern capitalism. The economic principles of the ancient economy excluded any predominantly competitive and market economy; likewise, the guilds were committed to a restrictive economy and, in the capitalist era, one could find workshop enterprises operating on cooperative lines.

Sombart, therefore, looked for the economic principles at work in an economy rather than their particular organizational forms such as the enterprise, the household, the manor or the factory. His major idea was that two principles need to be distinguished in explaining the rise of western capitalism. One was the principle of the satisfaction of need ('Bedarfsbe-friedigung'), the other was the acquisition of wealth as an end in itself ('Er-werbswirtschaft'). Each of these principles came to define their respective economies. 'The purpose of a capitalist factory producing boots is not the making of boots but rather the raising of profit; the purpose of a peasant's own economy is equally not to produce boots but to protect the feet from the wet and the cold.'[14] This is the difference between a traditional economy and a modern capitalist economy. The traditional economy, in its various forms, is based on the motivation of fulfilling immediate needs, and it is characterized by a limited division of labour. The modern capitalist economy is psychologically driven by a desire for profit as an end in itself, irrespective of what good or service is provided.

Sombart's main question is what causes the changeover from the prin-ciple of the satisfaction of need to that of the acquisitive principle, which, as Parsons pointed out in an early paper, is the *Kapitalismus* problematic.[15] The crossover was triggered in the late Middle Ages by a heightened sense of consumption and wealth, after Europe had made contact with the Near East and the depredations of the Crusades and the later expeditions to find new sources of wealth in the colonies. In place of an economy regulated by tradi-tion, there arose, says Sombart, a new lust for wealth – 'auri sacra fames'.[16] The motivation of greed, followed by a new 'economic rationalism' centred on double-entry book-keeping (introduced by Luca Paciola in 1494), opens the door to the calculation of profit. Modern capitalism therefore originated in the Italian towns that had grown rich on trade, had adopted the techni-calities of profit calculation and were freed from traditional restraints in their search for wealth.

'Geist' plays a major conceptual role in Sombart's explanation, especially with regard to the move from one economic principle to another. Part Three of his exposition is entitled 'Die Genesis des kapitalistischen Geistes'. It com-prises two chapters: one on the awakening of 'Erwerbstriebes', the other on the formation of economic rationalism. Sombart frames the problem of the emergence of modern capitalism in terms of psychological motives, econom-ic principles and the resultant organization of economic forms in terms of norms and regimes. (Indeed, it is not a little Parsonian in method.) Sombart uses the phrase 'psychogenesis' to conceive the sea-change in psychological motivation that was taking place by the end of the Middle Ages.[17]

Weber disputed a particular aetiology in Sombart's account. As we have seen, Sombart's aetiology turned on the new 'auri sacra fames' – the ac-cursed lust for gold. Chapter 14 of *mK* raises alternative possible causes and dismisses them. Sombart dismisses religion as a possible cause.

> It also seems insufficient to me to locate the nature of modern capitalism through the belonging to specific religious communities. That Protes-tantism, particularly in its variants of Calvinism and Quakerism, has significantly supported the development of capitalism is a well-known

fact but one that also needs to be further established . . . the Protestant system of religion is the consequence rather than the cause of the modern-capitalist spirit.

Sombart, like Weber, quotes (in a footnote) Eberhard Gothein's contribution to the debate.

> Whoever will trace the origins of capitalist development, in whatever country of Europe that may be, is always impressed by the same fact: the Calvinist diaspora is at the same time the breeding ground ('Pflanzschule') of the capitalist economy. The Spanish expressed this with bitter resignation: heresy supports the spirit of trade ('Handelsgeist').[18]

What, however, is required to avoid such an error, says Sombart, is a closer examination of the actual historical constellation in order to draw a satisfactory answer for the rise of modern capitalism.

The scientific significance of what Sombart and Weber were attempting turns on getting the causation correct. An unbridled acquisitive urge (Sombart) or inner-worldly asceticism (Weber) was the decisive motivational principle that moved the economic development of western Europe into a new phase and new dynamic. The new capitalist spirit (however described) is part of the cultural genealogy of modernity. Both Sombart and Weber were conducting a historical exercise to isolate this cultural 'gene' in the make-up of modern capitalism.[19] If, as they argued, it were decisive and distinctive, then it would also shape the behavioural patterns of contemporary economic behaviour.

Weber's dialogue with Sombart's *Der moderne Kapitalismus*

A close reading of Weber's Chapter Two, 'The "Spirit" of Capitalism', in relation to Sombart's *mK* reveals it to be a critical dialogue with Sombart's position on the motive forces of economic behaviour. Weber's chapter heading deliberately echoes Sombart's own title for Part 3 of *mK*, 'The Genesis of the Capitalist Spirit'. Weber apologizes for the pretentiousness of the term 'spirit' but curiously fails to acknowledge that Sombart had already coined the term two years previously.[20] Weber uses the case study of Benjamin Franklin to illustrate what he means by the new spirit of capitalism. It is a systematic work ethic driven by an ethical attitude to the world.

> the summum bonum of this ethic, the earning of more and more money, combined with the strict avoidance of all spontaneous enjoyment of life, is above all completely devoid of any eudaemonistic, not to say hedonistic, admixture. It is thought of so purely as an end in itself, that from the point of view of the happiness of, or utility to, the single individual, it appears entirely transcendental and absolutely irrational.
>
> (PESC, p. 53)

Weber disputes the significance of one of Sombart's prime examples of the new acquisitive spirit. Sombart placed on the frontispiece to Book 2 ('The Genesis of Modern Capitalism') a quote from the memoirs of Anton Fugger: 'but Herr Jacob Fugger had always given him the same answer: . . . that he was of a different mind, that he wished to turn a profit as long as he lived'.[21] The questioner was a business colleague who had already retired and had asked Jacob Fugger why he did not do likewise as he had already made a tremendous fortune. (Jacob Fugger [1459–1525] belonged to one of Europe's greatest business dynasties, making money as merchants, bankers, tax farmers and money lenders to kings and emperors.) The high-profile argument between Sombart and Weber concerned the motivation of Jacob Fugger. For Sombart, it was a spectacular example of the new acquisitive spirit and the new business mentality spreading north to Catholic Bavaria from the Italian cities. Jacob Fugger's comment could serve as a motto for the capitalist entrepreneur, notes Sombart, where calculation, speculation and business become a way of life in itself.[22] For Weber, while Fugger embodied mercantile daring and risk-taking,[23] he lacked the sober and systematic attitude to business exemplified by Benjamin Franklin. The latter embodied the modern attitude, while the Fuggers stood for premodern merchant aristocracy.

On the matter of work 'as an end in itself', Weber is saying the same thing as Sombart. But of course, what Weber has to establish is that this is religiously driven and not a lust for profit in its own right. Weber demands the specific historical origins of this religiously derived spirit be confirmed, because the later development of capitalism through its inevitable secularization of religious discipline into capitalist discipline obscures the specific historical origin. This leads to the mistake, made by 'naïve historical materialism', of reversing the causal relation, i.e. a type of religion produced the capitalist spirit, and not capitalism a religious attitude. What Weber spells out as a mistake was the very position articulated by Sombart, who, as we have seen, dismisses the influence of Protestantism and Calvinism as a causal factor.

Weber next takes up Sombart's key description of the emergence of the lust for gold, which distinctively stands out in both men's text as a Latin tag: 'auri sacra fames'. Sombart locates this in the late Middle Ages, whereas Weber notes that 'it is as old as the history of man' (PESC, p. 57). This means, for Weber, that there is nothing new about it, so it has to be discounted as a new factor. Sombart's acquisitive spirit can be found all over the world – in an Italian as well as a Chinese cab-driver, craftsmen in southern Europe and Asia, etc. 'At all periods of history, wherever it was possible, there had been ruthless acquisition, bound to no ethical norms' (PESC, p. 57). Weber then takes on Sombart's argument that an adventurer capitalism developed from the European experience of the Crusades. Against this, Weber asserts, 'Capitalist[ic] acquisition as an adventure has been at home in all types of economic society which have known trade with the use of money . . .' (PESC, p. 58). 'Absolute and conscious ruthlessness in acquisition has often stood in the closest connection with the strictest conformity to tradition' (PESC, p. 58). Sombart sought to contrast traditionalism with the new acquisitive spirit. For Weber. the traditionalism of unscrupulous adventurer capitalism has to be combated with a new ethical style of life. So what Sombart takes to be novel (acquisitiveness). Weber takes to be age-old; also he insists that what was age-old – a traditional attitude to acquisition – had to be converted by the emergence of a new ethical style of life. At this point, Sombart has made no formal appearance in the main text, although Sombart is clearly the critical object of Weber's own exposition.

A few pages further on, Weber formally disputes Sombart's division of economic motivation into satisfaction of need and the 'new' acquisitive spirit. Sombart, as we have seen, had put considerable effort into a dual articulation of enterprise, both within the framework of craft mentality (production for need) and within the capitalist spirit (the struggle for profit freed from needs). Weber appears to bend towards Sombart's position, equating production for need with what he (Weber) terms economic traditionalism. This, for Sombart, is the precapitalist world that is to be transformed. Weber likewise is focused on the transformation, but he brings in the concept of traditional capitalism. This introduces a new axis of articulation: capitalism can exist in traditional form either side of the historical line (or watershed) of the transformation into modernity. One can adduce historical examples of capitalism in the medieval and ancient world that are traditional in orientation. 'Enterprises, namely, which are carried on by private entrepreneurs by utilizing capital (money or goods with a money value) to make a profit, purchasing the means of production and selling the product, i.e. undoubted capitalistic enterprises, may at the same time have a traditionalistic character.'[24] Sombart is right to note what Weber terms an 'adequate relationship' between capitalist spirit and the capitalist enterprise – they do go together in the modern era. But this is not a 'necessary relationship', says Weber. One can have a capitalist workshop in the ancient world run on traditional grounds. Conversely, within the period of modern European history, it is common to find capitalist enterprises run on traditional principles.

Weber uses the example of the textile industry in the nineteenth century, in order to ram home the argument that capitalist businesses are frequently traditional and lack the dynamic impulse to ever-expanding growth. The linen business was a cottage industry and used middle men to process the raw material. 'The form of organization was in every respect capitalistic; the entrepreneur's activity was of a purely business character; the use of capital turned over in the business was indispensable; and finally, the objective aspect of the economic process, the book-keeping, was rational' (PESC, p. 67). Book-keeping was a central feature of Sombart's account of economic rationalism. But, despite these features, the linen business remained locked into a traditionalist phase. Weber continues to labour the point over the next few pages and is, in effect, trying to bury Sombart's distinctions.

Weber next takes a point already established by Sombart: that it is not the availability of money that is the vital prerequisite for the development of modern capitalism, but rather the attitude towards business. 'The question of the motive forces in the expansion of modern capitalism is not in the first instance a question of the origin of the capital sums which were available for capitalistic uses, but, above all, of the development of the spirit of capitalism.' This is exactly Sombart's argument but, of course, Weber wishes to denote a different spirit. Weber seeks to establish that it is the ethical qualities informing the spirit that are crucial (PESC, p. 69). The capitalist system 'needs devotion to the calling of making money' (PESC, p. 72) that the previous era with its 'auri sacra fames' would have found 'perverse'.

Weber, again without mentioning Sombart, turns to the Church's attitude to money-making in relation to the Italian cities in the late Middle Ages. For Sombart, as we have noted, the Italian cities were the location of the new capitalist spirit. Weber asserts, on the contrary, that the Church's influence was decisive in making the unrestrained search for profit an object of deep shame and unworthiness.[25]

Chapter 2 finally ends with another reference to Sombart. 'The attempt has been made, particularly by Sombart, in what are often judicious and effective observations, to depict economic rationalism as the salient feature of economic life as a whole' (PESC, p. 75). Weber admits economic rationalism to be a central component of 'modern bourgeois society' (PESC, p. 75). Weber even offers that it might seem that 'the development of the spirit of capitalism is best understood as part of the development of rationalism as a whole, and could be deduced from the fundamental position of rationalism on the basic problems of life. In the process Protestantism would only have to be considered in so far as it has formed a stage prior to the development of a purely rationalistic philosophy' (PESC, p. 76). As can now be expected, Weber dismisses this train of thought on the grounds that rationalism is not a uniform movement in European history. Roman law attained a high degree of rationalism but, in the modern era, it had little impact on capitalist development.

At almost every stage of Weber's exposition in Chapter 2, Sombart is the mostly hidden object of his argument, and so the structure of Weber's argumentation derives from Sombart. Weber alters, quite crucially, the terms of the argument: from adventurer capitalism to ethical lifestyle, and from modern acquisitiveness to universal acquisitiveness. Weber redistinguishes Sombart's conceptual categories, and he is also more incisive in his definition of capitalism (but not in his definition of 'Geist'). But we should not lose sight of the fact that motive ('Geist') is established as a new way of thinking in national-economy by Sombart. Weber may differ in terms of the contents of the argument, but the (hidden) underlying structure of thinking about the relation of economy to economic subjects in comparative perspective is Sombart's.

Simmel's *Philosophy of Money*

We have seen that Sombart's *moderne Kapitalismus* sought to establish 'spirit' as the decisive force in releasing the dynamic of modern capitalism, and we have seen that Weber directly confronted Sombart's attribution of greed as the driver of the acquisitive economic principle ('Erwerbsleben'). In both Sombart and Weber, there was an acceptance that psychological motives were the key to any understanding of the rise of modern economic life and, in both men, there was an acceptance that the ends of economic behaviour – in the fulfilment of needs – had been decisively altered by an economic system that placed the emphasis on penultimate ends, the search for profit regardless of economic use and need. Greed linked to economic rationalism, for Sombart, drove the search for profit and, for Weber, Puritan asceticism led to the concentration on work as an end in itself. Final purposes such as consumption, want satisfaction, expenditure to demonstrate status distinction or waging wars became displaced by the economic mechanism itself. Sombart's merchant and Weber's Puritan had, through their disregard of the ends of economic activity, entered a wholly new disposition in western civilization.

Both authors, especially Sombart, acknowledged their indebtedness to Georg Simmel for the insight that final ends could be thought of as being displaced by mechanisms that take possession of the mind and behaviour of economic actors.[26] The work to which they referred was Simmel's *Philosophy of Money*, a 550-page treatise that was first published as a book in 1900. This project had first surfaced in 1889 as an essay, 'Zur Psychologie des Geldes', published in a journal edited by Schmoller.[27] During the 1890s, Simmel had developed many of the themes of the book as separately published essays, and it is reasonable to infer that both Sombart and Weber were aware of Simmel's project during the 1890s.[28] Indeed, we know that Weber read the book on its appearance in 1900, for Marianne Weber tells us that, during his convalescence in Rome in 1902, it was one of the first books he read at the start of his recovery.[29] Further, if we pair Simmel's book with the 'English texts' also being read by Weber in Rome, one begins to sense the immense straddling operation that he was putting into place. One very large foothold is the German debate over capitalism, the other not yet significant foothold is the revolutionary (and inwardly heroic) potential of the Puritan achievement that made modern capitalism a possibility. Both Sombart and Weber acknowledge *Die Philosophie des Geldes*.[30]

Simply stated, the argument that Simmel delivered was to show how money developed into a powerful mechanism enabling a huge range of economic transactions and that, as an instrument for economic process, it inserted itself as a determinative force into the quality and structure of the social relationships of people. If greed was a prime psychological driver for Sombart, then money was its object, and it was Simmel who pointed out how intimate this link was. And if the Puritan in his economic behaviour could change the texture of economic activity from the mundane to the inner consolation of salvation anxiety, then it was Simmel who had shown how such psychological displacements were possible. Through his analysis of money, Simmel is the first social theorist to place the stress on the centrality of mediating mechanisms, that the medium becomes determinative of the ends of action and that a means under certain circumstances becomes an end in itself. It was also Simmel who established the usage of the word 'Geist' as a set of psychological attributes that had to be analysed in relation to the nature of money.[31] There is more than a hint of the magical and Faustian in the choice of the term 'Geist'. Money is a type of alchemy that transforms the normal social and economic relationships between people into something slightly beyond their own control; in enabling so much, it enables too much.

Chapter 3 of the *Philosophy of Money*, 'Money in the sequence of purposes' ('Das Geld in den Zweckreihen'), is a crucial reference point for both Sombart and Weber. It provided the pretext for thinking about modern capitalism as the pursuit of money as an end in itself. It also provided a theory of social action, as it is now termed. Sombart had already built some of its features into his own schematic account of economic principles, motivation and organizational norms. Weber, in favouring a psychologistic account of inner-worldly asceticism, had not built a theory of social action into PESC, although, as the comparative sociology of religion project got under way, his own theory of social action appeared in his 1913 essay for *Logos*. Weber is generally regarded as the initiator of the theory of social action, but Simmel produced the first clear outline in his *Philosophy of Money*. Weber acknowledged Simmel's importance at the start of his *Logos* essay.[32]

The language of 'causality' with regard to human action is highly varied in the philosophy of social science and, to make comparisons across philosophical positions, we need to be alert as much to underlying models of action as to terminology. Simmel realizes this at the outset. 'The great antinomy in the history of thought – whether the contents of reality are to be conceived and interpreted in terms of their causes or their consequences ('Folgen') (i.e. the opposition between a causal and a teleological approach) – finds its original expression in a distinction within our practical motivations' (p. 204). Do we, asks Simmel, adopt an approach that sees human action 'caused' by factors outside our control, or are we conscious beings, intentional and in control through the pursuit of our own aims?[33]

Simmel distinguishes instinctual from planned or intentional action. For example, eating wild strawberries is an instinctual response to hunger. Planting strawberries in spring is a purposive activity.

In both these cases (instinctual and intentional actions), Simmel stipulates that energy is expended. Instincts cause the release of pent-up energy, and intentions that are realized also involve the expenditure of energy. An intent could remain an 'ideal representation of action and events' – 'it . . . can become real only to the extent that it is endowed with real energy, in the same way as justice and morality, as ideas, have no historical influence until they are adopted as determinants of action by real powers'. The results of action, says Simmel, here exist in a psychologically effective form before they acquire an objective existence. In both cases, the real status of action is confirmed by the expenditure of energy. All human action, therefore, will leave an energy trace, and it is up to the social scientist to attribute that energy to motive in pursuit of an objective or as instinctually caused. In this way, the expenditure of energy as common to both action complexes, the debate between causality and teleology, is reconciled, asserts Simmel.[34] The energy component of action needs to be linked up to Simmel's discussion of desire as value realized against resistance. Desire implies that work (the expenditure of energy) needs to be accomplished before satisfaction is reached; so seduction, cuisine, cultivation are all forms of energy expenditure in the pursuit of objects in the world, whose instant gratification – as sex, fast food, prettiness – would devalue desire.

This is an extraordinarily neat and compact theory of action. It is not particularly sociological. It asserts some psychological cause (intentional or instinctual), which is worked out in the world, producing specific results. Weber omitted the energy component when he developed a similar theory of action (in 1913). In the PESC, it was sufficient for his thesis to treat psychological motivations and compulsions as causally effective.

Simmel becomes sociological in his argument when he acknowledges that realizing an aim or purpose in the world involves the mediation of the subject who makes that aim happen in the world. 'Our actions are the bridge that makes it possible for the content of the purpose to pass from its psychological form to a real form. Purpose is necessarily bound up with its means' (p. 206). We have to engage with the objective world to attain our aims, and this involves complex means–end complexes. In order to achieve D, 'a chain of mechanical processes A, B, C has to be produced so that B is caused by A, C by B and D only by C . . .'. In other words, if I wanted to go to the Football Cup Final, I have to actualize my desire by ringing the box office, buying a ticket and then getting across London to Wembley. In doing this. I will use tools or instruments – the telephone, a credit card and a transport system. A tool for Simmel is an intensified form of means, and money for Simmel is the purest example of a tool. 'Here, finally, we reach the point at which money finds its place in the interweaving of purposes'. Money 'is an institution through which the individual concentrates his activity and possessions in order to attain goals that he could not attain directly' (p. 210).

The nature of money as a tool for the attainment of aims leads Simmel into an interesting digression on the congruence of strangers and money – with Puritans as a particular example. 'The importance of money as a means, independent of all specific ends, results in the fact that money becomes the centre of interest and the proper domain of individuals and classes who, because of their social position, are excluded from many kinds of personal and specific goals' (p. 221). There are, then, social groups who are excluded from full rights and benefits of citizenship. The Quakers in England are an interesting case because they voluntarily renounced political participation.

> After the Quakers had already attained full political equality, they themselves rejected the interests of others: they did not take an oath and therefore could not accept a public office; they refused everything that was associated with the adornment of life, even sport; they even had to give up their farming because they did not want to pay tithe. Thus, in order to retain an external interest, they were directed towards money as the sole interest in life to which they had access.
>
> (p. 222)

Simmel makes the same point with regard to the German Pietists and Herrenhuter, whose 'naked acquisitiveness' stands out as their only practical impulse when these communities denied themselves an 'interest in the sciences, the arts and cheerful sociability'.

Simmel, then, provides more than hints (about Puritans) for the Protestant ethic thesis; he provides a philosophy of social action. This is rooted in a theory of desire, resistance, realization and value and, overall, it can be said to be psychological. Perhaps it is in this connection that Weber raises his objection in 1913 that Simmel does not differentiate sufficiently the subjective from the objective (see note 25). But in 1904–5, Weber himself is operating with psychological motivations in the absence of his own theory and model of social action.

Some interim conclusions

Two main points can be drawn from the above analysis and exposition. First, Simmel, Sombart and Weber all use the concept 'Geist' as a form of explanation, and all three have in common its use in a predominantly psychological manner. Simmel stands out through his intensive discussion of the psychology of motivation and how it may be developed as a philosophy of social action. This has methodological consequences for Weber that will be discussed in the next chapter. At this point, however, it is premature to speak of a sociological theory of action in either Simmel or Weber (although if one chooses to read more of Sombart, a credible basis for an economic sociology will be found at the start of *mK*).

Second, Simmel's discussion of the role, function and philosophy of money enters into a *diffuse* account of historical development. There is an implicit assumption in *The Philosophy of Money* that barter and the absence of money characterize prehistory and simpler societies and that fully developed money characterizes modern society. But Simmel himself provides no clear periodization in the way proffered by authors such as Marx, Rodbertus, Bücher, Sombart and Weber.[35] My argument throughout this chapter has been that, although we have a precise grasp of the nature of Weber's explanation, the same specification does not apply to what is to be explained. I have outlined the contours of the capitalism problematic ('Fragestellung') in Weber's lectures as a national-economist, as the central topic in the younger generation of the *Verein* and as the advertised object of study in the *Archiv*. PESC is an essay that contributes to the much wider capitalism debate, and this becomes particularly clear when its relation to Sombart's *mK* is fully articulated – something Weber was less than forward about. There is therefore a lack of symmetry in the PESC between Weber's care in expounding his explanation and the assumed and imprecisely indicated nature of what exactly was being explained – and, as noted by Nipperdey, Weber used a postgraduate dissertation on late nineteenth-century occupational divides by way of an explanandum.[36] As we will see, Weber had to rectify this asymmetry outside the original text of PESC. He took up the methodological problems in his 'Objectivity' essay of 1904, which, following the suggestion by Lehmann, can be seen as the followthrough of a suggested division of labour with Brentano. He attempted to answer his critics in a series of anti-critiques, after which he redefined his research orientation in terms of a comparative sociology.

A final point remains to be considered. Weber and Sombart were reliant on Simmel's exposition of means and ends and how money is able to reconfigure the actions of individuals and groups. But *The Philosophy of Money* did not conform to the capitalism debate in the way I have surveyed it above. Simmel was quite explicit about this at the outset and, in an often quoted section of his Preface, he wrote, 'The attempt is made methodologically to construct a new storey beneath historical materialism such that the explanatory value of the incorporation of economic life into the causes of intellectual culture is preserved, while these economic forms themselves are recognized as the result of more profound valuations and currents of psychological or even metaphysical pre-conditions.'[37] Historical materialism or Marxism famously developed the divide between a material base (the economic relations of class society) and the superstructure (state, politics, culture, religion), and either directly or indirectly the base determined the superstructure. For example, for Marx, the state was nothing but the executive committee of the ruling class. What Simmel proposes is to insert a new level of analysis beneath the base and its superstructure. It is a statement of some verve in taking on the central tenets of Marxism, and it is somewhat cheeky as this is about the only direct reference to historical materialism in his book.[38] Moreover, he also states in the Preface that, 'Not a single line of these investigations is meant to be a statement about economics.'[39] So we have an engagement with Marxism, but of what sort? Overtly, it is not that of a national-economist.

Simmel's reply is to refer to 'psychological or even metaphysical pre-conditions'.[40] While we have examined the psychological preconditions, what are those metaphysical preconditions? It is here that 'Geist' comes to be more than psychology. Money, by being the measure of all things, combining form, function and substance (latterly symbolic), becomes a universal means. It combines in itself the extension of mind as abstraction, as 'Geist', and the value standard of things. There is in Simmel's exposition a dualism (derivable from Spinoza): the world of mind and the world of things can never be reconciled because of their radically different ontologies. But money is an instrument that can equilibrate between the valuations placed on objects and things when they are exchanged by people. Money has no substantive value itself but acts as a universal measure of value where value is only objectified through the process of exchange, so realizing the subjective values of the desires and preferences of individuals. Money, here, can be thought of as a new plane of existence – the point at which the plane of mind has conjoined with the plane of things. Although Simmel did not go in for reflections about the distinctiveness of the west, the development of money by modern man would count as a singular event in comparative perspective. This, I think, is the attractiveness of Simmel's analysis for Sombart and Weber. Where they could not follow Simmel was into the area of philosophy and his assertions of ontological planes – of mind and things – for these are metaphysical speculations off-limits to national-economy.

Weber and Sombart instead tried to provide a historical aetiology for the rise of the means–end mentality. They moved national-economy towards thinking about what sociological and historical conditions would satisfy the problematic of modern capitalism. The explanandum that required an explanation was the emergence of an extended division of labour, production for profit and means–end calculations in which both people and things are treated as means to a further end. Both Sombart and Weber drive their analysis (of greed and of asceticism) to fit the Simmelian means–end schema. But, in being drawn to Simmel's philosophy, Weber and Sombart were attempting to confront a question of origins that, as one reads Simmel more intensively, lay beyond historical representation. For money could be conceived as a new 'media res', a new plane of existence, determining but not itself historically determinable.

A recent essay by the sociologist and theologian Martin Riesebrodt succinctly states the position developed in this chapter. '. . . Simmel, Sombart, and Weber all understood themselves as further developing Marx from a critical perspective, not as refuting him'. 'Weber's generation of scholars identified the weakness of the Marxian approach most in need of further development to be historical materialism understood as a doctrine, . . . instead of as a method of inquiry.'[41] Weber, Riesebrodt continues, sought to widen the materialist perspective through the consideration of ideal factors (i.e. inner-worldly asceticism). In this, he followed Simmel, who argued that, in history, 'material and ideal factors engage in a dialectical relationship in which neither one is first or last'.

However, Riesebrodt goes on to conclude of Simmel, 'The difference between materialism and idealism is not an ontological one, but a methodological one.'[42] This is true of Weber and Sombart, but not of Simmel. His book was titled *The Philosophy of Money* precisely because he wanted to go beyond the layer of positivist economic science into a consideration of ontology. Moreover, there is not a methodological solution to the issues raised by Simmel, only philosophical ones. Weber's methodology, as it developed from 1904 onwards, wanted to treat ideal factors as causes, not as philosophical inquiry.

3 The Protestant Ethic and the 'Spirit' of Capitalism

Max Weber published *The Protestant Ethic and the 'Spirit' of Capitalism* in two instalments in November 1904 and June 1905. He called it an essay. Most readers assume that it is a book they are reading. It has the structure of a research thesis. Its opening chapter outlines what is to be explained: the much-noted link between economic progress and populations that are Protestant in orientation. Chapter 2 exemplifies but does not define what Weber means by the spirit of capitalism. Chapter 3 develops the argument that the idea of occupation is religious in origin, as indicated by the concept of vocation or calling ('Beruf'). Chapter 4 deepens the argument through an exploration of Christian calling as practised by four different Puritan sects, and this practice is defined by Weber as inner worldly asceticism. Chapter 5 concludes the study by arguing that a religiously derived asceticism constitutes the mentality of modern capitalism. The study is supported throughout by highly detailed and scholarly footnotes, which sometimes reduces the main text to a few lines in the original German edition. So, is it a book or an essay?

This is a slightly unfair question, because what Weber meant by an essay was not the relatively brief exposition of ideas that we take an essay to be. He meant an exploratory investigation rather than a systematic treatise, and the investigation would not be limited in length or in penetrative depth. Most commentators agree that it is unrivalled as a penetrating study of the roots and significance of the western capitalistic work ethic and, indeed, as a study of just what it is that characterizes the uniqueness of modern western civilization or 'Kultur' as Weber termed it.[1] In these senses, it is *taken* to be 'a classic', i.e. widely acknowledged to be outstanding in value and to possess additional qualities of proportioned and harmonious structure befitting one of the foundational texts of sociology and, more widely, the social and cultural sciences.

The critical reaction to the study, both positive and negative, bears out the proposition of its classic status. Within six years of its first appearance, it had attracted a body of critical literature to which Weber replied in a series of anti-critiques. Some of the major figures in economic history (Lujo

Brentano and Werner Sombart) as well as some of the more minor figures (Karl Fischer and Felix Rachfahl) ignited a debate that made Weber's study one of the more controversial issues of the day in the German-speaking academic world. A later German editor of Protestant ethic studies, Johannes Winckelmann, gathered some of these critiques and the anti-critiques together[2] as a supplementary volume, and it came out longer in length than the original studies.[3] Throughout the twentieth century, there have been waves of international debate – some of these collected together in a reader by Green[4] – and in the centenary years (2004–5) of the first appearance of the essay, there have been at least three publications devoted to it.[5] As recently as 1992, Hartmut Lehmann and Guenther Roth published a major scholarly reconsideration of the Protestant ethic. Interest in the subject is likely to be rekindled by the imminent publication of *Die protestantische Ethik und der 'Geist' des Kapitalismus* in the German complete works of Max Weber (Max Weber Gesamtausgabe), complete with introduction and scholarly apparatus. And a fourth English translation of the work is soon to appear.[6]

In the academic world, most debates move on, through scientific resolution, through paradigm change or through exhaustion of the subject. The Protestant ethic debate is one of those few that refuse to lie down and die. I will argue in this chapter that this is in part related to the question already posed: is it an essay or a more systematic academic book? In particular, I will examine the claims that Weber makes for his study, which are somewhat contradictory, and I will argue that these contradictions derive from the origins and construction of the study. And in these respects, while it is a work of outstanding value, its structure is less than classical, and what is taken by sociology to be one of its founding texts in fact has a number of pronounced oddities.

In my original draft for this chapter, I attempted to survey the methods employed by Weber in PESC as a way of teasing out these oddities. It proved to be an almost impossible task. In contemplating my failure, I came to fathom just why Weber's PESC has a perennial ability to weather criticisms. My plan was to reread PESC, and extract and list what seemed to be the principal methods used by Weber. Then, I would compare these methods with what he had to say about them in his methodological writings. I wanted to create a situation similar to Durkheim's where there is a systematic linkage between methodological rules and substantive work. With Durkheim, he wrote his *Rules of Sociological Method* and, then two years later, he produced *Suicide*, which was a near perfect exemplification and vindication of his new scientific method. I knew I would never obtain as perfect a match between method and substantive study in the case of Weber, but assumed this was because Weber did not, or could not, operate in the same planned and integrated way as Durkheim did. Nevertheless, I reckoned that there would be enough of a match to reveal how PESC exemplified Weber's own innovative thinking in methodology. Like any teacher of social research methods, I was aiming to make transparent the combination of methods and practice.

But Weber's PESC resists any such treatment. Methods cannot be separated out from the substantive arguments because Weber had fused them together, and this fusion was a condition of the work's own creation. My argument now is that Weber went beyond methods and created something much more than cultural science – his own designation of what he was doing. To an extent, he had created a work of art, and it is to those methods and skills we have to turn if we are to understand what sort of work of art it was – and still is.

'Theory and method' in PESC

My survey of PESC produced the following list:

1   causal links and causal mechanism;
2   the historical individual and genetic ideal types;
3   hermeneutics;
4   'Verstehen'.

This was drawn up from the following brief audit of Weber's methods.

Chapter 1 of PESC, 'Religious Affiliation and Social Stratification', uses survey data on occupational statistics to establish the argument that Protestant populations are more strongly associated with economic development than Catholic ones. Survey data and the establishment of non-random variability between factors or variables is the dominant style of today's social research. Weber, however, wants to go beyond the results of survey data. He asks: 'why were the districts of highest economic development at the same time particularly favourable to a revolution in the Church? The answer is by no means so simple as one might think'. Weber raises an issue that still bedevils much survey-based research. How do we know what is cause and what is effect? Statistical data can be tabulated and reformatted in all sorts of ways in order to reveal a non-random relationship between variables. Statistically significant correlations between variables, such as religion and occupation, can be found. But the question still remains as to the nature of the relationship and causal priority. Weber will argue that, in initial outline, the causal linkage goes from reformed church to higher economic development in comparison with the unreformed church and the economic character of its population(s). But he immediately acknowledges the counterhypothesis: that higher economic development could attract Protestant populations as more adapted than their

Catholic counterparts. The causal sequence then becomes: the causes of economic development lie outside factors of religion, i.e. they could be endogamous to the economic sphere concerned with trade routes, financial innovation, technological progress, etc. And once economic development is under way in its recognizably modern capitalistic form, then the outlook and habits of Protestants are drawn to the new centres of commerce.

Actually, in a reworked version, this argument is far more potent than Weber allows. But the point is that Weber has flagged up the crucial importance of some kind of underlying model that provides an explanation of how the causal linkages operate – the links or mediations in the argument as well as the directionality of causality. Swedberg and Hedstrom have recently given a very cogent summary of why causal models are required to make sense of statistical data.[7] They call for the explication of the causal mechanism. This is what Weber proposes to do in PESC. He intends to spell out the causal mechanism. This will establish the direction of cause and effect, not beyond scientific doubt, but beyond any uncertainty in his own argument. And he will articulate a chain of causes and effects – a recognition that the causal mechanism will be complex and subtle.

Right at the start of Chapter 2, 'The Spirit of Capitalism', Weber presents the reader with a fairly tricky proposition. The 'spirit' of capitalism – 'a somewhat pretentious phrase', says Weber – can only be understood as 'an historical individual'. It is the novelty of this suggestion that trips the reader up, because not a person, nor a thing, but a 'spirit' is to be thought of as a 'historical individual'. Obviously, then, this is not individual as in a person – such as Fred Smith – but more in line with an individual event. But it is a complex of events that, taken together, would seem to be historically unique or 'individual'. Weber could have referred the reader to his colleague Heinrich Rickert, who originated the concept. But he doesn't and instead provides his own parenthetical definition: 'i.e. a complex of elements associated in historical reality which we unite into a conceptual whole from the standpoint of their cultural significance'. The point about these 'historical concepts', says Weber, is from the methodological point of view 'not to grasp historical reality in abstract general formulae, but in concrete genetic sets of relations which are inevitably of a specifically unique and individual character' (p. 48; all page references are to the Parsons' translation of PESC unless otherwise footnoted). Weber could have saved himself and his book much misunderstanding by going on to explain this more fully, for it entails a central tenet of neo-Kantianism, which was the theory of knowledge that in part underwrote Weber's new approach to the historical and cultural sciences. At the very least, Weber should have referred the reader across to his 'Objectivity' essay, which handled some of these novel methodological issues, including what he meant by 'genetic'.[8] At this juncture, I only list 'historical individual', 'genetic' and 'cultural significance' as requiring further explanation.

Weber then immediately launches into his famous exposition and analysis of Benjamin Franklin. We have already seen why Franklin is central to his argument, for he represents the new spirit of commerce over the old ethos of capitalist traditionalism (and obviously I do need want to repeat Weber's argumentation in this chapter). The methods deployed at this point by Weber concern the interpretation of historical texts. Weber wants to draw out the inference, which for him is crucial, of what Franklin wrote or what was said and reported about the merchant aristocrats, the Fuggers. On p. 71, Weber makes a glancing reference to Franklin, in embodying the new entrepreneurial spirit, as an 'ideal type'. This is not explained, as surely it needed to be. The interpretation of meaning, and in textual expression, is normally known as hermeneutics. Chapter 3, 'Luther's Conception of Calling', is a further, and brilliant, example of hermeneutics, and is a reminder that the technique called hermeneutics was developed within theology and the reading of sacred texts.

Chapter 4, 'The Religious Foundations of Worldly Asceticism', contains the central part of his argument, specifically the sequencing of causes in their roots in Puritan theology to their realization in the conduct of everyday economic life, which as Weber notes is a move from dogmatic origins to non-dogmatic practice. Weber announces at the start of the chapter that: 'In history there have been four principal forms of ascetic Protestantism . . .' (p. 95), and these were Calvinism, Pietism, Methodism and, lastly, the sects growing out of the Baptist movement. Weber, briefly, warns the reader that he 'can of course only proceed by presenting these religious ideas in the artificial simplicity of ideal types, as they could at best be seldom found in history' (p. 98). So, we should briefly follow through and see how Weber handles Calvinism.

Its 'most characteristic' dogma is that of predestination. In the sixteenth and seventeenth centuries in the most highly developed countries of the day – the Netherlands, England and France, this doctrine was subject to 'great political and cultural struggles'. For example: 'The schism in the English Church became irrevocable under James I after the Crown and the Puritans came to differ dogmatically over just this doctrine' (p. 99). Weber shields the reader at this point from the extraordinary political, theological and social complexity of the historical record. Today, as in Weber's days, professional historians can devote a lifetime's scholarship to this period, probably concentrating on just one country. Weber extracts what he takes to be predestination in about three pages, citing, or rather excerpting, the Westminster Confession of 1647 as his main source.[9] He then elaborates or interprets what this means for the religious person and, over the next dozen pages, he elaborates in some very fine writing the deeper significance of this for the persons concerned. This is the place where Bunyan's dilemmas and terrors are outlined. The method being used here, broadly speaking, is an interpretative one, but it subdivides into hermeneutics and the ability to place oneself in the position of someone like Bunyan – the method otherwise known as 'Verstehen'. Then, at the start of Chapter 5, 'Asceticism and the Spirit of Capitalism', Weber has to complete the transition from dogmatic to everyday ethics, and it is here that he expands on manuals of practical instruction, such as Bayley's *Praxis Pietatis* and Baxter's *Christian Directory*. In a sociological sense, he also has to ensure through some empirical verification that working men did, in large numbers, read and follow these instruction manuals.

Weber places his own methodological emphasis, such as it is, on items 1 and 2 – causality and genetic ideal types – and very little about items 3 and 4. Some years later, in connection with his move towards sociology around about 1912, he would have more to say about 'Verstehen'. And right across his oeuvre, he makes hardly any mention of hermeneutics. Not to be systematic and integrated 'as in Durkheim' is allowable, but for Weber to say practically nothing about his principal methods is very strange. What makes it stranger is that his whole intellectual formation came out of a golden age of hermeneutics and 'Verstehen'. Marianne Weber, in her biography, tells us that 'when Weber returned to academic writing around 1900', he started with some methodological writings,[10] and that the leading figures and basis for discussion lay with Dilthey, Windelband, Simmel and Heinrich Rickert.[11] Windelband and Rickert were philosophers who had developed the theory of knowledge, working out the rules and limits of science in the area of history and the cultural sciences. Simmel, as we have already encountered him in the company of Sombart, was a deeply gifted analyst of human behaviour and human motivation and the consequences of action. Wilhelm Dilthey

– and this is where the real surprise lies – not only formulated the grounds on which 'Verstehen' could claim to provide a scientific basis for what he called the human sciences, but was also the leading commentator and theoretician of hermeneutics. Yet, apart from some passing references in an early methodological essay, Weber never refers to him. I shall return to Dilthey in the next chapter but, in the field in which Weber was working, it is reasonable to argue that Dilthey was a massive presence.

So why do items 3 and 4 not receive any explicit attention from Weber? My answer is that Weber had not only absorbed the 'methodological' lessons from Dilthey, but went beyond them as a *practitioner* of hermeneutics. One of the biographical challenges of Max Weber is to realize something akin to what Dilthey achieved with Schleiermacher. Dilthey had established hermeneutics as part of a long tradition in European thought, originally stemming from the interpretation of a sacred text – the Bible – where the explication and understanding of the meaning of a text had become an *art* of interpretation. This is the definition of hermeneutics: the art of interpretation. PESC is peopled with leading interpreters of texts – Luther, Calvin, Zwingli, Wesley, Baxter; these are some of the leading religious figures of the Reformation which, just to point out an obvious and large fact, came about through and depended on the reading and interpretation of the Bible. Weber also engages critically with some of the leading academic theologians of the nineteenth century whose work concerned the historical interpretation of meaning. Weber is such an accomplished and powerful interpreter of meaning that he himself joins the ranks of the hermeneutical tradition. He himself becomes canonical in the interpretation of religious text and religious expression. He becomes the Luther of the secular age, in the John Lennon sense that more people read Weber today than they do Martin Luther. Weber determinedly held on to items 1 and 2 in the list, regarding himself as a proponent of a new causal method in the cultural sciences. He failed to recognize the sheer achievement of his own essay and just how much of his own heart and soul he had poured into the creative outburst that is PESC. Weber's own insistence on the sober, objective and restrained habitus of the 'Wissenschaftler', his own favoured image, is continually belied by his eruptive genius that has left its mark on the European historical consciousness of modernity.

'Der geniale Hermeneutiker'

In this section, I shall give some examples of Weber's interpretative genius, and then I will outline the methodological tradition he was part of, yet went beyond as a practitioner of the art of interpretation.

Weber's treatment of Benjamin Franklin seizes the reader at the start of Chapter 2. Weber, quite dramatically, presents a series of excerpts of Franklin's sayings. Initially, Weber does not tell the reader who the author is or the source. The reader is presented with a series of statements that will produce various reactions in the reader, from strong recognition through to strong incredulity (depending on the reader's exposure to Protestant work values). 'Remember, that *time* is money.' 'Remember, that *credit* is money.' 'Remember, that money is of the prolific, generating nature. Money can beget money, and its offspring can beget more, and so on.' 'Remember this saying, *The good paymaster is lord of another man's purse.*' Weber unleashes the full rhetorical and literary force of Franklin upon the reader. The starting injunction – 'Remember' – repeats like hammer blows. Franklin was also master of the aphorism and, of course, his sayings have entered popular language. What today's readers may have heard their grandmother saying is re-presented by Weber in its pristine form. Franklin ties the getting of money to all other departments of life in a striking, even outrageous, way. The literal implication of Franklin's injunctions is to reduce the waking consciousness of a person to one aim alone, thinking how to make more money.

Weber does not modify his presentation in any way. 'To understand the object of investigation [spirit of capitalism]', he says, 'we turn to a document of that spirit which contains what we are looking for in almost classical purity, and at the same time has the advantage of being free from all direct relationships to religion, being this, for our purposes, free of preconceptions' (p. 48). Weber is being insouciant here. There is some debate about just what Franklin's attitude was. To call it 'classical purity' is to misdirect the reader from Franklin's artfulness. Franklin knew his English was mimicking the religious/Christian form of the Bible 'thou shall do this & thou shall not do that'. Franklin was not a believer, as Weber notes, but his employment of this homiletic form has an air of the not quite serious. Weber takes Franklin to be what we would today perceive as the style of an earnest and evangelical business guru. Franklin, however, was too much of a man of the world (so the debate argues)[12] to take himself this seriously. Rather, a serious point, about how to save in difficult circumstances, is being made in a semi-humorous but memorable way. It has more to do with mnemonics than 'classical purity'.

Weber also does not situate Franklin in his historical setting – mid-eighteenth-century Boston – an economic environment of small traders, producers and shopkeepers. The linkage between Franklin's spirit and any potential seeding of modern capitalism in North America is ignored. Instead, Franklin becomes the embodiment of the spirit of capitalism, period. The pattern of Weber's argumentation, and one comes across this repeatedly in his oeuvre, is to contrast Franklin's attitude with another person's – first Ferdinand Kürnberger and then Jacob Fugger. Kürnberger gave a satirical account of America in his *Picture of American Culture*, which was published in 1855. Weber introduces him as going too far in portraying the American culture as completely materialist. And Fugger, as we have seen, is introduced to show a non-modern business ethos. These two references, historically hundreds of years apart, serve to throw the distinctiveness of Franklin's ethos into relief: 'the earning of money within the modern economic is . . . the result and expression of virtue and proficiency in a calling; and this virtue . . . is the real Alpha and Omega of Franklin's ethic, as expressed in the passages we have quoted . . . ' (pp. 53–4). Through a skilful use of figures who embody differ- ent ethoi – through Franklin, Kürnberger and Fugger – Weber establishes his central point with the reader: '. . . duty in one's calling . . . is an idea which is characteristic of, and indeed in a certain sense of constitutive significance for, the "social ethic" of capitalistic culture' (my translation, p. 54).

Weber is keen to stress the historicity of vocational calling, which has been taken for granted in modern times. It is something he will trace back 'to a time previous to the advent of capitalism'. This (historical) exercise will show just how peculiar an idea vocational calling is. He draws out a powerful historical paradox. This constitutive and historical idea is now no longer required.

> Still less, naturally, do we maintain that a conscious acceptance of these ethical maxims on the part of the individuals, entrepreneurs or labour- ers, in modern capitalistic enterprise, is a condition of the further exist- ence of present-day capitalism. The capitalistic economy of the present day is an immense cosmos into which the individual is born, and which presents itself to him, at least as an individual, as an unalterable order (Gehäuse) of things in which he must live (p. 54).

This is the first appearance of the trope of the immutable shell/steel housing/iron cage of a giant capitalism dwarfing the individual. It is a trope of fear, of helplessness in the face of an impersonal order, of the loss of a personal ethic to an anethical machine. Weber legitimately wants to locate and exemplify what he takes to be the spirit of capitalism, but he does this by playing the reader backwards and forwards through time, pointing him squarely, through passing allusions, to the idea of duty in one's occupational calling. This is not manipulation of the reader, but also it is not without art. Weber's depiction in the rest of the chapter of medieval and Catholic attitudes and traditionalism of work is equally skilful in his use of illustrative examples.

Chapter 3, 'Luther's Conception of Calling', is almost exclusively con- cerned with hermeneutics. It is based purely on textual exegesis and in- terpretation. Weber's argument is that it was Luther who first introduced the idea of work as possessing a religious connotation. Luther, through his translation of certain passages of the sacred texts (ben Sirach and Paul's let- ter to the Corinthians), elided the idea of God's calling of man to salvation ('Ruf') with that of vocation ('Beruf'). Weber establishes this point through a comparison of the original Greek and Latin versions of the relevant sacred texts (and, in the 1920 version of PESC, the Hebrew version) and transla- tions prior to Luther's. The sense in all these languages of a passage, selected by Weber from ben Sirach (Chap 11, verse 20), advises the believer to stay in his job/task/work. Whether 'ergon', 'opus' or 'Pflicht', the sense of these words had no religious connotation. Luther, however, translated this as meaning stay in your 'calling' ('Beruf'), whereby a job or work is now given a religious revaluation.

There are many hermeneutical aspects to what Weber is undertaking. Weber establishes the new meaning of 'Beruf' through a comparison of previous texts both in German and in the first language versions of the sacred text (Greek and Latin). The meaning of a word – here one word – is established in relation to a sentence. The previous normal sense of the sentence is established through its various translations. Luther alters the word and, from that point onwards in Protestant Bibles, the new sense of 'Beruf' is conveyed. Hermeneutics operates by discerning the meaning of a word by placing it in a sentence. It is placed in a known context. That text is also placed in the context of the author. Weber makes the crucial point, both for his own argument and for the operation of hermeneutics: 'but the fact that the word [Beruf] in its present meaning derives from the *translations of the Bible*, in fact from the spirit ('Geist') of the translators, not from the spirit of the original'.[13] Weber, I think rather lazily, does not inform us of Luther's new spirit – presumably a tendency to accentuate work and its sense of joint community. The context, though, is Luther's intent, and this gives Weber and other exegetical commentators the ability to note a semantic shift in an important Biblical word.

Harry Liebersohn, coming to this passage in PESC by another route – a critique of meanings as derivable from ethnic primordialism – has this to say:

> The act of translation disrupts the continuum of culture and introduces a new concept. The search for origins does not lead to a primordial linguistic past but is arrested at a specific moment in Luther's work. Weber's survey of linguistic evidence goes on the assumption of the instability of linguistic meaning over time; he delineates how social and political institutions provide the proper frame of reference for the interpretation of words, whose meaning depends not on linguistic essence or folk spirit, but on social convention.[14]

Hermeneutics, then, proceeds by teasing out meaning or a shift in meaning through relating a word to its surrounding words (a sentence) and outwards to the intent of the author, and still further to the context of the author.

This interpretation of the meaning and significance of 'Beruf' is an absolutely critical stage in Weber's argument. Luther switched the meaning of a concept, and the world in its Protestant sphere was set on a different path. Weber cements his argument by making a contrast between the medieval worldview of Dante and the new Puritan worldview expressed by John Milton. Weber assumes his readers already know the last canto of Dante's *The Divine Comedy*. Weber therefore refers back to the reader's own knowledge and understanding, inserting an emphatic point of his own argument. This barely works for today's reader because a knowledge and appreciation of poetry has been marginalized in favour of a more utilitarian curriculum. *The Divine Comedy* is a cosmological epic in which the poet is guided first through the inferno, then purgatory and, finally, into paradise where, right at the end, the poet looks upwards into the heavens, describing the divinity of God and the state of his own being. Weber could have explained to the reader that the poet's vision and ecstasy is other-worldly and involves a mystic union of poet with the divine, where, through divine benefaction, the poet's will and desire become perfectly reconciled. It is a kind of cosmological nirvana, an inverse of what Weber was later to term, in relation to Buddhism, an acosmic love where pure contemplation replaces the Christian notion of pilgrimage, of a necessary arduous and long journey before sight of the divinity is obtained.

Milton's *Paradise Lost* has the same structure of an epic as Dante's *Divine Comedy*, but the cosmological psychology is entirely different. The worlds of heaven and hell are not invested with liturgy, magic and an intense devotion towards sacred objects and people. In a sense, the medieval Christian outlook tended to assimilate the supernatural into the everyday. For the Puritan, this was not allowed. His or her problem was not so much to attain a psychological state through mysticism, ecstasy and their accompanying techniques of sensory deprivation and intensification, but rather to ensure salvation after death. Weber quotes the passage where Adam and Eve are expelled from paradise, a simply unutterable thought for Dante as the culmination of a religious life was to gain some inkling of paradise. Milton allots some measured sorrow to Adam and Eve as 'They looking back all the eastern side beheld/Of paradise so late their happy seat,'; 'Some natural tears they dropped, but wiped them soon:'. Weber places the next two lines in an emphasized font (which has been accidentally omitted in the Talcott Parsons' translation). 'The world was all before them, there to choose/Their place of rest, and Providence their guide.' The archangel Michael gives them some advice, a list of virtues they will need to get on in the world outside, saying with these they will not be sorry to have left paradise, 'but shall possess/A Paradise within thee, happier far.' Weber also emphasizes these lines (p. 88).

Weber's final comment reads, 'One feels at once that this powerful expression of the Puritan's serious attention to this world, his acceptance of his life in the world as a task, could not possibly have come from the pen of a mediæval writer.' This is something of an understatement about a topic that could have been explored more extensively and more profoundly. Instead, Weber invokes the reader's own poetic imagination and memory to mark the transition point between the medieval and (for Weber) modern sensibility. Weber's interpretation of the meaning of these passages is dependent on the reader's own knowledge and understanding. In the two paragraphs above, I have interposed my understanding of the gulf that stands between Dante's climactic of paradise and Milton's endorsement of work as an alternative for the loss of paradise. As we shall see, this constitutes a permanent feature of hermeneutics.

Puritanism revisited

One of his English texts for PESC was Edward Dowden's *Anglican and Puritan*, which was published in 1900, and whose importance for Weber at a critical stage in his life has been noted by Peter Ghosh.[15] Its chapter on John Bunyan is well worth reading, for it recreates the imaginative world of seventeenth-century English Puritanism. The chapter also advances some of the ideas that Weber integrates into his conceptualization of Puritanism. For us (c. 2006) to enter into Dowden's evocation of Bunyan will take a little imaginative effort of our own. In my education in a Christian school, I do not remember reading Bunyan. I suspect this was because he was regarded as a little too desperate in his religious enthusiasm and his literalism – he was not a suitable role model. My students today are Islamic or Jewish or Christian in faith, or have a multifaith education. This raises the question of how an empathetic connection can be made with a seventeenth-century Puritan? And, more generally, how do we understand another person's faith, or the absence of faith?

Dowden has a phrase to describe this problem – 'the parallax of truth'. Bunyan was the most popular author of middle and late seventeenth-century England – 'who will not say that in the religious passion of an Englishman of the mid-years of the seventeenth century that the parallax of truth was not considerable?'[16] So, from where a Puritan stood in the seventeenth century, what Bunyan wrote had the absolute conviction of truth. Moving forwards in time to 1900 and Dowden registers a problem that the parallax of vision is no longer looking straight ahead, but is looking backwards or not in a straight line. The credibility of Bunyan as an author does not convince in the same way. 'If the deep realities of Puritanism remains – its seriousness, its ardour, its plea for the loins girt and the lamp lit – yet its exact modes of thought and feeling, which did their work and have been replaced by others, can no more be revived than its exact forms of speech.'[17] Dowden himself exemplifies the problem of which he speaks. 'Loins girt and lamps lit' is the language of the seventeenth century. Dowden is being ironic, and he knows his readers will know he has 'patched' into the idiom of early modern English. Of course, it does not really work for us in the twenty-first century (other than through Shakespeare who, as a world author, keeps this language alive).

Dowden regarded Bunyan as having a particular genius. 'Had he interpreted what was peculiar to a special period and a particular phase of religious thought and feeling, what he has written might still be valuable as a document for historical students, but it could not be a living power with successive generations of readers of every class and in almost every region of the world.'[18] Weber, as will be seen, called this a 'transcendental presupposition'. This means that, although we are no longer contemporaneous with past events, we can still understand what animated Bunyan's writings.

Bunyan has an intense feeling of holiness. Religion for him was 'a personal unique experience'. He did not receive his religion through the organized Anglican Church which, with 'its appointed bounds . . . forms and ceremonies [as] an aid to spiritual life', was a form of 'cultivated community'. Bunyan stood for the rawness of direct belief in his God. He found the deepest community 'not in institutions, or corporations, or Churches, but in the secrets of a solitary heart'. This individualized belief gave 'an incandescence of the inward life . . . which touches heights and depths beyond what can be safely approached in forms suited for the general and habitual uses of religion'. Bunyan constructed an inward literary drama of his belief, which featured himself, God and Satan. He, as a solitary soul without help of church rites and ceremonies, has to escape the City of Destruction and journey to the Celestial City. It is a journey from everyday temptation and sinfulness to a realm of purity and salvation. In describing this journey, Bunyan reveals his most private experiences. Bunyan shared his experiential journey by writing *Pilgrim's Progress*, a best-seller in the seventeenth century. He also wrote an autobiography, *Grace Abounding to the Chief of Sinners*, that chronicles the psychological mood changes of his journey: a 'history of a soul struggling from darkness to light, from confusion to clearness, from weakness to strength . . .'. He wrote in Bedford jail in 1666, locked up for the zealousness of his religious convictions and the intolerance of government (whose laws were ameliorated in 1687).

In speaking of the 'disillusioned and pessimistically inclined individualism' and the 'deep spiritual isolation' of the Calvinist, it is Bunyan whom Weber cites,

> To see the specific results of this peculiar atmosphere, it is only necessary to read Bunyan's *Pilgrim's Progress*, by far the most widely read book of the whole Puritan literature. In the description of [Mr] Christian's attitude after he had realized that he was living in the City of Destruction and he had received the call to take up his pilgrimage to the Celestial City, wife and children cling to him, but stopping his ears with his fingers and crying, 'life, eternal life', he staggers forth across the fields. No refinement could surpass the naive feeling of the tinker who, writing in his prison cell, earned the applause of a believing world, in expressing the emotions of the faithful Puritan, thinking only of his own salvation.
> (PESC, p. 107)

Grace Abounding shows that Bunyan was possessed by a literal and vivid understanding of heaven and hell, and his psychological states alternated between a visceral fear that he might die and descend to the tortures of hell, or the intensely felt joy that he might be saved and that his lonely earthly existence would be replaced by entering the communion of saints and God in heaven. The Bible was more than a book of scriptures, it was, says Dowden 'the authentic voice of God'. It was not something to be interpreted by priestly experts, but it was the 'sayings of the divine word; they leaped out upon him, now like angels waving swords of flame, now like winged messengers of consolation'.[19] Bunyan was both a martyr to and the glorified child of Puritan scripturalism, notes Dowden. Bunyan describes what would now be called neurotic and obsessive thoughts. When playing cards in a public house, a voice came into his head and spoke to him – 'Wilt thou leave thy sins and go to heaven or have thy sins and go to hell.' He enjoyed bell-ringing but, on occasions, he could not put out of his mind the idea that the bells and steeple were about to collapse on him, and the fear of this forced him to run out of the building. As he walked along the country roads of Bedfordshire tormented by the psychological agony of whether he was a sinner or whether he could be saved, he would seek a miraculous signal that he was after all to be saved. He would say to the puddles 'be dry' and to the dry patches 'be you the puddles'. Bunyan was what Dowden terms 'otherworldly'. He was always preoccupied by his own goodness or badness and his possible fate when he died, which in his neurosis he always imagined to be at any moment. Yet Bunyan describes this spiritual journey in a completely practical way. It is an empirical world of roads, trees, birds, animals, houses, family, friends and types of person. He lives in this world but is always thinking of another world.

What caused Bunyan a particular sort of ever present terror was the thought that God had already decided who had received His grace and would join 'the elect' in heaven, and that he Bunyan was not among them. He was already, whatever his struggles, doomed to die a sinner and go to hell. The theological term for this is predestination, and its rationale follows from the idea that, if God knew everything, that he was omniscient, he would already know who was destined for salvation and who for damnation. Among the Puritan sects, it was the Calvinists who made predestination a central feature of their faith, unlike the mainstream churches who allowed the idea that, through good works, prayer and confession, all sinners might be saved. This particularly vicious piece of theology had reduced Bunyan to a psychological wreck. And it is an interesting psychological dilemma: if you personally are responsible for your sins directly to God without any intervention of priest, liturgy or confessional, yet God has already decided your fate, just what do you do? Deliverance came, literally, through the Bible. He read 'Behold, thou art fair, my love . . . thou art my love.' This was a message from God to him that he was saved. He was unable to save himself, which as Dowden notes is a form of spiritual egoism. To achieve this, Bunyan tells us, he abandoned his self to the righteousness of God. Bunyan tells us that in this state of grace he *saw* Jesus at God's right hand, i.e. he had attained an extraordinary psychological state. The idea of deliverance, redemption and abandoning oneself to a higher force is well captured in the German word 'Erlösung'. When Weber refers to 'Erlösung', the straight translation is 'salvation'. But Bunyan exemplifies, almost in a psychopathological way, the psychological dimensions of falling into salvation.

Dowden's recreation of Bunyan's faith as psychological drama and crisis would, I suggest, have had a significant impact on Weber in his psychologically prostrated state. This points not simply to Weber's own receptiveness to the otherwise strange world of English Puritanism, but also to Dowden's imaginative powers in retelling Bunyan's story. Of course, today, we are far less receptive. Bunyan comes across as naïve, simple and somewhat unhinged. His language and images seem strange if not bizarre. While the contemporary urbanite may believe in good and evil, the literal visual presence of heaven and hell may well seem far-fetched. However, central to Weber's method is the acceptance that we can imaginatively recreate the psychological attitude, values and outlook of another person, across time and even across cultures. Ten years later, Weber was recreating the mentality of the Confucian in ancient China, the Hindu mystic, the Islamic warrior and so on. The grounds and reasons for this capability raise some interesting questions.

Weber used the case of John Bunyan sparingly, mainly to illustrate the condition of spiritual isolation (as quoted above). In order for Weber to advance his study on the economic effects of religious belief, Weber required more practical attitudes. Bunyan was too extreme a case, bordering as we have seen on the psychopathological and certainly the neurotic. All the main ideas of Puritan behaviour are there in Dowden's study. What we need to see next is how Weber reassembled them. Weber needed to demonstrate the psychological attitude of the mass of Puritans as a more normal phenomenon. When Bunyan was in jail, his wife brought him two books to read: Arthur Dent's *The Plain Man's Pathway to Heaven* and Bishop Bayley's *Practice of Piety*. These texts were manuals of instruction and spelt out just exactly how one could and should behave in everyday situations. Weber used Bayly's *Practice of Piety* and another work that was extremely popular in the seventeenth century, Richard Baxter's *Christian Directory*. This latter book, technically known as a casuistry, is in the format of frequently asked questions. If you lend someone money, should interest be charged upon it? Under what circumstances should beggars be aided? This sort of book is far less fervent and far more a practical guide to everyday conduct. The readers inhabited the same set of Puritan beliefs as Bunyan, but here behaviour is both normalized and disciplined.

Weber makes the point about Bayly (Weber uses the spelling 'Bailey') that, although doctrinal beliefs such as predestination were central to Calvinism, religious writers such as Bayly placed the emphasis not on doctrine but on how one practised one's religion. 'The emphasis was placed so strongly on the *praxis pietatis* that doctrinal orthodoxy was pushed into the background; at time, in fact, it seemed quite a matter of indifference.'[20] And on Baxter, he 'stands out above many other writers on Puritan ethics, both because of his eminently practical and realistic attitude, and, at the same time, because of the universal recognition to his works, which have gone through many new editions and translations.' '. . . like so many of the best spirits of his time, [he] gradually grew away from the dogmas of pure Calvinism.' 'He sought his field of labour most especially in the practical promotion of the moral life through the Church.' 'His *Christian Directory* is the most complete compendium of Puritan ethics, and is continually adjusted to the practical experiences of his own ministerial activity.' Baxter would preach to the weavers and other trades of Kidderminster in the English Midlands, forcefully telling them how they should behave in all practical aspects of life.

Weber, then, combines a keen sense of the psychology of the Puritan predicament with its practical resolution. The principal theme of this resolution was work which, as Weber notes, has in many other religious situations, especially monasticism, been used as a way of controlling the emotions. Puritanism as a doctrine turned away from emotional display, it had a horror of sensuous and sexual enjoyment, it regarded art as frivolous, and regarded idleness as one of the greatest sins. If we accept that man and woman are sensual beings in their make-up, Puritanism can be seen to go against the grain of human nature. 'To put this is in our terms', writes Weber,

> the Puritan, like every rational type of asceticism, tried to enable a man to maintain and act upon his constant motives, especially those which it taught him itself, against the emotions. In this formal psychological sense it tried to make him into a personality (*Persönlichkeit*). Contrary to many popular ideas, the end of this asceticism was to be able to lead an alert intelligent life: the most urgent task the destruction of spontaneous, impulsive enjoyment, the most important means was to bring order into the conduct of its adherents.[21]

Understanding Calvinism

Weber also uses the same passage to indicate the gulf between the Lutheran and the Calvinist outlook. 'But it [life in the world as a task] is just as uncongenial to Lutheranism, as expressed for instance in Luther's and Paul Gerhard's chorales.'[22] The reader, again, has to supply his own meaning, for Weber has assumed his reader attends, or has as a child attended, church services where this music is sung. The reader is meant to infer that participation in Luther's church music 'was to be the liturgical counterpart to his theological doctrine of the communion of all believers'.[23] Calvinism, however, is absolutely severe and far more abstract in its notion of divinity. Strict Calvinist churches play no music (just as they have no altars, stained glass windows or any other sensual evocation of the sacred). Milton was a Calvinist, although in later life, he escaped its full rigour. With this literary flourish, Weber turns the essay away from Luther (allowing, of course, his crucial admission of 'Beruf' into German language usage) and comes to what he says is 'the starting point in the investigation' – 'the relationship between the old

Protestant ethic [Lutheranism] and the spirit of capitalism in the works of Calvin, of Calvinism, and the other Puritan sects' (p. 89).

Weber goes on to state the main methodological purpose of his investigation. 'The following studies could, then, perhaps play a modest part in illustrating the manner in which "ideas" become effective in history.' Weber's academic or 'sociological' treatment of religious ideas was something new c. 1900. He has to reassure his readers that he has no interest in religious ideas for their own sake and, against materialist interpretations of history, he wishes to make two things clear. First, he rejects 'any notion that economic changes could have led to the Reformation as a "historically necessary development"'. Second, he has no intention of defending 'the foolishly doctrinaire thesis' that the '"capitalist spirit" (as always in the provisional sense of the word in which we are using it), let alone capitalism itself, *could only* arise as a result of certain influences of the Reformation'.[24] 'For we are merely attempting to clarify the part which religious forces have played in forming the developing web of our specifically worldly modern culture, in the complex interaction of innumerable different historical factors' (p. 90). From Weber's methodological standpoint, what mattered was not being taken for an idealist, nor for being anti-materialist. His novel suggestion was that ideas could be treated as effective in history, one factor in a constellation of others. Weber is pushing for a more complex grasp of causes and their outcomes. Yet the identification and isolation of the ideas themselves, how they are articulated and expressed in texts, and how taken up within the practical behaviour of people also remains a methodological challenge about which Weber has little to say.

Chapter 4, 'The Religious Foundations of Wordly Asceticism', presents two major challenges for the interpretation of meaning. Weber requires that his analysis of Calvinist theological texts pronouncedly displays the idea of predestination, and then he needs to show how the acute psychological problems presented by predestination are dealt with in everyday conduct. In respect of the first issue, I will discuss his interpretation of the Westminster Confessions and, for the second issue, I return to Richard Baxter.

In Weber's argumentation, Luther had no interest whatsoever in economic development. In economists' terms, he was a traditionalist. However, within the realm of Calvinist doctrine and practice, a fundamental change in attitude towards business and work occurred. Weber quotes directly six statements from the Westminster Confessions of Faith of 1647 as evidence of the Calvinist dogma of predestination, and mentions in support the international synod held at Dordrecht in 1618 that formulated the principle tenets of Calvinist dogma. Actually, in the light of Weber's eloquent discussion of the effects of Calvinist belief, the Dordrecht synod supplies the full tenor of predestination – more so than the Westminster Confessions. Diarmaid Mac-Culloch, a historian of the Reformation, writes of it, 'The Synod formulated conclusions under five headings which would remain the reference points of developed Calvinism: the unconditional decree by God of election, the limiting of Christ's atoning death for humanity to those elect to salvation, the total corruption of humankind, the irresistibility of God's grace, and the unchallengeable perseverance in saving grace of God's elect.'[25] As, today, only some few isolated communities live under the terror of this doctrine, it is probably necessary to probe some of the irrationalities of predestination. Following the writings of St Augustine of Hippo (fourth century CE), church doctrine has held that humankind had fallen into sin, 'into death' as the Bible quaintly puts it. Adam and Eve were the perpetrators of original sin and, hence, their mythical and poetical status in Christian belief. The Christian Church, however, offered forgiveness of sin through the performance of good works – charity, behaving in a Christian manner – and confession. Sins could be absolved in a person's lifetime, even up until death. The Church in countless ways was the beneficiary of this contract. Calvinists considered the Church, under its papal leadership, an abominable interference in the word of God as revealed in the Bible. The Bible teaches that the Christian God is all powerful and all knowing; therefore, in a display of devilish consistency, the Calvinists argued God had already determined everything that could happen, and it was already chosen who were the damned and who would be saved, irrespective of people's actual behaviour. Doctrinal points that the Calvinists and other sects frequently visited were whether a person chosen for election to heaven could, through their wickedness, alter that judgement (was it irresistible?); when God had first decided on the elect – at their birth, at their baptism, at some existential point when they received God's grace (i.e. have been chosen), or even whether God's soteriological lottery had been implemented prior to the appearance of Adam and Eve. The Calvinists were a new sect (under way by 1560), marginalized in Europe and frequently persecuted. So, by word of explanation, the social psychology of this belief system excluded any intellectual doubt about salvation and demanded complete confidence of its members that they should act as if they were predestined for salvation.

Weber's use of the Westminster Confessions can be criticized for its partiality. The full doctrinal extent of Calvinism could have been better presented, for instance through the Dordrecht synod. This would have better underpinned Weber's wide-ranging subsequent discussion. Malcolm H. MacKinnon has criticized Weber's partiality in another way.[26] In his excerpting of the Westminster Confessions, Weber mistook the main doctrinal thrust of the document. The statements that Weber quotes are a kind of preamble of what everyone already knew. They are of less significance than what follows. The real message of the Westminster Confessions was an amelioration of the doctrine of predestination in favour of God's providential guidance of mankind. Providence still asserts the denial of free will to people in the face of God's all powerful status, and it is God who will decide the fate of each individual irrespective of their attempts to influence his decision – a guilty thought or single bad deed can still lead to damnation. But God's decision has not been predetermined. This offers a slightly more liveable contract, or covenant as it was known, of Calvinists with their God. MacKinnon goes on to argue that this reduces Calvinists' anxiety over their salvation, so the psychological tension that Weber argued for as crucial to disciplined conduct was historically inaccurate.

There have been a number of assessments of just how damaging the MacKinnon critique is for the Weber thesis.[27] The technique of hermeneutics has the ability to resolve the MacKinnon/Weber dispute in terms of the interpretation of meaning. A principle of hermeneutics is to relate individual words, sentences and paragraphs within the whole text; also, the intentions of the authors of a text should be taken into account. If Weber were to provide an anti-critique to MacKinnon, he would have to follow such a procedure.

MacKinnon also pursues Weber over his interpretation of Baxter and Bayly. It will be recalled that Weber's final empirical proof for the effects of belief on conduct rested not on dogma but on how the lay population were guided in their practical behaviour. This is one reason for Weber's justification of his reluctance to become too deeply involved in religious dogma. The doctrinal points that priests argued over, while of interest to theologians, have only indirect relevance for the economic historian. But MacKinnon argues that, if the true import of the Westminster Confessions allowed the idea of 'effectual calling', through correct spiritual exercise a person could influence their fate, then the task of Richard Baxter in his pastoral preaching was less daunting.[28] MacKinnon's reading of Baxter is that a temporal calling is just another term or description for occupation with none of the religious overtones imputed by Weber to Luther. Also that Baxter and other Puritans distinguished between temporal calling and spiritual calling. It was the latter that was the object of Baxter's ministry. Temporal calling was considered to be part of natural life and a matter of indifference in spiritual terms.

MacKinnon's critique has, in its turn, been subjected to a penetrating critique by David Zaret, who seeks to reinforce Weber's view that Puritanism was 'an anxiety-inducing creed' and to restore Weber's arguments on the 'spiritualization of secular employments'.[29] Once again, matters turn on the interpretation of documents, and Zaret notes that, within a proper selection of documents, there will be contradictory evidence, interpretations for both strict determinism and providential statements. Zaret puts his methodological requirements in the language of current qualitative social research. All researchers are faced with the problem of 'exegetical selectivity' – which texts and documents to present and which to leave to one side. This does not permit selectivity that eliminates the ambiguity of the original documents and discards any interpretation that goes against the researcher's own favoured line of argument. The criterion of reliability stipulates thatnother researchers who come along and reassess the data would not expect to find marked biases of interpretation in the account of the first researcher. Obviously, there will be biases according to viewpoint, but science does not permit all evidence against a viewpoint to be dropped into the trash can, and all evidence for to be ruthlessly extracted from the overall text. Second, the process of inference of behaviour from belief systems requires 'triangulation', that is 'corroborating interpretations of formal writings by consulting other types of textual data such as autobiographies, biographies, letters, juridical records, contemporary accounts, and so on'.[30] Third, when a document is studied, it is necessary to take account of the context in which it was written.[31]

Weber's own presentation and the numerous subsequent debates demonstrate that one of the primary methodological fields in PESC concerns the interpretation of meaning. Before turning to Weber's reluctance to make this an explicit topic in his methodology, I will finish this chapter with some observations on the rhetorical force with which Weber conveys his arguments.

'Der Rhetoriker'

In the interpretation of the significance and meaning of Puritan texts and religious praxis, Weber appears to follow the obvious procedure of presenting a text and then moving on to critical commentary of it. But his commentary quite quickly becomes a strongly moulded set of arguments whose purpose and endpoint are to offer a 'characterology' of the ascetic Protestant. Weber's own argumentation is eloquent and is not without rhetorical flourishes. His method of exposition is highly effective, and he leaves the reader very much in possession of a fully explicated 'character'.

His discussion of Benjamin Franklin falls into this mode of interpretative procedure. Probably the most impressive example is his analysis of Calvinism. The Westminster Confessions are excerpted, some textual analysis occurs and then, around page 103 in the Parsons' translation (which best picks up Weber's eloquent flow), Weber launches into an almost intimate portrait of the predicament of the Calvinist. 'For the damned to complain of their lot would be much the same as for animals to bemoan the fact they were born as men.' Weber is paraphrasing Calvin, but is it Weber's voice or Calvin's voice we are hearing?[32] Weber acknowledges the majesty of Calvinist doctrine, almost personally. 'In its extreme inhumanity this doctrine must above all have had one consequence for the life of a generation which surrendered to its magnificent consistency. That was a feeling of unprecedented inner loneliness of the single individual' (p. 104). Here, Weber references Edward Dowden's depiction of the Calvinist as a 'solitary soul'. Of that inhumanity for the lone individual, Weber enthuses:

> No one could help him. No priest, for the chosen one can understand the word of God only in his own heart. No sacraments, for though the sacraments had been ordained by God for the increase of His glory . . . they are not a means to the attainment of grace . . . No Church, for though it was held that outside the Church there is no salvation . . . , nevertheless the membership of the external Church included the doomed . . . .

Finally, even no God. For even Christ had died only for the elect, for whose benefit God had decreed His martyrdom from eternity.

(p. 104)

The repetition of the negative followed by the explanatory clause is, of course, a cadence much used in the Bible itself, although Weber keeps his rhetoric within the bounds of ostensibly cultural science.

Weber then moves on to the sensuous side of the Calvinist character: 'the corruption of everything pertaining to the flesh, this inner isolation of the individual contains, . . . the reason for the entirely negative attitude of Puritanism to all the sensuous and emotional elements in cultural and in religion . . .' '. . . it forms one of the roots of that disillusioned and pessimistically inclined individualism' (p.105). In this vein, friendship is mistrusted, for a Calvinist should place his trust exclusively in his God. Confession was disallowed. 'The means to a periodical discharge of the emotional sense of sin was done away with' (p. 106). Weber relentlessly heightens the sense of being shut off from all normal physicality, contact and pleasure and, at this point, introduces the figure of Bunyan, a man so obsessed with salvation that wife and children have to be left behind for its immediate search. Weber then enters into a number of literary comparisons on the matter of ultimate existential choices. The true Calvinist's fear of death is like Döllinger's description of Alfonso of Liguori. Bunyan is also like a character in one of Gottfried Keller's novels, but he is quite unlike Machiavelli's citizen who would place 'love of their native city higher than the fear for the salvation of their souls'. And the Calvinist is even further away from the mock feudal fatalism of Wagner's Siegmund 'before his fatal combat' (examples, p. 107). Some of these comparisons will not work for the current reader because he or she will have a different universe of historical and literary references. But what Weber is establishing with the reader is a sense of the position of the Calvinist as a character type in relation to other types.

Weber enters into a four-way comparison: the Calvinist, the Lutheran, the Catholic and the monk. The Calvinist is wrenched away from the close ties that would normally bind him to the world. As an elect, predestined to heaven, his only way to realize the glory of God, which was a commandment, was to labour in a calling. The Lutheran, who also has to bear the sense of sin, can simply trust in God's grace rather than trying to 'prove it' through labour as does the Calvinist. Work for the Lutheran can be a straightforward sense of brotherliness. Weber is drawing what for him was to be an important contrast of types. The religious believer can ensure a state of grace 'either in that he feels himself to be the vessel of the Holy Spirit or the tool of the divine will. In the former case his religious life tends to mysticism and emotionalism, in the latter to ascetic action. Luther stood close to the former type, Calvinism belonged definitely to the latter' (pp. 113–14). With these types is contrasted 'the normal Catholic layman' who 'lives ethically, so to speak, from hand to mouth' (p. 116), that is in his secular and temporal work, 'did not necessarily form a connected, or at least not a rationalized system of life . . .'. Against these, 'the moral conduct of the average man [Calvinist] was thus deprived of its planless and unsystematic character and subjected to a consistent method for conduct as a whole' (p. 117). In this respect, as a planned form of asceticism as a way of seeking to ensure grace, it comes close to western monasticism. Western monasticism 'developed a systematic method of rational conduct with the purpose of overcoming the *status naturae* . . .'. Active self-control, as developed in the monasteries, became 'the most important practical ideal of Puritanism'. The respect for 'quiet self-control . . . still distinguishes the best type of English or American gentleman to-day' (p. 119).

Weber's writing of these passages is masterful. He combines theological, ethical and practical precepts in developing a characterology or a series of character types: the average medieval layman, medieval monk, Puritan and Lutheran. Weber focuses the Puritan character in the reader's mind through a series of well-handled comparisons. 'The Puritan, like every rational type of asceticism, tried to enable a man to maintain and act upon his constant motives, especially those which it taught him itself, against the emotions. In this formal psychological sense of the term it tried to make him into a personality' (p. 119). Asceticism, a practice, is made into a living thing, breathing form into the Puritan. Weber makes his characters, as average types, come alive for the reader. Given the complexity of the materials and the history with which he is working, this is a formidable achievement. He lodges these characters in the reader's mind, and they become fixed reference points for an understanding of Reformation history and its long-term effects.

In his summation of his essay, where Weber seeks to further emphasize his argument, he chooses the theme of the imposition of Puritan asceticism turning 'with all its force against one thing: the spontaneous enjoyment of life' (p. 166). Weber selects the episode in which King James I and Charles I of England tried to stop the Puritans' banning of all popular pastimes on the sabbath. Enjoyment of life versus rational asceticism becomes a defining moment in the characterology of early modernity. Weber pursues this theme with considerable literary skill in the field of culture and arts. 'Here asceticism descended like a frost on the life of "merrie Old England"'. 'The Puritan's ferocious hatred of everything which smacked of superstition, of all survivals of magical or sacramental salvation, applied to the Christian festivities and the May Pole and all spontaneous religious art.' 'The theatre was obnoxious to the Puritans, and with the strict exclusion of the erotic and of nudity from the realm of toleration, a radical view of either literature or art could not exist.' Warmth, sensuality, enjoyment on one side, and hoar frost on the other – the argument with its use of this imagery becomes irresistible in its rhetorical force. Asceticism was an attack against a universal character, the average sensuous living human being. 'That powerful tendency toward uniformity of life, which today so immensely aids the capitalistic interest in the standardization of production, has its ideal foundations in the repudiation of all idolatry of the flesh' (pp. 168–9).

Weber's essay ends in pages that are now so well known that they have become etched upon our own consciousness. He does this by bringing together his historical characters and some of his recurrent images. Weber has related a story of where capitalist spirit originated from, how it entered the lives of the Puritans and was transferred into methodical conduct of the utilitarian outlook of the nineteenth century, and then that spirit disappearing from the human being as an animating principle to become the spirit inherent within the capitalistic economic cosmos of industrial capitalism; becoming, as if it were, the ghost in the machine. Weber, almost arrogantly and certainly in a Nietzschean flourish, discards the notion of a meaningful, animating sense of vocation for the modern professional. They are 'sensualists without heart, specialists without spirit'. Weber conducts his argument through a deft handling of his historical characters pulling them onto a fast-moving historical stage whose backdrop is images of the human form, clothing, confines and machinery.

> The Puritan wanted to work in a calling; we are forced to do so. For when asceticism was carried out of monastic cells into everyday life, and began to dominate worldly morality, it did its part in building the tremendous cosmos of the modern economic order. This order is now bound to the technical and economic conditions of machine production which to-day determine the lives of all the individuals who are born into this mechanism, not only those directly concerned with economic acquisition, with irresistible force. Perhaps it will so determine them until the last ton of fossilized fuel is burnt. In Baxter's view the care for external goods would only lie on the shoulders of the 'saint like a light cloak, which can be thrown aside at any moment'. But fate decreed that the cloak should become a casing as hard as steel.[33]

In a recent contribution, Donald A. Nielson argues that Weber's PESC is a 'grand narrative'. It cannot be considered a narrative in the normal sense as understood by historians, as it fails to adhere to any consistent time line. Weber's examples shift backwards and forwards through time and place – Franklin in the eighteenth century, Baxter and Bunyan in the seventeenth century, the Wesleys in the nineteenth century and so on. But Nielsen suggests that, if the topics were joined up, then his thesis could become 'the grand historical narrative of European civilization's inner life'.[34] Nielsen rearranges Weber's major topics and produces the following temporal series: monastic orders, Luther's idea of calling, Calvinist teaching, Puritan ethics as an everyday accomplishment, Benjamin Franklin, Methodist workers, the iron cage of industrial capitalism. Nielsen's perception is interesting, because it poses the question: just what would a narrative of a civilization's inner life consist of? To make it 'grand' would surely lead such a historian into an idealist and essentializing methodology, as if there was a continuous mentalist thread to be grasped.

Weber does not do this. An alternative way of approaching this is through Wilhelm Hennis, who has argued, in a series of provocative and authoritative essays, that Weber is conducting throughout his oeuvre a form of philosophical anthropology. It is the human being who always stands at the centre of Weber's interests. The materials Hennis brings together go far beyond the subject of this chapter, and he constructs a sociology of orders around the concept of the human being ('Mensch'). His viewpoint, which he strongly attributes to Weber himself, is that the concept of the human being, or man, belongs to a long tradition of political thought from the Sophists, to Aristotle, to Machiavelli and to classical political economy, where the questions of politics – how should we live? – is always interlinked to a concept of man as a human being living together in society. This can be termed philosophical anthropology to the extent that the human being, as a living physical and cultural entity, is a constant reference point for study and for education; although Hennis would not accord a cardinal priority to anthropology separate from the political. The individual, as a human and cultural being, needs to be studied in relation to the social and political orders within which he and she is always to be found.

On the basis on the PESC text alone, it goes too far to say that Weber was engaged in a philosophical anthropology. But Hennis has observantly noted that there is some sort of characterology at work here and that Weber is always concerned with living individuals and not an abstract entity like 'homo sociologicus' or 'homo œconomicus'.[35] If a search is conducted using the prefix 'Leben-' ('life'), the word is rife throughout PESC: 'Lebensführung', 'Lebensinhalt', 'Lebensbeziehung', 'Lebensfremdheit', 'Lebensreglementierung', 'Lebenstechnik', 'Lebensbedürfnisse', 'Lebensstil', 'Lebenstempo', 'Lebensgenuß', 'Lebensarbeit', 'Lebensideale', 'Lebensfreude', 'Lebenspraxis', 'Lebensstellung', 'Lebensstimmung', 'Lebenszweck', 'Lebenshochmut', 'Lebensweisheit', 'Lebensglück', 'Lebenslage', 'Lebensgestaltung', 'Lebenszeit', 'Lebensanchauung', 'Lebensauffassung'. 'Lebensführung' occurs over 65 times in the text.[36]

We should agree that the living individual in his and her inner and outer life is a central concept of PESC. To call it a grand narrative or a philosophical anthropology does not quite designate what Weber was doing in PESC. My conclusion from this chapter's analysis is that Weber is presenting to the reader a set of characters who come to personify in their views, their behaviour and their outlook a series of historical types whose distinctive characteristics are revealed and thrown into relief through their comparison. In presenting these characters, Weber goes beyond the art of interpretation (hermeneutics) and offers the reader something closer to the art of the novelist. Imagery, rhetoric, eloquence and the play of character are all used to impress Weber's cardinal aim: conveying to the reader the full significance and meaning of a crucial stage in the formation of modern rationalistic capitalism and culture. Weber gave a copy of PESC to Mina Tobler, who was a close and amorous friend of his. Tobler wrote to her mother on 6 October 1912:

> Isn't that splendid, such an historical chain of arguments in which each part is remorselessly pieced together without any gaps, where, as in this case, 'the writer' makes himself totally invisible but nevertheless everything that is there is involuntarily animated by the heartbeat of a grand personality. He said I would find it boring, and I have read it as if it were a good novel.[37]

Professor Lepsius notes of Mina Tobler that she 'could not provide Weber with any intellectual resonance, or act as a critic; she reacted spontaneously and emotionally'.[38] The academic criticism, as we have seen, is relentless in pointing out the various shortcomings of the PESC. But Tobler identifies the sense that PESC has for the first-time reader. It does read like a novel with a thread of arguments drawn together by the writer's artistry. In expressing her views Mina Tobler was re-living the spontaneity of Weber's original creativity. That for Weber probably concerned a mix of intellectual emotions – dread, joy, admiration, aspiration – emotions not unconnected to his own predicament in 1900. These he used to re-live and re-create the experience of Puritan beliefs and practice. Tobler reminds us that the interpretation of meaning is always about re-animating the experiences of not a dead past, but a past brought to life. This is what Dowden did, and what Weber did in his turn. And whether these works still speak to us will depend on our imaginative resources and circumstances.

4 'Wissenschaftslehre'

Tying PESC down to any specific method, or even set of methods, is a futile undertaking. As we have already noted, it is a fusion of methods and a highly imaginative intellectual project. Weber was offering a new solution to a wide-ranging debate on the origins and significance of modern capitalism. His originality lay in offering a new explanatory variable – 'kapitalistische Geist' – placed within his own framework of investigation. He used every available intellectual means to investigate and convey his thesis: statistics, philology, historical scholarship, theology, hermeneutics and a highly figurative and, at times, rhetorical mode of delivery. His work fell into no recognizable school of thought or discipline, yet it revolutionized how historians, cultural scientists, economic historians and sociologists would think about their subject. Weber had exceeded by far what had, up until then, been achieved in this subject area – and especially in the manner he had accomplished this.

What I want to examine in this chapter is, broadly put, what Weber thought he had achieved. On a personal level, he had come back from academic oblivion, having lost his university chair as a full member of the faculty through illness, and established his reputation for originality, scholarship and the sheer imaginative power of his work. But he had also put himself in a new intellectual territory. While he may have started out as a national-economist, after the completion of his essay he was in a new but undefined territory. He was not a sociologist. Not for him Durkheim's systematic steps of founding a discipline first through definition of rules and, second, by brilliant vindication and realization of those rules. Weber had started on some methodological reflections in 1900 – a series of three essays on the 'old' 'Nationalökonomie', which took him five years and then remained uncompleted. They were highly discursive, overly complex and still remain a topic of some scholarly despair among experts today – little Gallic illumination shines out. He also composed, in consultation with his fellow *Archiv* editors, a supposedly programmatic introduction on the occasion of assuming the editorship of the *Archiv*. From these writings, one can establish what he disliked and what were the new tasks, but they do not adequately explain what he was doing in PESC. And from within PESC, the reader is given little practical guidance as to his own method of proceeding and, frequently, the reader is simply assumed to be informed about contemporary debates. An instance of this is the throwaway reference to the 'historical individual' – a less than intuitive concept formulated by the philosopher Heinrich Rickert.

In this chapter, I give an exposition of some of the principal ideas of Wilhelm Dilthey, and I argue that they are the most relevant for what Weber achieved in PESC, especially the manner in which he did this. I examine critically the accepted position that Weber adhered to Rickert's philosophical position on the validity of knowledge in the historical and cultural sciences. For reasons that have yet to be completely explained, Weber followed Rickert's critical distance to Dilthey's *Introduction to the Human Sciences*, even though that work presented the fundamental issues of how a science of mental life was both possible and necessary. Weber devised his own methodology of meaning and causation and, in his essay on 'Objectivity', he showed how progress in social science was possible – and transitory.

The word itself – methodology – is fairly horrendous. Marianne Weber used the term 'Wissenschaftslehre' when referring to her husband's 'methodological' writings, and this was the title she gave to the collection of those writings. 'Wissenschaftslehre' was already a 'heritage' word when Marianne Weber chose it (in 1922). She took it from the title of one of Fichte's lecture courses in Berlin c. 1800, i.e. at the start of the whole revolution in method and techniques that so distinguished German academic knowledge throughout the nineteenth century.[1] Marianne Weber was alluding to the agreeable idea that 'Wissenschaftslehre' denoted an idea of knowledge and a way of learning; something one would do throughout one's life as a developing potential and that would contribute to knowledge and culture in its turn. Methodology can, of course, be technical but, when the term is used in relation to Max Weber and his contemporaries, it still retained some component of learning as part of life and culture. Its Fichtean legacy concerned ontology – statements about the nature of reality and being – and epistemology – theories on the status of knowledge. In addition, there was a concern with the validity as well as the relevance of knowledge, where validity concerned the philosophical justification of knowledge itself.

Marianne Weber, in resorting to Fichte's Berlin lecture course ('Wissenschaftslehre'), also makes the link between learning and a new national awareness. Fichte established patriotism among the educated middle class at the time of the Napoleonic rule of Prussia. From these small beginnings began the ascent of the idea of Germany as a cultural nation and the role of the educated middle class in propagating those ideas through a distinctive idea of learning ('Bildung'). Education and, by implication, 'methodology' had a decidedly emancipatory flavour. Some of this emancipatory fervour is still detectable in Weber's methodological essay on 'Objectivity' when setting out the agenda of the relaunched *Archiv fur Sozialwissenschaft und Sozialpolitik*. Hence, when the word 'methodology' is used in this chapter, it is quite capacious in its various senses.

The study of methodology also has an unfortunate tendency to place people in schools and to create divides after the event. Weber himself, especially in the field of the philosophy of history, was a polemicist. But much of what Weber achieved came from his ability to synthesize different methods. Some care, therefore, has to be taken in inferring what positions, at the time, were complementary, what were compatible and what were truly opposed. I will outline the field of methodological forces at work; 'in play' would be a better phrase, because positions had not yet solidified. For example, when Weber does cite Dilthey or Husserl or Vossler, it would be a mistake for us to conclude that somehow Weber should be considered to be sympathetic to vitalism, phenomenology or linguistics respectively. The period c. 1900 was awash with new ideas and new approaches, and it is only later rationalizations of academic knowledge that have retrospectively codified these fluid positions into opposed schools.[2] We also need to take on board recent work by Austin Harrington who argues that, in the subsequent codification of debates, false oppositions have been created – crucially, between hermeneutics and objectivity; equally, the work by Michael Friedman that points out that the split between 'analytic' and 'continental' philosophy occurs was not as clear cut in the period in which Weber was writing, and Stephen Turner, who argues the relevance of Weber's philosophy of social science in connection with recent work on action, explanation and cause. In the formation of later positions, each side drew from a common store of philosophical presuppositions.[3]

I present the main elements in the methodological field of debate, in which it should be noted that Weber himself is an interacting and not yet stabilized element. The main figures include Wilhelm Dilthey, whose whole approach to academic knowledge insisted that we, as academic writers, are embedded in the flow of life and this affects how we revisit our subject material, for example history. Georg Simmel is an important referent, because he had already articulated the validity grounds of knowledge in cultural science and sociology in *The Philosophy of Money* (which we have already discussed in relation to the debate over modern capitalism). Both Dilthey and Simmel were drawn to certain ideas of Friedrich Nietzsche who, from a methodological point of view, can be regarded as something of a 'wild card'. His thinking injected creativity and instability into the force field. Carl Menger, who we have already encountered, offered Weber the heuristic option of modelling the complexity of social reality. Lastly, the Baden epistemologists, Wilhelm Windelband and Heinrich Rickert, attempted to impose their own philosophical order on the field. They stood in the Kantian tradition that the flux of reality had to be tamed through the imposition of categories, classifications and judgements. This, to repeat, is schematic in presentation, and one has to remember that the German tradition was rooted in a very keen sense of the history of philosophy, including classical Greek philosophers and schools. Weber can at times be quite disconcerting, plucking ideas or concepts unreferenced (because he expected his readers to know the reference) from both the history of philosophy and his own contemporaries.

Wilhelm Dilthey

Dilthey is the most intriguing influence. He is mentioned least by Weber, he is usually presented in opposition to Weber, yet PESC is the most 'Dilthey-an' of all Weber's works. Anyone who doubts Dilthey's pervasive influence need only consult a glossary of his terms in order to realize their take-up in writers such as Max Weber: 'Bedeutsamkeit', 'Bedeutung', 'Erfahrung', 'Erklärung', 'Erlebnis', 'Geist', 'Geisteswissenschaften', 'Gemeingefühl', 'Handlung', 'Herrschaft', 'Kausalzusammenhang', 'Kulturwissenschaften', 'Leben', 'Lebenseinheit', 'Lebensführung', 'Lebensgefühl', 'nachfühlen', 'psychophysische', 'Sinn', 'Sittlichkeit', 'Stellung', 'Trieb', 'Urteil', 'Verhaltung', 'Verstand', 'Verstehen', 'Weltbild', 'Wirklichkeit', 'Zusammenhang', 'Zweck'.[4] Many of these words are simply common German words. 'Verstehen' is the verb 'to understand'. But it is the use to which Dilthey puts them that marks them out as part of his conceptual vocabulary. They are all used, often in a reconceptualized form, by Weber. Translating the above list of terms, it will be seen that many of them are everyday terms: 'Significance', 'meaning', 'experience', explanation', 'lived experience', 'spirit' or 'mental life', 'the sciences of mental life', 'feelings held in common', 'action', 'power over somebody', 'causal nexus', 'life', 'the individual as an entity', 'conduct of life', 'feeling of life', 'to re-experience feeling', 'psychophysical', 'sense' or 'meaning', 'ethical life', 'attitude', 'drive', 'judgement', 'behaviour', 'comprehension', 'understanding', 'worldview', 'reality', in the sense of what (the social scientist) wishes to designate as real, 'an interrelated context', 'purpose'. Most of these words belong to the language of life, and their usage by both Dilthey and Weber demonstrates that a social or cultural science will operate with words that are commonly used by people themselves. Unfortunately, it is not quite that simple, because their use within science involves treating them as concepts with fairly precise definitions, and procedures have to be followed within research in order to ensure accuracy and truthfulness. The language of life confers its own relevance on study, but the social and cultural science has its own ways of proceeding.

Dilthey (1833–1911) belonged to the generation before Max Weber's. In fact, he was a friend of Weber's father in Berlin in the 1860s. The young Max Weber visited Dilthey as a sixteen-year-old during a walking tour in Bohemia. In his letters home from the walking tour, he treats Dilthey with some familiarity.[5] In the 1860s, Dilthey worked as a journalist before establishing himself in an academic position and, as a philosopher, he still continued writing articles for newspapers on a huge range of topics: culture, literature, science, politics, religion. He was a voracious reader and followed developments in both humanities and natural sciences. These last two terms are common to the Anglophone world. Dilthey argued for a cultural science alongside natural science. Both would be sciences, and the German word 'Wissenschaft' allows this latitude as well as indicating that science was also knowledge and learning. 'Humanities' in the Anglophone sense would remain for literary and cultural studies, but a science of culture or of human and mental life he termed 'Geisteswissenschaft'. This, as befitting a science, would be as systematic, objective, reliable and truth establishing as the natural sciences; however, the cultural and natural sciences each had their own subject material and would therefore pursue their broadly similar goals through different routes and methods. The subject material of the natural sciences was matter, whereas in the 'Geisteswissenschaften', what was studied was the expression (in language, text, artefact and art) of human mental life. 'These are only accessible to understanding and require interpretation.'[6] Dilthey was the first person to establish a rigorous set of criteria for distinguishing between the natural and the cultural sciences and their respective approaches. Simmel, Weber, Windelband and Rickert all followed his lead in making this distinction, even though they introduced qualifications, amendments and objections of their own. When Max Weber speaks, successively, of a cultural science, a social science and a sociology, it was Dilthey who provided the gateway into a scientific approach that placed meaning and cultural significance at the heart of the enterprise.

While understanding and interpretation may be thought of as normal words and everyday accomplishments, Dilthey specified their operation within the 'Geisteswissenschaften'. Central to the cultural sciences is the interpretation of meaning. Human activity has the capability of communicating meaning. The method of comprehending these meanings is hermeneutics. Dilthey saw this as a rigorous and difficult accomplishment, as equal to corresponding activity in the natural sciences. Writing at the end of the nineteenth century, he keenly appreciated the advances that had been made in philology, law, history and theology from the start of that century. In theology, close textual analysis of the Bible in its various original languages (Greek, Hebrew, Aramaic and Latin) had identified the history of its compilation – that the first five books of the Old Testament were not the oldest parts as the Genesis story would imply, and that, from the literary styles of the New Testament gospels, much could be learnt about their authors and their intentions. While for the believer the Bible was the word of his or her God, for biblical scholars, the historicity of its origins could be established. In history and law, the study of historical documents, records and inscriptions allowed the actual history of, say, ancient Rome to be ascertained in place of literary treatments of a mythical past and romantic ruins. Likewise, the history of the German language could be traced from its earliest appearances, a scholarly exercise that was crucial to an emergent sense of a German cultural heritage. These achievements for Dilthey rivalled those in natural science which had emancipated itself from medieval theories of substances and essences, from alchemy and from religion.

In his *Introduction to the Human Sciences*, Dilthey writes with as much confidence as a Comte or Durkheim.

> The sciences which take socio-historical reality as their subject matter are seeking, more intensively than ever before, their systematic relations

to one another and to their foundation. Conditions within the positive sciences are working in this direction together with powerful forces stemming from the upheavals in society since the French revolution. A knowledge of the forces that rule society, of the causes that have reproduced its upheavals, and of society's resources for promoting healthy progress has become of vital concern to our civilization. Consequently, relative to the natural sciences, the importance of the sciences dealing with society is increasing. On the large scale of modern life, a transformation of our scientific interests is taking place comparable to that which occurred in the small Greek city-states in the fifth and fourth centuries B.C . . .[7]

Like Comte and Durkheim, Dilthey insists that the study of history, society and culture will be a science. It will be 'a complex of propositions 1) whose elements are concepts that are completely defined, i.e., permanently and universally valid within the overall logical system, 2) whose connections are well grounded, and 3) in which finally the parts are connected into a whole for the purpose of communication.' In a further comment, Dilthey wrote: 'Thus, all philosophy of science is governed by the concept of scientific certainty in its various forms, such as the conviction of reality in perceptions, evidence in reasoning, and the consciousness of necessity in accordance with the principle of sufficient reason in knowledge.'[8]

Unlike Comte or J.S. Mill, whose works Dilthey had studied closely, the sciences of society, culture and history – the human sciences ('Geisteswissenschaften') will not be based on 'a definition of knowledge which arises from a predominant concern with the natural sciences . . .'. It is because of this mistaken identification of social with natural science – an 'arbitrary concept of knowledge' says Dilthey, 'some have shortsightedly and presumptuously denied the status of science to the writing of history as it has been practiced by great masters . . .'.[9]

The human sciences are faced with difficulties of their own, but this should not be used to deny their scientific approach and ambitions. History, social science, sociology, the study of culture, the moral sciences – these all have in common a concern 'with the facts of the human spirit' ('geistigen Lebens'). A science of this spirit ('Geist') has 'the advantage of appropriately characterizing the central sphere of facts in terms of which the unity of these disciplines was actually perceived, their scope outlined, and their demarcation from the natural sciences established, no matter how imperfectly'. This unity resides in 'human self-consciousness'.

Dilthey's programme will establish how 'human self-consciousness' may be scientifically studied, how this will be constitutionally different from the natural sciences, and how this study undergirds the unity of the human sciences. The quality of human self-consciousness Dilthey refers to as 'geistlich'. This is the same word that Max Weber used in the title of PESC – *Die protestantische Ethik und der 'Geist' des Kapitalismus*. Weber placed 'Geist' in inverted commas, and we have seen that this could have been a direct reference and distancing from Sombart's use of the same phrase. Equally though, we come to the issue of how the facts of human self-consciousness can be studied, which is the challenge Dilthey sets out to answer. 'Spirit' as a translation misleads. What Dilthey is trying to grasp by scientific means can be termed, alongside human self-consciousness, a quality of mental life, or the psychological medium of cultural communication between individuals. We can intuitively understand what Weber is conveying in his term the 'spirit of capitalism'. It is a specific type of human self-consciousness shared through the medium of religious practice by a large number of people. Dilthey's task is to demonstrate how there can be a robust science of what is intuitively obvious to us as social and cultural beings – something Weber presumes (on the basis of Dilthey I will argue) rather than explains.

Dilthey's *Introduction to the Human Sciences* has the sense of a pioneering work. There have been advances in both the natural sciences and the humanities, and his chosen task is to place a science of mental life on firm foundations. Initially, he circles around his task, pointing out the difficulties that are peculiar to studying human and social life. The individual is able to reflect on his or her own experience, yet is also aware that the facticity of that existence is tied to a biological body with its own demands and constraints. Psychological reflection, what Dilthey terms the 'psychic', cannot be separate from the body: there is a 'psychophysical unity of human nature'.[10] 'Psychophysical' was the term Weber also used, realizing that the study of meaning could always be overshadowed by the determination of the physiological.[11] Dilthey continues to the capability of the individual to have 'sovereignty of the will, a responsibility of actions' that distinguishes him from the rest of nature. 'He exists in nature as a realm within a realm . . .'. 'Thus from the realm of nature he distinguishes a realm of history, in which, amidst the objective necessity of nature, freedom is manifested at countless points. In contrast to the mechanical course of natural change which at the outset already contains everything that follows from it, acts of will exert force and involve sacrifices, whose meaning is evident to the individual in his experience and which actually produce something.'[12] In Weber's essay on the logic of the cultural sciences, he took up the same theme that the individual person is both an agent of his or her own destiny as well as being controlled by both natural and social processes.[13]

Dilthey raises the difficult issue that people are evaluating, opining and judging creatures. His solution here is to offer a threefold analytical differentiation. There can be a science of cultural life and history that is concerned at one level with facts, at another with theories and at a third level the judgments people make. 'The human sciences consist of these three classes of statements: facts, theorems, value judgements and rules.'[14] This is recognizably the same as Weber's later distinction between the empirical, the ideal typical and value judgements in his essays on 'objectivity' and value freedom.

Dilthey's concentration on 'spirit' and 'Geist' should not be confused with the 'spirit of the people' ('Volksgeist'). This quite major part of German nineteenth-century thinking is quickly dispatched to the trash can. The events and outcomes of a people or nation can come to possess a common genealogy – Dilthey has no objection to that (and nor I think should we). There can be no commonality based on 'somatic constancy' (what we today would term gene pool); instead, 'historical and spiritual physiognomy creates ever more refined differences in all the various spheres of the life of a people'. In our terms, the contingency of history and the agency of decision supervene over any primordial nation. Dilthey is harsh in his criticisms of those attempts to appropriate the concept of 'Geist' into a romantic, essential spirit. 'The individual unity of life in a people that is manifested in the affinity of all its life expressions, such as its law, language, and religion, is mystically expressed in terms such as *Volksseele, Nation, Volksgeist,* and *Organismus.* But these concepts are no more usable in history than is the concept of life-force in physiology.'[15]

Dilthey also eliminates approaches which for him cannot succeed with his chosen subject of study. In considering the psychic dimension of human life, a descriptive psychology is allowed, but an explanatory psychology based on the assumption that the individual is some mechanical unit about which assumptions are based and conclusions drawn about human nature is dismissed.[16] This point needs registering in light of subsequent critical attacks on Dilthey for his 'psychologism'. The ambitious scientific systems of Comte and J.S. Mill are rejected. 'In the spirit of eighteenth-century French philosophy, Comte's sociology subordinated the historical world to the system of the natural sciences. Mill retained and defended the idea that at least the method of studying the facts of the human world should be subordinated to the methods of the natural sciences.' 'In Comte's view, the study of the human mind is dependent on the science of biology, and the uniformity that can be detected in a succession of mental states is the effect of uniformities of bodily states. Thus he denies that lawful relations between psychic states [Dilthey's project] can be studied.'[17] Dilthey dismisses Comte for the presumption that the whole of social reality was amenable to the science of sociology – a critique later expounded by Karl Popper under the pejorative term of 'holism'.[18] Both Mill and Comte are taken to task for their misuse of natural scientific methods.

> Especially in Mill do we hear the monotonous and tedious clatter of the words 'induction' and 'deduction' which now resounds around us from all neighbouring countries. The entire history of the human sciences stands as a refutation of the idea of such an accommodation. These sciences have a wholly different foundation and structure than the natural sciences. Their subject matter is composed of unities that are given rather than inferred – units that are understandable from within.[19]

This is not the place to enlarge on Dilthey's quite expansive critique of Comtean positivism. It was a line followed by Weber who, in referring to positivist sociology, would usually have Comte in mind, whose mistake, for Weber, was on the basis of a deductive science to derive laws of society from which individual behaviour would be inferred. In his later comparative studies, Weber did, however, absorb some of J.S. Mill's methodology. Whatever their faults, it should be noted that both Comte and Mill offered the largest and most coherent account of a positivist scientific account of society, culture and history. In dismissing them, Dilthey signals his own ambitious plans for a unified science of cultural and human sciences, and Dilthey's writings here far outstrip any of his contemporaries.

So, how does a science proceed from an understanding 'from within'? An object of study is created in the human sciences in one or other of two ways: 'either when a purpose grounded in some aspect of human nature – which for that reason is enduring – relates psychic acts in different individuals to join them into a purposive whole ("Zweckzusammenhang")'. This, says Dilthey, creates a cultural pattern within society. Or 'when enduring causes bind the wills of many into a single whole, whether these causes be rooted in the natural articulation of social life or in the purposes which drive human nature'. This latter option creates the 'external organization' of life 'which man has created for himself. The latter consists of states, associations . . .'. Dilthey continues that, when the enduring volitional bonds between individuals are probed, this brings us to the various forms of association of society – the basic relations of power, dependence, property and community.[20]

This is fairly dense writing and it needs to be 'unpacked' somewhat. The two options, the either/or, both produce what Dilthey terms a 'Zusammenhang'. Dilthey's translator renders this as 'system', but this goes too far. Both options create an interconnected entity made up of the purposive activities of individuals. Dilthey says, at one level, this produces a cultural entity (or 'system') and, at a level external to the individual, a state and the forms of society.

Later in his exposition, Dilthey makes clear that the distinction between the external level of institutions such as the state, law or ethics as an external 'system' enforcing, for example, conscience within the behaviour of individuals, and the more associational and immediate linkages between individuals, which he designates as cultural life, is not an absolute one. In the sphere of ethics, individuals act from their own ethical volition as well as reacting to the force of ethical injunctions. In one form, ethics 'appears as a living force of motivation, in the other as the force that responds from without', approving and disapproving of the behaviour of individuals. 'In this twofold form, ethical consciousness permeates the overall life of society in an infinitely complex play of impulses and reactions.'[21] Law is also characterized by the same twofold form. In customs, common law and feelings such as the sense of justice, it is a cultural form of the psychic–cultural life. When codified or '"objectified and compressed in the smallest possible form, i.e., the shape of legal constructs"' (here, Dilthey is quoting the legal theorist Jhering), it is like the state and represents an organization external to the individual.[22] And even that state itself has limits. 'The volitional relation of power and dependence is limited by the sphere of external freedom' just as 'the relationship of community is limited by the sphere in which an individual exists for himself'.[23]

Individuals, in interrelating their mental behaviour in a purposive way, create culture, society and state. This can be taken as a protosociology of social action – a forerunner of what Weber constructed more systematically. But Dilthey refuses to call his analysis sociology. That, for him, meant either organicist accounts such as Shäffle's and von Mohl's or positivist schemas such as Comte's. Dilthey's ambition is to construct the mentalist ('geistlich') basis for all the human sciences: anthropology, economics, psychology, law, ethics, politics, sociology, etc.

Dilthey has more to say about purposive behaviour and its formation of interconnected entities ('Zusammenhänge'). This can be represented as propositions, 'but propositions of very diverse kinds. Depending on whether the psychic elements connected in the purposive system belong predominantly to thought, to feeling, or to will, we must differentiate between truths, expressions of feelings, and rules respectively.'[24] Purposive behaviour, therefore, comprises thought or intentional action, feelings or some sort of emotional action, and will or what an individual wants. This remains some distance away from what Weber was to develop into a theory of social action, and it is probably wrong to force this connection at this juncture. The substratum, though, of Dilthey's claim to create a human science is that (1) individuals are volitional and purposeful, (2) this covers a range of behaviour including the rational, affectual and evaluative, and (3) the ways in which the volitional behaviour of individuals combines in 'systems' or (sociological) entities gives us culture, the forms of society and the external organization of the state.

Dilthey provides the reader with an interesting illustration of his approach. Theories can be generated from 'systems' or entities. Within a 'system' or set of purposive psychical or pyschophysical elements, certain dependencies can be generated. Individuals can express religious feelings as purposeful activity, for example through the feelings generated by congregational worship, and these can exist in a dependency relation to religious dogma and their worldviews. Dilthey refers to the work of Schleiermacher at this point as an exemplar of such a theory.[25] Dilthey does not offer complete clarity as to what he is saying here, but it is not impossible to read in this a methodological justification of Weber's PESC. A dependency relation exists between the religious (predestinarian) feelings of Puritans, on the one side, and the conduct of life, on the other. Dependency relationships, which for Weber become causal relationships, can be adduced from the interactions of individuals (socially groupable) at the psychic or psychological level.

One would not single out Dilthey's account of psychophysical life as the clearest statement of a theory of social action, which Weber was to achieve with a far tighter focus. But the two accounts of human action indicate that Dilthey's *Introduction to the Human Sciences* was a not incompatible starting point for Weber's own deliberations. Also Dilthey, in his *Introduction*, established the key principle that its 'logic' was to be built on the propositional statements of individuals in their lives. Social and cultural scientists should take statements such as 'I want such and such', 'what I feel is such and such', 'I accept the prince's authority as absolute', 'I judge this person in such a way' as their datum. These are the statements that the social or cultural scientist will use in their relational interdependence to construct purposeful edifices of sociopsychic life. It is Dilthey who insists that a future science of mental life will work with the language of life.

Hermeneutics

In the last chapter, the question was raised about whether Weber's interpretation of predestinarian doctrines and everyday practices could be accepted. Was he correct and how would we adjudicate this? Dilthey is the author who has most to offer on the subject. Dilthey's starting point here is the interpretation of texts, and his inspiration was the advances made by historians, theologians and philologists in their interpretation of historical documents, sacred texts and ancient languages. In these situations, the meaning has to be deciphered and thought about, and it is in these non-transparent situations that Dilthey worked out the rules or methods of interpretation.

It is important to grasp the thrust and impetus of this background that had developed spectacularly over the nineteenth century. Hermeneutics enabled classical historians such as Niehbuhr to assemble the first reliable account of the history of Rome. It enabled theologians and philologists to work on the historical stages of the composition of the different books of the Bible and to distinguish between apocryphal and traditional religious texts. In philosophy, the writings of Plato were placed within the context and traditions of Greeks schools of thought and the practice of learning and disquisition. In philology, the genealogical history of languages was being established. Documents, inscriptions, texts all provided the source material for gaining a scientifically reliable way of establishing 'what really happened', to use the historian Ranke's famous phrase. And what really happened was pieced together by correctly extracting the information contained in the various forms of historical evidence. This procedure was taught and transmitted in the university seminar. The professor had mastered the sources of evidence in his field, and his students had to demonstrate their own competence (or incompetence) in their interpretation of historical (primary) sources. Weber himself was a product of this system, which had come to define the university during the nineteenth century. He worked with historical law documents with Frensdorff and other legal scholars at the University of Göttingen.[26]

To an extent, it was a tradition and procedure that Weber could well have taken for granted in his own writings. It was a technique and discipline that had to be mastered as part of an academic's training, rather than standing for a methodological novelty (now designated as working with 'primary sources').

Dilthey took what many practitioners would regard as a necessary skill and made it into a component of his philosophical approach to the human sciences. He makes the point that, just as the natural scientist has the experimental method as a way of establishing truth, so the human sciences have hermeneutics as the art of interpretation. If this statement is read through the lenses of Heidegger, Gadamer and Derrida, who have come to characterize the hermeneutical operation over the twentieth century, an opposition between science and art will be assumed. Science is concerned with exact certainty, whereas in the humanities, everything is subject to interpretation, and the meaning inferred will be highly dependent upon the interpreter's own situation. Dilthey's own writings can be pulled in the direction of the arbitrariness of viewer (as opposed to the object studied for its meaning), and this relates to one of the weaker flanks of Dilthey's position (which we will consider shortly). But the opposition between science and art is not Dilthey's point. Science and art are equivalents in the search for truth. The German word for art, 'Kunst', denotes not only art in the aesthetic sense but also art in the sense of skill, as in 'artistry'. The art of interpretation has been developed to 'crack open' documents and all expressions of the human spirit that had remained indecipherable, misunderstood or have received mistaken readings. Such procedures do not eliminate all ambiguities, and major debates are sometimes required before contradictory interpretations are resolved. But the whole tenor and practice of hermeneutics was to establish certainty of meaning. It is a standard that most professional historians still adhere to.[27]

In a lecture to the Prussian Academy of Science in 1896, which was published in 1900, Dilthey noted that 'philology and history rest on the assumption that the understanding of the unique can be made objective'. Disciplines in the human sciences, such as history, 'depend for their certainty on the possibility of giving general validity to the understanding of the unique'.[28] Data in the human sciences derive from the expressions and utterances of other human beings, and these do not face the investigator, as in the natural sciences as an insensate reality, but can be understood from within. The 'systematic understanding of recorded expressions we call exegesis or interpretation'. 'The art of understanding therefore centres on the interpretation of written records of human existence.'[29]

> The art of interpretation has developed just as slowly, gradually and in as orderly a way as, for example, the questioning of nature by experiment. It originated and survives in the personal, inspired virtuosity of

philologists. Naturally it is mainly transmitted through personal contact with the great masters of interpretation of their work. But every skill also proceeds according to rules which teach us to overcome difficulties and embody what can be transmitted of a personal skill. So the art of interpretation gives rise to the formulation of rules. The conflict between such rules and the struggle between different schools about the interpretation of vital works produces a need to justify the rules and this gives rise hermeneutics, which is *the methodology of the interpretation of written records.*[30]

At a technical level, these rules involve what today is called triangulation (see above p. 67) – a number of methods are used in combination to pin down the exact place and meaning of, say, a text. Hermeneutics can be seen 'as an edifice of rules – the parts of which – the individual rules – were held together by the aim to achieve a valid interpretation. It had separated the functions which combine in this process into grammatical, historical, aesthetic-rhetorical and factual exegesis. From the philological virtuosity of many centuries it had crystallized the rules according to which these must function.'[31] By grammar, Dilthey means a given language – its syntax, vocabulary and range of meanings have to be learnt. The first recognizably modern theorist of hermeneutics, Schleiermacher, argued that this occurred through an iterative process of relating a part of a text to the whole – of a word within a sentence, an expression within a language. Only by going backwards and forwards between part and whole can a language and, therefore, the meaning of a word or text be established. The historical meant that the historical origins of a text have to be established. A book might come down to us as a seemingly unified entity, but historical analysis can reveal it to be a composite of texts from different periods and pens. Texts convey their meaning, as communication, through the use of imagery, tropes and rhetorical devices. Aristotle was the first analyst to provide an inventory of rhetorical devices. These have to be recognized and, to an extent, put on one side in order to study the factual or substantive level of the text.

In the development of hermeneutics over centuries (from the second and third centuries BC), there is, says Dilthey, a history of wrong-headed interpretation, of what Dilthey refers to as 'allegorical' interpretation. Allegory is used as a way of avoiding the truth of what is stated or written down. Veracity is abandoned, often in the face of religious, political and other subversive pressures, in favour of interpretivist accounts. In Christianity, the New Testament is seen as following on from the Old Testament. In particular, the prophecies scattered over the Old Testament have to be made to conform –when clearly many of these do not – to Jesus Christ as the foretold messiah. Historical theological scholarship points to the lack of fit, when the text is read for what it actually says; the imperatives of revelatory belief mean that these inconsistencies have to be explained away through fanciful allegories.

This, for Dilthey, would be an interpretation of meaning but not herme-neutics. Another and more relevant example concerns the Christian Refor-mation. In the face of Jean Calvin's interpretation of the sacred texts, which also at points explained the rules of interpretation, the Catholic Church asserted that the scriptures were 'obscure' and had to be interpreted through Catholic traditional doctrine. The Lutheran theologian Flacius understood the need to demonstrate that the scriptures could be interpreted correctly and, in doing this, 'he became conscious of [new] methods and rules which earlier hermeneutics had not elicited'. 'It was Flacius who was also the first to grasp the significance of the psychological or technical principle of inter-pretation according to which an individual passage must be interpreted in terms of the aim and composition of the whole work. He was the first to use methodically the insights of rhetoric about the inner units of a literary product, its composition and effective elements for technical interpreta-tion.' Flacius used the methodical aids of 'context, aim, proportion and the consistency of individual parts or links in determining the definite meaning of passages'.[32] Dilthey follows the history of the development of biblical hermeneutics through to Schleiermacher at the beginning of the nineteenth century. Schleiermacher is a pivotal figure for Dilthey, and this is where his account stops, but Dilthey could have traced the continuation of Protestant historical theology in the figures of Harnack, Ritschl and Troeltsch. Herme-neutics had a mission within Protestant theology – of combating tradition with the presentation of the truth of the text. This was a trail that led directly to Weber's academic front door.[33]

One section of Dilthey's thinking can help with our treatment of Max Weber in the last chapter. In writing on methodology, there is a tendency to-wards the pedagogic exposition of rules – hence, the rules of hermeneutics. With Schleiermacher, Dilthey encountered someone who had not only ab-sorbed these rules but, through his inspirational gifts, had gone far beyond them. We can refer to this as the virtuoso 'problem'. When we read Erving Goffman, Richard Sennett or Harry Braverman, it is possible to specify their methodological procedures but not, however, to account for the extra bril-liance that suffuses their writings and explanations. There may also be a difficulty, as with Weber, that what they say they are doing and what they are actually achieving can be (artfully) different.

Dilthey is adamant that hermeneutics involves more than the specifica-tion of rules which 'only produces blind windows through which no one can look. An effective hermeneutics could only emerge in a mind which combined virtuosity of philological interpretation with genuine philosophic capacity. A man with such a mind was Schleiermacher.' 'He recognized that the imaginative consideration of the creative process through which a vital work originates was the basis for appreciating the process by which we understand the whole of work from its written signs and from this the purpose and mentality of its author.' Reading a text (or, more widely, read-ing a sociological situation) should at its best involve creativity. 'Receptivity and creativity cannot be separated.'[34] A literary text possesses the creativity of the author.

> Such a work meets with the insatiable desire of the reader to supplement his own individuality through contemplation of that of others. Understanding and interpretation therefore are constantly alive and active in life itself, but they are perfected by the systematic interpretation of living works and the unity they were given in the author's mind. This was the new conception in the special form it assumed in Schleiermacher.[35]

The last part of this statement says that the researcher has to penetrate the writer's own mind and intentions, and to recreate the vision and outlook of the author if the full sense and meaning of the text is to be garnered. In terms of social research, an investigator has to give something creatively of his or herself in the process of interpretation. The realm of public, social and civic life that Sennett brings to life in his *Fall of Public Man* had to be creatively reconstituted. The documents and testimony drawn on by Sennett were not ready and waiting in the archives, requiring only presentational display. A breath of inspiration, the creativity of the investigator to imagine how it might have been, and was, in revolutionary Paris was required. On this basis, it is what the student brings creatively to interpretation – in conjunction with mastery of methodological rules – that always makes possible the next masterpiece. In Weber's case, penetrating the mindset of the seventeenth-century Puritan and bringing it alive to the twentieth-century reader would fulfil the full creative potential of hermeneutics for Dilthey (although it should be added that we do not know what he thought of Weber's masterpiece).

There is a case for stopping the methodological exposition at this point. There are rules, and those who can go beyond them (without egregiously breaking them) fall into the master class. Methodology cannot legislate for this extra brilliance; all it has to do is allow it to happen. To an extent, Dilthey himself rests the argument at this point. For him, what is important is that a linkage is made between a past or objectivated expression of human consciousness and the self-awareness of the researcher in his or her world. Understanding is a living process, where one person creatively relives the outlook and expression of another era ('nacherleben') through a process of ascribing. Ascetic (English) Protestantism was not an academic construction for Weber in c. 1900, it was a significant part of his own self-conception, indeed, if not an ideal that he would have preferred more of his fellow countrymen to have experienced.[36] It is on this basis that Weber was able to bring his Puritan character to life on the academic stage. These creative academic works add to the canon of a society or civilization's own heritage, self-awareness and educative potential. This is the completion of the hermeneutical task for Dilthey.

But Dilthey does not allow this creative 'loose end' to remain unsecured.

He wants to tie it into a complete philosophy. His argumentation here displays vulnerabilities, which will be quickly sketched before moving on to some of Dilthey's more academicist critics (with whom Weber is more usually aligned).

Schleiermacher had expanded the rules of interpretation (more accurately 'explication'/'Auslegung') to include the psychological motivation of an author and his place in historical context; this involved a creative act of understanding.[37] This, for Dilthey, is an act of artistic fusion. 'The concepts which guided him [Schleiermacher] in his brilliant works on Greek poetry, Goethe and Boccaccio were: the inner form of the work, the development of the author and the articulated whole of literature.' Schleiermacher 'rejected the division of the exegetic process into grammatical, historical aesthetic and factual interpretation', for this has to be combined with psychological interpretation that penetrates the inner creative process.[38] In philosophical terms, Dilthey terms this, with critical intention, transcendental idealism: that the creative act itself gives one access to the mental expressions of any other human being and time. And underlying this assumption is the further opinion that human beings as natural beings have access to an understanding of nature, and that the world of spirit and that of matter are not necessarily apart. This philosophical doctrine owed more to poetic influences such as Goethe than it did to philosophy proper. Dilthey knew this and set about reworking the philosophical basis of what may be termed transcendental understanding. This becomes a validity question: how can we know that we have this ability to reach across from our own world to penetrate the outlook of another era or social world?

This is a question that is more strictly formulated in the philosophy of Locke and Kant respectively. In the English tradition of Locke and Hume, what our minds know of external reality remains a philosophical mystery, simply because our minds are separate and different from reality 'out there'. We obviously receive sensations from reality, but our thoughts and ideas can only be said to be fading reflections of sensations which, by their nature, are only momentary. I leave the seminar room to allow my students to discuss the topic, but how do I really know they are still in the seminar room when I have shut the door? All I have is the fading impression of what I, in the seminar room, immediately knew. This is philosophical scepticism. Dilthey is pretty scathing about this approach because it conceives reality 'out there' in physicalist terms. Reality is also, for Dilthey, the life of the mind, so why reduce it to pale and wan impressions of sensate data? This is no way to think about ideas, culture and all the expressions of the mental capacity of human beings. Immanuel Kant attempted to secure the faculty of reason in the human mind in the face of the rather depressing implications of Humean scepticism. Reason gives us the ability to think rationally and to act morally, and the mind also has the capacity of aesthetic appreciation and ennoblement. Kant argued that, although we only apprehend the appearances of a reality 'out there', we – everyone – do have root mental capacities that allow us to order that reality in terms of fundamentals such as the passing of time, spatial awareness, causality. These properties of mind Kant termed transcendental categories. Overall, it needs to be noted that these problems are designated, both now and by Weber and his contemporaries, as dualism; there is the perceptual world of the human being and there is a world of external reality. Weber's friend, the philosopher Emil Lask, referred to this as an unbridgeable gulf – a 'hiatus irrationalis', and Weber agreed with this stance.

Dilthey is dismissive of philosophic dualism. In the Preface to his *Introduction to the Human Sciences*, he notes:

> Although I found myself frequently in agreement with the epistemological ('erkenntnistheoretischen') school of Locke, Hume, and Kant I nevertheless found it necessary to conceive differently the nexus of facts of consciousness . . . No real blood flows in the veins of the knowing subject constructed by Locke, Hume and Kant, but rather the diluted extract of reason as a mere activity of thought. A historical as well as psychological approach to whole human beings led me to explain even knowledge and its concepts (such as the external world, time, substance, and cause) in terms of the manifold powers of a being that will, feels, and thinks.[39]

Dilthey's solution is to lay aside transcendental categories in favour of categories of life. Instead of making the Kantian assumption of transcendental categories, Dilthey holds that these categories are part of our existence as human beings. We all experience time, its passing and its duration and sense of present and future, we are all in our lives exercising our capacity to understand and make sense and meaning of the world in both its parts and whole, and we all make positive and negative valuations of the world around us.[40] This is ingenious and it added considerably to the methodological field, where other attempts – most notably phenomenology and pragmatism – were being undertaken not to solve the dualism problem but to go around it and render it irrelevant. In this light, Dilthey may be referred to as post-Kantian. Weber, in his explicit epistemological ('erkenntnistheoretische') writings, remained locked into the dualism problematic, although as I have suggested in the previous chapters, PESC should be regarded as his most hermeneutical work.

Dilthey wanted to push philosophical thinking into the language and experience of life itself.

> I will relate every component of contemporary abstract scientific thought to the whole of human nature as it is revealed in experience, in the study of language, and in the study of history, and thus seek the connection of these components. The result is that the most important components of our picture and knowledge of reality – our own personality as a living

entity, the external world, other individuals, their temporal life and their interactions ('Wechselwirkung') – can be explained in terms of this totality of human nature.[41]

This was a prefatory statement, one of ambition rather than its realization, so we cannot adequately assess Dilthey's success in this enterprise (which he never completed, leaving as he did many unfinished manuscripts).[42] Nevertheless, we can glimpse how the enterprise could founder: by collapsing the issue of the categories of knowing into an insufficiently distinctive conception of 'life itself'. Such a judgement cannot be made here, and it would be contingent on an assessment of how Dilthey handled the relation of the parts of the world to its whole.

The neo-Kantians

The neo-Kantians, Windelband and Rickert, colleagues of Weber at the universities of Freiburg and Heidelberg, are Kantian in the following respects. Scientific work has to proceed through the construction of concepts in order to perceive and make sense of reality, and a philosophy of knowledge has to be used to impose some sort of ordering of scientific work in the cultural and historical sciences. In Rickert's hands, a highly detailed 'logical' account is given of how the investigator relates to the subject being researched and how the dualistic split between concept and reality is to be handled, so preserving the scientific validity of work in the human and cultural sciences. Rickert was critical of the efforts of Dilthey, regarding his underpinning of the validity of knowledge as 'ontological', i.e. the categories of life. Rickert advocated quite prescriptive procedures for ensuring the validity of scientific knowledge in the cultural and historical field. This is the sense in which Rickert is termed a neo-Kantian – the abiding concern is how to secure the grounds on which scientific claims for knowledge can be made, once the duality and scepticism of the observer–world split are admitted. Dilthey, as we have seen, was quite aware of this issue but chose to treat it as, in large part, solved by academic work using the methods of hermeneutics and as, ultimately, a condition of human existence, whereas Rickert turned to logical or formal solutions.

Quite an amount of tension sprang up between the Rickert and Dilthey approaches, but it is important to recall that they had a common enemy in the positivistic conception of natural science. Scientific advances in evolutionary biology, embryology and cellular research, electromagnetism, entropy in physics, the bacterial origins of diseases, and the support given by the Prussian Ministry of Education to research institutes and professorial chairs in the natural sciences had placed the humanities on the back foot. The balance of influence and prestige was moving from the seminar to the laboratory and, unless a claim for the scientificness of historical and cultural disciplines could be advanced, their standing within the university system and as a cultural force within society would be diminished. Another

Comtean moment had been reached. The genius of the young Comte in his *Discourse on Positivist Philosophy* (1822) had provided a conspectus of recent scientific advances and had perceived the shift from 'Aristotelian' substances and teleology to a proper understanding of causation in the physical world; for Comte, this was the move from the metaphysical to the positivist conception of knowledge, and the new science of society, sociology, would model itself on the same scientific principles.

In Germany at the end of the nineteenth century, the Comtean moment appeared in the guise of scientific monism. The dualistic notions that there exist scientific theories and hypotheses, on the one side, and the ultimately unknowable world of brute reality, on the other, were being swept aside by scientific discoveries and a rapid progress, which suggested to some that all that was needed was the laboratory, technology, experiments and the gathering and analysis of facts and the laws of the natural world would be revealed. Regularities of law-like certainty were a feature of physical reality. It was not brute, chaotic or unknowingly noumenal; properly addressed, it revealed its secrets. Furthermore, the psychophysical human being could best be explained through its natural properties. The human being was a product of biology, of cellular embryology, and consciousness through experimental methods would be shown to operate in terms of stimulus and response. A scientific psychology started by Fechner and Wundt would demonstrate how thinking and feeling were constituted and produced in the psychophysical organism.[43] The human being possessing the sovereign faculties of reason – Kant's postulate – could be dispensed with. The autonomy of will – thinking, feeling, wanting, valuing – was to become subsidiary to causal determination. A monistic conception of science held that the human being was reducible to the rest of physical reality, which, when approached with the instruments of natural science, would reveal its laws and mechanisms. While Dilthey's 'Geisteswissenschaften' is now translated (not wholly satisfactorily) as 'human sciences', there were major efforts around 1900 to create the human sciences through a reduction of the human organism to physicalist mechanisms.

Much of Weber's 'Wissenschaftslehre' is taken up with very combative refutations of the claims and illusions of a unified science of 'Natur' and 'Mensch' on monistic principles. (And, by implication, there is far less writing – than we might wish – devoted to practical methodological issues in the social, historical and cultural sciences.) Weber attacked the startlingly ambitious programme of the evolutionary biologist and chemist, Ernst Haeckel, who in his book *The Riddle of the Universe* saw monism rather in the way Comte came to inscribe positivism as a controlling 'Weltanschauung' with its own priesthood. Karl Lamprecht is vituperatively rubbished for his grandiose schema for outlining in his *Deutsche Geschichte* the laws of succession of culture and the determining mentalities of each epoch. Economists are attacked for believing that utility maximization will be secured through psychological laws of diminishing response to stimuli. The legal theorist

Stammler is demolished for asserting that legal norms are a reflection of the materialist laws of society – this was monism though the evolutionary Marxism of Engels and Kautsky. In the same vein, the older generation of national-economists, Roscher and Knies, are criticized for securing their theories to evolutionary entities seen in organic terms, where 'Volksseele' and 'Volksgeist' become real and growing objects. And Ostwald's championing of entropy as the key to a unified science is revealed as an extraordinary gambit.

Weber's place in the force field of debates on the nature of science should be seen as the major antagonist in favour of a culturalist approach and against an encroaching monism. All the academic writers discussed so far – Schmoller, Sombart, Simmel, Dilthey, Windelband, Rickert – align with Weber against a positivizing approach to science. By comparison with this major division, the neo-Kantian direction is significant but represents a minor divide.

In opening the neo-Kantian case in 1894, Windelband acknowledges a generic point. The cultural and historical sciences have to lay claim to their own legitimate place as science in the face of the natural sciences, which make that claim by a different route. Windelband makes his, by now famous, distinction between idiographic science that focuses down on the singularity of phenomena and nomothetic science whose goal is to explain by showing the operation of laws and their causal effects. The nature of the object being studied determines the particular method of investigation. History, for example, studies particular events, personalities and their motivation, and the contingency of processes. Explanation tends to reside in the in-depth knowledge of these topics. Unlike natural science, the materials studied do not offer up striking regularities that can then be formulated as laws. This opening has much in common with Dilthey's own setting out of the issues (at roughly the same date – 1893).

Having made the case for the difference between, but equivalence of, the two approaches to science, Windelband had little to contribute on just how the idiographic would secure its scientific validity. This was developed by Heinrich Rickert in *The Limits of Concept Formation in Natural Science*, published in 1902. Weber read it in Florence in 1902 while recuperating from his illness. He pronounced it as 'very good' in a letter to his wife, although his subsequent comments were less approving.[44] Hence, we know he had read Rickert, also that he took over some of Rickert's terminology, but just how much of Rickert's solution to the epistemological problems of the cultural and historical sciences Weber took over into his own work will require consideration below.

Rickert framed the problem, 'in what areas the formation of concepts of natural science makes sense, and in what areas the sense of that kind of concept formation is by necessity lost'.[45] Rickert treated the world of reality 'out there' as being composed of objects that were innumerable. In physics today, especially particle physics, this is a reasonable proposition – the idea that reality can be broken down into ever smaller objects, until they are infinitesimally small. Rickert asserts this as a logical proposition that, in the dimensions of both time and space, the objects that could be perceived are infinite. In this respect, reality cannot be cognized in its complexity. We use words to reference objects in this infinitely complex reality, and scientists use concepts, which give precise definitions of objects. Again on formal or logical grounds, Rickert asserts that, in the natural sciences, concepts can group together objects that have common properties. These concepts in their turn can be fitted together to arrive at laws describing the regularities of objects. Concepts in the natural science, therefore, tend to an ever increasing abstraction of reality. In the study of social and historical life, 'objects' are individual, that is they do not present commonalities that allow them to be grouped together under abstract concepts. This presents two classes of concepts: those that travel away from reality in the direction of abstraction; and those (in the historical sciences) that attach themselves as closely as possible to the individuality of the past. Individuality – and this works slightly better in its Latin form – should be understood as the individuation, or the dividing up, of reality into specific objects.

So informed, it is now feasible to return to Weber's usage of the term in PESC. Introducing the phrase 'the spirit of capitalism', Weber says of it,

> If any object can be found to which this term can be applied with any understandable meaning, it can only be an historical individual, i.e. a complex of elements associated in historical reality which we unite into a conceptual whole from the standpoint of their cultural significance.
>
> Such an historical concept, however, since it refers in its content to a phenomenon significant for its unique individuality, cannot be defined according to the formula *genus proximum, differentia specifica* . . .
>
> (PESC, p. 47)

The Latin phrase means that individual specifics can be grouped together to produce more general concepts, i.e. the method of increasing abstraction. This cannot be done with historical concepts, which have to attach as far as possible to the object's unique reality. Rickert therefore introduces the term a 'science of reality' ('Wirklichkeitswissenschaft') to depict this movement towards objects. It is a term that Weber himself deploys in his essay on 'Objectivity' in the social sciences. Because reality ('Wirklichkeit') is not subsumable under general concepts and is infinite, in both time and space – what Weber refers to as 'extensive and intensive infiniticy'[46] – the historian is forced to be selective in approaching this infinite multiplicity.

Selectivity is a fairly open-ended notion. Selection could mean selection to your point of view or opinions. This is not what Rickert, or Weber, meant. Many histories are written from an opinionated standpoint or with a blatant bias that leads to absurd situations. For example, a Catholic historian will write a history enumerating Catholic martyrs and their torture in the

Reformation, whereas a Protestant historian will do the same but for Protestant martyrs, and no doubt an atheistic historian would argue that religion is bad for your health.

Rickert argues for something far more neutral, what he calls value orientation. Human beings are purposive, and they make evaluations of the world. Reality, argues Rickert, with regard to history only has meaning for the purposive and active human being in so far as it is unique.[47] This line of thought is not dissimilar to Dilthey's recreation of the historical through the historian's own values of life. But Rickert turns what sounds like a practical evaluation into what he terms a 'value relation' ('Wertbeziehung'). This means it is worthy of interest, although what practical evaluations may be drawn is a different matter – one to do with what Weber termed value judgements. Both Weber and Rickert insisted on the distinction between value relation and value judgement and, without the insistence, the distinction easily falls back to a more encompassing 'point of view'.

Rickert also argues that what is of interest to the historian must be a reflection of what is of general interest to the community of historians and their public. This gives a value relation a general validity, and it is not hard to trace the Kantian influence here. Kant had argued that practical reason derives validity in the applicability of a (moral) rule as being true for all members of a community, indeed as universally valid. In a more restricted community – of historians – validity is conferred through some sort of consensus, as opposed to the possibly idiosyncratic view (value relation) of the lone historian. In passing, one cannot help but observe that this would seem to condemn value interest to the conformity of the generally accepted, and that innovation in historical science could not be generated from what initially might seem to be obscure and of no interest.[48] Also, it would seem to beg the question of what constitutes value in the first place. The obligation of the historian, writes Bruun about Rickert, is 'always to let his value relations be guided by values which are generally (empirically) valid in the "Gemeinschaft" [community] for which his account is written . . .'.[49] Empirical validity here means the values actually held by a community. Furthermore, these values, insofar as they can claim validity, are general values. Each community for which a historian writes and, by this, Rickert means Church, state, law, science and arts, hold values that are 'cultural values'.[50] History must therefore be oriented to culture. And, because these values are general to each community, they have normative force. It is this aspect of selection, a difficulty that applies to both natural and historical sciences, that confers empirical validity and so objectivity to history. The selection is empirically valid because it is a reflection of the relevant values of the normative community of historians. This, it should be noted, is not how methods in history would be thought of today. Actual methods of interpretation and verification would be emphasized – for example, is the document original and to be trusted, what are its origins, who or which persons wrote the document and for what purposes, and so on? Rickert turns the emphasis around, pinpointing an exercise – that of selection – that most historians ignore or remain unaware of. But in choosing a subject, and bringing certain value questions to bear on it, for Rickert, this is to confer an empirical validity on the topic selected.

This, I think, takes Rickert down an overly prescriptive road incompatible with other scientific values of spontaneity, creativity and the ability to cause value positions to be changed within a public. Kantian imperatives might be considered as a viable system of ethics but, within the sphere of science, at the operational level, i.e. choosing what to study, this meeting of validity claims involves too much of a sacrifice of the historian's own individuality. The anarchic spirit of Nietzsche – to ask the questions that nobody else permits themselves to ask – would be appalled. Rickert was concerned to exclude just that sort of arbitrariness in which question, judgement and evidence are reduced to an aphorism; however memorable the aphorism might be, it could be no substitute for scientific procedure. Rickert would also be able to point out that historians in their periodizations and dividing up of the historical past into topics, such as legal history, ecclesiastical history, economic history, etc., are proceeding in the way he suggests and prescribes. But, in following this procedure, it can be noted that Rickert clearly separates his procedure from that of Dilthey's, for whom the movement between investigator and objects studied is far more fluid. It allows the researcher freedom and creativity to move back into any aspect of historical and cultural life, and to reanimate for himself and perhaps to create a new audience and field of interest. Rickert's concern is to place the epistemology on a more specified basis.

In relation to Dilthey's work, it is worth noting where Rickert himself places the stress. He agrees that the division between the science of nature, concerning non-meaningful objects, and the science of mental life, which concerns meaningful behaviour, can be a common starting point for epistemologists. History 'is primarily concerned with cultural realities that are meaningful and mental. For this reason, a representation of this object requires a value-relevant, individualizing concept formation. The domain of nonmeaningful "nature", on the other hand – in other words, everything whose existence independent of value and meaning – intrinsically conforms to a system of general concepts.'[51] On the basis of 'the distinction between meaningful and nonmeaningful realities' that forms 'the real core of Dilthey's theories of the human sciences . . . there can be no question of a fundamental opposition between Dilthey's ideas and those set out here'. What Dilthey fails to provide, says Rickert, is a 'clear conceptual analysis of the essential feature of his principle of demarcation'.[52]

Their differences, in Rickert's hands, are quite subtle though important. (And they should not be depicted unsubtly, as many commentators do,[53] as an opposition between an expressive, relativistic 'Lebensphilosophie' and the tight conceptual formulation of Rickert.) Having made the meaningful–non-meaningful distinction, Rickert goes on to insist that meaning is a non-real and transcendent category. It is not an empirical and objective

category. Only when meaning is ascribed through value relation to a historical object does it take on the status of the empirical; otherwise, it is a free-
floating supposition. The historical individual as a topic, period, personality,
etc. contains value in itself, asserts Rickert, and the historian is informed by
his or her own value community. The value relation that connects these two
is an empirical one, opening the way to establishing questions of objectivity
and of what is true and false. Values in themselves can claim to be valid (as
truth, as aesthetic, as moral, etc.) but in themselves are not real.

> Values as such are never real. On the contrary, they hold validly. In other
> words, the values themselves cannot be real, but rather only the things
> ('Güter') in which they are 'realized' and in which we discover them. In
> the same way, the *meaning* reality acquires with reference to value does
> not itself fall within the domain of real existence. On the contrary, it
> obtains only in relation to a valid value. In this sense, the meaning itself
> is unreal. In consequence, by culture we understand, first, real histori-
> cal *life* to which a meaning is attached that constitutes it as culture. In
> addition, we can also understand by culture the nonreal 'content' itself,
> conceived as the *meaning* of such a life that is detached from all real
> existence and is interpreted with reference to cultural values.[54]

Rickert adds that, although 'meaning' and 'value' interpenetrate our sense
of life, in theoretical terms, they should be distinguished.

Undoubtedly, there is a strangeness to Rickert's argument and its Kantian
style and the way in which he deploys the categories of value.[55] It is by these
means that he hoped to place the cultural sciences on a more objective basis,
even though it is quite hard to discern just how his conception of objectivity
is made to work. In particular, Rickert addresses Dilthey's lecture (1900),
outlined above, accusing him of over-reliance on the re-experiencing of inner experience as the basis of understanding. He quotes Dilthey: 'We call
that process understanding in which we acquire knowledge of something
that is inner on the basis of externally given signs.' Of this, Rickert opines,
'We know how vacuous the concept of an inner process is.' 'The signs that
are "externally" given must make it possible to acquire knowledge of more
than a real "inner" process. Otherwise they will remain unintelligible.'[56] The
simple Diltheyan riposte to this is that the interpretation of inner experience attaches to its objects of expression – texts, pictures, gestures – and the
interpretation of authorial intention has to be inferred from the historical
situation. And if we revisit Dilthey's sentence, in the official translation, it
reads: 'On the logical side of this process [the possibility of valid interpretation deduced from the nature of understanding] is one of coming to know
a whole context from only partially defined signs by making use of existing
grammatical, logical and historical knowledge.'[57] Hermeneutics, for Rickert,
would seem to include the art of paraphrase.

This is not the place to argue out the dispute over the best scientific treatment of the meaningful in history, other than to note that it was a sophisticated debate and that neither side had abandoned objectivity and truthfulness. Reading much of interpretative sociology today, of which Weber is said to be a founder, it would be a complete misreading to assume that Weber is arguing that 'subjective understanding' equates with the subjectivity or relativism of truth. He is part of a tradition whose concern was to establish objectivity through a proper conceptualization of values.

Weber's critical distance from Dilthey

Pietro Rossi points out that Weber acknowledged Dilthey's work, and that his knowledge of his works was quite comprehensive. It included *Introduction to the Human Sciences, Ideas on Descriptive and Analytic Psychology* and his lectures on 'The Origins of Hermeneutics' and 'Studies towards the Foundation of the Human Sciences'. These references occur in the footnotes of Weber's methodological essays on Roscher and Knies. They acknowledge Dilthey's importance but are accompanied by references to Rickert. Dilthey was the first to establish the division of the sciences, but it was Windelband and Rickert who revealed the 'logical distinctiveness of history'. Weber, following Rickert's argument, noted that Dilthey's distinction between 'inner "experience" ("Erlebungen")' and 'outer appearances' was not just 'logical' but 'ontological'. Weber continued that he favoured Rickert's logical and conceptual approach to the study of history.[58]

Hence, Weber's comments on Dilthey are meagre, not fulsome, and critical of his ontology. It is a difficult judgement to make, but how much of that eruptive work of genius – *The Protestant Ethic and the Spirit of Capitalism* – was reliant on Dilthey's expansive intellect and how much on Rickert's logic? It was Dilthey who opened the door to the in-depth exploration of the inner life and meaning of historical lives and documents, and it was he who underlined the importance of hermeneutics and 'Verstehen' as a reliable method of study. Dilthey also supplied an embryonic sociology that was able to link the internal dimension of people's actions with the external structures of society that surrounded them. Rickert supplied a way of using concepts that neutralized the observer's engagement with history, and so offered the assurance of objectivity in place of a subjective engagement with the lives and artefacts of the past. Dilthey's imaginative and energetic intellect celebrated our ability to make just such an engagement. The question, which I leave on the seminar table for discussion, is: what kind of exercise was Weber pursing in his imaginative and energetic engagement with Puritan history?

The actual dynamics of this debate – its cross-currents, debates and conversations – have yet to be fully investigated from a history of ideas standpoint. Toby Huff's discussion of the Weber–Dilthey relationship points out the complexity of the debates and the large number of other actors, minor and major, who were also on stage. For Huff, the critical split, which he terms a 'theoretical gulf', was over the issue of psychologism. When Dilthey published his *Ideas on Descriptive and Analytic Psychology* in 1895, it was critically taken apart by Ebbinghaus. Dilthey immediately withdrew from any further work in that direction. I am not sure whether this provides enough evidence to locate the split in terms of psychologism.[59] Dilthey's *Introduction to the Human Sciences* places the emphasis on descriptive psychology, simply in the sense that the historian needs to recreate the thoughts, ambitions and feelings of historical personages. No 'scientific' discipline of psychology is alluded to as providing an explanatory tool. Dilthey's move into 'analytic psychology' did make that move – but then he withdrew from such a project.

I would hypothesize that psychologism was a more general threat, seen by a large number of academics as the next big breakthrough in the human sciences. Dilthey might have given hope to those ambitions, and hence he was suspect. But, in his lecture on hermeneutics, I do not see how calling for the motivation behind a work of art also to be taken into account constitutes a cardinal sin. It is abundantly clear that Weber did not like psychologism, and he spent a considerable amount of methodological ink in condemning it. The principal object was that a science of psychology – and it would be based on natural scientific procedures – could provide a royal road into the human and cultural sciences; in the same way, today, evolutionary psychology offers that possibility. Very many economists persevered with the idea that a psychology of stimulus and response would explain the underlying mechanism of desire, utility and its satisfaction.[60] Weber disagreed with this on the grounds that social economics provided the basis for imputing desires and motives to economic actors; this was a sufficient explanation. In the area of 'Verstehen', so crucial to Weber's cultural science, psychologism offered not so much a science as a loose account of how re-experiencing and empathy operated.

Simmel was one of the worst offenders in this respect. In his 1892 publication of *The Problems of the Philosophy of History*, Simmel wrote:

> We must be able to recreate the mental act of the historical person. As this is sometimes expressed, we must be able to 'occupy or inhabit the mind of the other person'. The understanding of an utterance entails that the mental processes of the speaker – processes which the words of the utterance express – are also reproduced in the listener by means of the utterance.[61]

For Weber, and hermeneutics in general, both the subjectivity of the speaker and the objectivity of the utterance are important. The mistake is to short cut from the subjectivity of the person, whose mind we in some wise inhabit, to the objective meaning of what is said – or expressed in writing or in artefact or in observed behaviour. Simmel was guilty of taking this short cut. Intuition, sympathy and feeling were the ways into the mind of another person and, in so understanding the mind of another person, their utterances could be understood. With Weber, motives have to be inferred, and what is said as an utterance, having an objective empirical existence separate from the intentions of the speaker, has to be interpreted; what Weber does not say is – interpreted according to hermeneutic rules. Simmel was capable of assuming a spirit world of the soul as a common property of humankind; hence, empathy was always possible and self-evident. For Weber, it can only be taken as an unprovable assumption that such understanding of motives and feelings is possible. This is the transcendental presupposition. What then matters is the procedure, which has to be critical not credulous.

It was Simmel who used the example 'one does not have to be Caesar in order to understand Caesar', in *The Problems of the Philosophy of History*.[62] Weber agreed with this as a possibility and uses the phrase himself. But as Huff points out, Simmel gave validity to this process by virtue of feeling alone. He quotes Simmel: '. . . the kind of general validity that is at stake here is a psychological property of mental activity itself. It is a feeling immediately given in mental activity' (p. 65). Weber's and Rickert's methodology was designed to place this possibility of understanding on a sounder and more objective basis. Huff notes, 'In short, Simmel substitutes "feeling" for objective and logical criteria of "validity"' (p. 66). I think Huff is correct in presuming that this not minor methodological difference is the basis for Weber's very prominent disavowal of Simmel's subjectivity. In Weber's two sociological essays – 'Some Categories of Interpretive Sociology' and 'Basic Sociological Concepts' – Simmel is both acknowledged and reprimanded in the opening preamble. 'I deviate from the method adopted by Simmel in his *Sociology of Money* in that I make as clear as possible a distinction between *intended* and objectively *valid* "meaning" ("*Sinn*"), a distinction which Simmel not only sometimes fails to make, but often deliberately runs together' (EW, p. 311). Simmel, it seems to me, redeems himself through his depiction of objectification as well as the central feature of his sociological and cultural analysis, the reciprocity of life and its forms.

Weber's distrust of Dilthey, I suspect, stems from the issue of vitalism. Simmel's psychologism and subjectivism are ways into what interests him most of all, the energy and creativity of life itself. Weber never reconciled himself to this feature of Simmel's work. Yet the word 'life' ('Leben') and its compounds are central to Weber's own work. It is perhaps here that Weber's preference for Rickert over Dilthey should be sought. Dilthey, as noted in the preceding section, effectively collapsed his hermeneutic method into the 'categories of life'. This was as much a move into vitalism as it was a psychologism. It was a move incompatible with the ambitions for a science of human and cultural life with any claims to validity in terms of critical distance and objectivity. It was just this distancing of the investigator from the embrace of vitalism that Rickert supplied to Weber.

There is an important corollary to this debate, which was conducted as much covertly as textually explicitly. Weber, so to speak, sheltered behind Rickert rather than directly engaging in methodological debate with Dilthey. Weber also seized hold of the method of causal attribution. Neither of these manoeuvres obviates the need for a critical discussion of hermeneutics. I flag this up for future discussion, and I agree with Huff's recommendation that the work of recent language philosophy, particularly Donald Davidson,[63] will show the way forward – in a way that accords with Weber's ambitions for 'objectivity' in the human sciences.

The 'objectivity' of knowledge

We do not have to make Weber conform to either the Diltheyan or the Rickertian line. He does need, however, to be placed in the extraordinarily rich context of methodological work that was reflexively coming to terms with a century of academic progress in the historical and cultural disciplines and with the recent challenge of the all too successful natural sciences.

Key to Weber's views is his essay 'The "Objectivity" of Knowledge in Social Science and Social Policy'. This is a massive essay in its length, topics and issues covered, and its innovative approach. In terms of pedagogic understanding, it is probably one of the more difficult pieces of his writing and one lecturers probably have the most difficulty teaching, even though it will always appear in a 'theory and methods' syllabus. It contains just about all the ideas and concepts of Weber's thinking on methodology, although we need to make the proviso that he had not at this point developed a theory of social action. It has no subtitles, and it certainly should have them, because of its large array of topics. There is some evidence that it was written under pressure in order to front up the relaunch in 1904 of the *Archiv für Sozialwissenschaft und Sozialpolitik* by its new editors, Max Weber, Werner Sombart and Edgar Jaffé.

It was composed in order to raise and answer questions at a number of levels. It takes until the halfway point of the essay before the topic of 'objectivity' and the issues related to PESC are discussed. It is preceded by an introduction signed by all the editors ('Die Herausgeber') that signals the change of direction in the journal. Under its old editor, Heinrich Braun, its major orientation was the labour question ('Arbeiterfrage'), and the journal had had an explicit reform agenda, which it promoted through the publication of details of labour statistics and labour legislation. Under the new editors, the labour question is widened and deepened to consider the origins and consequences of the revolutionary process of capitalism on economic life and to consider this in the interaction of the social with the economic. The editors wrote as economists ('Nationalökonomen') but in the pursuit of the study of the 'general cultural significance of capitalist development'. A theory of the social would establish the specific meaning of the social phenomena of culture ('Kultur'). This, in its turn, demanded a consideration of the relation between conceptual constructs ('Begriffsgebilde') and reality ('Wirklichkeit'). This was necessary if the journal was to meet scientific standards and, hence, the introduction would be followed by an essay by one of the editors (Weber) on 'Erkenntniskritik' (epistemology) and 'Methodenlehre' (research methods).[64]

So Weber's essay on 'Objectivity' emerges within the context of the capacious manifold of national-economy, a reform-oriented analysis of modern capitalism and a commitment to science. While it was written at the same time as PESC, the essay does not have a specifically cultural, religious or sociological focus. PESC can be placed within the new programme of the *Archiv*. It would be an example of the cultural determination of the economic development of capitalism. PESC might exemplify the new programme and its approaches, but it did not constitute a new disciplinary departure in the social sciences. While, as we have seen in the last chapter, PESC does indeed have major implications for social and cultural science, Weber's overall methodological comments keep his cotemporaneous essay within the bounds of the scientific project of the new programme for national-economy.

Weber's essay opens with an aggressive attack on the prevailing orthodoxy in national-economy and social science. This attributed too much faith to the explanatory power of science, assuming that, once the laws of societal development or the laws of the mind derived from biology, then all sociopolitical decisions and ethical choices could conform to scientific analysis. Weber terms this historical relativism, and he applies this critique to historical materialism as well as Spencerian evolution.

Value judgements

His other associated main theme is value judgements. Science, Weber says, can establish what is, but it cannot prescribe what we should do in the light of scientific information. The ends of our actions, our goals and purposes, belong to a realm separate from that of science. Science can tell us how to pursue an end and the consequences flowing from the achievement of that end. Science can analyse *means*, but *ends* belong to the purposive activity of human beings. Weber had a huge fight on his hands in advocating this position. The general public (then, as now) was quite happy to accept the scientific logic of statements such as 'scientific research has shown, for example, smoking damages your health' and therefore we ought as a society to adopt the recommendations of scientists. For Weber, something like 'smoking damages your health' might be demonstrable and 'self-evident' through research, but what we choose to do about it as private citizens and public governments is another matter. Professors, whether in public health or social science, in his day saw no point in conducting research unless they could tell or prescribe what people and governments ought to do. The economists, of all persuasions, were especially inflexible. Forces of economic determination, for Weber, clearly could not be denied, but how citizens and governments reacted still remained a realm of freedom of choice within certain boundaries, i.e. capitalism could not be reversed, but it could be shaped, and the direction of its shaping was a matter of citizen/political debate. It was on this front that the *Archiv* wanted to open up the subdiscipline of social economics. Weber's remarks remain persuasive today. East coast US economists in the early 1990s demanded, on the basis of free market economic theory, neo-liberal solutions for the ex-Soviet Union, and they did this in the certainty of scientific truth – which for Weber would have been a value judgement. In a Weberian scientific world, neo-liberal recommendations would be analysed as one policy option with certain benefits and disadvantages and, crucially, they would be compared with alternative economic prescriptions (EW, p. 362), both open to public debate.

In very broad terms, Weber's position on value judgements is considered Kantian in that it follows in the footsteps of Kant's threefold analysis of cognitive (pure) reason, moral (practical) reason and artistic judgements.[65] Each of these spheres has its own philosophical logic. In contrast, the dominant Anglophone philosophy of utilitarianism tends to collapse these categories: what a person finds rational tends to coincide with what he or she wants, and what gives pleasure is what he or she fancies, whether aesthetic or any other cultural good. In the sense of this gross contrast, Weber is Kantian. But, on the formation of value judgements, Weber is not strictly Kantian.

> The fate of a cultural epoch that has eaten from the tree of knowledge is that it must know that we cannot read the *meaning* of world events out of the results of any analysis, no matter how complete that might be; but that it has to be prepared to create such a meaning itself, that 'worldviews' can never be the product of enhanced experiential knowledge, and that therefore the highest ideals that move us most strongly are forever formed in struggle with other ideals, ideals which are as dear to others as ours are to us.
>
> (EW, p. 364)

We cannot decant our view of the world from scientific knowledge. But for Weber, our view of the world may well be in opposition to another one and, in this sense, we assert our meaning against other viewpoints. It is an agonistic or competitive vision. In the Kantian and more ordered world of Rickert, value judgements would emerge from values that were held in common by a community, and they would be prioritized according to areas of life.[66] Habermas, one of the most prominent critics of Weber in this respect, argues that moral values and norms should emerge from an open discussion within any one community and that their validity derives from a procedure that can produce a consensus within a community. Habermas criticized Weber for his 'decisionism' – that ethical and political judgements are reduced to individual decision-making unreflective of wider group norms. And, in later work, Habermas specified the procedures whereby those norms could best be realized within groups.[67] With Weber, the formation of value judgements appears to rest on the desirability of commitment, that one set of values are supported while openly recognizing that others commit to opposing value judgements. Kant's moral philosophy endorses the community consensus because it can secure a more universal basis, and so validity. Weber endorses the heterogeneity of values that may exist in perpetual conflict rather than being resolvable to any one consensus.

Weber insists that 'a social scientific periodical as we understand it should, inasmuch as it is *scientific*, be a space where truth is sought, truth which can claim to be a valid conceptual ordering of empirical reality . . .' (EW, p. 365). Truth is a scientific standard that is universally valid. Weber continues that two obligations follow from the inability of scholars to refrain from introducing value judgements into their work.

> First of all, both readers and editors should be at all times entirely aware *which* standards are here applied for the measurement of reality, and from which a value judgement is derived; contrasting with the all too frequent practice of an imprecise mingling of the most diverse values, confounding the conflict between ideals in an effort to 'offer something to everyone'.
>
> (EW, p. 366)

Secondly, value conflict should lead to a clear 'confrontation' of value standards.

> Any meaningful *evaluation* of alien *aspirations* can only be a critique formed from one's own 'worldview', a struggle against *alien* ideals on the basis of one's *own* ideals. *If* in individual cases the ultimate value-axiom underlying a practical aspiration is not only identified and subjected to scientific analysis, but its relationships with *other* value-axioms made clear, then 'positive' criticism of the latter through systematic exposition is unavoidable.
>
> (EW, p. 366)

Education and science, then, will form the basis for a critical debate over policy issues. A strong commitment to wealth creation is not necessarily reconcilable with egalitarian viewpoints. In this 'confrontation', scientific analysis would remove empirical errors and lack of clarity in arguments; it would not remove the underlying convictions that may be deeply held, but it could place the debate on policy on a new footing.

Weber is eloquent and insistent on this issue for many pages, very much aware of the opposition he would face. As the policy and social sciences were new and innovative, there was a belief that they would change the world for the better. This was an aspiration held in various policy forums such as the *Verein für Sozialpolitik* in Germany, the *L'Anneé Sociologique* in France and the Fabian Society in Britain. Weber's scepticism on values was later to lead to a major crisis (1909–14) in his relationship with the German Sociological Society and the *Verein für Sozialpolitik*. At this point, however, his insistence on scientific standards will be pursued. Bruun pertinently notes that the separating of value judgements from scientific analysis has the corollary that greater emphasis is placed on the objectivity of knowledge – the title of Weber's essay.[68]

The challenge

Weber was facing a major challenge. He insisted on scientific validity in the sense that the truth of empirical facts in the social and cultural world can be established and that truth will be universally valid. He is not able to fall back on a 'correspondence' account of empirical truth, that facts 'speak for themselves' – 'naïve self deception' (EW, p. 381). Rickert had put this issue beyond contention as, in the infinite nature of the world, there are a number of facts that can be presented, and the procedure becomes one of selection of facts and the aspectual character of what we know. There is no 'real' underlying structure to the world whose nature is presented to the scientist through unambiguously true facts. Weber also follows Rickert on the conceptual dualism that an ontological gulf separates the mind of the observer from reality itself ('Wirklichkeit'). If anything, Weber stresses this gulf even more than Rickert. Weber takes the reality 'out there' to be an irrational chaos, and holds that the role of the social and cultural scientist is to impose some kind of ordering.[69] Weber also assumes that people make evaluations and hold to deeply held beliefs and convictions. These, however, need not coexist in some kind of order, in the way in which Rickert sought to structure values. Heterogeneity of values is the assumption that Weber makes, what he would later call the polytheism of beliefs.[70] Weber belongs to the philosophical tradition that the human, social being is a feeling, wishing and evaluating entity.[71] In his refusal of reductionism, and this is how he uses the term 'relativism', Weber continually insists that the acting human being – what Spinoza termed the 'conative' part of being – cannot be explained away as determined by forces of biology, evolution or materialism.

Weber cannot, therefore, follow the full Rickertian programme of securing some kind of ordering among scientists and citizens, which then confers some kind of validity upon the process of selection. Weber's position – and solution – is unique to him, and he carries a fairly minimal amount of baggage as measured in presuppositions or 'a priori' assumptions. The 'Objectivity' essay marks the coming of age of twentieth-century social science and the removal of the comforts of positivism, naïve empiricism and the transcendentalism of ideas and values.

The only existing English translation (until Keith Tribe's translation in 2004[72]) rendered the title, ' "Objectivity" of Social Science and Social Policy'. Edward Shils, its co-editor and co-translator, was a forceful advocate not only for social science, in post-1945 North America and Great Britain, but for a Weberian conception of it. In his Introduction, he speaks of a marriage of policy and science and, to a certain extent, he forces the linkage of these two – and this appears in the English title. The German runs, 'Die "Objektiv-ität" Sozialwissenschaftlicher und Sozialpolitischer Erkenntnis': 'The "Objectivity" of Social Scientific and Social Political Knowledge'. Weber's intent is to separate policy from science and to downplay the claims of science. Weber does not use the term 'science' ('Wissenschaft') in the title, he uses 'knowledge' ('Erkenntnis') and, whether science or knowledge, the word is dropped entirely in the Shils and Finch edition.[73] 'Erkenntnis' has the sense of the getting of knowledge, and its English equivalents from a standard dictionary read: 'realization', 'recognition', knowledge' and (in philosophy) 'cognition'. 'Science', in contrast, has a spurious finality.

It is in the second part of the essay that Weber gives his solution. Weber defines the object of study as 'socioeconomic' in character. In meeting their economic needs, people engage in 'careful forethought, effort, a struggle with nature, and the need to work in association with people'. These phenomena have no inherent objectivity. Rather, study 'is determined by the direction of our cognitive *interest*, arising out of the specific cultural meaning that we attribute to the individual process in question'. Where a specific event or process has such a meaning, a social scientific problem is found. This problem and its circumstances then becomes a task for a discipline that seeks to clarify the problem and its 'underlying circumstances' (EW, p. 368).

Because the essay is directed towards how people meet their external physical needs, i.e. economics in its widest sense, Weber places stress on economic motives but also their interaction with cultural life more generally. In this more general field, a topic only becomes an object of study when it becomes 'problematic', and what the *Archiv* considers to be problematic is 'the constellation of interests and conflicts of interest arising out of the leading role played by capital in search of investment opportunities in modern developed economies ("moderne Kulturländer"), their present significance and their historical formation'. This leads to a subset of problems, such as the labour question or tariff question, that are 'formed by the particular nature of the economic foundations of our culture, and hence specifically modern cultural problems' (EW, p. 371).

The creation of an object of study, therefore, is not the free play of academic discourse but something far more 'hard-nosed'. Weber was slightly premature in his diagnosis of the carving up of the world into investment opportunities (although not in its colonial phase), whereas today this is happening with a frightening intensity and speed. Today's satisfaction of material, and ideal, needs generates enormous problems and, for Weber, inevitable conflicts – now, for example, the desire for motor cars and a clean environment, or the interests of the developed world and those of the developing world. The *Archiv*'s general problematic has become even more pressing and urgent. Socioeconomic life generates issues which then become objects of disciplined methods and study. 'Scientific domains,' says Weber, 'are constituted not by the "*objective*" (*sachlich*) relation of "things", but by the relationship of *problems* in *thought*: a new "science" emerges wherever new methods are applied to a new problem and, in this way, truths discovered which disclose significant and new perspectives.' So, for example, climate warming 'objectively' had been occurring throughout the twentieth century. It was only when it was defined as a problem in the 1970s–80s that the swathe of environmental subdisciplines were created.

Weber is scathing about the scientific priority that investigators allocate to their subject in the name of 'objectivism'. He has in his sights the (Marxist) materialist interpretation of history where everything is reducible to the circumstances of economic motives and interests; likewise, theories of race rooted in the objectivism of biology. What is required in their place is 'the enlargement of the possibility of certain imputation of individual *concrete* cultural events occurring in historical reality to *concrete*, *historically* given causes through the acquisition of *exact* observational material furnished by specific perspectives' (EW, p. 372). Racial biology – 'a product of the modern rage for founding new disciplines' – fails as a science because it misplaces the role of science, which is exact method and not 'objective realities'. The modern rage for sociobiology on genomic principles would equally have incurred Weber's ire.

> There is no absolutely 'objective' scientific analysis of cultural life . . . there is no 'objective' analysis of 'social phenomena' *independent* of special and 'one-sided' perspectives, on the basis of which such phenomena can be . . . selected as an object of research, analysed and systematically represented. The reason for this arises from the specificity of the cognitive aim of social scientific work which seeks to move beyond a purely *formal* consideration of legal or conventional *norms* governing social association.
>
> (EW, p. 374)

This passage points both towards Rickert's principle of selection and against any formalism of pre-existing norms, of which the study of law, or of theology, would be examples. 'The social science that we wish to pursue is a *science of reality* (*Wirklichkeitswissenschaft*). Our aim is an understanding of the uniqueness of the lived reality within which we are placed . . . to understand the context and cultural *significance* of individual phenomena in this lived reality – and, on the other hand, the reasons for their being historically so and not otherwise' (EW, p. 374). Weber squarely places the enterprise as a science of lived experience, of life, but the epistemological route for apprehending reality follows Rickert.

> All cognitive knowledge of infinite reality by the finite human mind thus rests upon the implicit presupposition that at any one time only a finite part of this reality can be subjected to scientific scrutiny, that only this part is 'material' in the sense of 'worth knowing'.
>
> (EW, p. 374)

This is close to Rickert's distinction between the real and the non-real. For

Rickert, what is worth knowing is valid but not real, but through the process of selection of infinite reality, it attaches to a segment of material reality. Weber draws the same sort of contrast as Windelband and others between a science framed in laws and a science that seeks out the individuality of phenomena. Astronomy conforms to the former and is quantitative, whereas social science is concerned with the qualitative. In dealing with mental processes ('geistiger Vorgänge'), understanding ('Verstehen') is gained through re-experiencing ('nacherlebend') (EW, pp. 375 and 386). This is a sentence straight out of Dilthey, who put forward a method of empathy and re-experiencing as a way of connecting the investigator to the expressive human subject. In the social sciences, although there might be regularities falling short of laws, these would not constitute, or point to, a topic worth studying. Instead, it is the investigators' own evaluation of what is of interest that confers cultural significance upon reality.

> The *significance* inherent in the formation of a cultural phenomenon and the *bias* for this significance cannot be taken, founded and rendered intelligible from a system of law-like concepts, no matter how complete, for the significance of cultural phenomena implies a relationship to *evaluative ideas* (*Wertideen*). The concept of culture is an *evaluative concept*. Empirical reality is for us 'cultural' in the sense, and to the extent that, it is related to evaluative ideas; it comprises those elements of reality rendered *meaningful* by this relationship, no more.
>
> (EW, p. 377)

It takes a little concentration at this difficult juncture of the 'Objectivity' essay to grasp that Weber is using terms very close to Rickert's terminology, but is not following in his exact footsteps. Key to Rickert's argument was the term 'Kulturwerthe' but, with Weber, this has become 'Wertideen'. Rickert's cultural values structure and impose validity on 'Wirklichkeit'. Weber's 'Wertideen' cannot perform this task, because Weber has already admitted to the heterogeneity of values. Instead, they become for him the pretext for selection in terms of meaning from the complexity of 'Wirklichkeit'.

Of course, this is not made any easier to follow by the slightly contrived nature of Rickert's own argumentation. The issue of concern here is the Hume/Kant one of epistemological dualism. Dilthey had one solution, Rickert another. What was Weber's? This matters because on it hangs Weber's methodological treatment of the meaningful. Weber got more from the analysis of the meaning and significance of culture than just about any other practitioner in the social, cultural and historical sciences. Weber produces colour where other social scientists manage tones of grey. If the social sciences were to deal with its subject matter, as defined through the process of selection as being of evaluative worth – and hence concerned with a meaningful segment or aspect of culture – what makes this 'objective', even within scare quotes?

Reading this section of his essay, a clear answer is not to be had – if one is looking for a philosophical answer to epistemological dualism. Weber appears to be saying that we throw or project our own ideas of value against a brute complex reality and so illuminate it, in some aspect, as meaningful. But the underpinning operation is left unresolved, neither Rickert's validity of cultural values nor Dilthey's categories of life. Weber presses on to provide other forms of assurance in the form of research techniques that are more clearly in line with how objectivity is secured in current research practice. One conclusion, however, is that Weber is giving himself covert Nietzschean licence. To make a value relation and confer value is tacitly to re-evaluate; not in Nietzsche's own 'über' sense of the aesthetic or the will to power, that is of imposing oneself – as a higher being – on brute reality, but nonetheless having the freedom to decide oneself what is of cultural value and thereby becoming an object of study. This gives Weber room for his own undoubted creativity and also contributes to his own powers of attraction to his audience.

Validity questions pertained to causation, not meaning and values. Weber follows the Rickertian line that causal explanation occurs only when attached to the individual event or fact. Concepts of increasing generality, as in physical laws or, indeed, in the mass regularities of exchange behaviour, contain less explanatory power the further removed they are from concrete individual events. 'The more general, that is the more abstract, that the laws are, the less work they do for the requirements of causal imputation of *individual* phenomena, and hence indirectly for the understanding of the significance of cultural processes' (EW, p. 379).

Weber applies the argument that only historical causation is a real explanation. He uses the example of exchange behaviour. 'The cultural significance such as exchange in a money economy lies in the fact that it appears in the form of a mass phenomenon, which is a fundamental component in modern cultural life. But if we are to understand the cultural *significance* of the *historical* fact that it plays in this role, then its historical emergence has to be causally explained' (EW, pp. 377–8). The money economy, like modern capitalism, is a system that has specific causal/historical origins – the invention of money, or the rise of the Puritan middle class, for example. However, like the orbit of a comet in the natural sciences, price and exchange behaviour will take on regularities that can be explained by theories such as the quantity theory of money or market behaviour. But the actual position of a comet or the actual price of a commodity is the real that is caused by the antecedent events. In a diachronic analysis, history matters, because certain historic events have long-term repercussions. In synchronic analysis, the regularities occurring at a point in time provide the social scientist with powerful explanatory theories. Weber's answer to these arguments would be that all reality is diachronic – every event and every fact has a history – and this is the only 'real' there can be, and hence is the site of causal explanation. If one wishes to choose to divide time and space up into the diachronic and synchronic, the social scientist can do this, but these divides would be purely concepts not descriptions of an indivisibly complex reality.

Weber's radical insistence on the unknowability of the infinitely complex real forms the basis of his discussion of where he wishes to place the emphasis of 'objectivity' – on causal adequacy and ideal types. Before turning to this, it is worth reflecting on Weber's style or way of arguing. He refers in passing to logical developments in the theory of knowledge. But he fails to provide bibliographic references, and this applies to both Rickert and Dilthey. His transposition of Rickert's argument on values to causality and meaning is hard to discern. He has denied Dilthey in the name of Rickert, and he has replaced Rickert's strict treatment of values by inserting in their place the Diltheyan emphasis on meanings. He hopes to secure his position with the empirical testing procedures of causation of concrete events.

Reasons and causes of action

In the continuous war of a positivistic versus an interpretivist version of social science, one of its front lines has been the dispute about whether human behaviour is 'caused' by factors external to the individual or whether a person is a participating and, in principle, freely deciding member of a culture and society. It is a debate that sets in, on one side, with scientific earnestness with Comte, and continues through Durkheim, behaviourism and current versions of sociobiology and evolutionary psychology. And those positivistic claims are resisted by the humanities, by the 'scientific' humanities (Dilthey) and the long interpretivist tradition of the twentieth century that originates in the phenomenology of Edmund Husserl and Alfred Schutz. The methodology wars of the twentieth century have disputed every term in the lexicon of social research. Precise definition of terms, their operationalization, hypothesis forming, empirical proof, causal explanation belong to positivism. The understanding and elucidation of meanings, how they are shared and how they affect individuals and groups belong to the interpretivist account. It is one of the heavy burdens of postgraduate training in social research methods that some part of this conflict has to be imbibed (even though the slightly more farcical situation seems to have been reached where these debates now come down to a choice between 'hard' quantitative methods versus 'soft' qualitative methods; a choice that makes risible any credible claim to research design).

Weber simply walks across this line, seemingly unaware of the sound of gunfire. As the champion of meaning, he moves straight to the assertion that individual actions are 'caused'. Yet the language of causation belongs to the natural sciences and the nomological. If we follow Martin Hollis' highly commended essay 'Models of Man', in which the two opposing schools are schematically represented as 'autonomous man' (the interpretivist account) and 'plastic man' (the positivistic account), some care is exercised by Hollis in his own use of terminology. In the former account, individuals have 'reasons' for acting; in the latter, they are have 'causes' for action.[74] This, incidentally, is not a debate about free will versus determinism. Durkheim and Weber both agreed that people are placed in sociological situations that are beyond their making, but within which they can exercise free will.[75] And Marx said a similar thing in his theses on Feuerbach. But each of these social theorists operates with different and opposed methodologies of causation.

Weber is impervious to this methodological divide. For him, even if there were nomological regularities in social science, these would not explain the actions of individuals. This he asserts on the grounds of the non-real status of concepts. Causal forces, like Durkheim's suicidogenic currents, have no ontological validity for Weber. It is, however, permissible to *attribute* to individuals the reasons/causes for their observed behaviour. In this way, a reason for acting becomes an *imputed* cause for Weber. Causality becomes a retrospective operation and can never be a predictive science. In his causative model, the situation offers various 'objective possibilities'; sociologically, we do not live in a realm of freedom but of constrained choices. Causal explanation operates through imputing or attributing causes to actions. In an English coroner's court, the 'objective possibility' facing an inquest is the person was murdered or died of natural causes or took their own life. In reaching a verdict, the coroner imputes a possible cause. The coroner may well turn out to be wrong in his or her attribution, but this highlights the nature of probability in sociological judgements. Hence, the judgement from a social scientific perspective, which would, optimally, operate to higher levels of evidence and investigation than an average coroner's court, is that someone *probably* took their own life. Weber expects the social scientist to imagine the range of possible causes of an event on the basis of his or her experience of life and accumulated academic knowledge. These form the basis of objective possibility, a term not dissimilar to counterfactual possibility, i.e. the course of action could have been 'a', 'b' or 'c' but, on the basis of the evidence, a cause is attributed to an outcome.[76] 'Concepts of this sort are constructs in whose terms we formulate relationships through the employment of the category of objective possibility; and these constructs are *judged* with respect to their adequacy by an *imagination* oriented to, and guided by, reality' (EW, p. 390).[77]

After some few pages in which Weber berates the claims of abstract theory as being able to deduce causal explanation of 'real' events and actions (and a reflection of the eruptive debates in German-speaking national-economy), Weber outlines the ideal type. Weber has, so to speak, prepared the epistemological ground for this and, conversely, it is not advisable for a student to look this term up in the index and expect to comprehend what is at stake! It is in the nature of social science that the researcher has to be content with choosing an aspect of reality as worthy of study and, in this sense, all theory is one-sided; this would apply to Marxism as much as to marginalism, for neither can validly claim to be a comprehensive account of reality. Marginalism as much as Marxism is a theoretical or accentuated account of reality. In this sense, both are conceptually utopian – they do not exist in reality and neither can they be produced out of history. We can, says Weber, have an ideal grasp of processes of markets, commodities, exchange, competition and rational action.

> This construction brings together certain relationships and events of historical life into an internally coherent *conceptual* cosmos. This construction has the substantive idea of a *utopia* arrived at by the conceptual accentuation of particular elements of reality. Its sole relation to the empirically given facts of life is where relationships there represented abstractly, i.e. events related to the 'market', can be *identified* or *supposed* as existing in reality; and we are therefore able to make the characteristic features of this relationship pragmatically *lucid* and understandable in terms of an *ideal type*. This procedure can be of value, even indispensable, heuristically as well as in exposition. The concept of the ideal type can direct judgement in matters of imputation; it is not a 'hypothesis', but seeks to guide the formation of hypotheses. It is not a *representation* of the real, but seeks to provide representation with unambiguous means of expression.
>
> (EW, p. 387)

Weber himself notes the ambiguity of the term 'ideal' in ideal types. Ideal types can be constructed just as much from saintliness as from prostitution. Perhaps it would have been better for Weber to call them heuristic types, an adjective he uses on a number of occasions. Ideal types seek to accentuate meaning, but note that the word hermeneutic never crosses Weber's lips. We can only guess that hermeneutics belongs to a sort of preliminary enterprise, and belongs to the researcher's accumulated understanding, knowledge and experience of the world. An ideal type is a sharp conceptual instrument for the purpose of elucidation. Hermeneutics belongs to the exegesis and explication of the text and other cultural artefacts. Heuristics is a conceptual contrivance for shaping and dissecting cultural meanings, while hermeneutics has to attend to the facticity of the artefact. While I have drawn this distinction, so to speak on behalf of Weber, I would not myself like to defend the distinction as hard and fast, for both would seem to involve parallel, if not overlapping, conceptual operations. Weber has his gaze firmly set on causal explanation as the standard of objectivity and of science. But to do this, he has to interpose hypothesis construction between ideal types and causal explanation. Were the Herrnhuter a sect? In ideal–typical terms, this cannot be answered but, if we hypothesize certain characteristics, indicative of and drawn from the ideal type of sect, the empirical facts of Herrnhuter could be said to meet those characteristics. Weber says very little on the subject of hypothesis formation, although he does say that the overall aim is to compare (EW, p. 396) or even confront (EW, p. 402) empirical reality with ideal type. This is not terribly satisfactory, and modern methodology in social research has not fared terribly well either in working out the relation between concepts of meaning and the investigation of empirical reality

– as debates over 'grounded theory' and 'sensitizing concepts' have shown.[78]
Weber is aware that problems remain to be elucidated on the relation of ideal
types to other seemingly similar concepts such as ideals in life, like Christian ethics, collective concepts, normative concepts of value as in economic
theory or normative concepts of the state. But, he says, 'we must simply
abandon any ambition of seriously examining in any greater depth practical methodological questions that are here only briefly *exposed* . . .' (EW,
p. 397). One is tempted to observe that methodological questions can only
be practical and that Weber remains delinquent on how to investigate how
values are empirically attached in the world.

Weber does offer a very brief discussion of the role of ideas in history, a
topic which unsurprisingly was going to occupy more of his attention in the
light of the publication of PESC: 'the causal relationship between a historically existing *idea* that rules men, and the components of historical reality
from which its corresponding ideal *type* can be abstracted, can be formed in
quite various ways' (EW, p. 391). Weber, needless to say, stresses the procedure of abstracting the ideal type of ideas from their complex manifestations
in history. '. . . the "ideas" that govern the people of a given epoch . . . can
(where a degree of complexity of thought construct is involved) only be
grasped with any kind of conceptual clarity *in the form of an ideal type*, since
this idea empirically inhabits the heads of an indeterminate and constantly
changing number of individuals . . .' (EW, pp. 391–2). And, 'the empirico-
historical process in the heads of human beings has to be understood as a
*psycho*logical process . . .'. 'Ideas are historically effective, and they live on
in the minds of men long after the fundamental "idea" has . . . died out . . .'
(EW, p. 392). This is unambiguous. Ideas are causally effective, existing as a
psychological reality in the minds of men and causing them to act in certain
ways.

The progress of knowledge

Weber has a number of scattered remarks about how knowledge advances.
This has become one of the major themes of the philosophy of science, especially in the second half of the twentieth century. Here, as in much else,
Weber anticipates future developments. When his remarks are brought together, a motif can be discerned, which I think comes to be a characterizing
feature of Weber's own creation of social scientific knowledge.

This can be envisaged, mentally rather than diagrammatically, as a background reality of continuously flowing space and time coordinates. The
investigator occupies a 'pod' in this reality that is filled with his or her experience and knowledge. Around this is a larger pod of the scientific or
disciplinary knowledge. The investigator shines a torch (powered by evaluative ideas) on to the otherwise impenetrable complexity of reality. This
cognitively defines and fixes an aspect of reality. This is then subjected to
the dual operation of ideal type and causal analysis. The result could be
prosaic or highly creative. If the latter, then it feeds back with considerable

impact into the scientific/disciplinary pod and as a cultural product to the researcher himself. The process could then repeat, for example as critique and anti-critique, as it did in the case of PESC itself. The epistemology of this has been outlined above. But the temporality of knowledge is worth noting. Knowledge is never secured to time and place and, in this sense, it cannot be 'objectively' banked. The researcher lives and works in the continuous flow of time, and this temporality characterizes both what counts as scientifically interesting and the results of scientific investigation in the cultural and historical fields.

This would seem to be the 'model', although Weber puts it far more eloquently. For the normal researcher, evaluative ideals lead to selection and the attribution of meaning, so 'the direction of his personal belief, the refraction of his values in the prism of his mind, gives direction to his work'. 'And the values to which the scientific genius relates the object of his inquiry may determine, i.e. decide the "conception" of a whole epoch, not only concerning what is regarded as "valuable" but also concerning what is regarded as significant or insignificant, "important" or "unimportant" in the phenomena' (EW, p. 381). Essentially, this what I have argued in Chapter 3 with regard to Weber's own scientific genius and achievement with PESC.

Weber goes on to argue that a closed system of knowledge cannot be achieved. 'The stream of infinite events flows constantly towards eternity. The cultural problems that sway humankind are constantly renewed and reformulated . . .'. 'The points of departure for the cultural sciences remain mutable throughout an endless future, so long as a Chinese ossification of intellectual life does not render mankind incapable of posing new questions to eternal, inexhaustible life' (EW, p. 383). Specialization can lead to the consolidation of knowledge. 'And that is a good thing. But at some point the atmosphere alters: the significance of viewpoints used unreflectively becomes uncertain, the path becomes lost in twilight. The light cast by the great cultural problems has moved onward. Then even science prepares to shift its ground and change its conceptual apparatus so that it might regard the stream of events from the heights of reflective thought' (EW, p. 403).

The body of knowledge and procedures known collectively as 'science' is itself a floating temporal object in the flow of time. Science, as Weber was later vigorously to assert, only arose in the Occident and was particular in its maturing to a period and place. 'For scientific truth is only valid for those who *seek* truth' (EW, p. 383). The resurgence of anti-modernity at the beginning of the twenty-first century unfortunately gives this insight added weight. Science *tout court* is an evaluative idea that confers a particular sort of significance upon reality – it brings, to quote Weber, 'order out of chaos', and without the evaluative idea, no science.

Conclusions

A great many ideas and projects in the philosophy and methodology of the social sciences can be traced back, or at least imputed, to this transformative essay that so confounds the claims of scienticism, empiricism, reductionism, idealism and evolutionism. The traceable ideas include Popper's conjectures and refutations as the solution to Humean scepticism, Kuhn's idea of paradigm shifts as an account of 'progress' in science and Rorty's anti-foundationalism and the wider field of pragmatism, to name the most prominent.

Equally, the essay offers little support to an interpretative project concerned with meanings *per se* and understanding (without causal explanation). The consolidation of this split between positivistic explanation and interpretative understanding postdates Weber, so was obviously no concern of his. The split, as it predated him, no doubt he reckoned to have handled authoritatively, indeed muscularly. But some confusion and difficulty remains and, reading the essay, it is a reasonable inference to say that Weber was looking for various solutions in the course of writing the essay itself. In particular, how is meaning and its interpretation assessed prior to being incorporated into a cultural science?

At the end of the essay, Weber provides a sort of summary, more in the way of looking back and assessing the long route he has taken.

> We have come to the end of this discussion, the only purpose of which has been to trace the fine line that separates science and belief, and makes clear the meaning of the search for socio-economic knowledge. The objective validity of experiential knowledge rests, solely rests, upon the fact that given reality is ordered by categories which are in a specific sense *subjective*: they represent the *presupposition* of our knowledge and are based on the presupposition of the *value* of those truths which experiential knowledge alone is able to give us.
>
> (EW, p. 402)

This part is Diltheyan. Scientific questions originate in life, but they cannot be validated by the empirical material.

> The 'objectivity' of social scientific knowledge depends rather on the fact that the empirical given is always related to those evaluative ideas which alone give it cognitive *value*, and the significance of the empirically given is in turn derived from these evaluative ideas. But this empirical given can never become the pedestal upon which is based an empirically impossible proof of its validity.
>
> (EW, p. 403)

Objectivity is constituted by something outside the empirical – this part is an adaptation of Rickert on empirical validity. Our highest and ultimate beliefs, in which, says Weber, we 'anchor our being', do not exclude the notion that we can always change our scientific viewpoint. The transitivity of viewpoints and the corresponding transitivity of reality is Weber's 'base-line' (or anti-foundationalist) position, and it underwrites and promotes progress – if one chooses to believe in science.

> life, in its irrational reality and its store of *possible* significances is inexhaustible, the *concrete* formation of value relations remains therefore fluid, subject to change in the distant future of human culture. The light given off by these highest evaluative ideas falls upon an ever-changing finite part of a monstrously chaotic stream of events that flow through time.
>
> (EW, p. 403)

5 The reluctant sociologist

From the Protestant ethic to the *Grundriss der Sozialökonomik*

This chapter, and the following, covers an extensive segment of Weber's intellectual life (1905–14), in which he made a number of intensive commitments to a variety of projects. The chapter will register the various phases of this period in terms of the goals and markers Weber had set down in PESC and the essay on 'Objectivity'. The phase up until around 1909 is marked by unsuccessful attempts to answer his critics. Weber's difficulties stem from the difficulty of solving the highly problematic issue of multiple causation. The second phase (1910–14) is a creative convulsion taking his work way beyond the Protestant ethic studies. There are a number of trajectories which, I shall argue, we should not try to arrange into a neat order. One strong dynamic of the second phase, however, is developmental history on a comparative basis bringing with it a further, but not final, elaboration of methodology. It is here that Weber has to construct a sociology of his own making and for his own needs.

The Protestant ethic thesis is not an easy matter to grasp and the grounds for mistaking what kind of thesis it was are not minor. As has been argued, it offered an explanation as a contribution to a wider debate, which was not in itself visible from the text of PESC. It could be mistaken in the appearance of its arguments as a narrative history, which was not its intention. It presented itself as an ideal type of a historical individual, a self-presentation that has continually failed to secure widespread comprehension and acceptance. It was an exemplification of the ambitions laid out in the 'Geleitwort' of the 'Objectivity' essay and explicated as a new methodological way of doing cultural science in that essay. But the connection – between PESC and 'Objectivity' – was not a programmatic formulation. Finally, through its rhetorical verve, PESC dazzled its critics, leading to them to praise or blame features that were not necessarily core to the thesis.

PESC suffers an inconsistency between the boldness and ambitions of the thesis, on the one hand, and the caveats and qualifications that are introduced, on the other. In addition, Weber announces at the beginning that his main concept, the spirit of capitalism, cannot receive a final definition until the end of the essay (PESC, p. 47). But at the end, he says that systematic work in a worldly calling was the most powerful factor contributing to 'that attitude toward life which we have here called the spirit of capitalism' (PESC, p. 172). At this point, the spirit of capitalism still awaits its definition. And right at the end, he writes that 'one of the fundamental elements' of the spirit of capitalism was 'rational conduct on the basis of the idea of calling' (PESC, p. 180). From these statements, one concludes either that, in the end, Weber failed to provide a definition, or that what definition he did provide seems in part to include the causal factor (religious calling) that is meant to explain the spirit of capitalism. The latter option comes close to being an identity and not a causal relationship. This is a very large weakness to expose to your critics. The thesis can, however, be saved because it is not hard to assemble from Weber's incisive argumentation the characteristics of the spirit of modern capitalism, i.e. systematic and rational attitude to life and work, unceasing labour, asceticism of conduct, the concentration on means and technique over ends. These are the ingrained attitudes of those who work and live in the modern capitalist economy and culture. Weber offers up Benjamin Franklin in his systematic and rational search for profit as an illustration of the spirit of capitalism (PESC, p. 64). But much ink and controversy would have been spared if a complete definition of this concept had been supplied – preferably at the outset where the reader would expect it.

Weber writes that his study 'may thus perhaps in a modest way form a contribution to the understanding of the manner in which ideas become effective in history'. Hartmut Lehmann points out that Weber insistently refers to his 'provisional remarks', 'provisional illustration' of the spirit of capitalism and 'provisional' definition of traditionalism.[1] To this he adds another caveat that he did not subscribe to the 'foolish and doctrinaire thesis' that capitalism as an economic system is a creation of the Reformation (PESC, pp. 90–1). The second statement certainly qualifies the scope of the thesis. The thesis is not an idealist theory of history. What it seeks to do is 'ascertain whether and to what extent religious forces have taken part in the qualitative and the quantitative expansion of that spirit over the world'. This reads like a caveat. Just like the 'modest way' the study would be a 'contribution', but equally they can be read in their own terms as very strong propositions. Was PESC just another bit adding its own causal factor in the edifice of European historiography, or was it boldly reformulating the hitherto hidden realm of effective ideas in history? If Weber is arguing for the interaction of material forces and effective ideas in history, as he undoubtedly is, can we formulate the (null) hypothesis boldly and sharply in these terms: no Puritanism, no ascetic practice, no spirit of capitalism, no modern capitalism as we know it? This formulation of the hypothesis is not without its own problems, but it does illustrate the ambiguities that come to the surface when critical questions are asked of the thesis. I will in due course return to the null hypothesis (no Puritanism . . . no modern capitalism) in a discussion of what I term the singularity argument. Against the bold hypothesis, and when read in the light of the essay on 'Objectivity', PESC is slight in its intentions. Weber found Puritanism to be a subject of value to be studied, whereas before it had been neglected; he isolated an aspect he found significant and offered it as a contribution to the development of modern capitalism. This combination of methodological slightness and boldness of hypothesis has created confusion and difficulties in the critical interpretation of the thesis.

In his replies to his critics, Weber consistently, and sometimes angrily, insisted that they had misunderstood what he was saying. In the next section, I will focus on his inability to provide the 'killer' answer to his critics, and will suggest that this inability is inherent in PESC itself.

Weber replies

A Dr Karl Fischer, about whom not much is known, posted the first review in 1907 and in the *Archiv*. He was the first of many to take the thesis as an idealist account in place of a materialist one. Because Weber, as we know, devoted some pages in PESC (pp. 90–2) specifically arguing for the combination and interaction of material and ideal forces, he could rebut this suggestion. But the amended position – ideas as 'effective forces in history' – would still require a more robust methodology than the couple of references to ideal types.

Fischer raised a valid point about Weber's interpretation of Luther's translation of work as 'Beruf' (see pp. 56–7). 'For how did Luther arrive at the idea of using *Beruf* for his translation of the passage in Jesus Sirach? Presumably, he could not have meant his Bible translation to create a religious system in which even work in a worldly calling was to have a place. Rather, he must have thought that by using this common expression, he was choosing the best, most easily understandable term for ordinary people.'[2] The point Fischer was making was that economic development had already preceded the Reformation, and that Luther's use of terms was a reflection of existing use of meaning, i.e. 'Beruf' had already taken on the connotations of calling *prior* to Luther, therefore he, or the movement of Protestantism more generally, did not amount to the effective force of an idea in history.

Fischer also raised the question of the psychogenesis of modern capitalism, referring to Sombart's *moderne Kapitalismus* on the origins of acquisitive behaviour in Europe. Fischer correctly identified the psychological explanation of motivation as central to the thesis. It is interesting to see that Fischer was unable to discern the Sombart–Weber linkage on psychogenesis, and Weber is forced with some asperity to acknowledge his link 'to my good friend Sombart' (PE Debate, p. 32). Fischer drew on the English utilitarian tradition as formulated by J.S. Mill and Herbert Spencer to suggest that, if the acquisition of money as an end in itself is the thing to be explained, then 'we can understand it in terms of the pleasure of the individual in active exertion of his powers' (quoted by Weber, PE Debate, p. 35). The pleasure of exerting oneself is a generality that hardly applies to the 'reigned-in Puritans'. Weber reckoned himself to have refuted such simplistic psychological explanation elsewhere (in his 'Objectivity' essay and his articles on Roscher and Knies). This, though, still leaves the door open to the more complex question of how historical situations come to determine the psychological outlook and thinking of social groups.

Weber's response is to accuse Fischer of not providing any evidence for his argument. 'Philological findings may obviously correct my conclusions at any time. However, as the evidence stands, this certainly cannot be done merely by asserting the opposite' (PE Debate, p. 32). Weber certainly closes down this avenue of criticism, but it still remains an interesting conjecture worth exploring in its own right – despite Fischer's failure to substantiate it. Meaning could well be given by ordinary (German) language use. David Chalcraft notes in his introduction to Weber's replies that much of the debate turns on misunderstandings, and therefore on hermeneutics. Weber, notes Chalcraft, finds debates on terminology sterile. 'Yet, when discussing the meaning of a Franklin, or a Luther or a Sir William Petty, it is clear that what is said in particular places and contexts *in their texts* is at the heart of the matter.' Chalcraft concludes that one searches in vain for a consistent hermeneutics' in Weber's replies (PE Debate, p. 14). What is consistent about the replies and PESC is that Weber does not enter into the field of Diltheyan hermeneutics, despite his dependence on such procedures.

Weber's strategy is to focus debate on the role of causation in history, the groundwork for which he had laid down in the 'Objectivity' essay. Fischer remained unsatisfied with Weber's reply and, in 1908 in the *Archiv*, he published a rejoinder, in which he accused Weber of being 'temperamental' – no doubt because Weber, fairly roughly, accused him of being ignorant of the historical facts and misunderstanding his approach. Fischer said there was no doubt that Puritanism strengthened the methodical conduct of life, but the issue still remained to be debated about 'the genesis of the spirit of the methodical conduct of life in this period' (PE Debate, p. 41). To settle the genesis question, Fischer said Weber would have to eliminate other possible causes in order to show that only religion remained as the prime determinant of life conduct. (To an extent, this is how Durkheim proceeds in *Suicide*, eliminating possible alternative explanations, leaving his own favoured one as the sole survivor.) Weber resiled, pointing out that the historian could scarcely be expected to take on 'the negative burden of proof'. 'Normally he works the other way, investigating the effects of the *other* causal components positively [the economic, political components, etc.]. In this way, he will arrive at an ever more comprehensive (but never entirely self-sufficient) attribution of causes . . .' (PE Debate, p. 46).

The issue of causality arose again when Felix Rachfahl, a historian specializing in German and Dutch history, made a number of objections to the Protestant ethic thesis, of which he designated Troeltsch as well as Weber the authors. Rachfahl noted that economic development had occurred in France and the Low Countries prior to Protestantism, and that, in the case of England, the decisive move in economic development occurred in the eighteenth century under entirely different religious influences. And in North America, capitalism did not accelerate until the late eighteenth century and then under the influence of secular rationalism. Rachfahl contended that a methodical conduct of life was the result of the development of business as a vocation in the Renaissance period prior to Protestantism. He also objected to Weber's use of an abstracting ideal type, when what was required was country-specific historical analyses in order to handle the complex factors at work.

Weber's response here, as with Fischer, is to assert the ascendance of the causal change he had sketched out, i.e. religious vocation → conduct of life → spirit of capitalism. He refers his critics back to a key passage, on multiple causality, in PESC.

> In view of the tremendous confusion of reciprocal influences emanating from the material base, the social and political forms of organization, and the spiritual content of the cultural epochs of the Reformation, the only possible way to proceed is to first investigate whether and in what points particular *elective affinities* between *certain* forms of religious belief and the ethic of the calling can be identified. At the same time, the manner and general *direction* in which, as a result of such elective affinities, the religious movement influenced the development of material culture will be clarified as far as possible. Only *then* can the attempt be made to estimate the degree to which the historical origins of elements of modern culture should be attributed to those religious motives and to what extent to others.[3]

Fischer's method of elimination cannot operate because of the confusion of reciprocal influences. It remains methodologically impractical, even impossible, to isolate a cause, such as prior economic development, and its effect upon the conduct of life. Weber's tactic is to assert his historical grasp of the linkages, and his opponents' weaknesses in this department. The onus then rests upon the critics to come up with a better historical account. Weber, no more than his critics, has not solved the conundrum of multiple causality. Having established the positive linkages, he does concede it would be necessary to go back and investigate a different train of linkages, for example the economic and material factor operating upon religious influences. Weber never denies the converse: that material factors shape religion. It is just that he reckons he has established the superiority of his explanation over competing accounts.

Methodologically, what Weber proposes is akin to principal components analysis (or multifactorial analysis). Suppose the thing to be explained is the incidence of heart disease in a population. In a research design, various factors are held to account in different measure for its incidence. So smoking may come top of the list, followed by diet, followed by exercise. Applied to the Protestant ethic thesis, religious influences take priority over economic, political and social factors. The technique is to demonstrate that one factor takes priority over another. The other factors cannot be eliminated; also because they may be co-relational and co-terminous, the principal factor cannot even be isolated – it is probable that smoking will co-relate with bad diet and the two remain inextricable.

Weber, of course, did not have the luxury of thinking in terms of principal components analysis (which is, in addition, wholly dependent on statistical inference. Rachfahl did in fact suggest using statistics on economic growth, and Weber rightly points out that motivational influences in the past would not be susceptible to such analysis; PE Debate, p. 70.) Weber was in something of a quandary on the issue of competing causes, as no answer – then or now – can put the issue to rest. He makes two further responses. He places a greater emphasis on causal adequacy. Rachfahl had contested the linkage between capitalism as an economic system and the 'spirit of capitalism'. Weber replies that particular historical forms of capitalism have to be discussed in relation to different kinds of spirit, and he makes this point in contradistinction to talking of capitalism in general across history and place.

> A historically given form of 'capitalism' can be filled with very different types of 'spirit'; this form can, however, and usually will, have different levels of 'elective affinities' to certain historical types of spirit: the 'spirit' may be more or less 'adequate' to the 'form' (or not at all). There can be no doubt that the *degree* of this adequacy is not without influence on the course of historical development, that the 'form' and 'spirit' (as I said previously) tend to adapt to each other, and, finally, that where a system and a 'spirit' come up against each other, there ensues a development of (even inwardly) unbroken unity similar to that which I had began to analyze.[4]

An 'elective affinity' was a peculiarly nineteenth-century way of speaking about chemical bonding. Whereas today, we think in terms of two oxygen electrons binding together with a hydrogen nucleus (to form water), Goethe, reflecting his scientific knowledge, spoke of elective affinity ('Wahlverwandt-schaft'); it was also the title of one of his novels that catalogued friendship between two people – indeed, in Goethe's hands, as a new literary genre. So, individuals are drawn to each other in the strong sense that chemical elements bond together. Weber asserts that this reciprocal bonding lies at the heart of his research: modern capitalism and the vocationally specific spirit of capitalism. Weber allows the complexity of factors in play that have to be sifted by the historian, but what he has discovered is an immensely strong linkage. Weber's usage of 'causal adequacy' goes somewhat beyond imputation here. He is close to saying that this linkage is a real occurrence in history – a standard of objectivism he has already rejected.

His other reaction is to signal a retreat from the Protestant ethic thesis. He had intended to expand the scope of his studies. At the end of PESC, he wrote that 'it would be further necessary to investigate how Protestant asceticism was in turn influenced in its development and its character by the totality of social conditions, especially economic' (PESC, p. 183). He also referred to the period prior to the Reformation when the interaction of economic development and religion would become 'a further chapter' (PESC, p. 284, n. 118). This same note also registers Weber's distaste for writing big books 'I have no great inclination . . . to write heavy tomes'. Weber intended in 1907 to make further clarifications of PESC for its publication as 'a separate edition' (PE Debate, p. 34). In 1908, he referred back to his previous statements in PESC 'about future investigations for completing, interpreting, and testing it further' (PE Debate, p. 45).

During this period, Weber's close colleague at Heidelberg, Ernst Troeltsch, was also working intensively on Protestantism. He gave a lecture entitled 'The Significance of Protestantism for the Origins of the Modern World' at the Historians' Conference in 1906. (This was translated into English in 1912 as *Protestantism and Progress*.[5]) Hans Kippenberg notes of this lecture that Troeltsch was elaborating Weber's distinction between the capitalist system and the spirit of capitalism as it occurred in Holland, England and America, and that Troeltsch was indicating that, as the historical and theological expert, this was *his* field of specialism. Troeltsch was also publishing a series of articles in the *Archiv*, covering all aspects of Protestantism and western Christianity. (These later became the book *The Social Teachings of the Christian Churches*.) Weber had indicated in 1908 that there was an unnecessary duplication of work between himself and Troeltsch and, effectively, he was bowing out to the specialist theologians.[6]

But, if we read his second and last reply, in 1910, to Felix Rachfahl's critique of PESC, Weber's own stance to further research in this field remains unclear. He admits that further specialized research is required, and goes on: 'However necessary (indeed substantially *more necessary*) it may be to *compare* the various characteristics of the individual countries influenced by ascetic Protestantism (which alone will help explain evident differences in development), the most pressing questions for me lay and lie elsewhere.' Weber then goes on to specify where further research needed to be done. 'First . . . I needed to differentiate the various effects of Calvinist, Baptist and Pietist ethics on lifestyle, much more deeply and in detail than had been done before. We must also investigate thoroughly the beginnings of similar developments in the Middle Ages and early Christianity, as far as Troeltsch's works still leave scope for this – which will certainly require very intensive collaboration with theologians.' (Weber inserts a footnote here on his relation to theologians.) He continues, 'Then we need to consider how best to explain, from the *economic* standpoint, that ubiquitous elective affinity of the bourgeoisie to a definite kind of lifestyle . . .'. 'Numerous things have been said from many different quarters about this more general problem, but much more remains to be said – including, I believe, all that is fundamental.'[7]

In his footnote on his relationship to theologians, Weber says that – in contrast to the criticisms of the bungling, amateur and dilettante Rachfahl – his PESC had been well received. 'However,' he goes on, 'such merely "sociological" work must also be carried out – as it has been done by some of the theologians themselves, pre-eminently by Troeltsch. It should surely be done best by the specialists, to whom we outsiders can just here and there offer possible *perspectives on the problem* . . .'.[8] There certainly is an element of Weber giving the problem back to sociologically attuned theologians, pre-eminently Troeltsch.

But Weber also says fundamental work still remains to be done. I take Weber here to be referring to his own plans. The Protestant ethic studies can be interpreted as still remaining a focus for his research programme, but the specialist historical work on the Puritan sects would be accomplished by others. The Protestant ethic essay never did become a stand-alone book, as his publisher fervently hoped.[9] The enlargements, as promised, never did materialize. Peter Ghosh has observed that, by the time Weber had replied to his critics, he had exhausted the subject of capitalism and its relation to ascetic Protestantism.[10] This comment cannot, I think, be extended to Weber's interest in capitalism as a socioeconomic phenomenon subject to cultural influences, because the period 1910 onwards represents just such a commitment but now on a universal–historical scale. It is difficult to reach a conclusion. Had Weber effectively retreated in the face of the demands of his critics, especially in respect of the highly problematic field of multiple causation? Or was he about to rework the problem of causation through comparative analysis? It is probably a mistake to search for continuity, and we need to register the author's discretionary right to switch fields, not least as a new energizing source of enthusiasm. This does not, however, make the problem of multiple causation go away; rather, it moves it to a higher, and no less problematical, level.

The agrarian regimes of ancient civilization

Rachfahl's criticisms had prompted from Weber a reflection on the analysis of European-specific capitalism and whether other historical, but ideal–typical, constructs of capitalism could offer a point of comparison. This, he says, 'is what I tried to do for the "capitalism" of the ancient world as an economic system, although certainly in a very incomplete way (see my 'Agrarverhältnisse im Altertum' in *Handwörterbuch der Staatswissenschaft*, third edition, Vol. 1, 1909)' (PE Debate, pp. 74–5). The comparison would operate by presenting features 'not so present in other epochs'. Hence, both early modern European development and antiquity could be constructed as types of capitalism, but one (antiquity) would lack the 'spirit of capitalism'. The implication – and this is all it is at this stage in Weber's thinking – is that a missing cause will have missing effects, so throwing into relief their presence in Protestant Europe. This represents a new approach, as yet not clear in its logic, to the methodology of causation.

But Weber himself admits in his 1910 reply to Rachfahl that his attempt was incomplete. 'Agrarverhältnisse im Altertum' was not written with comparison in mind. It belonged to a series of initiatives and projects, like his intensive involvement in the literature coming out of Russian in 1905 on revolutionary activity and like his study of the industrial psychology of workers in 1907, that led him away from ever completing the promised additions to the Protestant ethic 'sketch'.

'Agrarverhältnisse im Altertum' was a commissioned entry for an encyclopaedia, and this meant that it had to conform to a format, title and style laid down by the editors of the *Handwörterbuch*. This placed constraints on Weber's ability to pursue his favoured methodology of the ideal type. The encyclopaedia format was very popular in the German universities – as it is again today. The whole approach favours the reader who, essentially, is able to find information on an indexed or alphabetical system. The format tends to the presentation of reliable and accessible knowledge rather than the more usual academic habit of getting embroiled in controversial debate.

The *Handwörterbuch der Staatswissenschaft* in its third edition was a well-established and respected encyclopaedia. Weber had provided short entries of eighteen pages for the supplementary volume of the first edition in 1897 and an amended version for the second edition of 1898. This probably explains Weber's sense of obligation to contribute to the third edition of 1909, but not why his entry was so extensive. Weber's entry ran to 136 double-columned pages. By comparison, the entries by Karl Lamprecht on agrarian regimes in the Middle Ages ran to three pages and agrarian regimes of modernity by Freiherr von der Goltz ran to eighteen pages. The entry title was given to the author: 'Agrarian regimes in the ancient world'. An introduction was required: 'on the economic theories of states in the ancient world'. Part 2 provided a breakdown of the agrarian history of ancient civilization ('alten Kultur') – in Mesopotamia, Egypt, ancient Israel, Greece, Hellenism, Rome and the basis of development in the Roman Empire.

So, it was a commission, for a dictionary/encyclopaedia, and had seemingly little connection to seventeenth-century Protestantism. Where, it might be asked, was Weber going with this academic enterprise? Initially, he considered it an obligation he could not refuse and that he would return to the Protestant ethic. On 26 December 1907, Weber wrote to Oskar Siebeck (his PESC publisher) that the article for the *Handwörterbuch* was a 'terrible obligation' that he could not decently refuse to do. He thought he would be finished in a few weeks, and then he would concentrate on a separate publication ('Sonderausgabe') of the 'Geist des Kapitalismus' for Siebeck. Weber never delivered on that promise, and one implication is that his move into comparative historical sociology blocked his return to the Protestant ethic study.[11] 'Agrarverhältnisse im Altertum' is a work that is held in some awe by classical historians. Alfred Heuss considered it 'the most original, daring and persuasive analysis ever made of the economic and social development of Antiquity . . . the area in which Weber's judgement, especially in the details, was most sovereign and surefooted . . .'.[12] And the foremost classical scholar of the twentieth century, Moses Finley, wrote, 'When I read in Marianne Weber's preface that Max Weber's *Agrarverhältnisse* was the result of four months' intensive work, I react as to one of the miracles of the Bible. It takes me four months to study Demosthenes.'[13] Marianne Weber, when she had the article reprinted, added a footnote at the start saying its contents far exceeded the prescribed title – it was 'a social and economic history of antiquity'.[14]

This raises a large question about what is meant by the term 'history', especially at this juncture in Weber's intellectual career. I think Guenther Roth is right to say that Weber was advancing 'a limited developmental scheme' or, more simply, 'developmental history'.[15] This is the direction of travel in another of Weber's enterprises that he agreed to the year before, an encyclopaedia under his own editorial control, the *Grundriss der Sozialökonomik* (which is considered in the next section). Heuss refers to Weber as being 'sure-footed' in the field of classical studies, but his last effort in this field was a lecture in 1896 and his 1897 entry to the *Handwörterbuch*. What has to be grasped here is that Weber's footwork allowed him to change direction at will and to generate enormous impetus in a very short space of time – another of his 'temperamental' qualities. During the period 1909–14, Weber generated a truly enormous output of material that can be broadly described as developmental history. Considered from the stance of 1904 and 1905, this was tangential, even perverse. The strategy then was not history *per se* in its narrative traction and multiple complexity, but by a point of view determined by the author's value-signifying discernment and deployment of the thrown net of the ideal type. In 'Agrarverhältnisse im Altertum', Weber is not allowed to roll out his pet method of ideal types – just three mentions, and one of these in the bibliography.

I have translated 'Agrarverhältnisse' as agrarian regimes. The difficult word here is 'Verhältnisse' whose literal translation is 'relationships' or, more loosely, 'organization'. 'Regime' suggests itself because, while Weber does not ignore the agricultural dimension – the topography of garden culture, cereals, forests, rivers, irrigation, coastal settlements etc. – he is much more interested in the arrangements for the delivery of agricultural and economic goods. He is concerned with the relationship between landlord and serf, freeholder and renter, estate owner and slave, monarchs and taxation, land grants and their legal conditions. It is the power and status distinctions that structure the delivery of agrarian products that Weber works with. In this sense, he is concerned with the regimes of agrarian societies.

Weber would have been approached by the editors of the *Handwörterbuch* (Conrad and Lexis) as an agrarian expert.[16] His postdoctoral thesis ('Habilitationsschrift') on the changing legal forms and economic conditions of Roman agriculture was based on the analysis of primary documents (laws, legal documents, wills, inscriptions). And, as a national-economist in the 1890s, Weber's empirical inquiries on agrarian conditions had established him as an authoritative expert. It is this expertise that Weber delivers to the *Handwörterbuch*.

Turning, at random, to the section on Mesopotamia, how does Weber proceed? First, he indicates the state of the historical sources – the development of cuneiform scholarship. Throughout the section, he refers back to the sources available, for example the laws of Hammurabi. Weber was not equipped to read the primary sources but, as his bibliography shows, he was up to date with the German, French and American scholarship.[17] Weber then fashions this source material to the ways in which he thinks about the agrarian economy. As might be expected, he starts with a (brief) description of agriculture – domestication of animals, horticulture, irrigation – but then he quickly turns to the political system of the monarchy and its economic base: how taxes and labour services were delivered by the different status groups (slaves, serfs, landowners and subjects). The economic resources of the temple are mentioned as are the military campaigns to acquire booty. The basis of the military system of obligation is outlined (mercenaries, vassals, community forces). The economy is discussed in terms of what could be inferred from documents: the forms of property – the 'oikos', the ownership of private land and the limitations placed on its sale (alienation). Subsections follow on the organization of the family and the status of women, slaves and wage labour, rental agreements on land, the existence of money and its restricted use as an indicator of value of bartering, loans and money transactions, trade in benefices as a form of interest-bearing bonds and the regulation of prices.

This may well seem prosaic, but it is where Weber's historical expertise lay. Weber makes some acute judgements. He notes the danger of basing arguments using analogies from modern states, yet inevitably he has to draw on the language of modern economic usage. A 'money man' in ancient Mesopotamia is someone who does not act as buyer and seller but is an estimator of value in a predominantly barter economy. And, under old Babylonian law, caravans were given commissions to 'buy at the going price'. This was not evidence of a free market economy, but an instruction to buy at the 'price set by the royal or temple storehouse' (AS, p. 104). Weber was working with very few translated documents, yet he is able to discern and mark out the principal legal, social and economic forms and the undergirding structure of economic obligations between status groups. Weber processes the existing source material to a very high level of intelligibility and, if one consults, in contrast, the 1911 *Encyclopaedia Britannica* entry on Mesopotamia, it is a mass of undigested philology, dates and genealogies.

The *Handwörterbuch* article reminds us that Weber was ever the national-economist and agrarian expert. He had accumulated over the decades of the 1880s and 1890s a fund of knowledge and expertise that he could draw on at will; or at least the ability to update his knowledge in a very short period. Having noted this, though, it is still permissible to ask in which direction this work was leading him. Recent work by Hinnerk Bruhns, Luigi Colognesi,

Jürgen Deininger and Mohammad Nafissi alerts us to Weber's continuing engagement with the 'Kapitalismus' problematic.[18]

In his few uses of the ideal type, Weber enters into a discussion of whether there is a generic ideal type of capitalism. From his 1898 Lecture Outline, it is clear that Weber was fully informed about Bücher's division of economic history into three stages: the 'oikos' economy, the city economy and the national-economy. Weber was probably agreeable to this as a useful periodization, although he would have rejected a theory that held this to be a kind of evolutionary necessity. 'Oikos' is a 'Wirtschaft' or an 'economy' (indeed, it is the Greek root word for 'economy'). An 'oikos', for Bücher, was an economically self-contained, rural-based estate headed up by a patriarch. The patriarch or head of the household would rule, organize and look after the needs of his family, personal retinue, serfs and slaves. While an 'oikos' might make a surplus, this was stored rather than traded or invested. Bücher held that the 'oikos' was the main economic institution of the ancient world of Greece and Rome, its use of slavery being particularly characteristic. It was preceded by a form of tribal and clan organization. The 'oikos' stage marked a decisive step forward from the 'primitivism' of the clan. An 'oikos' was embedded in a wider political community, which in Greece culminated in the 'polis' (that, in Athens for a brief period, initiated and attained a democratic form). The city economy pertained to the Middle Ages, differentiating itself from feudal and manorial regimes. The national-economy started to become the predominant phase in the modern period, fostered by absolutist states from the sixteenth century onwards.[19]

The classical historian Eduard Meyer challenged Bücher's construction of the 'oikos' as the dominant economic form of antiquity. He disputed the emphasis that Bücher placed on slavery, and his ignoring of the role of free labourers, markets and factory enterprises. Mohammad Nafissi refers to Meyer as a 'modernist'. Meyer regarded it as acceptable to use modern economic terms to describe the ancient world. His argument was that the ancient world had attained a high level of economic development. 'Meyer pointed to widespread commerce, developed accountancy systems, and transportation networks linking various centres of the pre-classical ancient Orient from the third millennium BC to the fall of the Persian Empire more than two thousand years later.' 'By displaying the breadth and depth of commercial activity in the ancient Near East, Meyer at the same time painted Greece and Rome as inheritors of a process of commercial and cultural development spanning over two millennia rather than as recent offspring of fairly primitive kinship formations.'[20] As Nafissi shows, Bücher's attempt to encapsulate the 'oikos' economy of Rome and Greece as an autonomous development from its preceding simple clan society fails. Meyer substitutes instead a pre-existing economy stretching across the Near East and Mediterranean. Meyer made the dramatic claim that 'the seventh and sixth century of Greek history corresponds to the development of modernity in the fourteenth and fifteenth century after Christ; the fifth to the sixteenth.' And he went on later to claim that Athens 'stands under the banner of capitalism just as much as England since the eighteenth century, Germany since the nineteenth.'[21]

In 'Agrarverhältnisse im Altertum', Weber was forced to reconsider his own position that, as set forth in 1896, was close to Bücher's. Weber had emphasized the predominant place of the 'oikos' and an economy based on slavery. Indeed Weber's account of the decline of the Roman Empire depended on the centrality of slavery. While the civilization based on Athens depended on trade between city and countryside as well as the existence of international trade along the Mediterranean coast, the later Roman Empire shifted the economic centre of gravity inland where transport was difficult and trade limited. The huge geographical expansion of Roman rule was motivated by conquest and the demand for slaves for the emerging large estates ('oikoi'). 'Wars served as slave hunts and were followed by confiscation of lands; the lands were formed into domains, and leased by exploitation to wealthy contractors' (AS, p. 395). 'Thus the slave owner became the dominant figure in the economy of Antiquity, and a slave-labour system became the indispensable foundation of Roman society' (AS, p. 396). There were, however, limits to the expansion of empire and its military capability. This led to the drying up of the supply of slaves and, in turn, led the (late) Roman Emperor, Diocletian, to issue bureaucratic ordinances forcing people to remain in their place of origin, so severe became the shortage of labour. At this point, the empire was already set upon the path of decline and the rural stultification of the Dark Ages.

Meyer's argument also related to Sombart's articulation of capitalist profit as the defining feature of modern capitalism, as opposed to industrial workshops that existed in the medieval period but did not operate according to the principle of profit maximization (see Chapter 1). The same issue arose in Antiquity. Industrial workshops had operated within the 'oikos' and in the cities. Did this make the ancient economy capitalistic, especially when the existence of markets, trade, transportation and banking are noted?

Weber notes that the question of using concepts drawn from later economic periods had been debated 'with vigour and sometimes with passion during the last century'. 'The starting point of this controversy was the theory of Rodbertus, according to whom all Antiquity was dominated by what he called an "oikos" economy', one in which production centred around the household and the household was extended to include unfree workers. He argued that division of labour in Antiquity was essentially only specialization within the great slave households, and that commerce was only an occasional and secondary phenomenon, serving merely to dispose of the excess production of the great households. Hence, Rodbertus argued for the 'autarky of the "oikos"; he regarded the great households of Antiquity as in principle economically self-sufficient' (AS, pp. 42–3).

There is slightly more to say about Rodbertus than Weber provides. He was a country squire, a conservative and favoured a version of state socialism. He held to a historically undifferentiated version of the whole of Antiquity in which, to quote him, 'nowhere does buying and selling intervene, nowhere do goods change hands. Since the national dividend never changes hands, it nowhere splits up into various income categories as in modern times . . .'.[22] The intellectual significance of Rodbertus is not simply Bücher's relationship to him, but Karl Marx's adoption of some of Rodbertus' principal ideas. In the 'oikos', the patriarch could decide who (slaves, retinue and family) got what. In the modern economy, surplus is distributed not through personal rule, but is divided up between rent, rent on property, interest (on capital) and profit, and a fixed constant, which went to wages. Despite improvements in technology and productivity, wages remain the same – at subsistence – while rents increase. Rodbertus argued for the (Prussian) state to intervene and reallocate a taxed portion of rent to the workers. Marx's thinking about surplus value – how the capitalist class expropriates the value produced by the working class – is obviously proximate to Rodbertus' thinking. This genealogy of ideas had implications for the 'Kapitalismus' debate at the end of the century. Bücher as well as Sombart were products of this genealogy, but as much through Rodbertus, who was no revolutionary, as through Marx. In other words, they participated in a labour theory of value and circulation without belonging to the Marxist camp.

So, in acknowledging Rodbertus as a forerunner of Bücher in the 'oikos' dispute, Weber would have taken these implications as commonly understood. Weber continues his outline of the 'oikos' dispute:

> Karl Bücher accepted Rodbertus' account of the *oikos*, but with a difference. His view may, I think, be interpreted – on the basis of his own statements – in this manner: he considered the *oikos* as an 'ideal type', denoting a kind of economic system which appeared in Antiquity with its basic features and characteristic consequences in a closer approximation to its 'pure concept' than anywhere else, without this *oikos* economy becoming universally dominant in Antiquity, either in time or space. One may add with confidence that even in those periods when the *oikos* was dominant this meant no more than a limitation on commerce and its role in meeting consumer needs. This limitation was, to be sure, strong and effective, and caused a corresponding economic and social degradation of those classes which would have otherwise carried on a more extensive trade.
>
> (AS, p. 43)

Weber effectively saves Bücher's generalization of the 'oikos' economy from Meyer's criticisms through the device of the ideal type. And Meyer is criticized for suggesting that it was necessary to use the concepts of 'factory' and 'factory worker' to analyse Periclean Athens. Weber agrees with Meyer that capitalism existed in the ancient world. There were workshops, free and semi-free workers as well as slaves; there were banks and credit, and there was extensive trade and merchants. But capitalism in its modern form did not exist. This leads Weber to conclude that capitalism did exist in the ancient world, 'Where we find that property is an object of trade and is utilized by individuals for profit-making enterprise in a market economy, there we have capitalism.' This is Weber's generic definition of capitalism. But capitalism in the ancient world was entirely different from modern capitalism. 'We must avoid exaggeration. In particular it is necessary to show the specific peculiarities of the various types of capital goods, and the manner of their valorization, which determined the course of ancient economic history' (AS, p. 51).

The merchant and the owners of capital, whether in the form of land, workshops or treasure, were never in a position for a great many reasons to invest profit with the expectation of expanding production and increasing profit. Over some sixteen pages (AS, pp. 42–68), Weber elaborates the principal differences between ancient and modern capitalism. Factories did not exist in the industrial sense of size, continuity of operation and a technology reliant on fixed capital, division of labour and its concentration in the factory workshop. Treasure was not advanced as capital, but stayed within the palaces and temples – it was thesaurized. Capital in the form of ownership of slaves was a highly unstable mechanism for advancing a business, and the vagaries of supply added to this. There was no reliable cost accounting. Guilds in Antiquity were a state organization for performing public tasks, and nothing like the medieval independence of guild masters appeared. The cities were centres of consumption not production and, where free labour existed, it nowhere amounted to a proletariat defined through its productive role.

> To sum up, the most important hindrance to the development of capitalism in Antiquity arose from the political and economic characteristics of ancient society. The latter, to recapitulate, included: (1) the limits on market production imposed by the narrow bounds within which land transport of goods was economically feasible; (2) the inherently unstable structure and formation of capital; (3) the technical limits to the exploitation of slave labour in large enterprises and (4) the limited degree to which cost accounting was possible, caused primarily by the possibility of strict calculation in the use of slave labour.
>
> (AS, pp. 63–4)

Weber's long list of differentiating factors that marked out the ancient economy as different can be read the other way round: their absence signals what defines the nature of modern capitalism. Through this simple method of difference, Weber was addressing the 'Kapitalismus' debate as a national-economist.

Weber writes here very much as the national-economist, essentially reverting back to his teaching role in the 1890s. However, the point, of course, is that Weber had never left off being a national-economist. The academic footprint of the 1890s contained the periodization of the ancient economy, the medieval economy and the modern national-economy. Bücher had unwisely turned this periodization into a series of necessary stages – from the 'oikos' economy, to the city economy, to the national-economy. Weber shared the periodization, as did most national-economists, but maintained that the dynamics and the characteristics of each period were far more complex. It was through the analysis of the differences between the ancient and the modern economy that the distinctiveness of modern capitalism was ascertained. Weber's outlining of these differences creates the reference point for what were the characteristic features of modern capitalism. This was the same 'Kapitalismus' debate that preceded the writing of PESC. Did capitalism emerge in the fifteenth century with the accumulation of treasure and a new acquisitive instinct, as argued by Sombart, or was it a later development subsequent and intrinsic to the Puritan reformation, as argued by Weber? Through these comparative analyses, the distinctiveness of modern capitalism was to be established.

Weber speaks of the 'oikos' economy of Bücher's, as already noted, as an ideal type, and the 'urban economy' as it appeared 'in a great many medieval cities' as an 'ideal type' (AS, p. 48). By the standards of PESC and the 'Objectivity' essay, this is misleading. There, the ideal type refers to cultural meanings – the spirit of capitalism and the vocational ethic. In 'Agrarverhältnisse im Altertum', capitalism as an entity or system is put forward as a theoretical model. In addition, what emerges from Weber's discussion is the distinctiveness of a *regime* – the conditions of status inequality and the mechanisms through which economic needs are met. Within these regimes, the attitudes, reasons and motivations can be subjected to ideal typical treatment as a cultural heuristic. But Weber actually makes very few references to attitudinal dispositions of the vocational sort. The 'moral qualities' of slaves render them 'amenable to exploitation' but make them 'most inefficient as workers in a large enterprise' (AS, p. 55). 'The ancient businessman remained no more than a "common tradesman" in his own eyes and in the eyes of his contemporaries.' This contrasts with early modern times when the 'rationalization and economization of life were furthered by the essentially religious ideas of "vocation" and the ethic derived from it, but nothing similar arose in Antiquity' (AS, p. 67).

It is an important switch of emphasis on Weber's part to start referring to what are effectively definitions of different regimes as ideal types. 'Agrarverhältnisse im Altertum' undoubtedly represents a widening of scope as well as a more muscular way of handling the historical materials, but the ideal type was now being merged into history and its developmental sequences. But the ideal type, in its original formulation, distanced the investigator from the sheer facticity of history and privileged his or her own standpoint in terms of what was seen as worth studying and as conferring significance. Within the constrained framework of an encyclopaedia entry, it could perhaps be argued that Weber was simply using the concept of the ideal type as a convenient way of handling an extraordinarily complex set of materials. But, when we examine Weber's growing preoccupation with developmental history on a comparative basis, the ideal type appears to operate more as a modelling device than as a cultural heuristic.

Developmental sequences comprise the end of Weber's introduction to the 'Agrarverhältnisse im Altertum'. Weber reports that little is known of the prehistoric period of the agrarian societies of the ancient world. 'But one thing is clear: there are certain *stages* of organization, and these appear to have been repeated by all the peoples in Antiquity from the Seine to the Euphrates among whom urban centres developed' (AS, p. 69). In summary form, these stages were:

1 Walled settlements providing defence for essentially kinship-orientated groups.
2 The fortress with more urban characteristics and ruled by a king.
3 The aristocratic city state of the 'classical' age. This was a feudal nobility emancipated from kingly rule, possessing slaves and serfs, and where rank was determined by military criteria: 'these cities were not administered by bureaucracies, a fact of decisive importance'.
4 The bureaucratic city kingdom. This represents an alternative developmental route from stage 2. 'If the king gained sufficient economic resources to become master of his retinue and army to the extent that he could bind them to his own person, then he was able to take a step of fundamental importance: create a bureaucracy entirely subordinate to himself and organized on hierarchical principles. With the aid of such a bureaucracy the king could govern his subjects directly and the city then became no more than the royal capital where he and his court resided' (AS, p. 72).
5 The authoritarian liturgical state. Here, the economic relationship of king to subjects underwent 'rationalization', becoming a tax and liturgy regime. Subjects were forced to pay taxes or to provide labour services directly to the court and state, the state ran monopolies for which subjects were forced to provide labour services, and there was a system of taxation backed by punishment. Outside these liturgical obligations, commerce was encouraged, because it offered another source of revenue. ' "Enlightened despotism" of this sort generally developed in the ancient Near East directly out of the more primitive forms of the bureaucratic city kingdom, and indeed differed from the latter type only in its more rationalized organization' (AS, p. 74).
6 The hoplite 'polis' of the Mediterranean lands. Hoplites were independent farmers who owned their own land. They were soldier citizens, and they overthrew the aristocratic clans.
7 The democratic citizen 'polis'. Citizenship rights were no longer dependent on the ownership of land. 'All citizens could become eligible

for office without regard to property qualifications.' Laws were passed to create a stable social order where creditors were no longer allowed to reduce peasants to debt slavery. Weber refers to this as the amelioration of class conflict in the ancient world, although it was a tendency that 'never wholly triumphed'; equally, that conflict could intensify with land ownership being held by a wealthy elite.

At one level, as Weber insists, these seven stages are just types that 'seldom existed in complete isolation. They are "pure types", concepts to be used in classifying individual states. They simply allow us to ask whether a particular state at a particular time more or less approximated to one or other these pure types.' This, says Weber, is only an approximating exercise, 'for the actual state structures in the most important phases of history are too complex to be comprehended by so simple a classification as the one used here'. This statement should be taken at face value. The types, which Weber fails to designate explicitly as 'ideal types', are organizing ideas or concepts to provide some kind of framework to a very far-reaching dictionary entry.

As a developmental series, there is a clear impulse to move from simple kinship (stage 1) to higher stages. Weber's developmental stages cannot be used as an argument for linear developments. Stages 6 and 7 are historically contingent upon circumstances, and the history of the later Roman Empire shows the complete reversal of an independent arms-bearing peasantry. In addition, there is the much commented upon bifurcation at stages 4 and 6. One leads to the authoritarian liturgy states of the Near East – Mesopotamia and Egypt – the other to some kind of (feudal) democratization of rule on the basis of independent property and reaching its high point in the Athenian 'polis'. This bifurcation in developmental paths is highly consequential for the history of the Occident and the Near East.

The split is complicated by 'the manifest and latent struggle between theocratic and secular-political forces'. Weber, at this point, wants to factor in 'developed theology and educated priesthood' which, through functional specialization (or 'differentiation' in the later terminology of modernization theory), had attained some degree of independence. The priesthood could act as a competing centre because it possessed three sources of power: economic – from its ownership of temple lands and income; religious – through the ability to offer salvation in cases of sacrilege (i.e. ritualistic 'sins' not ethical sinning); and literacy, which was either a monopoly of learning belonging to the priesthood or one held in competition with secular officials.

Weber does not systematically follow through the permutations, making instead particular developmental paths contingent upon conflict between the various sources of power.

> Hence certain conflicts are characteristic of early Antiquity: temple priesthood versus military nobility and royal authority in bureaucratic monarchies; commoners ('nichtadligen Bürger') versus the monopoly of

legal knowledge enjoyed by noble priests in aristocratic states. All sorts of alliances occurred. These conflicts influenced social and economical developments, especially in periods of general secularization or restoration; the latter were usually due to usurpers striving for legitimacy. There were important differences in this respect between oriental and occidental civilizations, and these will be discussed below.

(AS, p. 79)

Weber, then, was entering into one of the great fault lines in world historiographies – the bifurcation between east and west – using a 'simple' classification of types with the role of the priesthood as determinative, but in an unspecified way. Contemporary historical sociology operates very much in the manner of Weber's realist analysis of competing sources of power and their outcomes.[23] But, for Weber himself, it has to be noted that he had rapidly moved away from the causative role of religion in the period of early modernity in Europe and its ideal type methodology.

The ideal type method in 1904 and 1905 had produced cultural heuristics – the religious nature of vocation, the spirit of capitalism – against which empirical reality could be assessed. If there was a closeness of fit (which of course could never be a verified certainty), then it could be said that certain ideas worked out in people's behaviour may well have given the capitalist system its distinctive character. While this in itself was a scientific achievement of a high order, Weber was not able to assess just how consequential the religious derived spirit of capitalism was for the development of the whole system. In his qualifications of the extent of the thesis, Weber had to forgo an assessment of the emergence of capitalism as an entity. As he put it in his first reply to Rachfahl in 1910:

> Now just a few more remarks about the relationship of the 'spirit' of capitalism to capitalism as an economic *system*.
> Werner Sombart has made a study of this subject (Archiv, XXIX:689ff),[24] which in its broad agreement on all significance points, especially methodological, relieves me of the obligation to go into detail. Both the concepts of 'capitalism', and even more so, 'spirit of capitalism', can be construed as 'ideal-typical' constructs of thought.
>
> (PE Debate, p. 74)

This absolved Weber from entering into the analysis of capitalism as an economic system. What Weber had supplied was an important cultural determinant in its development. But, if it was important, the next question is how important?

The move into comparative studies offered one way of supplying an answer. Early Rome and Periclean Athens had capitalism but lacked any 'spirit of capitalism'. J.S. Mill, who was well understood by German national-economists, had offered a 'method of difference' as a way forward. The historian might be in a position to operate a quasi-experimental method. If two historical situations were roughly similar, but differed in respect of one factor, then a causal linkage could be asserted if the crucial factor (spirit of capitalism) produced dynamic rational capitalism in one setting and, in the other setting, where it is absent, then no dynamic capitalism appears. By this experimental method, some sort of proof would be established. The closest Weber came to doing this was in his comparative study of Puritanism and Confucianism at the end of his study *The Religion of China*.[25] As an economic system, China was more advanced than Europe c. 1400, but Confucian mores and life conduct could not psychologically push the system into a higher gear. In Europe, there was sufficient economic development plus a spirit of capitalism that 'kicked in' in the seventeenth century. The causal inference, under Mill's method of difference, is that the 'spirit of capitalism' is an effective cause. There are a great many objections that can be mounted against this way of proceeding, and the comparative historiography of China and Europe can hardly be said to endorse Weber's argument in the conclusion of *The Religion of China*. All this being noted, it is possible to see how Weber would be drawn to a stronger comparative programme, even though it exceeds the ambitions of 1904–5. It would provide a further justification – or what would now be termed triangulation – of the Protestant ethic thesis. In PESC, Weber demonstrated a positive factor and, in China, that factor being missing, further support was offered to the thesis.

As far as I know, J.S. Mill's programme has never been successfully realized in the field of comparative historical sociology, and it is easy to understand why. Finding two historical situations that are alike, but in one respect or factor, is almost impossible. The similarity will only be proximate and, without complete knowledge of all the factors at work, the researcher can never know for sure whether just one factor has been isolated. For example, a very well-known argument for China's slowness to emerge as a dynamic capitalist force was its aversion to expansion overseas. This is the result of fairly recent research, of which Weber whad no knowledge. Weber might think that Confucianism was a factor, but the crucial causal factor might have been naval policy. In a multicausal world, the sheer unknowability of the variability of factors at work reduces positivist ambitions to a heuristic.

The intriguing question is why Weber was embarking upon a comparative method, even of his own devising. He had found the solution to causality in the methodological essays of 1904–5. Causal links are attributed after the event according to the evidence as structured and clarified by ideal typification. This is the best that can be achieved (one is tempted to say, period), and it was a position he was to reaffirm in 1918–20.

The comparative role of towns

The role of towns, trade and townspeople differs markedly between the ancient economy and the inland manorial regime of the European Middle

Ages. This is a developmental comparison that Weber sets forth in his 'Agrar-verhältnisse' article and pursues in his writings on law and on the towns. In both historical situations, feudalism existed. A warrior stratum was main-tained by grants of land, received rents or compulsory service from depend-ent subjects. And in both settings, there was a similarity of urban conditions – ownership of property, market activity, accumulation of property through trade, the acceptance of landless peasants as 'guests' in the towns, the obliga-tion to townspeople to make payments to the city lord and a military stratifi-cation between foot soldiers and horsemen. 'All these elements were present in the early stages of the medieval town just as they were in the early period of the ancient polis' (AS, p. 337).

The distinguishing difference was the relation between the cities and the countryside and their associated regimes. In the ancient 'polis', lordship and forms of rule remained in the towns – they remained predominantly sites of urban feudalism and controlled the surrounding countryside and its obliga-tions. In the European (early) Middle Ages, feudalism or 'Grundherrschaft' was rural. The towns remained isolated enclaves of limited political and economic freedom within a political economy of manorial feudalism, where obligations to the feudal lord were paid mainly in kind in order to support a stratum of knights. The new foundations of towns in medieval Europe and the emergent town economy were dependent in political terms on the local lord ('Grundherr'), but the town itself was not, as in ancient Greece, the site of political power. The townspeople were only of economic interest to rural lords. As long as rents and taxes and the profits of justice were forthcoming, the townspeople were allowed to organize their own courts, raise their own taxes and run their own administration. This enabled the two to develop a qualitatively different urban existence from that of the ancient city. 'That the "Stadtbürgerschaft" had increasingly enlarged its autonomy within the rul-ing groups of the state ("staatlichen Verbände") up until the fifteenth century while the Hellenistic and Roman cities had been absorbed into monarchical states, has its basis in the contrasting structure of the state in which both were embedded' (AS, pp. 345–6). Across the ancient world, the internal life of the town was unfavourable to the continuous production enterprise. For example, the self-equipped hoplite army passed laws against the accumula-tion of property. This contrasted with Europe. Prior to their incorporation into the absolutist and bureaucratic states of the sixteenth century, there occurred a vital breathing space. 'During both the early and high middle ages the self-developing city is given time for the unfolding of its own decisive characteristics: the main carrier of a money economy and connected with this administrative obligations, and the (in general) exclusion of the burgh-ers from the surrounding hierarchy of the power-based relationships of the feudal and service regime' (AS, p. 346).

This same argument is repeated in Weber's 'The City', which is usually taken in some way to be part of a larger work *Economy and Society*.

The special position of the medieval city in the history of political development does not, in the last analysis, derive from the essentially economic contrasts between the urban burghers and the non-urban strata and their economic life styles. The crucial element was, rather, the general position of the city within the total framework of the medieval political associations and estates. It is this aspect which differentiates the typical medieval city most sharply from the ancient city . . .

(ES, pp. 1339–40)

Weber continues that 'The political situation of the medieval townsmen determined his path which was that of a *homo economicus*; whereas in Antiquity the polis preserved during its heyday its character as the technically most advanced military association: the ancient townsman was a *homo politicus*' (ES, p. 1354).

Economy and Society: initial drafts and plans

While the strong developmental 'logic' of the differential paths of the ancient and medieval cities enter through 'The City' into the analysis of *Economy and Society*, the so-called 'older part' of that work is not designed primarily with this in mind. 'The City' works with a range of classificatory types not unlike, nor unconnected to, the seven stages outlined at the start of 'Agrarverhältnisse'. Weber calls them types but, again, as in 'Agrarverhältnisse', they are devices for modelling complex material, and the culturally heuristic impulse is missing. The phrase 'ideal type' does not occur in 'The City'. These classificatory models cut across historically contingent developmental paths. Weber is quite happy to classify the citizen democracies of the ancient and medieval city together. This, as we know, goes against their contrasting developmental paths. Therefore, it would seem permissible to regard 'The City' as a conceptual grid with rows cross-cutting different civilizations and columns as developmental paths; although, having said this, Weber gives priority to rows over columns, and we seem to have arrived at a new stage in his thinking about comparative history.

'The City' also relates back to the lectures on national-economy (see p. 23). It sits quite well with §11 (the city economy and the origins of modern enterprise). §11 itself sits within a developmental sequence of §8 (the typical forerunners of the economy), §9 (the economic development of ancient coastal civilization), §10 (the agrarian basis of medieval inland civilization) and, following on, §12 (the origin of the modern economy). 'The City' opens with a very Weberian approach to national-economy. Its first section is titled 'Concepts and Categories of the City'. Sociologically, the city is defined as a 'settlement of closely spaced dwellings which form a colony so extensive that the reciprocal personal acquaintance of the inhabitants, elsewhere characteristic of the neighbourhood, is lacking.' The city is defined in an economic sense if its inhabitants live 'primarily from commerce and trades rather than from agriculture' and if the city is 'a market center' (ES, pp. 1212–13). Weber goes on to discuss the city's relationship to the surrounding lordship as well as its relationship to agriculture. Cities are economically classified into consumer, producer and merchant cities. (Actually, this threefold distinction was first elaborated by Sombart in the second volume of his *moderne Kapitalismus*. Weber takes it out of its modern European context and applies it in a universal manner across civilizations and time periods.)[26] Weber also discusses the urban economy 'as a stage of economic development'.

> The relation of the city as the carrier of the craft and trading activities to the countryside as the supplier of food forms one aspect of that complex of phenomena which had been called the 'urban economy' (*Stadtwirtschaft*), juxtaposed, as a special economic stage, to the 'household economy' (*Eigenwirtschaft*), on the one hand and the 'national-economy' (*Volkswirtschaft*) on the other . . .
>
> (ES, p.1218)

This is a clear, but unfootnoted, reference to Bücher's schema. Weber does not discuss the matter in terms of time and sequential stages, but in terms of contiguity. He analyses how the town economy seeps into the rural economy and how the density of settlement marks it out from the village economy.

Throughout 'The City', there is a continuous concern with political forms: within the city itself, to the surrounding centres of power, and the role of ruling bodies within the towns in terms of the furtherance of their own interests as well as the regulation of economic activity.

The attentive reader may well be suffering from overload at this point. It has just been argued that 'The City' is consistent with national-economy and Weber's periodization of economic history. The theme of developmental history has been pointed out. And in 'The City', Weber seems intent on cross-relating the city economy to the relevant sociological and political forms, and the work opens with a flurry of 'concepts and categories'. In which direction, it might well be asked, was Weber's argument, which is quite obviously comparative and of some complexity, heading? I will delay my attempt to answer this question, for we have arrived at the 'big bang' phase of Weber's career.

Der Grundriss der Sozialökonomik

The German editor of *Die Stadt* for the Max Weber Gesamtausgabe writes in the opening paragraph of his preface, 'This volume contains Max Weber's uncompleted study "The City" which was first published in the *Archiv für Sozialwissenschaft und Sozialpolitik* in 1921 and then again as a chapter of *Economy and Society* in 1922.' In the first paragraph of his introduction, the same editor, Wilfried Nippel, writes, 'Max Weber's posthumously published and uncompleted treatise "The City" exists in a state of preparation that can be dated to the period between the end of 1913 and the middle of 1914. It cannot be unambiguously decided for what context Weber wrote the study and, after its possible completion, how he would have wished to use it (MWG, I, 22-5, p. 1).

When we push open the study door marked 'Economy and Society. The Older Part', a quite alarming number of texts with similar introductions awaits the reader. Alongside 'The City' are the texts on communal groups, the sociology of religion, the sociology of law, the sociology of rulership, the sociology of music and an article on the categories of interpretative sociology. There is a scholarly dispute about what should and should not be included in this list and even the naming of the texts is problematic. It is known that Weber started to rewrite the whole *Economy and Society* project in 1919, and he published it in four chapters in 1920 just before he died. The older, probably discarded, manuscripts were retrieved from desk drawers by his wife Marianne who had them published after his death. The strong inference is that Weber himself would not have published them, and certainly not in the state Marianne found them. They are an amazingly rich store of special 'sociologies' written from the historical and comparative viewpoint. After their publication in Germany, they have been translated into many languages, although rarely initially as a 'complete' work. Guenther Roth and Claus Wittich boldly put together a full set of translations of Weber's final version, the so-called 'Part One', along with the texts of the earlier versions, the so-called 'Part Two'. It was published as *Economy and Society* by Bedminster Press in 1968. Weber's reputation in international social science was established and cemented by this scholarly 'tour de force'. The main overall difference between the final version and the earlier texts is one between schematic abstraction and historically rich conceptualization. Many scholars and users have a greater fondness for the earlier versions, which are information and hypothesis rich, rather than the later final version, which for many are too dry and casuistic. Looking for an overall pattern for the earlier texts is considered by some an illegitimate activity as they are disparate and may be abandoned texts. Working out the 'logic' of the final version is no easy task either, but it can be legitimately presumed that there is rationale behind it.

The period when Weber was writing the earlier versions of *Economy and Society* overlaps with the start of another project, 'Economic Ethics of the World Religions' – hence the phrase 'big bang'. Professor Lepsius, a senior editor of the Max Weber Gesamtausgabe, reckons that Weber was writing up to four manuscripts at the same time during this period. Hence a dramatic expansion had occurred compared with the scholarly monograph of the Protestant ethic study. Against this statement, however, it has to be held in mind that the framework of the lectures on national-economy (1898) outlined a set of interrelating topics that, in its scope (though obviously not content), rivalled the ambitions of *Economy and Society*. Weber had always thought on the large scale.

When Marianne Weber published as much of Weber's work as she could lay her hands on in the early 1920s, she was (successfully) securing his legacy. When the German editors of the Max Weber Gesamtausgabe came to publish the early versions of *Economy and Society*, they were faced with a series of quite punishing dilemmas. If there was some discoverable plan or immanent textual unity, then obviously this should be respected. But if there was not, how should the texts be treated? Wolfgang Mommsen, a senior editor of the Max Weber Gesamtausgabe, comments:

> Marianne Weber's assumption that the so-called older section of *Economy and Society* which she edited from Weber's papers constituted part of one comprehensive project was obviously mistaken. In fact the earlier texts were little more than a heap of manuscripts, many of them incomplete, most without definite titles or no titles at all.
>
> Furthermore, there was no indication of how they might have been arranged for publication. They represent an earlier version of Weber's sociology.[27]

The Max Weber Gesamtausgabe have made the decision to break up the first drafts into five subvolumes, under the running heading of 'Wirtschaft und Gesellschaft. Die Wirtschaft und die gesellschaftliche Ordnungen und Mächte. Nachlaß' ('Economy and Society. The Economy and the Orders and Powers of Society. Posthumous Work'). The five subvolumes are entitled: 'Gemeinschaften', 'Religiöse Gemeinschaften', 'Recht', 'Herrschaft' and 'Die Stadt' ('Communities', 'Religious Communities', 'Law', 'Domination' and 'The City'). Within some of these subvolumes, for example 'Herrschaft', the continuity of chapter headings, which is presented in Part 2 of *Economy and Society*, is abandoned for freestanding chapters with their own editorial introduction.

Against this decision, Hiroshi Orihara has argued that the first drafts were nearly completed and that there does exist an inherent textual unity. Max Weber repeatedly cross-referenced to the various components of 'The Economy and the Orders and Powers of Society' (as he had entitled his contribution in 1914), as in 'this has been discussed above' or 'see the discussion on this below'. Orihara says there are 447 of these cross-references, all but six of which he has identified in the texts. These cross-references provide the basis for reconstructing the structure and the sequencing of 'The Economy and the Orders and Powers of Society'. Orihara, therefore, sharply criticizes the editors of the Max Weber Gesamtausgabe, in their 'Overview of the Text of Economy and Society', for their decision to dismember the textual corpus.[28]

The matter is further complicated because *Economy and Society* is not a stand-alone project but part of a far wider programme, known as the

Grundriss der Sozialökonomik. Paul Siebeck was the publisher of Gustav von Schönberg's *Handbuch der politischen Ökonomie*, and on the death of Schönberg he offered its editorship to Weber in August 1908. Weber agreed to this in January 1909 on the condition that, while he might be the lead editor, the project should be carried forwards as a joint project of all the academic contributors. Effectively, though, it was Weber, in consultation with Paul Siebeck, who determined the coverage and scope of the new edition of *Handbuch der politischen Ökonomie*. The national-economists Georg Bücher and Eugen von Philippovich played supporting editorial roles to Weber. By May 1910, Weber had produced an outline plan for an overall conspectus of national-economy with publisher's contracts ready to go out to forty, mainly German, national-economists.

There was a protracted and bitter dispute with the representatives of Schönberg's estate as to whether it had residual rights in the new *Handbuch*. The previous four editions had come to be known as *Schönberg'sche Handbuch*. To emphasize the change of editors, the new *Handbuch* under Weber's direction was called *Grundriss der Sozialökonomik*, and it was specifically stated in its preface (in June 1914) that the attempt to publish a fifth edition of Schoenberg's *Handbuch* had failed and that the *Grundriss der Sozialökonomik* was a brand new departure.[29]

Social economics was Weber's new way of approaching national-economy and, as already noted above, the discourse of political economy had already been displaced in Weber's circle of national-economists. What Weber planned and intended by the term 'social economics' is a major intellectual endeavour that I can only indicate (in this book). Initially, it is easier to think about *Grundriss der Sozialökonomik* as an extensive exercise in national-economy.

Weber divided up the field of national-economy into five books:

1 Economy and the science of economics.
2 The specific elements of the modern capitalist economy.
3 The individual areas of production in the modern market economy and the domestic economic policies of modern states.
4 The international-economy and the foreign economy and social–political policy of the modern state.
5 The social relations of modern capitalism and the domestic social policy of the modern state.

This outline is recognizably similar in scope to the lecture course outline of 1898. There is less emphasis on the historical and more detail on the specific industries and regulatory problems of the modern economy. Weber had returned to his didactic task as a lecturer in national-economy, but this time drawing on the talents of specialist economists. The outline is a massive confirmation of Weber's abiding interest in capitalism and its development and the corollary for its study, national-economy. It also confirms that

Weber's essayistic treatment of the spirit of capitalism in PESC was built on a secure and continuing knowledge of just about everything that was then to be known about capitalism. Bücher was commissioned to write on the epochs and stages of the economy as well as trade; the Austrian von Wieser to write on price theory; Joseph Schumpeter to write on the history of economic doctrines; Werner Sombart to write on the principal character of modern capitalism as a historical phenomenon. Other authors wrote on the institutions of finance, transport, industry – their types and location, mining, agriculture, forestry, hunting and fishing – housing and insurance. The *Grundriss der Sozialökonomik* would provide the reader and the student with a comprehensive presentation of the modern capitalist economy.

Weber put his own name down for a variety of projects. Just to list these entries, they comprise: economy and race; economy and society; the methodology of economics; the modern state and capitalism; modern communication and news services and the capitalist economy; the limits of capitalism in agriculture; obstacles and reflex effects in the development of the modern capitalism; agrarian capitalism and population grouping; capitalism and the middle class ('Mittelstand'); social position of the working class; and monopolistic, communal and bureaucratic tendencies in capitalist development (with Alfred Weber). It seems to me unlikely that he would have gone through with all these entries, probably at the initial stages indicating his commitment to the project before finding other authors. But, on the other hand, there is no reason to doubt his expertise in all these areas.

Much of the material under these headings found its way into what has been published as *Economy and Society*. In the Outline of 1910, the actual heading of 'Economy and Society' appeared in Book One under Weber's name. It is worth giving the major sections and subsections of Book One. Its formatting has to be understood if the rationale of *Economy and Society* itself is to be grasped. The breakdown of the subject of social economics is handled systematically by Weber, and the sequencing of materials also has to be understood.

Book One. Economy and Economic Science

I   Epochs and stages of the economy (Prof. K. Bücher)
II   Economic theory (value and price theory, distribution, exchange, etc.) (Prof. v. Wieser)
III Economy, nature and society
    1   Need and consumption as conditions for and as parts of the economy (Dr Oldenberg)
    2   The natural conditions of the economy
        a   Geographical conditions (Prof. Hettner)
        b   Economy and population (Prof. Mombert); economy and race (Prof. Max Weber)
    3   The technological conditions of the economy

  a Economy and technology (Prof. v. Gottl)
  b Labour and the division of labour (Prof. Herkner)
 4 Economy and society
  a Economy and law (1. principal relations, 2. stages in the development of the present situation) (Prof. Max Weber)
  b Economy and social groups (family and local groups, estates and classes, state) (Prof. Max Weber)
  c Economy and culture (critique of historical materialism) (Prof. Max Weber)
IV Economic science
 1 The object and logical nature of (scientific) questioning ('Fragestellungen') (Prof. Max Weber)
 2 Epochs in the history of methods and general theory (Prof. Schumpeter)
V Paths of development in economic and sociopolitical systems and ideals (Prof. v. Philippovich)[30]

In Parts I and II, the economy is defined, its development outlined and economic theory is introduced. By Part III, then, the economy is established in its own right, and the task is to cross-relate it to economic geography, technology and society. Society is handled by Weber according to a modest set of categories (law, social groups and whatever lies behind the critique of historical materialism). Wolfgang J. Mommsen has argued that, at this stage (1910–12), Weber's principal concern is to cross-relate the economy to the main communal forms of society – kinship groups, neighbourhood, family. A probable example of this phase of Weber's writing is reprinted as Chapter 3 of Roth and Wittich's edition of *Economy and Society*.[31] The original German editors supplied, or interpolated, the chapter heading and section titles.

If we read the opening section of this text, we can obtain a pretty good sense of what Weber was trying to achieve. It has to be remembered that, while the scope of the *Grundriss* was extensive, its individual entries were meant to be didactic and not weighed down by theory or statistics. *Economy and Society* adheres to an encyclopaedia format, and its organization of materials was meant to aid accessibility and easy comprehension. Weber starts by making things easy for the reader. He will not examine 'the specific, often highly complex effects of the ways in which social groups satisfy their economic wants'. A systematic classification of social groups 'according to the structure, content and means of social action – a task that belongs to general sociology' will be abandoned.

> Only the relationship of the economy to 'society' – in our case the general structure of human groups – will be discussed here and not the relationship between the economic sphere and specific areas of culture – literature, art, science, etc. Contents and directions of social action

are discussed only insofar as they give rise to specific forms that are economically relevant.

(ES, p. 356)

The social groups he then discusses in relation to the economy are the household, the neighbourhood (farm, village, city street, slum – and, in the year 2006, it is pertinent to note there now exist a quarter of a million slums in the world) and kinship group.

This already tells us a great deal about *Economy and Society*. It was not a general sociology. The basic perspective is how specific social groups meet their economic needs and, under that perspective, Weber sets out the basic organizational forms of social groups and how they operate. These are classificatory forms, not ideal types in the 1905 usage of that heuristic; likewise, there seems little to connect *Economy and Society* and the *Grundriss* to PESC. The materials Weber introduces are very historical – clearly predating modern capitalism – and this is slightly strange, as the general focus of the *Grundriss* is the modern economy. But it does demonstrate that Weber remained fairly committed to the periodization we have already seen in the outline of his lecture course and in Bücher's stage theory.

This is just a snapshot of what Weber must have been writing in the first phases of *Economy and Society*, but the pattern of what he is doing is clear, and it repeats through his other areas of interest – law and culture. So, on the legal and economic order, he writes that social economics 'considers actual human activities as they are conditioned by the necessity to take into account the facts of economic life' (ES, pp. 311–12). Weber then discusses the principal legal forms – legal norms, laws, customs and conventions – as a prelude to considering their interaction with economic life. In establishing the basic forms, whether they are communal or legal, Weber is unable to stop himself from entering into long definitional passages, where he pins down the different senses of law, convention and custom. The main task of *Economy and Society* would surely be to move to a discussion of law in relation to economy, for example how community law is related to the village economic activity in certain ways, or how merchants have recourse to city or to canon law. It is a pronounced feature that definitions become a thing in themselves for Weber, something he himself recognized when he referred ironically to his 'casuistry'. This feature of Weber's writings, to an extent, detracts from accessibility criteria and the overall pedagogic function of the *Grundriss*.

When the first volume of the *Grundriss* to appear was published in 1914, it carried a new plan of the entire work ('Einteilung des Gesamtwerkes'). It shows that Weber withdrew from some of his projected entries and had greatly expanded his contribution to *Economy and Society*. The plan is a crucial guide for the overall structure of *Economy and Society*, as Weber was writing it in the period before the First World War. Most of the texts that were published in the Roth and Wittich *Economy and Society* as 'Part Two' can be related to this plan. *Economy and Society* now occupied a third of Book One, as Section C. This section was split into two.

C. *Economy and Society*

I   The economy and the orders and powers of society (Weber)
II The developmental paths of economic and sociopolitical systems and ideals (Philippovich)

Subsection II remained the same as in the outline of 1910, and it was to be written by Philippovich. Subsection One, in English the so-called Part Two of *Economy and Society*, is in fact called 'The Economy and the Orders and Powers of Society'. Strictly speaking, this is the title of the older parts to the extent that they formed a unity. This indicates a bolder conception. The economy is to be related not just to legal and social forms (as in 1910), but society is conceived of as having orders and powers ('gesellschaftlichen Ordnungen und Mächte'). Weber provides the following breakdown of topics under this heading.

1   Categories of the orders of society.
    Economy and law in their principal relations.
    The economic relationships of groups ('Verbände') in general.
2   Household, 'oikos' and enterprise.
3   Neighbourhood group, kinship groups, local community.
4   Ethnic relationships of community.
5   Religious communities.
    Class conditioning of religions; the religions of civilization and economic mentality ('Wirtschaftsgesinnung').
6   Formation of market relationships ('Marktvergemeinschaftung').
7   The political group ('Verband').
    Developmental conditions of law. Estates ('Stände'), classes, parties. The nation.
8   Rulership ('Herrschaft'):
    a   Three types of legitimate rulership.
    b   Political and hierocratic rulership.
    c   Non-legitimate rulership.
        Typology of cities.
    d   The development of the modern state.
    e   Modern political parties.

Because 'Part 2' of *Economy and Society* provides some of the most read and applied passages of sociology, and has done for decades – for example, the excerpts on nation, ethnic groups, class and status groups – it is important to realize that they do belong to an overall framework, the 1914 Outline Plan. Like the section on law and social groups, these passages can of course be read for their own sake as freestanding parts. Weber, in writing these sections, himself becomes absorbed in the development of his ideas – another of his 'temperamental qualities'. Although he disclaims writing a general sociology, he certainly created a series of special sociologies that, in the American *Economy and Society*, extends over a 1000 pages. The overall plan makes clear the interrelation of the sections and, above all, that there is a continuous reference point in all these writings, the economy, even though that reference point may disappear for long stretches of the work.

One reason for the increase in length at this stage was that Weber had been let down by one of his principal authors, Karl Bücher. Weber, as we have seen in the 'Agrarverhältnisse', had 'saved' Bücher by turning his stage theory of economic evolution into ideal types. The tripartite distinction between the 'oikos', city and modern economies was a pivot on which Weber's own thinking as a national-economist turned. That is why Bücher was given 'pole position' in Section One, Book One in the *Grundriss*. Unfortunately, Bücher had slowed up, he was ill and ageing, and he had belatedly delivered only twenty pages of dry economic reasoning. The *Grundriss* was already behind schedule, and Weber had to make good the difference himself in his section. Weber wrote to Paul Siebeck (30 December 1913) to explain and announce the reason for his own ballooning contribution.

> Because Bücher's 'Stages of Development' is wholly insufficient, I have worked out a unified sociological theory and presentation, which places all the main forms of social groups ('Gemeinschaftsformen') in relation to the economy: from the family and household to the 'enterprise' ('Betrieb'), to the clans, to ethnic groups, to religion (*all* main religions on earth comprising: a sociology of salvation doctrines and religious ethics, – what Troeltsch has done but now for *all* religions, but much shorter), finally a comprehensive sociological theory of rulership and the state ('Staats- und Herrschafts-Lehre'). I should say that *nothing* like this has been done before, not even in outline.[32]

(The reference to Troeltsch was the latter's *The Social Teaching of the Christian Churches*.) Weber also added a footnote to his letter to Siebeck. 'Later at some point I hope to provide you with a sociology of culture, its contents (art, literature, Weltanschauung) – not part of this work or only as a free-standing supplementary volume.' This was a remarkable statement of his ambitions, creativity and, one should add, a mind that was looking around for new avenues of investigation. Weber never achieved this goal, although he did mention it again as an ambition around 1920.

The extra historical material (sections 2 and 3 in the 1914 Plan) was inserted because Bücher had failed to deliver it. The deficiency Weber was in part making up for concerned Bücher's notion of 'primitivism'. Classical Mediterranean societies had achieved the social and economic forms of the 'oikos' in its urban and rural forms. Something still remained to be said about more basic communal and localist forms such as the household, neighbour-hood and an earlier epoch of clans. Weber was able to draw upon previous work he had done in conjunction with the publication of Marianne Weber's *Wife and Mother in Relation to the Development of Law.*[33]

Section 4 on ethnic communities appears to exist in a fairly fragmentary state, and it relates in part to household and family, through a discussion of racial intermarriage, and in part to ethnic communities and their relation to the nation. Section 6 would appear to be fundamental to the project of social economics as it purports to deal with the social nature of market relation-ships. And then we come to the fairly clearly defined sociologies of religion (section 5) and power and rulership (sections 7 and 8).

An interpretative sociology

Weber's preoccupation with sociology dates from 1910, and it emerges out of his massive project on, and commitment to, social economics. We might even describe Weber as a reluctant sociologist. In December 1913, he wrote to his fellow *Grundriss* contributors to explain the name change from *Hand-buch der Politischen Oekonomie* to *Grundriss der Sozialökonomik* and to up-date them on publication plans. Because of the non-submission of important contributions (a veiled reference to Bücher), Weber says he will make good the deficiency himself in the section on 'Economy and Society'. His piece would be 'a pretty comprehensive sociological discussion' and, apart from the circumstances outlined 'he would never have taken the task on' (MWG, II, p. 427). The task that had fallen to him was to relate economy to the prin-cipal orders and powers of society. Here he required a sociology to handle the major social forms of human life. It is quite noticeable that Weber has no prior account or grand theory of society as an entity. He was still stand-ing by his distaste for the 'bad authors' in sociology. What he required was a way of particularizing the nature of the social relationship as it existed, and as it changed, in a variety of settings: for example, the clan, the 'oikos', cit-ies, political groups, structures of power, religious communities, etc. These elements became a grand design – the orders and powers of society – in the plan of 1914. And from this, we derive the grand sociologist, Max Weber, from the publication of *Economy and Society*. But it has to be understood that he is most directly concerned with the nature of social relationships as these exist in the various areas of social life: household, law, religion, poli-tics, economy.

1910 also marks his commitment to sociology by becoming a founder member of the German Sociological Society. This met for the first time in October 1910, providing a forum for those who wanted to discuss 'the prob-lems of living in modern society', as Marianne Weber puts it in her biogra-phy.[34] Its emphasis was on contemporary problems, and the first conference took as its themes technology and culture, race and society, the sociology of panic, economy and law, and legal science and sociology. The problems of living in modern society, broadly conceived, relate to the 'Kapitalismus' problematic. For Weber, who was closely aligned with Simmel in the founding of the Society, the material, psychic and technological problems faced by the individual in contemporary science were treated as problems of modern culture. Lawrence Scaff argues that, at the first meeting, Weber 'took it upon himself to identify the specific problems of modern culture as the relationship between the technologies and form of objective culture on the one hand and the subjective "conduct of life" on the other . . .'. Weber wanted culture to be made a thematic focus of the conference.[35] This picked up the theme outlined at the end of PESC, where Weber dramatizes the fate of the individual in the face of the giganticism of an impersonal economic order (PESC, pp. 181–3). Weber invested considerable effort and time in trying to get an inquiry of the press under way (although was ultimately unsuccessful in this). The press represented one of the major shapers of objective culture. Weber proposed the questions, 'What does the press contribute to the formation of modern humanity?' 'What kinds of mass beliefs and hopes, of "feelings towards life" (*Lebensgefühle*) as one says today, of possible points of view will be destroyed or created anew?'[36] The answers to these questions threw the emphasis on to how individuals were able to shape their lives and, hence, a concern with subjective culture.

Scaff quotes an interesting remark from a letter of Simmel's concerning the planning of the second conference of the German Sociological Society in 1912.

> In my opinion for meetings where discussion is expected one should avoid everything that can or even must lead to a quarrel over concepts and definitions. In sociology we have in this regard suffered to the point of suffocation, and a discussion about what folk, nation, or race 'actually are' would be deadly for our session . . .. What do members think of the theme, the relations of handicraft industry to individual spheres of culture, that is, to political organization, to art, to relationships with foreign countries, to the nature of the family, etc.?[37]

This statement could stand for Weber's own view of sociology – that it would be a relational study. In Simmel's example, he uses artisanal industry as a topic for study, and the relational questions become ones of its influence on art and politics and so on. These relationships could only be particularized and could not be contained by discussion of the nature of social groups. In Weber's own intervention from the floor in the first conference, he discusses technology ('Technik'). Weber discusses a series of possible relational links: technology and capitalism, technology and material determination, technology and art (and its formal values), technology and the modern urban sensibility.[38] Sociology then may be said to be the study of contemporary cultural problems in their relational connection; a study bearing a pronounced interdisciplinarity. There is little sense of Weber committing to a pure sociology as a freestanding discipline.

Weber resigned shortly after the second conference in 1912 following a heated conference debate on the permissibility of academics expressing normative viewpoints in the guise of scientific statements. Weber was committed to the *Archiv*'s stance, outlined in the introduction to the 'Objectivity' essay of 1904. Weber fought for the principle in another policy forum, the *Verein für Sozialpolitik*, in its 1909 conference in Vienna. Mixing science with value judgements, opined Weber, was 'the work of the devil'.[39] There had to be a clear separation so that questions of scientific validity could be assessed unclouded by value judgements, which remained a separate sphere of public debate. Weber was particularly concerned that this principle was incorporated into the statutes of the German Sociological Society. Sociology was a fledgling science, and the mixing of normative prescriptions with scientific analysis had to be avoided. For example, in the study of the press, it would be only too easy to condemn the content of certain newspapers. What was important, however, was to analyse the growth of press media and show how it shaped the individual's way of thinking regardless of normative content. Scientific comment here had to remain free from value judgements. Weber's stance was written into the first paragraph of the German Sociological Society's statutes.

> The aim is to promote sociological knowledge by the arrangement of purely scientific investigations and enquiries, by the publication and support of purely scientific works and by the organization of German sociology conferences to take place periodically. It will give equal space to all scientific directions and methods of sociology and will reject the representation of any practical (ethical, religious, political, aesthetic, etc.) goals.[40]

At the 1912 conference, Rudolf Goldscheid argued for a sociology based on the scientific study of biology. This, for Weber, was an example of hated monism, that physiological forces could extend their explanatory reach to parts of behaviour that properly belonged in the cultural sphere of meanings. Weber resigned in something of a rage that Statute 1 was not being observed. He unburdened himself in a letter to Roberto Michels.

> I resigned from the executive committee of the 'sociologists'. In a struggle in permanence my nerves aren't a match for such pesky insects as Herr Goldscheid – for his 'services' in good faith and his 'idealism' too! Now I am only still trying to organize the *scientific* activity as best I can. May these gentlemen, *none* of whom can stifle the impulse (for that's what it is!) to importune the public with his subjective 'valuations', all infinitely uninteresting to me, and *everyone* of whom *must* otherwise still turn his lectures into hard cash (this does *not* occur in the Verein für Sozialpolitik) kindly stay in their own circle. I am absolutely fed up with appearing time and time again as a Don Quixote of an allegedly 'unfeasible' principle and of provoking 'embarrassing scenes'.[41]

Like geographers who cannot read road maps in a car, one might observe that Weber was one of those sociologists who are not the most social animals. However, despite very obvious temperamental difficulties on Weber's part, his joining and leaving the German Sociological Society is an episode that underlines his very specific expectations for sociology, as a science. It was to do with cultural meanings and social relationships. The ideal type was its main instrument of investigation, and this coloured Weber's whole view of a science of society. Others, with more 'realist' or 'monistic' theoretical agendas, failed to understand and to agree with what they would have considered Weber's eccentric purism.

Weber's first major dedicated exposition of sociology occurred in his article 'Some Categories of Interpretative Sociology', which was published in the journal *Logos* in 1913. The fact that Weber chose to publish this text has detracted a little from the fact that it has very strong linkages to the manuscripts of the older parts of *Economy and Society* (which he did not publish). This is one of the reasons why the editors of the Max Weber Gesamtausgabe chose not to include it in the volumes dedicated to the older parts of *Wirtschaft und Gesellschaft*.[42] Hiroshi Orihara has convincingly argued on the basis of explicit references in the text, which can be cross-referenced to other parts of *Economy and Society*, that it stands as a 'head' in relation to the 'torso' of the other texts.[43] This is a scholarly and technical dispute, but both sides acknowledge that 'Some Categories of Interpretative Sociology' is a highly significant text in Weber's intellectual evolution – probably the most important essay since the 1904 'Objectivity' essay.

Weber, in his opening footnote, writes, 'The second part of the essay is a fragment from an exposition written some time ago that was to have served as a methodological basis for substantive investigations, among which is a contribution (*Wirtschaft und Gesellschaft*) to a forthcoming series of volumes and from which other parts will probably eventually be published elsewhere.'[44] This sentence (which I have retranslated more precisely) reveals that the second part of the essay was indeed a methodological statement intended for the *Grundriss* and related directly to *Economy and Society*. The 'other parts' that might be published elsewhere implies that pieces would be taken out of his writing of *Economy and Society* – with the inference that this writing could not be contained within howsoever Weber was planning his own contribution. Since the 'Categories' essay was published in 1913, it predates the plan of 1914, and so Weber was already thinking of off-loading material elsewhere.

The first part of the essay recapitulates material, for the *Logos* readership, that Weber had been dealing with in his 'Wissenschaftslehre' since 1900. The central issue is how there can be an interpretative science of human behaviour. *Logos* was a philosophical journal closely connected to Heidelberg circles, and it took as its starting point culture both as an object of investigation and as a means of knowing the world – it was another expression of Baden neo-Kantianism. Weber's task was, therefore, not so much to convince them of an interpretivist approach as the way to understanding as to show how this should correctly proceed and to differentiate his method from other similar but not always correct approaches. In his opening footnote, Weber references this general field. The list comprises Simmel, Rickert, Tönnies, Vierkandt, Gottl, Husserl and Lask who, in their different ways, took the individual, meaning and its expression, subjectivity and psychology as their subject matter.

It is not necessary to analyse the essay in detail. It is quite hard to follow all Weber's arguments, the exposition of certain points could be fuller, and the justification of certain arguments is sometimes lacking. He revised it comprehensively after the war, and this included a whole set of terminological changes. The later version, to an extent a new text, remains a challenging document, but it does have a strict logical structure of exposition and informative explanatory sections. The 1913 'Categories' essay is interesting for what it tells us about Weber's view of methodology at a point when his horizons had widened – first with the *Grundriss*, second the comparative historical sociology of *Economy and Society* and, third, his writings on the economic ethics of world religions, which he had also started. It is in this wider context of intellectual interests that sociology makes its first major appearance. The interpretative approach is now called sociology whereas, previously, especially 1904–5, it was an approach that was applied to the cultural sciences (and sometimes the 'Geisteswissenschaften').

Weber takes only a page to state the basic case for the role of understanding ('Verstehen'). This is an even more brusque treatment than in the 'Objectivity' essay where, as we have seen, Weber was less than fulsome in mentioning his methodological debts and sources (to Dilthey in particular). The first paragraph (of this not widely available essay in English), in its conciseness, is one of the most forward statements of 'Verstehen' to be found anywhere.

> Human behaviour ('external' or 'internal') exhibits both relational contexts ('Zusammenhänge') and regularities in its course, as do all occurrences. But what is unique to human behaviour – at least in its full sense – are contexts and regularities whose course can be *intelligibly* interpreted. An [intelligible] 'understanding' ('Verständnis') of human behaviour achieved through interpretation contains above all a specific quality of evidence ('Evidenz'), which varies greatly in degree. That an interpretation possesses this evidence in especially high measure does not in itself prove anything about its empirical validity. For identical behaviour, in its external course and result, can be based on the most varied constellations of motives whose most intelligibly evident quality is not always the one actually in play. Rather, the 'understanding' ('Verstehen' – inverted commas in original German) of the context must always be controlled as far as possible by the usual methods of causal imputation ('Zurechnung') before an ever so evident interpretation becomes a valid 'intelligible explanation'.
>
> (GAWL, pp. 427–8, my translation; see also Cat, p. 151)

The observer thinks the motive for action in a particular context is self-evident or immediately understandable, but this then has to be checked. On further observation and consideration, the motive attributed may turn out to be wrong, and another is imputed in its place as more valid.

Weber appears to preclude any discussion of hermeneutics, the art of interpretation, by simply saying it is evident and that validation belongs to causal attribution. But he then goes on to introduce a scale of interpretation. What is obviously evident is at the top of the scale. Instrumentally rational action – how best to achieve a goal – is an example of evident behaviour, as is our ability to understand behaviour motivated by emotion. Other forms of behaviour are less accessible to understanding, for example religious mysticism or that of small children. Abnormal behaviour is not in principle closed to understanding. Weber also cites here psychotic behaviour, a clear reference to Karl Jaspers' interpretative method and approach to psycho-pathology. At the bottom end of the scale are behaviours that completely lack the quality of self-evidence – they are incomprehensible. 'The object of the discussion, "Verstehen", is ultimately also the reason why interpretative sociology . . . treats the single individual and his action as its basic unit, as its "atom", if this questionable analogy is allowed here' (Cat, p. 158). Weber continues that there is a threshold, below which the sociological study of meaningful behaviour gives way to other disciplines that treat the individual as a complex of 'psychic, chemical and other processes'. Then there is a threshold above which the individual is treated. Action is comprehended 'in the guise of a persistent structure, either of a material entity, or of a personi-fied force leading a life of its own'. Jurisprudence will treat the 'state' as a legal personality. This is useful for jurisprudence because it 'deals with the interpretation of objective meaning, i.e., with the *normative* content of legal propositions'. Interpretative sociology, however, deals with 'certain kinds of joint human action' and not a normatively conceived entity such as the state or the association, or – for the historian – entities such as feudalism.

Sociology, then, sits between other disciplines such as law and sociobi-ology and treats the band of meaningful behaviour of people interacting with each other. Also, it does not deal with persistent structures, only joint behaviour of plural individuals.

Weber clarifies an intellectual pitfall. It is the illusion that, because we understand something as self-evident, the nature of the explanation rests with psychology. Weber is averse to this, and it was the common criticism levelled at Dilthey that his interpretative method was merely psychological intuition. It is here that Weber distances himself from Simmel who, in his *Problems in the History of Philosophy*, asserted that we understood the mo-tives of historical personalities because, at some deep level, which he called 'the soul', there is a common psychological substratum of understanding. This was Simmel's somewhat less than plausible transcendental basis for understanding the internal motives of historical actors. In its place, Weber asserts the need for causal imputation through consideration of the empirically ascertainable facts of the situation.

The essay picks up an increasing number of references to history, to religion, to the irrational basis of salvation beliefs, and to magic, to various types of economies, to racial and language communities and to law, power, coercion and rulership – signs of Weber's increasing comparative scope. How does an interpretative sociology help in this enterprise? This is the 'the sociological basis for the substantive studies' of *Economy and Society* that Weber mentions in his opening footnote, and it occupies the second half of the essay. The essay is a sustained deliberation on the forms and formation of social action that sustain the more obviously sociological character of institutions and social structures. To use Weber's own ('inappropriate') analogy, he is offering an account of the atomic basis of the orders and powers of society. This, he says, is the individual. I think it is worth insisting that this is not a claim for 'methodological individualism' – a phrase, incidentally, invented by Schumpeter not Weber. Individuals are particles that combine to create various sorts of social interaction, and the context of these interactions is saturated in meaning, to which 'particles' orient their behaviour. The reductionism, which is seen as a virtue of methodological individualism, is not a valid assumption for Weber's 'atomic' account. Certainly, individuals are the only units ('Einheiten') that can, for Weber, be legitimately used in sociological analysis, but they exist in a state of indeterminacy and openness. The nature of the interactions is never structured according to clear boundaries, there is always a fluidity between types of interaction. Weber insists upon this because he wants to eliminate top-down sociological theories. The state or law or the organization is a nominal entity produced by types of interactions working with specific textures of meaning. Political science or jurisprudence or organizational theory may choose to treat these entities as real – or, in the terminology of legal theory, to concede to them legal personalities – but this is inadmissible for sociology. These nominal entities should not be assumed to be real or, as Weber sometimes expressed it: they should not be hypostatized; individual behaviour cannot be deduced from these high-level entities, nor can higher level structures be induced from individuals.

What does remain a constant for Weber are interaction processes and contexts of meaning. This might seem a little perverse or anti-sociological. But, as we have seen in the last chapter with respect to J.S. Mill and Comte, once a methodology commits to either deductive or inductive (or variants thereof) accounts of individual and society, the justifying theoretical and epistemological scaffolding becomes extensive and vulnerable to some fairly basic objections – many of which were raised by Dilthey. The interaction processes in contexts of meaning do, however, result in regularities. Weber asserts this in the opening sentence of the essay, 'human behaviour . . . exhibits both relational contexts and regularities'.

In the 'Categories' essay, these regularities are shaped by three basic types of interaction: (1) Individuals might chose to form communal or social links. The German term that Weber uses is 'Gemeinschaftshandeln'. Literally, this means communal action, but what Weber is denoting by 'Gemeinschaft' lies semantically somewhere between the English 'social' and 'communal'. (2) Individuals might choose to form associational links ('Gesellschaftshandeln'). This behaviour is oriented to the assumption that some sort of order exists with a set of rules, which can be related to rationally. (3) Individuals might choose to forms links on the basis of coming to an agreement ('Einverständnishandeln'). Individuals enter into or become part of these three types, which are fluid between each other, from opposed or complementary interests – this is the aspect of external behaviour. In their 'internal' aspect, a variety of motives may be operant. These belong to the sliding scale already mentioned: subjectively instrumental motives, motivation driven by emotions, irrational motives extending to the psychotic and non-meaningful behaviour based on sheer unthinking habit.

This is, so to speak, a summary of Weber's atomic theory of social interaction. It is so densely written that it can scarcely be reckoned to be a success. It is an extremely pregnant essay with a wealth of ideas and quite fundamental thinking – one that could be profitably reworked in a number of ways. As I said, Weber rewrote it when he drastically revised the older parts of *Economy and Society* after 1918. The main function and purpose of the essay is to present interpretative sociology as the undergirding theory to the substantive part of *Economy and Society* – the various sociologies of the economy, law, religion, power and the state. The orders and powers of society are inevitably going to be discussed, by Weber and others, as possessing qualities of structure, order, hierarchy and boundaries. This is inevitable because most people will think of society in this way and, secondly, for the sociologist, it becomes a necessary shorthand. That being said, Weber is insistent that the structuring qualities are interaction processes in relational contexts of meaning. Weber's word for these power, order or institutional structures is 'Gebilde', which he often place in inverted commas. 'Gebilde' is a polyvalent word: its meanings include thing, object, construction, creation, pattern, shape, organization and figment (of imagination). Its ambivalence turns on something concrete yet something also being formed. For Weber, this indeterminacy is an inherent feature of structure.

In the last part of this section, I will highlight the (few) examples that Weber presents to link interpretative sociology to the substantive sociologies. 'We shall speak of "social action" ("Gemeinschaftshandeln") wherever human action is subjectively related in *meaning* to the behaviour of others. An unintended collision of two cyclists, for example, shall not be called social action.' But in the resultant aftermath, whether amicable or not, a meaningful, and so social, relationship is established. Social action can be oriented in its entirety to meaning, as in the case of devotion to (religious) values. An obvious example of 'association' action is the voluntary association. It is 'an associational action wherein *all* participants have rationally *agreed* on an order defining the purpose and the methods of their joint action' (Cat, p. 163). Agreement between economic actors in the case of a cartel is another example of associational action. Supermarkets, for example, might form an *ad hoc* agreement to fix prices. In Weber's day, the whole structure of production, pricing and sales was regulated by cartels with a permanent staff. The whole field of economic exchange throws up a range of examples of types of association. Some sort of permanent legal (and associational) order can guarantee the validity of exchange on the markets (with enforceable laws for breaches of agreements). Or, more minimally, economic actors may develop their own agreed rules for associating in exchanges. The associational nature of exchange does not generate, says Weber, enduring structures. Similarly, the history of the state originates in temporary associations, for example in military expeditions for booty and *ad hoc* defence associations that could cease to exist.

A language community is an example of agreed action ('Einverständnis'), ' "as if" those speaking were orienting their behaviour toward rationally agreed upon grammatical rules' (Cat, p. 167). Weber introduces this example specifically to reject alternative explanations of a language community. 'All analogies to the "organism" and to similar biological concepts are doomed to sterility.'

'Domination as the most significant foundation of nearly all organizational action, whose analytical problematic begins here, is necessarily an object of separate consideration not to be explained here.' This is an explicit reference to his (massive) sociology of 'Herrschaft' as he developed it in the early parts of *Economy and Society*. Its sociological analysis 'depends decisively on the varying possible subjectively meaningful bases of that *legitimacy* agreement . . .' (Cat, p. 177). Legitimacy was determinative for submission where naked power and coercion do not intervene. The varieties of legitimacy in his substantive sociology encompass the belief in tradition, the belief in the charismatic personality and the belief in rational legitimacy of an order of rules.

Although these examples, in their sparseness, may not strike us as completely persuasive of the worth of the approach (an interpretative sociology), Weber is offering, in principle, that any part of the substantive sociologies can be traced back to some type of interaction, or multiplicity of types, and the particular meanings that context interactions. An organization, a social group, a religious sect, a rational mechanistic bureaucracy, a retinue and so on, these are all to be approached through Weber's interpretative sociology. It is a frequent complaint that Weber failed to provide an adequate linkage between structural and substantive sociology – where wholesale rulerships and cultures take the stage – and his individualizing method. The 'Categories' essay supplies the answer to the complaint: the indeterminacy of interaction types and meanings underwrites more 'structural' sociology but refuses to confirm structures as entities in their own right.

6   *The Sociology of Religion*

The period 1910 to the summer of 1914 stands as a period of exceptional productivity. Weber had put on hold his Protestantism studies, only returning to them in 1919 to revise them for their inclusion in his 'Collected Essays in the Sociology of Religion'. In the last chapter, his move into an encyclopaedic charting of the principal relations of economy and society were outlined. Using an abbreviated version of the Outline Plan of 1914, I have listed the main headings of this in the right hand column of Figure 6.1. In the left hand column are listed his studies – actualised and planned – on the 'Economic Ethics of the World Religions'.

Feeding into this diagram are the 'Agrarverhältnisse im Altertum' and the essay 'Sociological Categories of Interpretative Sociology', both of which were discussed in the last chapter. I have not entered them into the diagram. The 'Categories' essay is central to this expansive period of Weber's writings. 'Agrarverhältnisse im Altertum' precedes the period, but sets up the scaffolding for a comparative approach. It provided a three-way comparison between Rome, Greece and the Near East. The analysis of the Near East offered a linkage in the form of the bureaucratic liturgical state to the ideal type of patrimonialism, and was able to include Chinese structures of rulership. Religion, which had only be touched upon in terms of the economic functions of temple treasuries and the place of priests within the ruling elites, was to be expanded as a set of sociological categories and applied to China, India, the Near East and the traditions of Christianity in the Mediterranean and inland Europe.

It is important to grasp the specific status of these texts and plans. There is a large discrepancy between what Weber intended and what was subsequently published. Weber planned to write works that he never got around to executing. And the converse is just as important: he wrote texts that were subsequently published but that he himself would not have published – and certainly not in the unrevised state in which they appeared after his death. This gives us three main categories of his texts and plans:

Collected Essays in the Sociology of Religion	Versions of Economy and Society for *Grundriss der Sozialökonomik*

Collected Essays in the Sociology of Religion:

Prefatory Remarks[3]

The Protestant Ethic and the Spirit of Capitalism[3]

Protestant Sects and Spirit of Capitalism[3]

EEWR

Introduction[3]

Confucianism[3]

Intermediate Reflection[3]

Hinduism and Buddhism[3]

Ancient Judaism[3]

Mesopotamia, Eygpt, Persia[1]

European Bürgertum[1]

Talmudic Judaism[1]

Islam[1]

Oriental Christianity[1]

Occidental Christianity[1]

The Sociology of Religion[2]

Versions of Economy and Society for *Grundriss der Sozialökonomik*:

Outline Plan of 1914

Economy and the Orders and Powers of Society

1. Categories of the orders of society[2]
2. Household, Oikos, and Enterprise[2]
3. Neighbourhood group, kinship groups, local community[2]
4. Ethnic relationships of community[2]
5. Religious communities[2]
6. Formation of market relationships[2]
7. The political group ('Verband') Developmental conditions of law Estates ('Stände'), classes, parties The nation[2]
8. Rulership ('Herrschaft'):
   a) Three types of legitimate rulership[2]
   b) Political and hierocratic rulership[2]
   c) Non-legitimate rulership[2] Typology of cities
   d) The development of the modern state[1]
   e) Modern political parties[1]

Economy and Society. Final Version (1920)

Basic Sociological Concepts[3]

Basic Sociological Concepts of Economizing[3]

Sociology of Domination[3]

Classes and Status Groups[3]

Figure 6.1 Publication plans.

1   Planned but unrealized texts.
2   Texts that were written but due to be revised, or not published at all, yet were published after his death.
3   Texts that were written and brought to publication by Weber himself.

Each of these categories is registered in superscript in Figure 6.1.

Moving to the columns, on the right is 'The Economy and the Orders and Powers of Society'. What has to be held in mind at this point is that it was essentially a commissioned work for the *Grundriss der Sozialökonomik*. As Weber was the lead editor for the *Grundriss*, he had considerable leeway to adapt his own contribution. We can see in his relationship, and correspondence, with his publisher (Siebeck) that the specifications of his contribution underwent a number of changes. There still remains, however, a tension between the encyclopaedia format of 'The Economy and Orders and Powers of Society' (hereafter EOPS), including the requirement that it relate to the overall architecture of the *Grundriss*, and the historical themes and ideal types that belonged distinctively to Weber's own plans. (One of Weber's major headaches here was inflation. In pursuing a number of not necessarily compatible goals, Weber tended to overwrite his contribution. This is one of the reasons why he needed to revise the manuscripts of the 'older part', and so these texts carry the superscript 2.)

The column on the left is headed 'Collected Essays in the Sociology of Religion'. The contents carry the superscript 1 and 3. The studies on Confucianism, on Hinduism and Buddhism and on Ancient Judaism are among the most famous and respected essays Weber wrote and, as such, do not require much additional comment here. Weber published them first in the *Archiv* and then revised them – the Confucian study considerably – for publication in his *Gesammelte Aufsätze zur Religionssoziologie* ('Collected Essays in the Sociology of Religion'). What stands out in the list are the titles bearing superscript 3 – the texts he planned but never wrote.

Between the two columns stands the work known in English as *The Sociology of Religion* and, in German, as *Religiöse Gemeinschaften. Typen religiöser Vergemeinschaftung* ('Religious Communities. Types of Religious Sociation'). Strictly speaking, it belongs in the right hand column and is the same as no. 5, as the title indicates. But Weber extracted whole sections from it and used them in the works in the left hand column, in particular the 'Introduction' to 'The Economic Ethics of the World Religions' and the 'Intermediate Reflection' essays. Marianne Weber published the old manuscript of *The Sociology of Religion* in its entirety after Weber's death, even though bits had already been published and the manuscript was unfinished. Weber would have had to rework the manuscript had he chosen to publish it in the revised *Economy and Society*, which he worked on in the last two years of his life. *The Sociology of Religion*, to give it its English book title translation, stands at the centre of the matrix.

It is quite hard to come to grips with this period of Weber's creativity, because of the sheer scale and depth of his researches. (Also, it should be noted, I have omitted from the diagram his study on the sociology of music, which Weber deliberately abandoned because of doubts about its value; also his study, on The City, which most probably belongs within this period, standing somewhere between the 'Agrarverhältnisse' and the manuscripts for 'The Economy and the Orders and Powers of Society'.) Some economy of mental effort might be had if the upper part of the right hand column is ignored on the grounds that Weber intended to revise those chapters. This is an unconvincing move for various reasons. The chapters have all been published, some as freestanding books – especially in translation – so some effort must be made to understand the original context. The right hand column operates as a counterweight to the studies on the world religions (in the left hand column). Then, finally, one has to be able to understand the rationale for Weber's late and uncompleted revision of the chapters in the right hand column. The final revision was a very intellectually assertive exercise, and it goes to the heart of how Weber thought modernity should be studied. The phase of 1910–14 had not quite found the right balance and method.

The interrelation between the left hand and right hand columns can be grasped if the correspondence between Weber and his publisher is followed. This has become available with the publication of most of the relevant volumes in the Max Weber Gesamtausgabe. As noted in the previous chapter, Weber wrote (in December 1913) to Paul Siebeck about the progress (or lack of it) of the *Grundriss der Sozialökonomik*.

> Because Bücher's 'Stages of Development' is wholly insufficient, I have worked out a unified sociological theory and presentation, which places all the main forms of social groups ('Gemeinschaftsformen') in relation to the economy: from the family and household to the 'enterprise' ('Betrieb'), to the clans, to ethnic groups, to religion (*all* main religions on earth comprising: a sociology of salvation doctrines and religious ethics, – what Troeltsch has done but now for *all* religions, but much shorter), finally a comprehensive sociological theory of rulership and the state ('Staats- und Herrschafts-Lehre'). I should say that *nothing* like this has been done before, not even in outline.[1]

Weber continued that in a fortnight he would send a table of contents. This has not been found, but the Outline Plan of 1914, which is reproduced in abbreviated form in the right hand column (see p. 145 for full outline), corresponds to what Weber lists in the above letter. Item 5 of the Outline Plan of 1914 'Religiöse Gemeinschaften' also includes 'The Class Determination of Religions. The Religions of Civilization and Economic Mentality'. Schmidt-Glintzer's comments that this indicates the insertion of Weber's comparative research on religion into the plans for the *Grundriss*. Weber's analysis would provide a critical analysis of both sides of the argument on determination – does class determine religion? does religion determine class? – and the analysis would involve material taken from the main religions of civilization.

Schmidt-Glintzer also comments that we cannot establish any chronological or substantive sequencing of the materials in both right and left columns. In the period 1910–14, Weber was writing for both the 'Economic Ethics' project and for his contribution to the *Grundriss*.[2]

The correspondence on the 'Economic Ethics of World Religions' is informative. Although these essays started to appear in October 1915 in the *Archiv*, it appears that they belong to the same period of composition as the *Sociology of Religion*. Weber volunteered for service duties the day after war was declared in August 1914, and he only turned back to academic work in the summer of 1915, and then only partially. He was not fully released from his hospital administrative post until the end of September. The *Grundriss* project was placed on hold until the war was over. Siebeck's were starved of copy. Weber wrote to the publisher on 12 June 1915.

> I would be prepared to give the *Archiv* a series of essays on the 'Economic Ethics of World Religions' which have sat here since the start of the war and only need to be read through for style – preliminary work and elucidation for the systematic sociology of religion in 'G. d. S. Ö'. They will have to appear as they are – with almost no footnotes, since at the moment I can't do any work *whatsoever* on them. They comprise Confucianism (China), Hinduism and Buddhism (India), Judaism, Islam, Christianity. I flatter myself that these essays, which bring to bear the general application of the methods of the essay 'The Prot. Ethic and Spirit of Capitalism', will likewise provide a strong contrast to the relevant volumes. They can be published separately later along with that essay, if you wish. But not now, since in their present form they are only appropriate as journal essays. As always I offer them first to the *Archiv*. If that doesn't suit – that is if you and Jaffé only want war-time issues, then I won't take offence and on this occasion perhaps try another journal.
>
> The essays are quite long. Some 4 essays of 4–5 Bogen. It will be good for the G. d. S. Ö. if they were published soon, at least some of them. For the publication in the G. d. S. Ö. will have to be more limited and 'systematic'. I've spoken to Dr Lederer about this. Please send this letter to Jaffé if you wish.
>
> (MWG, I/19, pp. 35–6)

It should be noted that Weber was offering his publisher studies on Islam and Christianity. While these were never published, the implication of the letter is that they were to hand. More still was to be offered. When the first instalment on Ancient Judaism was published in the *Archiv* in October 1917, its opening footnotes read, 'The following presentation is published omitting the debates on Egyptian, Babylonian and Persian circumstances. This will be added in a future collection and revised publication (including references for China and enlarged) together with older and some still unpublished essays.'[3] On 24 May 1917, Weber wrote to his publisher, 'The revision and expansion of the first essays for the Gesamtausgabe (if you wish the "Collected Essays" together with Kapitalismus and Protestantismus) will happen <u>after</u> the war. This could be three medium sized volumes if collection extended to study on Christianity.'

After the war, in August 1919, Weber informed his wife of his publishing schedule. 'I'm now getting to work on "Protestant Ethic" in preparation for printing. Then, the "Economic Ethics". After that the Sociology . . . I work slowly on the "Protestant Ethic" edition and other articles and will see through the other things.'

And on 11 September 1919, he wrote to Siebeck,

> The Preliminary Remarks (Vorbemerkung) is not yet written, it will follow soon after the manuscript of the revised 'Spirit of Capitalism' is ready. 'Church and Sects' will follow in 8 days.
>
> Then the essays of 'Economic Ethics of World Religions' would have followed. China (Confucianism) is already partly enlarged, but needs a few weeks extra work. India is ready for printing as it is, after proof-reading. Then an essay needs to be inserted, which is not yet written (but is in my head) over the general reasons of occidental separate development. Then follows Judaism (just has to be corrected).
>
> Of 'Wirtschaft und Gesellschaft' (GSÖ) I could send the start, but its continuation has still and unconditionally to be thoroughly revised.
>
> (MWG, I/19, p. 44)

For the 'Collected Essays in Religion', he wrote out the following advert, which was received by the publisher on 24 September 1919:

> Almost all the essays collected together have appeared in the *Archiv für Sozialpolitik und Sozialwissenschaft* but are now not only checked but enlarged through considerable insertions and the adding of material. At the start is the much discussed essay on 'The Protestant Ethic and the Spirit of Capitalism'. Then, following a sketch on the 'The Protestant Sects and the Spirit of Capitalism' (revision of an essay from the *Christliche Welt*), the essays on the 'Economic Ethics of the World Religions' enlarged with a short presentation of the Egyptian, Mesopotamian, and Zoroastrian religious ethics, but in particular through a short sketch – on the origins of the social distinctiveness of the Occident – of the development of the European Bürgertum in Antiquity and the Middle Ages. The presentation of Judaism stretches back to the beginning of the Maccabaean period. A third volume will contain the presentation of early Christianity, of Talmudic Judaism, of Islam and of Oriental Christianity, a final volume on the Christianity of the Occident. The overall subject concerns the question: What are the grounds for the economic and social *distinctiveness* ('Eigenart') of the Occident, as it has originated and, in particular, how it connects with the development of religious ethics.[4]

The various items in both columns can be checked against these letters. Very broadly speaking, the Economic Ethics of the World Religions in the left-hand column is concerned with the developmental history of whole civilizations. The right hand column with the first drafts (EOPS) and their later revision as *Economy and Society* were intended as Weber's contribution to the *Grundriss der Sozialökonomik* and, in that respect, would follow a more systematic format. Even though Weber did not meet his publication plans for EEWR, the inference is that these belonged to the period before 1914. The letter of 12 June 1915 indicates that Weber did not rigidly separate the two projects: the EEWR studies were preliminary studies for the *Grundriss*, almost implying that they were working papers. He allowed the *Archiv* to publish them as a wartime contingency, but they had to be brought up to proper publishing standard for the publication of the 'Collected Essays in the Sociology of Religion' in 1920. The *Grundriss* commanded priority in Weber's mind. He wrote to Siebeck, his publisher, in February 1917, 'If only the war would end then I could return to my Grundriss volume. But within myself it is just not possible and I prefer to pursue the articles on the Relig. Sociology further. But my desire is for the other.'[5]

The exact relationship of these two contemporaneous projects has been a source of some fascination to Weber specialists. Friedrich Tenbruck, in a seminal article, argued that Weber's main insights were contained in the studies for EEWR. Tenbruck was writing at a time when cultural analysis was not yet fashionable, and the full thrust of Weber's arguments were not fully appreciated (not least because of the vagaries of translation).[6] Tenbruck picked up on the simple but very powerful idea that worldviews, provided by religion and culture, structure people's actions at the level of perception and the interpretation of the meaning of the world. This contrasted with *Economy and Society* where the main determinants appear to be socioeconomic and political in nature. This set up a fairly stark debate between some sort of materialist/power analysis versus the role of cultural determination. Tenbruck himself inclined to a version of cultural conservatism and clearly felt that culture and civilization had to be assessed in terms of fundamental values. In this respect, a post-1945 civilization based on American values – material well-being and political democracy – seemed ill-equipped to ask the deeper, more Tolstoyan questions of the purpose of the conduct of life and the underlying nature of society. Only by grasping in a comparative manner the way in which cultures underwrote civilizations could some critical purchase be applied to a contemporary diagnosis. Tenbruck questioned whether modernity and progress could be so glibly equated, although at times his position verged towards an anti-modernity. While Weber on many occasions struck the pessimistic chord (usually most plangently), it would have been wrong for Tenbruck to term Weber an anti-modernist. The *Grundriss* was a wholesale document for the modernization of the German-speaking world by making available the most up-to-date social science knowledge. But Tenbruck did draw attention to a very Weberian theme. Modernity was not a given, it was the product of a historical and cultural determination, and this was a proper object of critical discourse. Even as his letters to Siebeck above show, Weber wished to advert to the singularity and distinctiveness of the Occident. Belonging to modernity meant knowing about its constitution and, through civilizational analysis, its alternatives.[7]

Johannes Winckelmann, the German editor of the fifth edition of *Wirtschaft und Gesellschaft*, unsurprisingly defended its claims as Weber's main work. Weber, as we have just seen, certainly saw it as his main priority. There is also, however, the undeniable point that Weber never finished it. Weber was not prepared to let it be published in its pre-1914 state – it had to be 'unconditionally' revised. But he revised in full only three chapters of a work that in 1914 was to contain eight chapters. Wolfgang Schluchter was the first scholar to outline meticulously the chronology of both projects, and he was able to show a high degree of interdependence between them.[8] Schluchter also worked his way through the conceptual arguments of both projects and was able to re-engineer a schematic presentation of all the main ideas and concepts that belonged to both projects. One perhaps unwanted consequence of this reconstruction was to bring the dry systematic character of *Wirtschaft und Gesellschaft* to the much more free-flowing and, at times, more passionately written studies on the world religions. The two projects might be related, but they belonged to two different intellectual styles within Weber's thinking. There is no standardized Weber analysis but, instead, a multiplicity of styles and formats.

The Sociology of Religion certainly gave Schluchter a substantial pretext, for it can be seen from the diagram to be part of both projects, thus furnishing arguments of interdependence. *The Sociology of Religion* is a brilliant, freely formulated text. It was also left unfinished, would not have been published without major revision by Weber and is, on first acquaintance, bewildering to follow. In what follows, I draw attention to some of its oddities and weaknesses rather than simply assuming that its textual status is an unproblematic basis for interpretation.

The Sociology of Religion was having to meet and satisfy quite a number of challenging demands. In the *Grundriss*, Weber's specific task was to follow the series of enduring institutions – household, neighbourhood, ethnic community, religious groups, market association, the political group, law, social stratification and the major types of rulership – and to show the various lines of co-determination of these institutions with the economy. This was the task of social economics and the rationale of the *Grundriss* itself. And, to perform this task, Weber had developed his 'Categories of Interpretative Sociology' to analyse more exactly the nature of the social interactions involved. *The Sociology of Religion* became a special sociology, like those of law and rulership. Like them, it became a book-length treatment. Partly, this was because Weber could not resist the legalistic casuistry of minute conceptual definition and accompanying explanations and examples; partly, because he was increasingly drawn into a comparative orbit beyond the circle of occidental history.

The Sociology of Religion, in going beyond its original basis, gave birth to the studies in the world religions. All the titles, both realized and planned, in the left hand column are mentioned, discussed and analysed in the *Sociology of Religion*. Whole sections in EEWR are lifted straight out of the text of the *Sociology of Religion* – in the 'Introduction', 'Confucianism' and the 'Intermediate Reflection'[9] – and hence there is some justification in thinking that it served as an outline sketch for thinking about other religions and civilizations and their development. And, in being pulled in this direction, it became a less systematic treatise on the relation of religion, economy and basic institutions.

Debates over religion in 'Religionswissenschaft'

The editor of the *Sociology of Religion* for the Max Weber Gesamtausgabe, Hans Kippenberg, has reconstructed the debates and the sources on which Weber drew. Kippenberg's work is a major scholarly intervention, because it shows how dependent Weber was on the new scientific study of religion when it came to dealing with the subject in comparative perspective. Because the *Sociology of Religion* has no footnotes, nor any kind of introductory literature review of current debates, it has been assumed that all the concepts were Weber's own. This is quite misleading, and it should also be remembered that Weber, while being highly original, was also a very reactive author. Also, there has been a tendency to assimilate his *Sociology of Religion* with his other writings. But examining his sources, and the major debates that were involved, a different picture emerges. Many of the major concepts that he took from 'Religionswissenschaft' were in themselves unresolved and still open. Despite the brilliance of some of his writing, *The Sociology of Religion* should be regarded as an exploratory work. In going comparative, Weber had logged into a new set of problems – and without properly escaping the issues raised by the critical debates over PESC. Much of the exposition of sources in this section is taken from Kippenberg's 'Einleitung' to *Religiöse Gemeinschaften* in the Max Weber Gesamtausgabe.

The major scriptural sources of the main world religions were being translated and commented upon by European scholars in this period. The German discipline of 'Religionswissenschaft' was developing an objective study of religion without prioritizing the revelatory superiority of Christianity. In particular, it was establishing the historical provenance of sacred texts – when they were written and under what societal circumstances. Much of the conceptual structure and terminology of the *Sociology of Religion* were taken directly from this academic context with which Weber had obviously been staying in close contact. The study of religion in Germany was guided by neo-Kantian methodology, and Rickert and Windelband were influential. At the first conference of the German Sociology Society in October 1910, an afternoon of debate was given over to religion. Troeltsch gave the opening paper on 'Stoic–Christian Natural Law and Profane Natural Law' and, in the subsequent (stenographically recorded) debate, Ferdinand Tönnies,

Max Weber, Georg Simmel, Martin Buber and Hermann Kantorowicz were contributors. Then there was the Eranos club in Heidelberg to which Weber belonged. From 1904 to 1908, a small group of professors would meet on a monthly basis in semester time to give papers on religion and society, treated historically and comparatively.

The conceptual train of Weber's argument in *The Sociology of Religion* can be aligned alongside contemporary approaches. Reduced to a conceptual skeleton, Weber argues that no definition of religion can be provided other than that it revolves around various attempts – religion, magic, frenzy, cults, totemism, etc. – to utilize, by coercion or by pleading, extraordinary powers for protection against nature or human foes. These attempts most usually concern goals in this world – prosperity, health, security – whereas developed religions tend to concern other-worldly goals such as immortality, the soul, nirvana and so on. What Weber wishes to explain is how the more frequent naturalistic state of 'religion', in which this-worldly goals are thought about as being deliverable by natural objects, is transformed into religions that are capable of devising abstract gods whose worship and attendance is oriented to godly purposes, not human needs in this world. For this to occur, personal bearers (charismatics, magicians) and ways of delivering extraordinary powers (frenzy, cultic rites) have, as religious action, to detach themselves from earthly ends. As Kippenberg summarizes Weber's argument,

> The sequence of magician–priest–prophet involves transferring the principle of religious social action from magic to that of cult, and of cult to that of ethics. The failure of the non-specialist magician worked in favour of the priests. On the orders of the political group, the priests did not wish to compel the gods but to influence them through the cult. It was they who conceive the world as a permanent and meaningfully ordered cosmos. They make the believers themselves responsible for misfortune in so far as they have disregarded the divine order. Prophets gave this declaration an ethical turn and integrated 'the relation of human beings to the world on ultimate and unified value-positions'. Around these are formed communities based on an ethic. The following distinction then becomes important: the prophet of the Near East, where the conception of a personal transcendental god predominates, is seen as the bringer of the word of god and a preacher of an ethic of obedience. The prophet in India, by contrast, where the idea of a divine cosmic order predominates, follows an exemplary life of flight from the world as the way to holiness – as in the example of Buddha. Prophetic communities can only become permanent, if the priests establish doctrine as binding and through preaching and the cure of the soul they have an effect upon the conduct of life of the laity.[10]

Once the idea of an ordered and divine cosmos has been established, which is no easy task and Weber is hesitant in his argumentation here, a second phase of the text starts. This is a discussion, in historical comparative terms, of the triangle of priests, prophets and laity. Societies are composed of negatively and positively social strata, and this affects their choice of religion and conduct of life. The laity are an independent agent in the take up of religious views of the world propagandized by priests and prophets. This section was reused and expanded in the 'Introduction' Weber wrote for EEWR. The third phase of the text concerns the relation of priests and intellectuals in constructing pictures of a meaningfully ordered cosmos. It is built on the premise that religion stands in opposition to the other orders of the world. Weber reused this section in the 'Intermediate Reflection' of EEWR.

The *Sociology of Religion* is a work that does not explain itself, and it pays to turn to its academic hinterland for clarification. One large question was how to analyse primitive societies. The anthropology of Edward Burnett Tylor and James George Frazer was evolutionary, and was influenced by Auguste Comte's law of three stages of how people thought about the world: from theological and the idiom of spirits, to metaphysical terms and, finally, to positivist terms and science. It was Frazer who, through his collection of data on folklore and ethnology, argued that magic and cultic practices, such as sacrifice, were used as a source of power over the natural world. In archaic societies, kings would control the weather – the rain maker – through the practice of magical rites and, for Frazer, this was the origin of political power. Tylor argued that the move from magic to religion was part of the evolution of culture, which he defined not in the normative sense of a superior civilization but, as Adam Kuper notes, in the German sense.

> Culture in this usage, included not only the products of élite civilization, but the whole gamut of learnt skills, habits, modes of communication and beliefs which went to make up a particular way of life, and it was the proper object of anthropological study. Cultures progressed along uniform lines, either as a result of borrowing or by independent inventions which took similar forms at particular levels of development.[11]

Frazer's major book, *The Golden Bough*, was first published in 1890, and Tylor's *Primitive Culture* in 1871. Hans Kippenberg points out that the criticisms of their work by Robert Marett had been republished in 1909 in the *Archiv für Religionswissenschaft*. Magic, for Tylor, represented a primitive form of belief in which objects were thought to possess spirits that exercised superempirical power. This was primitive mythic thinking. Marett argued that thinking about the natural world proceeded not through myths, but through the use of symbols where users were aware of the 'as if' status of symbolic knowledge. Early man could distinguish the symbolization from the real, whereas the attribution of myth to archaic societies imposed a false credulity. Marett, then, was providing early man with rational capacities in a world that lacked scientific explanation. In place of magic (animism – the belief in spirits), Marett advanced the idea of preanimism. He also rejected the evolutionary account of change in Tylor and Frazer.

Weber, of course, followed Marett in rejecting an evolutionary theory of religion. But many of the specific ideas in the debates are in evidence in the *Sociology of Religion*. Frazer's linking of power and magic and cultic rites provides Weber with his starting point. 'It is primarily, though not exclusively, these extraordinary powers that have been designated by such special terms as "mana", "orenda", and the Iranian "maga" (the term from which our word "magic" is derived). We shall henceforth employ the term "charisma" for such extraordinary powers' (SocRel, p. 2). The Melanesian term 'mana' and the Iroquois term 'orenda' described the attributes of power, supernatural, out of the ordinary that attached to people or to things. Tylor's idea of 'survivals' – magic and rite in the early modern world – is an evolutionary survival in the sense that rocks contain fossil 'survivals' from earlier aeons. Weber rejected the evolutionary method but repeatedly stressed that magic and rite are never eliminated by developed religions.

> To this day, no decision of church councils, differentiating the 'worship' of God from the 'adoration' of the icons of saints . . . has succeeded in deterring a south European peasant from spitting on the statue of a saint when he holds it responsible that a favour he sought did not materialize, even though the customary procedures were performed.
>
> (SocRel, p. 2)

Frazer's idea that Christianity was originally a cultic practice is a notion that Weber frequently alludes to. Eating together – commensality – is an early and strong form of social bonding based on the magical qualifications of the participants; Christianity was based on extending cultic meals beyond restricted ethnic and kinship boundaries. Weber actually pinpoints the growth of Christianity to Antioch when the apostle Peter tells Paul that he must eat with the uncircumcised, i.e. the ritualistically separate non-Jewish.

Edwin Rohde's book on frenzy ('Rausch') was also influential. Weber frequently notes that one way of calling up supernatural forces was through the route of ecstatic visions, voices, possession, which could be artificially stimulated through drugs, alcohol, overeating meat, dancing, music and sexual orgies. Weber often uses the term orgy, but it is less the sexual content as the creation of a state of frenzy through arousal.

Weber steers well clear of any one unifying theory whether evolutionary, or totemism, or primitive 'Rausch'. The whole opening section of the *Sociology of Religion* reflects Weber's reluctance to embrace any one theory, yet also to advance the claim of a range of practices as the manipulation of the superempirical for this-worldly and everyday purposes. To this day, anthropologists have shied away from committing to any one theory of magic, religion, rite, cult, totemism and taboo. No one theory can account for so many disparate phenomena, and the boundaries of what differentiates religion from magic, and both from social behaviour, have proved hard to define. As the anthropologist Maurice Bloch has observed: 'Anthropologists who specialize in the study of preliterate societies have always been faced with the difficult problem of defining what kind of phenomena can be called religious.'[12]

Weber faced a dilemma not too dissimilar from the controversy over Bücher's theory of evolution. Weber is dealing with three stages: (1) primitive practices – cults, taboos, totemism; (2) magic; and (3) religion. The stages overlap and have no necessity of succession on an evolutionary basis. He does not deploy the methodology of ideal type in order to say that these stages are a means of classification, as he did when defending Bücher in 'Agrarverhältnisse im Altertum'. Indeed, the ideal type does not feature at all. He does refer to 'pure types', for example of priests, magicians and types of prophets. But pure types relate to practitioners or bearers, not to a periodization. To an extent, he handles the problem by keeping the discussion to examples and case studies. When he talks about religions or magic or cults, he particularizes it to empirical data taken from history, ethnology and anthropology. Nevertheless, the thrust of *The Sociology of Religion* remains to outline the properties of the main world religions, which are markedly different in their internal dynamics when compared with magic and preanimism.

Weber writes,

> Transitions from pre-animistic naturalism to symbolism were altogether variable as regards specific details. When the primitive tears out the heart of a slain foe, or wrenches the sexual organs from the body of his victim, or extracts the brain from the skull and then mounts the skull in his home or esteems it as the most precious of bridal presents, or eats part of the bodies of slain foes or the bodies of especially powerful animals – he really believes he is coming into possession, in a naturalistic fashion, of the various powers attributed to these physical organs.
>
> (SocRel, p. 9)

A war dance at first is simply a heroic frenzy prior to battle – it is naturalistic and tries to evoke greater powers over the enemies. But a transition occurs when the patterns of a war dance become fixed through magical manipulation: 'mimetically anticipates victory and seeks to insure it by magical means'. Likewise, animals can be sacrificed but according to fixed rites. This is the threshold of the move to symbolism. By eating a sacrificed animal, the participants see themselves as being bonded together because 'the soul of the animal has passed into them'. This can be termed mythological thinking but, as Weber notes, the actual processes of transition from naturalism to symbolism are varied and complex (SocRel, p. 9).

The symbolism of rites and of magical practices is retained in religion, which is more obviously concerned with belief and dogma. Weber notes that controversy is often sparked by a change to symbolism rather than to doctrine. A schism was caused in the seventeenth century in the Russian Orthodox Church over how many horizontal bars the cross should have.

Weber has a similar problem in his discussion of gods. As with the concept of religion, which Weber refused to define, he expounds instead the large number of forms in which they are conceived. Gods may be naturalistic – in the Vedas, fire is god – they may be impersonal – 'numina' in Rome – or they may be personalized as in the Greek gods. 'The gods frequently constituted an unordered miscellany of accidental entities held together fortuitously by the cult, and this condition was by no means confined to periods of meager social development' (SocRel, p. 10). Weber points out that the sociological factors in the 'choice' of gods is by no means obvious. One would expect agrarian societies to honour chthonic deities – i.e. gods rooted in the earth such as the 'Mother Earth' cult – 'but such parallelism is not always direct' and, here, Weber enters into an inconclusive account of heavenly versus earthly (tellurian) gods. However, Weber does offer a limited formulation of the dynamics of god formation. 'Both the increasing objective significance of typical components and types of conduct and subjective reflection about them [gods] lead to objective specialization among the gods' (SocRel, p. 14). Some gods, by virtue of abstraction (Brahma) or priority (Janus), achieve supremacy over other gods. God formation is closely related to the need of the social group. Each group, whether household, clan or prince, requires its own god, for this unifies its members 'into a strongly cohesive group' (SocRel, p. 15). The political dynamics of a patrimonial leader being lord over other households leads to a situation in which his special god becomes superior over other domestic gods. Taken another step, the patrimonial ruler becomes the high priest, as in the case of the Chinese emperor and the Roman ruler ('princeps'). In the case of a confederation of clans, an oath may be taken to a god who then makes the federation sacred; the example Weber gives is of Jews with Midianites. The god – in this case Yahweh – imposes a contractual obligation on the peoples of Israel and 'from this, various ritual, canonical, and ethical obligations which were binding upon the human partner were presumed to flow' (SocRel, p. 16). In contrast, the Greek 'polis' did not allow the formation of an overarching priesthood, but remained a personal association of 'confrères with cultic associations related to tribe, clan and household gods'. Weber comments that this marked the 'polis' out as a group body ('Verband') rather than an institution ('Anstalt'), like the modern state.

In the next section of the *Sociology of Religion*, a stronger argument emerges. The endpoint of his discussion is monotheistic, salvation world religions, which is how Protestant Christianity is reconceptualized. First, the internal and external factors affecting the development of religion from local, to universal and, finally, to world status have to be outlined. Factors intrinsic to religion include consistency, and religions that are tied to stellar and planetary regularities achieve well. Monolatry, the worship of one god instead of many, and an ethical dimension also contribute. External factors consist of a religion being taken up by a dominant ruler. Judaism scores well on both sets of factors – Yahweh is occasioned through political federation and Yahweh also comes to demand ethical behaviour of his followers. Weber also suggests that one way of distinguishing sorcery from religion is whether priests and lay people attempt to coerce a spirit or divinity. Prayer, and religion, is an entreaty to a higher lord, whereas sorcery is a matter of routines and practices as devices to compel an extraordinary power to favour the practitioner. The common theme in both is to do something in order to get something back, and the overlaps between magic and religion in this respect are apparent. Silent prayer would count as religion, prayer beads or machines or prayer strips as magic.

Weber's own concept rationalization appears at this juncture. Sorting out a mass of gods into some kind of pantheon is an example of rationalization, or 'ratio' – a word he sometimes prefers. There is at work in religion 'a special evolutionary process' . . . , 'there is an ever-broadening rational systematization of the concept of god and of the thinking concerning the possible relationships of the divine' (SocRel, p. 27). There can also be 'primitive rationalism' – sorcery is a straightforward request for something. The end goal of religion, in contrast, is successively 'irrationalized' (a term Weber himself puts in quotation marks). The Puritan prays and behaves for otherworldly purposes, not daring to be venal enough to ask for good fortune. Judged comparatively, this is irrational and departs from the common reason for religion – to invoke out-of-the-ordinary powers to ensure good fortune. Rationalization, as 'ratio', is a mental or 'geistlich' phenomenon; hence, factors of rationalization intrinsic to religion as an intellectual product can be seen to drive it forwards. This is not, however, an inevitable process, because any number of contingent external circumstances can intervene to stop rationalization processes within religion. The most common is the demand of the laity for the retention of magical elements – 'an accessible and tangible religious object' rather than an abstract concept such as a monotheistic other-worldly god (SocRel, p. 25). There are, says Weber, very few consistent monotheistic religions: Judaism, Islam and Protestant Christianity. 'The Hindu and Christian forms of the sole or supreme deity are theological concealments of the fact that an important and unique religious interest, namely in salvation through the incarnation of a divinity, stands in the way of strict monotheism' (SocRel, p. 20). Elsewhere, Weber refers to Christ as a magician – useful for popularity, but not wholly consistent with the Abrahamic conception of god.

In the next section, Weber attempts or, rather, feels his way towards the distinction between magicians and priests. The exercise is not completely successful for, as Weber admits, the magical and the religious can rarely be absolutely separated; also, Weber is unable to pin down exactly what marks a transition point from magic to religion. Obviously, he was conscious that evolutionary manoeuvres were illegitimate. Weber's theory of transition is that they were rare and historically contingent, yet were in some way part of a process of rationalization whose dynamics Weber tries to specify. Those dynamics turn on the inability of magicians to rationalize belief in spirits into a 'rational' system of ethics and beliefs, which was an accomplishment achieved (in rare cases) by priests. Priests, in this reading, are a permanent enterprise ('Betrieb'), whereas magicians are more of an occasional pursuit. This is bound up with how to explain a move from trying to compel a divinity through sorcery and trying to influence a god through entreaty.

Another, and compatible, reading of this section of the text is its orientation to EOPS. Here, an extensive array of examples is outlined in the consideration of the role of gods in relation to, first, the social order and, second, the economy. He makes a principled statement about the requirements of the social order under conditions of: (1) large settled pacified political groupings for legislation; (2) the increased need of a rational comprehension of an external, permanent and orderly cosmos, and this relates to the (agricultural) needs for meteorology; (3) with increased human interaction, a dependence on conventional rules and that people observe these rules; and (4) a growth in the dependence of trust in the given word – between friends, vassals and lords, officials, actors in economic exchange and so on (SocRel, pp. 35–6). Weber does not say it, but this was the condition, historically, of settled agrarian societies from China to Europe. Weber here states an a priori case for the strengthening of the basis of order in societies based on increasing interdependence. Therefore, in Weber's argument, there was a predilection to attach the ethical systems of human interaction to cosmic accounts of obligations; calling up extraordinary power now extends to the social order itself.

Underlying these empirical observations is a neo-Kantian predilection to link meaning and order ('Sinn' and 'Ordnung'), a characteristic missing from the 'Agrarverhältnisse im Altertum', where external, structural factors prevail in Weber's analysis.

For the ancient Greeks, it was the idea that the gods to which they turned were in themselves 'subject to some social and moral order' – that order was ultimately predetermined by the fates ('moira'). Confucianism and Brahmanism were cases of theocratic strata upholding the social order to which is imparted cosmic authority and an ethical–rational character. In Hindu rites, a fixed order of religious ceremony, together with a fixed order of the cosmos, led to a fixed sense of human activity. This leads Weber to note that the important role of ethics could be supplied equally by magical practices alongside obedience to a religious law. Taboos are proscriptive, with evil consequences following their transgression. Totemism, the alleged powers of animal and natural objects, has a role in creating strong kinship bonds and kinship patterns. Taboos, when extended to dietary restrictions, define the inner group of those who eat together, and also add strength to caste systems. Moving the argument on to the economic consequences, a caste order leads to an immutable occupational system and a traditionalist economic ethic. The 'feng shui' system of spirits restricted the development of trade in China (although Weber predicts that the railway system would undermine both the caste system in India and the belief in spirits in China). Ascetic Protestantism stands out uniquely in giving ethical support to 'economic rationalism' (SocRel, p. 42).

This brings Weber up against the problem of how ethical religions can develop out of the more predominant mode of magic-based prohibitions – how 'the belief in spirits became rationalized into belief in gods', the move from coercive magic to prayer as entreaty (SocRel, p. 43), i.e. how does Weber initiate the developmental path of religion that would culminate, much later, in Protestant Christianity, which adhered so strongly to an ethical transcendental god and abhorred any vestige of magic? To answer this – it has to be said, at this stage, tentatively – he goes back to early developments in Judaism. The Old Testament or Hebrew Bible has a well-developed sense of good and evil as religiously buttressed. The question becomes one of returning to *before* good and evil and, here, Weber appears to offer an intermediate situation pitched between magic and religion. In magic, it is rational to ask and propitiate a god for victory over one's enemies. In this sense, salvation is the literal sense of being saved from one's enemies. 'In the Old Testament, the idea of "salvation", pregnant with consequences, still has the elementary rational meaning of liberation from concrete ills' (SocRel, p. 44). Propitiating a god is a form of piety, which Weber defines here as 'behaviour acceptable to a god'. 'In its earliest stages, the religious ethic consistently shares another characteristic with magical worship, in that it is frequently composed of a complex of heterogeneous prescriptions and prohibitions, derived from the most diverse motives and occasions . . . any infraction of an ethic constitutes sin.' It was the Israeli prophets, such as Isaiah, who convinced the believers in Yahweh that misfortune was the result of the people's sin. Sin at this point amounts to annoying a god who punishes his believers, and it does not have a metaphysical sense. Behaving correctly may be more important than believing properly. (Incidental to this, as Kippenberg notes, was Julius Wellhausen's scholarship that had established that the first five books of the Old Testament did not belong to the earliest history of Israel and Judaea. 'In the beginning' was not metaphysical belief and the awesome word of god instituted by Moses, but a collection of tribes pursuing magic and cultic gods.[13]) Holiness and piety tend to be associated with goodness, sin with evil. Even at this point, however, 'The conceptions of sin and piety as integral powers, envisaged as rather like material substances, still remained within the circle of magical notions. At this stage, the nature of the "good" or "evil" of the acting person is construed after the fashion of a poison, a healing antidote, or a bodily temperature.'

> It is a long way from the notion that the person who acts with goodness has received into himself a special soul of divine provenience . . . So

too, it is a far cry from the conception of sin as a poison in the body of the malefactor, which must be treated by magical means, to the conception of an evil demon which enters into possession of him, and on to the culminating conception of the diabolical power of the radical evil, with which the evildoer must struggle lest he succumb to its dangerous power.

(SocRel, p. 45)

The culmination of good and evil as something sublimated from its origins in this-worldly salvation and punishment is, says Weber, a road few ethics travel. Confucianism lacked a concept of radical evil, as did the ethics of Greek and Rome. Certain developments and contingencies are required. 'Prophets and priests are the twin bearers of the systematization and rationalization of religious ethics.'

At this stage in my exposition of Weber's *Sociology of Religion*, enough has probably been said to demonstrate the text's failure to fit the systematic criteria required for the *Grundriss*, but enough to show the many ways in which 'religion' might contribute to the developmental paths of different civilizations. The different world religions can be analysed to establish what is distinctive to them and, conceptually, Weber has the means to achieve this. Different notions of divinity, different ways of attaining salvation, the role allotted to priests and prophets – these are the analytical tools for distinguishing between the world religions. And in Chinese civilization, where magic prevailed in the relationship between ruler and people, this created a strong harmonious order with an aversion to change. Weber imports the same uncertainties of process into the separate studies of EEWR. Preanimistic or naturalistic understandings of nature are taken to be a stage common to all the world civilizations; the question then becomes one of trying to explain the major transformation process required to become a religion based on written doctrine and abstract belief, and how typical forms of conduct are generated that contribute to a particular social order. In one sense, Weber does not require a theory of the dynamics of transition, because he is content to write the studies as developmental narratives. How Christianity or Judaism developed becomes a theme in its own right; and we can see from the volumes he planned that he was quite happy to extend the narrative over different periods of Christianity and Judaism.

His method rested on an internal–external distinction. The science of religion ('Religionswissenschaft') in Germany provided an elaborate set of concepts for analysing the *internal* dynamics of religions. The debates over Frazer and Tylor have been mentioned. To this should be added Tiele's analysis of India and China as being transcendental impersonal rational world orders, and the Near East embracing a concept of transcendental personal god. Tiele also distinguished between local, universal and world religions. When Weber dove-tailed Troeltsch's Christianity-based split between mysticism and asceticism (the latter's contribution at the German Sociology Society conference) with Tiele's bifurcation, he had the basis of his own comparative developmental accounts: the mystical inclined to an impersonal transcendentalism of Indian religions, and the ascetic to a personal transcendental god of the Occident. Further conceptual advances were made by Hermann Siebeck, who advanced the concept of divine salvation ('Erlösung') as a way of denying the power of malificence and evil in the world; the believer looks beyond the world to the only real truth for him or her – salvation in another world. At this point, religion offered a new capacity of detachment – not only from evil but from social communities. In 'Types of Religion', Fabricius showed how a study of experiential piety could be related to life in the world. Piety was a behavioural attitude to the world and did not involve the difficulties of defining the essence of religion. By studying this attitude empirically, three types could be induced: conforming to the world ('weltförmig'); fleeing the world ('weltflüchtig'); and the overcoming the world ('weltüberwindend'). Respectively, conformity resulted in morality based on custom ('Sittlichkeit'); world flight led through asceticism to Christianity, and through mysticism to Buddhism. Christianity stood out as the only religion able to move to an active relationship to the world despite its otherworldly and world-denying beliefs. Troeltsch had handled the same issue in his distinction between different religious attitudes to profane natural law. The latter is the social order as it is and how it is governed. The strictly Christian attitude would see only a divine order, and that the social order on earth should be a reflection of this. In the Stoic tradition, however, there was a recognition that some compromise has to be made between heavenly and earthly orders. Under Christianity in the west, it was the Church that effected this compromise. It is not too hard to see the Puritans as a variant awaiting to happen: an asceticizing movement emerging within a Christian culture that was already heavily compromised with the orders of the world. When Weber returns to the theme of Puritanism, which he does in his comparison of Puritanism with Confucianism at the end of the China study of EEWR,[14] the panoply of 'religionswissenschaftliche' concepts are used. This can be judged if the concepts not deployed in PESC (1904–5) are picked out: disenchantment (which derives from the Chinese spirit-imbued magic garden), practical attitude to the world, rejection of the world, contemplation, hystericizing asceticism, pneumatic spiritual gifts, man as an instrument of god versus a vessel of the holy spirit, accommodation to the world, mastery of the world, ethical rationalization, transcendentally ordered rational ethic of Puritanism, and theodicy problem.

What is striking about the literature of 'Religionswissenschaft' is how much of importance had appeared in the collection edited by Paul Hinneberg, *Die Kultur der Gegenwart* (1906) and in *Die Religion in Geschichte und Gegenwart* published in five volumes by Siebeck from 1909 to 1913. While the interrelating of economic behaviour to Puritan doctrine had been Weber's own discovery in 1904–5, the study of religion on a comparative basis was an achievement within the academic community independent of

Weber. The question may be asked to what extent Weber was therefore a (willing) prisoner of tenets of German historicism that characterized the German academic study of religion. German 'historicism' is a fairly striking description, and is used by Hans Kippenberg to describe the approach of 'Religionswissenschaft'. It is composed of the following features.

Theory and classification are part of the attempt to make scientific sense of the vast variety of religious phenomena and willingness to debate and change concepts in the light of evidence presented. Theory excluded evolutionism, but did allow that developments in religions could be a product of internal dynamics. Weber went as far as anyone in this respect when he spoke of inherent logics ('Eigengesetzlichkeit'). Priests frequently push doctrine forward. For example, the relatively simple idea of Christian salvation could develop its own logic towards predestination in the hands of reformist thinkers, such as Jean Calvin. This intellectual rationalization occurs because priests at times attempt to achieve consistency of doctrine. If a god is all powerful and all knowing, it would therefore follow that he would know all events in the past, present and future and exactly which persons were to be saved. Whether and under what conditions the laity would wish to follow the consistency of this argument in everyday life stands as a separate variable in Weber's analysis.

Theory was offset by the more normally accepted sense of German historicism – an insistence on evidence, historical facts, philological skills in the reading and dating of sacred texts. The Indian Vedas, Zoroastrian Arvesta, Egyptian hieroglyphs and Mesopotamian cuneiform were being deciphered and translated. The importance of documents and evidence did not extend to the insistence on the uniqueness of each culture studied, a feature of early nineteenth-century historicism associated with Herder, for whom different cultures were 'equal in necessity, equal in originality, equal in value, equal in happiness'. Analytically, as the categories of preanimism, magic and religion show, similarities could be demonstrated *across* cultures. Weber explicitly refers to the preanimistic or naturalistic phenomena found in early phases of all the Abrahamic religions as well as in Buddhism and Confucianism. Preanimist cultic behaviour was a characteristic of early humankind, period. Herder's historicism saw culture as an emanation of popular spirit ('Volksseele') that was a living and growing entity. Weber had firmly rebutted such ideas in his Roscher and Knies essays.

Weber was dependent on secondary sources for his studies on world religions, and so on other scholars' translations and interpretations of texts. Hence, he was dependent on a slightly more controversial feature of German historicism, hermeneutics. As I have argued in Chapter 4 that hermeneutics was c. 1900 an essential part of philology and the establishment of the correct interpretation, there is no need to get too excited about this feature. The case of Julius Wellhausen is a case in point. Was his breakthrough in the dating of the books of the Old Testament reliant on philology or hermeneutics? One would say both, so it would be mistaken at this date (c. 1900) to separate the knowledge of languages from the interpretation of meaning. But, because Weber was not able to work with primary sources to the same degree that he did in the Protestant ethic studies, the emphasis on meaning and its interpretation ('Sinndeutung') could not be turned into the methodological question of causation in quite the same way. In the 'Objectivity' essay, Weber was able to distance himself from the neo-Kantian position of Rickert by tying interpretation of meaning to the attribution of causes through empirical investigation. Such a forensic approach to meaning can only operate if the investigator has primary access to empirical materials. Weber is remarkably acute in his assessment of the books and articles he was reading on the world religions and, for example, is only too well aware of the biases in the writings of missionaries. But to argue the long prehistory of the cult in Sinai and Judaea, he was dependent on Wellhausen and other scholars and their knowledge of Hebrew and other languages of the Near East. Weber is far closer to the neo-Kantian emphasis on 'Sinndeutung' in EEWR than he might have wished to be and, as will be noted shortly, his 'Introduction' to the EEWR offers another version of causation.

Die Religion in Geschichte und Gegenwart took Rickert as its methodological mentor, describing his approach: 'The justification of historical science in its autonomy and uniqueness is the purpose of his work . . . a theory of knowledge for history should attain and safeguard the particular right of the science of history.'[15] A scientific study of religion would be especially interested in a methodology that insisted on the separation of 'Sein' and 'Sollen', of what is and what ought to be. The empirical study of religions could operate according to academic rules of evidence, verification and falsification, and it would not be expected to make value judgements about the substance of religion – that Buddha was better than Christ. Doctrinal theology, as the exegesis of Christian thought as taken-for-granted revelation, was duty bound to make such judgements, explicitly or implicitly. But the neo-Kantian separation of the realm of values from the concrete empirical world meant that the pressure to 'prove' a set of religious values as more true or valuable than another set was removed. Values were non-real for Rickert. It was open to philosophy to prioritize and systematize values, and that is what Rickert outlined in his 1913 essay 'System der Werten'. Equally, it would be open to a philosophy of religion to debate the virtues of predestination over nirvana but, epistemologically, this sort of question would not be settled by a scientific treatment of the empirical. Philosophical questions and scientific questions belong to different orders with their own criteria of validity.

This falls far short of the requirements of a *sociology* of religion, because it is exactly how values impact upon human action and how internal religious values interact with external sociological factors that is its practical subject matter. No satisfactory sociological answer is forthcoming from Rickert – and this is one of the reasons why Weber, in his 'Objectivity' essay, pushes on beyond values to causation. But, for the scientific study of religion concerned predominantly with the internal dynamics of religious behaviour, the interpretation of meaning through Rickert worked very well. It was assumed that there was a subjective side to religious ideas, feelings and actions accessible to and comprehensible by the academic inquirer. For example, Hermann Siebeck (in his *Lehrbuch der Religionsphilosophie*)[16] interpreted what he called the 'natural religion' of early man as the belief that gods were able to ward off external evil. People's beliefs or values can be made sense of within their context, and this would extend without limit to magic, totemism, cult rituals or the salvationist contortions of Calvinist predestination. Siebeck had a concept of the objective – scriptures, doctrines, rites and so on. But the assumption was made that the inquirer, through intellectual imagination or re-creation, could envisage the perspective of all forms of religion. We have seen above how Weber thinks it possible to understand the 'rationality' of the head hunter or the magician, and to paraphrase him on Caesar, one does not have to be a Bornean headhunter to understand cannibalism.

Whether and how this assumption can be justified was discussed in Chapter 4 (in relation to the 'transcendental presupposition'). Its use for archaic societies and early man stands apart from English and French anthropological traditions. Evans-Pritchard criticized Weber for his 'intellectualism'.[17] By this, he meant that making sense of early kinship-based societies could proceed through mental re-creation alone. In the field, the anthropologist uses special theories and ways of gathering data (ethnography). In part, Evans-Pritchard's criticism is directed at the 'armchair' theorist; in part, for not recognizing that kinship patterns explain the functioning of society and that religion is integrated into kinship. Comparing Durkheim's theory of the role of the sacred and profane with Troeltsch's account of sacred and profane natural law shows that, in the French tradition, religion performs a societal function, and it can only do this by existing as a reality in its own right. Here, the subjective is not an understandable attitude to a body of doctrine, rites and ceremonies. Instead, the objective is the primary reality, which structures and codes the subjective attitudes of the community. The sacred and profane, for Durkheim, was a demarcation line specifying, with great strictness, actions that could and could not be performed. Practices such as totemism and taboo specified a whole range of rules that structured the patterning of kinship and sense of community. The sacred and profane were fundamental categories of thought that underlay the structuring of early societies. Troeltsch's argument on Stoic and Christian attitudes to the earthly social and political order is that the early Christians believed only in a perfect divine order and that earthly existence was worthless by comparison. Political power and law on earth had to be a direct reflection of the divine order, allowing no possibility for sin and evil. The German subjectivist approach tended to account for actions as flowing from beliefs. The Stoics had a greater acceptance of the imperfection of the world; therefore, their communities were open to the claims of political rulers. The Christians were absolutists and therefore chose to form sects apart from society. The Durkheimian response would be along the lines that the apartness of Christian sects was the primary sociological fact that was policed through a strict separation of sacred and profane in all areas of life, especially kinship.

It has been argued, for example by Donald Macrae, that Durkheim was the beneficiary and enthusiastic reader of contemporary ethnography, whereas Max Weber lay outside the English and French anthropological traditions.[18] Hence, he failed to appreciate the separateness and the extent of difference of early societies from other known historical societies. 'Verstehen' and imaginative re-creation could not be applied at a distance to what, for the anthropologist, would be a field study and expect to produce viable sociology. Hans Kippenberg's recent edition of the text qualifies this viewpoint. The debate on animism and preanimism was informed by recent ethnography. The work of Franz Boas, the pioneer of modern twentieth-century anthropology, and other ethnology was feeding into the German 'Religionswissenschaft'. Marett had assessed the respective claims of Durkheim against the British approach in anthropology.[19] The international debate did not go unnoticed in Germany. Their choice of approach was deliberate not uninformed.

Weber followed the strong tendency in German 'Religionswissenschaft' not to integrate religion as a functional disposition within society, but to treat it as a sphere in its own right – moreover, one in fundamental opposition to the other spheres of society. Tiele had argued that religions expand the number of their believers by escaping the chains of family, tribe, people and government. As religions expand beyond the narrower boundaries of institutions, they undergo a corresponding internal development. Natural religions, confined to clans, have magic at their core; prophetic religions represent another internal developmental stage – they attack magic and develop ethical religion, and so become first national religions and then world religions. These stages have their counterpart in Weber's less determinative transitions from magic to ethics and from ritual to prophecy. The rise of world religions involves a kind of emancipation from the closed institutions that would hold them back. In addition, the emergence of the ethical and other-worldly ideas of salvation directed behaviour to oppose the world. Taken to its extreme, in Buddhism and Christianity, the believer fled or turned away from the world and its orders. In Weber, magic is adapted to the world, in its instrumentalist guise – and hence is more integrationist; salvation religions represent an 'irrationalization' where the salvation goal lies beyond the world.

A similar argument was deployed by Hermann Siebeck in his engagement with Tiele's theories. Religion was a cultural factor alongside other factors such as language and custom, morality and law, family and state, school and education, art and science. But, unlike the spheres of (Hegelian) civil society, religion, in seeking to judge worldly life, stands apart. Religion perceives, unlike the other spheres, that cultural life is not unified but divided. And we have already considered Troeltsch's exposition on sacred and profane natural law, which is an elaboration of the same position. Mysticism, which for Weber stands predominantly for eastern religion, and asceticism are attitudes that represent a discomfort with the world as it is.

Windelband introduced the concept of antinomic orders – an idea used to great effect by Weber in his 'Intermediate Reflection' essay. As a neo-Kantian, he restated the –ultimately irrational – divide between the world as it is and how it should be ('Sollen und Sein'), and between the normative and the natural law. Human consciousness is marked by both the normative and the resistance to norms ('Norm und Normwidrige'). These are all antinomic spheres of existence, clashing against each other. Holiness or salvation ('heilige') is a transcendental concept operant in the cognitive, ethical and aesthetic spheres. Salvationism is everywhere and yet in opposition to all other worldly orders.[20]

What can be provisionally concluded from this discussion is that German sources had an internalist account of religious behaviour, placing an emphasis on the discovery of meaning within its context. Weber adds to this an insistence on external factors of economics and power. This does not create a unified theory because the internal and external belong to different dimensions. Unlike functionalist analyses in the French and British tradition, which can integrate theory as flowing from one standpoint, Weber leaves the exact linkage between the external and internal causation unresolved. Elective affinity stands in lieu of such integration, but it is not apparent whether this is a metaphor or a substantive theory of causation (see discussion below, p. 190). Also, culture exists as a set of meaningful values, constructive of order, but not functionally harmonious.

Thanks to Hans Kippenberg's scholarly introduction to MWG's *Religiöse Gemeinschaften*, Weber's close relationship and dependence on 'Religionsswissenschaft' becomes evident. In conclusion, I develop some points that come out of this discussion.

1. Actions, inner and outer states

Weber's sociological approach to religion is clearly signalled in his 'Categories of Interpretative Sociology' essay. While he is about to draw deeply from the new sources in the German academic study of religion, he also makes the subject his own and goes beyond previous work. He writes, 'in the sociological analysis of understandable relationships, rationally interpretable behavior very often constitutes the most appropriate "ideal type": sociology begins, as does history, by interpreting "pragmatically", that is, on the basis of rationally understandable contexts of action.' All types of religious phenomena, then, are to be placed in context, and it is assumed that the pragmatic reasons for actions are interpretable. The exotic and far distant in time or geography in principle do not resist interpretation for Weber. Interpretative sociology,

> because of its specific focus is not simply any kind of 'inner state' or outer behavior whatever, but rather, *action*. And to us, 'action' ('Handeln') (including intentional omission and acquiescence) is always intelligible behaviour toward objects, behaviour whose 'actual' or 'intended'

subjective meaning may be more or less clear to the actor, whether consciously noted or not. Buddhist contemplation and Christian asceticism are, for the actors, subjectively related to 'inner' objects; the rational economic transaction of a person with material goods is related to 'outer' objects.[21]

This is a crucial statement of method. The science of religion may certainly be concerned with religious ideas, but its sociology takes as its subject matter *action*. Action is revealed in the empirical world and, in principle, capturable by data-gathering methods, whether history, ethnology or sociology. Methods such as Simmel's intuition through psychology are by implication dismissed. Actions are preceded by subjective meanings that are interpretable, not through facile intuition of some inner state, but through the pragmatic assessment of action within its situation. This involves a retrospective attribution of causes for action. Action, by definition, is oriented to an object. There is a hint of Husserl in this statement.[22] Intentionality for Husserl was a mental state of feeling, wishing, believing, fearing, which should be studied not through a psychology of motives but because they had an object. For Weber, an object is the materialization of intended meaning. This is also the same argument of Rickert's that values in themselves were not real and had to be attached to some empirical referent. 'Kulturgüter' embodied values. 'Heilsgüter', one of Weber's genuinely puzzling terms, now begins to make sense. Salvation values – clearly part of the mental states of believers of certain world religions – can only be studied in the sociology of religion as objects of desire.[23]

In the 'Intermediate Reflection' essay, Weber summarizes the full intellectual scaffolding of his world religions project. It is a terminology of ends, means, routes, pathways. Take religious salvation, which, in non-Weberian hands, looms as a metaphysical property subject to doctrinal exegesis. With Weber, it becomes a desired end, a salvation good ('Heilsgut'); it is offered by someone (prophet or god) who is a saviour ('Heiland'); there are means for its attainment – magical rituals and ascetic or mystical ways of life ('Lebensführung'). Although all these processes stem from internal mental states, they have an external empirical reference because mental states of belief are realized through actions – the cult dinner, the officiating magician, the prophet at the king's court, the prophet in the countryside excluded from court, the church priest and the institutionalization of the distribution of grace (godly favour) and, above all – and this is Weber's sociological masterstroke – the actual conduct of believers in their daily lives: conduct of life. These are the experiential regularities of life itself. They form patterns and are noted by observers. They contribute to a historical record, to historical data. Take monks, who are one of the best examples of conduct of life or lifestyle – Weber uses both terms more or less interchangeably. The Indian wandering mendicant monk living only on what people give him or picking berries follows a style of life. In crude terms, this is determined by his beliefs.

Weber insists that the beliefs have to be interpreted through a framework of objects. From what is he fleeing (the world as a distraction) and to what salvation object is he oriented (a oneness with the universe) defines more precisely the pattern of behaviour. It is a pity that Weber never wrote a study on monasticism which, in some Christian versions, produced highly disciplined conduct. Flight from the world, salvation objects and means of attainment in part structure the conduct of life. In addition, techniques and rules are employed, as external means, to achieve conformity to a style of life. Internal goals and external techniques meet in the routinization of conduct. Franciscans broke the twenty-four hours of the day into religious duties – praying, singing, processing, fasting, not talking, reading, copying, labouring. This acted as an external discipline and, in the medieval idea of salvation, the monk worshipped each minute of existence as an affirmation of the divine. The case of Puritan asceticism was discussed previously. Worldly asceticism was disciplined through the rigour of work and the removal of idleness on a daily basis. The ideational spur to the conduct of life was the notion that, at any point, the Puritan might die and be called to judgement, not in a state of grace. This, it will be recalled, drove Bunyan close to psychosis. Interpretation inquires into the internal objects to which belief is directed. Its analysis requires an intellectual framework of magic and other religious phenomena – and this was elaborated by Weber in *Sociology of Religion*. Causal attribution is the investigation of empirical regularities, working 'back' so to speak (retrodiction) to infer internal mental states. In his EEWR studies, Weber has often to generalize this, dependent as he was on secondary sources.

2. Meaning and intellectuals

A common expectation of all the various and sometimes competing approaches to the 'Geisteswissenschaften' in the nineteenth-century Germanophone world was the emphasis placed on meaning. There was an obligation on the academic not only to interpret the world, but also to convey the significance of an interpretation to the reader. Historicism meant not only a commitment to historical context, but to relay this in terms that were meaningful for the audience. The 'bad' old evolutionists such as Hegel and later Roscher and Knies did this by running the past into the present. Spirit ('Geist'), whose substance was located in history, comes to unfold its potential in the present – as in, for example, the rather dubious anecdote that Napoleon was Reason on horseback. It is interesting to note that two of the MWG editors – Kippenberg in *Religiöse Gemeinschaften* and Schmidt-Glintzer in *Konfuzianismus* – do not dismiss Hegel in their introductions. Hegel had included the religions of India and China in his philosophy of history as a way of understanding the different realizations of religious spirit in history. It was Hegel's method that made him completely unacceptable to Weber. But Hegel's widespread diffusion in German thought derived from what was then accepted as a credible narrative of meaning.

Dilthey and Rickert turned this obligation to convey meaning into a methodological device. With Rickert, it was selection through values; indeed, determination by the contemporary 'communis opinio' of cultural values. Weber's methodology gives an explicit role to the academic as interlocutor between cultures. Weber's *Sociology of Religion* is self-consciously aware of the problems of intellectualizing non-intellectual cultures – in the debate over animism and naturalism. But, in his 'Introduction' to EEWR and in his 'Intermediate Reflection', he delivers interpretations of religious action as not just what they meant to historical actors but also what they might mean to a contemporary audience. Meaning, in this latter aspect, in Weber's hands, is a kind of value-added interpretation.

He imbues his discussion of magic with a tinge of romanticism. He constructs a universal of humankind's search for supernatural powers. In many cultures, this idea is expressed in folklore – the idea of harnessing spirits for practical purposes. Gad Yair and Michaela Soyer point out in German folklore the prevalence of the Golem myth and the Dr Faustus story.[24] The 'high' religions of Buddhism, Hinduism and Abraham saturate the world with meaning. These ideational structures of meaning were created by religious intellectuals – prophets and priests.

The modern capitalistic world is devoid of meaning, following on the historic consequences of Puritanism's exclusion of magic from the world. This is the move from magic garden to iron cage, and is appropriately termed the disenchantment of the world ('Entzauberung'). One consequence of the banishment of superempirical meaning is the fate of intellectuals. Prior to the modern, scientific world, they had a twofold task. First, to create rational structures of meaning and, by this, Weber is referring to some ability to make magical or religious ideas interrelate with some approximation of consistency. As often as not, this 'consistency' involves covering up lack of consistency, and the early church councils had to work hard to integrate an Abrahamic god, which met all the necessary requirements of belief, ethics and behaviour, with a charismatic magician and with a spirit life. Secondly, to make this meaningful to lay believers.

> The task of intellectuals has predominantly been to take the possession of religious salvation ('Heilbesitz') and to refine it into the belief in 'redemption'. [. . .] But redemption only achieved a specific 'worldview' ('Weltbild')[25] and the stance taken to the world. [. . .] What redemption could and wished to signify in terms of its meaning and its psychological quality has depended on that worldview and stance.
>
> It is the worldview that has directed 'from what' and 'to what' one would be 'saved' and, let us not forget, could be saved: whether from a political and social slavery to a messianic realm in this world; or from the defilement of ritual uncleanliness or from the impurity of being imprisoned within the body to the purity of body, soul and beauty and a purely spiritual existence; or from the eternal and senseless play of

human passions and desires to the calm peace of the pure sight of the divine; or from radical evil and the servitude of sin to the eternally free goodness in the arms of a fatherly god; or from the submission to the astrologically conceived determination of the constellation of the stars to the dignity of freedom and the partaking in the substance of a hidden divinity; or from mortality expressed in the constraints of suffering, privation and death and the threat of punishment in hell to an eternal bliss in an earthly or future existence in paradise; or from the cycle of rebirth and its pitiless revenge of living out time to the eternal peace; or from the senselessness of worry and contingency to a dreamless sleep. There are still plenty more possibilities. What stands hidden behind all of these examples is a position and stance towards something that was perceived as specifically 'meaningless' in the world. This resulted in the demand that the fabric of the world in its totality be in some wise a meaningful 'cosmos', or rather, that it could or should be. This longing, which is the nucleus of religious rationalism, has been invariably carried by the intellectual strata. The directions and the results of this metaphysical need, and also the extent of its efficacy, have varied greatly.

(EW, p. 69)

The content of religious ideas is the work of intellectuals, and it is the work of academics in the study of the science of religion to demonstrate how these structures of meaning operated. In the modern disenchanted world, the role of the intellectual becomes problematic. One of the key features of all the above instances of magic and religion is that they offer a theodicy. By this, Weber means a superempirical justification of why there exists an inequality in the human condition: why do some people have beauty and some ill-health, why do whole strata live in poverty while others are wealthy? The consequences do not follow from human worth, as goodness rarely translates into good fortune and evil often rewards well. An example of a secular theodicy is meritocracy – that everyone's status in society is due to ability and hard work. (Although this does not explain or justify the distribution of ability or the capacity to work.) All cultures have various cosmologically derived answers to this universal feature of societies. A universal problem requires a pragmatic solution. This is how Weber treats the religious construction of intellectuals.

One prominent secular theodicy in Weber's day was Marxism. It offered a scientific explanation for a social situation of extreme stratification, drawn from classical economics, and it offered the eschatology of utopia of a free and classless society. For Weber, Marxism was best understood through the categories of the sociology of religion as by political economy. Another new role of the contemporary intellectual was to re-enchant the world. At the end of the nineteenth century, art was seen as the substitute for religion, where the salvation benefits were derived from aesthetic and emotional sensibility. Symbolist artistic currents in Europe and America fed this demand.

Figures from this movement, such as the poet and magus Stefan George, irritated Weber, because he saw them as false charismatics. Had Weber been slightly more value neutral – as it was not for him to judge charismatic power except through the behaviour of George's followers – he could have allotted a larger role to re-enchanters. The phenomena would seem to be predictable in the face of disenchantment.[26]

Part of Weber's irritation was *his* role as an intellectual. The essential message, stemming from his Protestant ethic studies, was that the world could no longer be regarded as a meaningful cosmos underpinning ideas of progress, coherence, justice and ethics. Secularization, knowledge and science were driving out the illusionary ideas of a meaningfully ordered cosmos. Modernity, in its embrace of industry and cities, was turning away from the long era in agrarian settlements of gods and spirits. Weber's message as an intellectual was not to look for meaning beyond the empirical. Weber was slightly premature here in that he failed to anticipate the era of nationalism and the role of the intellectuals as ideologists of national consciousness and nation state modernization. He was not unaware of nationalists, but they also seem to have irritated him.

His intellectual message drew on the German tradition of religion standing in opposition and in conflict to the world. The 'Intermediate Reflection' essay is a disquisition on this theme: that where salvation ethics have created supra-institutional communities of believers, then there must be conflict with the powers and orders of society. The true believer places faith higher than family bonds; the realm of economic necessity detracts from the search for a transcendental salvation; the order of power and politics is a reflection of the corruption of humankind and is essentially flawed and beyond reform; aesthetics and sexuality have to be rejected as dangerous competitors to religious deliverance; and knowledge and its intellectualist demands remain an enemy of communicative consciousness with a god. Following on from disenchantment and cosmic meaning, these value spheres, as Weber terms them, have no necessary connection with each other. In modern life, there is no transcendent unity underlying what you believe in, how you earn your living, what your politics are, what your aesthetic tastes are and how you make love.[27] It might be thought that science, education and knowledge could provide new underpinnings. Weber, in his intellectual's role and giver of truth – in his lectures on science and politics to wartime students – declared that science cannot in itself generate the values by which we could lead our lives. How we lead our lives is a somewhat portentous theme and, here, Weber was looking to the Russian intellectuals Tolstoy and Dostoyevsky, whom he thought had gone furthest in probing the issue of meaning in the modern world. In Dostoyevsky, in a world of ethical irrationality, the analysis points to a realism shorn of illusions.[28] With Tolstoy, it becomes the basic question of life – how should it be led and, hence, his famous question – how it is to be lived (somewhat overshadowed by Lenin's 'what is to be done?').[29] Weber did not extend the question 'how should we live?' to 'how should we live together?' as the project of politics. Weber here never squared his intellectual objections to the illusion of political community and brotherhood with his rational obligation to participate in politics as a responsible citizen. (Weber's analysis of power is taken up in Chapter 8.)

3. Historical determination

In the EEWR, Weber is unable to deploy causal attribution as the decipher-ing of possible motives in relation to the situational context. He is dealing on a more wholesale scale with world religions, and he does not have access to primary sources and detailed situational information as he did in PESC. Whole social strata stand in as sociological actors, and the concept of car-riers ('Träger') becomes the empirical referent of religious goals. Different forms of religion have their own characteristic sociological proponents: the magician or sorcerer is the practitioner of magic, the priest officiates over the cult, and the prophet is the bringer of ethics. In the wider social structure seen comparatively,

> If one wishes to characterize succinctly, in a formula so to speak, the types representative of the various classes that were primary carriers or propagators of the so-called world religions, they would be the fol-lowing: In Confucianism, the world-organizing bureaucrat; in Hindu-ism, the world-ordering magician; in Buddhism, the mendicant monk wandering through the world; in Islam, the warrior seeking to conquer the world; in Judaism, the wandering trader; and in Christianity, the itinerant journeyman. To be sure, all these types must not be taken as ex-ponents of their own occupational or material class interests, but rather as the ideological carriers of the kind of ethical or salvation doctrine which most readily conformed to their social position.
>
> (SocRel, pp. 131–2)

This same exposition is taken into the 'Introduction' to EEWR and ex-panded. Weber has an obligation in his 'Introduction' to outline his main ideas to the reader, as it is a preface to the studies on the world religions. He cannot afford to be as discursive and exploratory as the *Sociology of Religion*. He has to establish how religions as sets of meanings and values can be thought of as exercising causal efficacy in the face of the material necessities of the world. As a national-economist writing in the *Archiv für Sozialwissenschaft und Sozialpolitik*, his subject was economic ethics.

> No economic ethic has ever been determined solely by religion. It is evi-dent that economic ethics possess to a high degree a lawlike autonomy ('Eigengesetzlichkeit') closely determined by economic geography and historical conditions in contrast to the attitudes of human beings to the world as determined by religious or other 'inner' factors of a similar

nature to religion. But it is true to say that among the determinants of an economic ethic – and these determinants it should be noted are *multiple* – belongs the religious definition of conduct of life.

Weber goes on to note that religious-determined life conduct is strongly influenced by 'geographical, political, social and national factors' (EW, p. 56). This produces the diagram in Figure 6.2.

Weber points out that it would be a 'never-ending task' to detail all the interactions involved in this model. He simplifies the problem to the conduct of life and some of their typical carriers. 'What is presented here is merely an attempt to bring to light only those social strata which, in giving direction to the conduct of life, have most strongly influenced the practical ethic of the relevant religion . . .' (EW, p. 56). This is a simple and robust model, and it allows Weber to make any number of comparisons across civilizations. The internal sources of action and religion have their own structure, their law-like character. This is the intellectual or rationalist character of salvation ideas or magical ceremonies or cultic rites. External factors are analysed according to the normal methods of the social sciences. Conduct of life is an observable regularity of actual behaviour and can be tied to a particular social stratum. Weber himself identifies the Confucian official, the Brahman, the Buddhist wandering monk, the Christian journeyman and the Islamic warrior as key strata decisive for the developmental path of those civilizations. Needless to say, other strata with other beliefs and external determinants and, therefore, with different conduct of life can be identified and their historical efficacy assessed. This then becomes a matter of academic debate. So, in the case of Islam as being carried by feudalistic warrior castes, there have been numerous challenges to Weber's interpretation. The town-based Islamic merchants, for instance, could equally be seen as decisive for the course of Islamic societies.[30] Weber could have been mistaken in his identification. But this does not affect the soundness of the model, only the empirical evidence and its interpretation. (In principle, the academic debate could be as intensive as the Protestant ethic debate. This is slightly alarming – for a sociologist! – as the major determining forces can become engulfed in disputes over historical detail. But this has to be allowed – especially by Weber's own methodology of scientific progress. A specialist will arrive and overturn previous assumptions, and the lines of the debate will have to be redrawn. Something like this occurred in the subsequent Protestant ethic

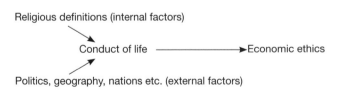

Figure 6.2 Determination of economic ethics.

debates, in which Weber's devout Calvinists were shown to be Erasmist humanists escaping economic persecution in the enforcement of Catholic dogma in the sixteenth century. Continuing in this vein, the whole of the world religions project could be redrawn, although whether in the strong Weberian brush-strokes seems unlikely.)

'Various efforts have been made to interpret the interrelationship between a religious ethic and the interest position of its carriers, so that the former appears only as a "function" of the latter.' Weber disputes the Marxist case here, and also Nietzsche's theory of 'ressentiment' – that religion is an expression of the impotent and the oppressed. His model brings to fruition the statement made in his 1898 Lecture Course that similar economic conditions give rise to entirely different cultures, and also to the subheading in the 1914 Outline 'The Class Determination of Religions'. Karl Marx's assertion that religion is epiphenomenal to class and that religion is 'the sigh of the oppressed creature, the heart of a heartless world, and the soul of the soulless conditions. It is the opium of the people . . .' was not directly confronted.[31] It is debatable whether Marx's writings on religion at that time formed a corpus worthy of academic attention. Instead, Weber, through his linking of economic mentality with religiously determined life conduct, demonstrates that the patterning and pathways of religious thought as they were constituted in people's actions and behaviour were extremely complex, and had developmental consequences. Rhetorical asides to opium are no more than literary flourishes compared with the actual use of opium in cultic practices. It might be thought that Weber is inverting Marxism in his terminology of salvation goods ('Heilsgüter') – as if religions sell salvation as a commodity. There is certainly something of the language of commerce and national-economy in Weber's usage. He was clearly aware that religions have to be marketed in order for them to have a mass appeal. 'Religions promise and offer different salvation goods ('Heilsgüter') . . .' (EW, p. 66). By this, Weber is indicating that, in comparative terms, salvation can be of this world or other-worldly, and different salvation paths are offered to the masses. It is an empirical matter for investigation. This also recalls Rickert's comment that cultural values ('Kulturgüter') have no validity until realized in empirical reality. Weber's usage, then, has a historical, empirical and (non-Marxist) materialist quality. A corollary of this is that his usage cannot be taken for being idealistic. While the German tradition had, to an extent, studied the content of religious ideas, Weber rendered them as ends of actions, objectified in social processes. This makes it harder (but not impossible) to mount a Marxian critique of Weber as an 'idealist' opposed to 'materialism'.

The role of intellectuals – priests, prophets and sorcerers – has already been mentioned in the construction of salvation goods and pathways – a process, Weber says, that attains its own inherent autonomy ('Eigengesetzlichkeit'). To this, Weber adds a cognitive component. 'But redemption only achieved a specific meaning when it became the expression of a systematically rationalized "worldview" ("Weltbild") [Weber's quotes] and the stance taken to the world.' 'It is the worldview that has directed "from what" and "for what" one would be "saved" and, let us not forget, could be saved . . .'. Weber does not define what a worldview is – neither does he say where he got the term from. It most probably derives from Dilthey's ambitions for philosophy. 'If', Dilthey wrote, 'we are to bear illness, death or banishment, a special frame of mind is needed in life. Most people receive this from religion; once dogmas have been discredited the educated classes need a substitute which is based on religious or philosophic reflection.'[32] This is quite close to being a secular theodicy. Individuals, in their lives, are faced by adversity, injustice and the workings of forces beyond their ken. Philosophy, for Dilthey, should be able to articulate a vision of the age in which people live, and provides guides for action. Weber uses the term 'Weltbild' in place of Dilthey's 'Weltanschauung' (view of the world, literally). Both terms are often given the same translation: 'worldview'. Weber did not share Dilthey's philosophical ambitions, and 'Weltbild' is a more neutral term. It is the notion of a framing device through which the world is viewed and made sense of. It is informed by values – religious or magical and, in the modern world, art rather then philosophy. In this framing sense, it would now be reckoned to have a cognitive aspect – although Weber did not himself explore the perceptual qualities of worldviews. (More is said about this in the next chapter.)

In his revision, in 1919–20, of the 'Introduction' to EEWR, Weber inserted a sentence between the two sentences on worldviews, quoted above. 'It is interests (material and ideal), and not ideas, that have directly governed the actions of human beings. But the "worldviews" that have been created by ideas have very often, like switchmen, decided the lines on which the dynamic of interest has propelled behaviour.' A switchman is, or rather was, the person who pulled the large metal lever to change the points on a railway track. It is a striking image and encapsulates Weber's thinking about the paths or tracks that developmental history follows. Take the late medieval European economy. Economically, this was building up considerable forward drive in terms of trading, money transactions, property rights, institutional changes, etc. In the fifteenth and sixteenth centuries, this was as much a south European as a northern European phenomenon. The Reformation intervenes, the path of development bifurcates between a new level of dynamism and stagnation. The switchman, for Weber, is Puritanism. Or take, at the same time, China and Europe. China had considerable economic advantages over Europe, but one track (Confucianism and the maintenance of harmony) is the slow or delayed train, while the other (switched by Puritanism) is the path of world-overcoming and capitalistic expansion.

It is only a sentence and not a methodological statement of causal verification in comparative history. Weber's methodology specifies the empirically attested attribution of motive and reasons to individual behaviour. Individuals as a mass of the similarly acting constitute a social stratum, so causation may be generalized to the group. That, as we shall see, is as far as Weber wants to proceed. But subsequent and recent work in comparative sociology, very much in the Weberian mould, has been far more preoccupied in coming up with an integrated theory of material and ideal factors. This is guided by the idea of factorial analysis – that somehow, in a multicausal situation, the various causative factors can be weighed against each other.

Weber did not have such an encompassing ambition. Turning points in developmental history were what mattered and could be empirically isolated and noted, e.g. the Christian apostle Peter at Antioch or Judaic legacy. Everything else remained history, intensively and extensively infinite in extent. There are material and ideal interests, not factors. Interests can be made sense of by the social scientist, and they have both consequences and meaning. Weber's final position on this in his 'Preliminary Remarks' to the 'Collected Essays in the Sociology of Religion' was to say that outcomes are the result of a concatenation of circumstances. In the examination of those forces, the obligation is to grasp the significance and meaning of historical development. Explanation resides in meaning, not in correct factorial analysis. The meaning that Weber draws out of occidental development is the imprint of rationalism. History may contain blind forces, but the switchman is not blind – he sees, or rather searches for, nirvana, a hidden god, paradise, earthly perfection, earthly satisfactions – and he prescribes the way of life or conduct for achieving these goals. The role of sociology is to go beyond events and to grasp types of social action displayed by social groups and social strata, and to understand their meaning and significance.

It is a mistake, therefore, to exaggerate the comparative ambitions of the studies in the world religions. It does look as though Weber wants to isolate the factor that accounts for the rise of the west by a process of elimination: the west had this crucial factor that the Orient lacked. In one sense the simple answer is western rationalism, but then this gives way to a more complex set of questions. For Weber, it is a concatenation of circumstances, or if one likes, an accident. But knowing how it came about and what ideal interests were implicated in its emergence is important and something that can be comprehended, and the accident is not without significance.

To say history in its developmental outcome is an accident is perhaps too strong a term. Conduct of life is a subjectively intended orientation in a situation and capable of sociological explanation; equally external factors such as economic and political forces and the environment of economic geography exert a discernible determination. How these two aspects interact, which they will do continuously, and what joint outcome is produced would be better termed fortuitous. In German, fortuitous and accidental is the same word: 'zufällig'. Fortuitous is better because it implies that things happen for a reason or reasons. In Weber's historical sociology, outcomes happen for reasons – motivational states and the pattern of external determination. But how they interact and combine is hard to predict.

Weber has an interesting discussion of this issue in his 'Categories' essay. The problem of fitting subjective motivation with the external play of forces would be solved if somehow intended meanings were 'objectively right' in the situation. But this is rarely the case. Weber outlines two possibilities, both of which illustrate the perversity of outcomes. 'On the one hand, there is behaviour that seems wholly irrational but has an unperceived ("disavowed") yet relatively extensive rationality; it is "understandable" because of that rationality.' Weber does not provide the example that this statement requires, although he could well have had a Freudian-type explanation in mind.

'On the other hand, there is the fact, substantiated hundreds of times (especially in cultural history), that phenomena apparently directly conditioned by instrumental rationality actually originated historically through wholly irrational motives; and subsequently, because changing conditions nurtured in them a high degree of technical "*correct* rationality", they survived as "adaptations" and occasionally became universal' (Categories, pp. 155–6). This takes us back to the Protestant ethic. The Puritans' rational, sober and systematic attitude to work appears to conform to the criteria of instrumental rationality: action that achieves its goal in the most effective and efficient manner. Benjamin Franklin, in his advice on how to get on in the world, offers an instrumentalist view of managing oneself. In PESC, Weber suggests a continuity between Franklin and Puritanism, as Franklin's father was a Calvinist. Franklin Sr's conduct of life was formed from an irrational motivation – predestinarian beliefs. Franklin Jr is brought up with the same mental outlook, and his behaviour will, as America's nascent capitalism gets under way, be 'adaptive'. W.G. Runciman has recently demonstrated how this can be underpinned by modern evolutionary theory.[33] Calvinism represents a cultural gene, or meme, to follow Dawkins. It does not necessarily fit well with the economy of early modernity but, over time and with capitalist development, it came to be highly adaptive in an economic world that demands a dedication to labour.

Weber himself was highly averse to evolutionary theory – for its monist, Hegelian and Comtean drawbacks – so the evolutionist concept of adaptation goes into inverted commas. Modern evolutionary theory, however, has a theory of change based on selectionism. There is no logic in history as in Hegel or Comte. Cultural forms, further down the historical road, prove to be adaptive to changing circumstances. This is a more theoretically reasoned account of historical change, for it seeks to explain fortuitous outcomes. In his 'Prefatory Remarks', Weber falls back on the concatenation of circumstances, i.e. it was a fortuitous set of conditions. Runciman draws an important contrast between 'selectionism' and 'elective affinity'.[34] The causal model in the former holds that a cultural attitude is empirically verified and is taken as a given rather than its causative effects being derived as immediately following. A cultural meme can lie, so to speak, 'dormant' for generations (although it does exist handed down over generations) before, under favourable circumstances, releasing its causal impact. For Weber, elective affinity is a coming together of circumstance and a culturally determined form of life conduct; the relational link displays what Weber terms 'causal adequacy', the one supporting the other. Culture ('Kultur'), for Weber, is always live rather than dormant, and does not exist as a rotating flywheel in neutral, so to speak, waiting its engagement with history. Culture embedded into life conduct is fate or destiny, and it is either realized or frustrated.

4. Value spheres and modernization

Runciman's use of selectionism is a fairly recent development in social theory. In the decades approximately 1955–85, neo-evolutionary sociological theories provided the basis for explaining modernization. Their key idea is differentiation. Modern societies are inherently complex and, to reach such a level, a process of differentiation has to take place. In Talcott Parsons' hands – by far the most influential theorist of the second half of the twentieth century in this respect – this differentiation proceeds according to the AGIL (adaptation, goal attainment, integration, latency function) schema. Parsons conceptualized modern industrial societies as a system that has differentiated subsystems: politics, economy, social institutions and culture. Each of these performs subfunctions that are integrated into an overall system. Politics is concerned with adapting the system to a changing environment, what Habermas was to rephrase as the steering mechanism of society. The economic subsystem is instrumentalist in achieving economic goals. The social subsystem organizes actors into role positions that fit them for the various institutions within a society – the family, the workplace, etc. Culture is a kind of coding mechanism that integrates system maintenance with individual behaviour in the subsystems.

Parsons did not regard his social system theory as antithetical to Weber's legacy. Parsons was a Weber scholar and translator of his work. It is not unreasonable to read *Economy and Society* as an account of fairly simple social institutions such as the clan, the neighbourhood and the household together with their relationship to cults and magic and how they are transformed under conditions of salvation religions, the rise of rationality and the emergence of contract and exchange relationships. This could be deemed as a move from simple to complex societies, and as an elaboration of Tönnies' communal groups bound by ties of blood and kinship to associational forms bound through rational association – the move from 'Gemeinschaft' to 'Gesellschaft'. Secondly, the 'Intermediate Reflection' essay would certainly seem to describe a process of differentiation even if Weber did not use this term. The early or archaic societies, in which clan, neighbourhood and household predominate, did not distinguish social relationships of kin, politics, economics, religion/magic and art. Weber says they have a primitive ('urwüchsig) natural attitude to the world. Only with the advent of salvation religions can a process of differentiation emerge. Religion as an autonomous value sphere stands in opposition to the values spheres of kinship, economy, politics and art. Thirdly, with his concept of 'Eigengesetzlichkeit' as well as rationalization, Weber would appear to permit autonomous mechanisms of development.

Hence, in Parsons' thinking, why not overcome Weber's aversion to evolutionary thinking and introduce differentiation as a process–concept in the way that Herbert Spencer and Emile Durkheim did? The move from simple to complex must involve phases of differentiation, and the task for Parsonian historical sociology is to show how increased differentiation makes complexity possible. Rainer M. Lepsius has recently suggested a similar manoeuvre at the level of institutions.[35] The actual terms that Weber uses in the 'Intermediate Reflection' essay are value spheres and life orders (of religion, economy, politics, culture, art and sexuality). If these are treated as equivalent to institutions, then a Weberian analysis can be built on institutional differentiation, each with their own ideal and material interests. These moves place Weber's sociology far more in accord with the preoccupations of late twentieth-century sociologists. As it stands, Weber's sociology is overly restrictive; for instance, not only does it not have a concept of societal differentiation, neither does it have a concept of role. Theories of role explain how the individual is able to operate across a range of institutional contexts –family, work, culture, politics – with some element of integration.

Weber's historical sociology is actually quite recalcitrant to such manoeuvres. In order to update Weber, cardinal emphases have to be removed. Weber's value spheres are denominated by values held by individuals. The individual occupies the central circle of a series of overlapping circles. The respective values of family, friendship, work, politics, culture and religion are all different, but the individual as a 'personality' experiences all these values – in their harmonies and in their conflicts. This is what gives his or her existence meanings. The human being is a thinking, feeling, wishing, affectual person, confronted with the various orders of the world. Weber refuses to turn the actual person into the abstract individual of 'homo sociologicus'. Value spheres are immediate to the individual, and they are not mediated by role playing. The antinomic stresses of values in conflict – brotherhood versus power for example – are parts of the conditions of existence. Parsons' subsystems create second-order spheres of values mediated by cultural pattern variables and roles. With Weber, existence, values and action are the stuff of the human or cultural sciences, and the precondition of their possibility. The scientist is part of the social world, he or she relates through values to other societies and cultures and, through academic study, draws out the significance of human existence. This position owes much to the German heritage, much of which has been referred to, and it also places blocks on the refinement of theories of society and societal change. One cannot move away from the base material of human existence – affectual and instrumental mental states in the face of the exigencies of the world. One might complain of want of further refinement in Weber but, equally, one might wish to recall Weber's judgement on religious intellectuals – overelaborate accounts of the meaning of the cosmos (society) tend to alienate the laity (public).

7   Going beyond Weber

The last chapter established that, although meaning and causation in Weber's historical sociology are not to be separated, the idea that *all* the factors behind developmental paths could be assessed and weighed is never
entertained by Weber. Equally, he dismissed evolutionary theories and would
probably have rejected neo-evolutionary theories of system differentiation.
The developmental pathways of different civilizations can be shown to possess a narrative of meaning (cyclical in India, harmony in China and rationalism in the west). This is not of itself determinative of outcomes and directionality. Outcomes are the fortuitous coming together of internal views of
the world and a variety of external forces. Some outcomes, which structure
future patterns of history, survive, and it would seem to be possible from
Weber's stance to allow an account based on new forms, or reforms, as being adapted to the environment – not by design but by fortuitous endurance.
History is not one damned thing after another, to paraphrase the playwright
Alan Bennett. It displays meaning, and the historian forges a value relationship between the contemporary reader and the past. PESC established that a
way of everyday life formed by Calvinism was both causative of capitalistic
modernity and significant for understanding the nature of modern society.
Origins determined the means–end mentality of modernity. In the EEWR,
a wider historical picture is drawn, in which certain key strata carried a
worldview that was causative for particular developments – itinerant artisans
for early Christianity, Calvinistic rising middle classes in the sixteenth and
seventeenth centuries – in the course of the long historical development of
the Occident.

In this chapter, I want to examine some of the implications of Weber's
expansion from the specialist, almost case study, approach of PESC to the
wide-ranging comparative approach of EEWR and, finally, to the summation
of his thinking on the distinctiveness of the west, in terms of rationalism,
from other civilizations or cultures. The expansion in the scope of Weber's
thinking should not be deliberated over as if it was a planned or precon-
ceived strategy. Rather, it is perhaps better thought of as an efflorescence
in Weber's remarkable capacity to develop an original thesis in a variety

of different contexts. The original explanandum was how to explain the origins of capitalistic modernity, and that is what he is still trying to explain in his final summation – his 'Prefatory Remarks' to the 'Collected Essays in the Sociology of Religion'. There is no one complete answer to the original question, although what does stay constant in his approach is the insistence that causation and meaning remain interlinked. That said, the causation–meaning linkage looks very different if Calvinism alone is being studied or if whole stretches of the development of western Christianity are being studied. To argue that the nature of western modernity originates in the fairly narrow particularism of Calvinism and certain Puritan sects, and then to go on to argue that western modernity is the outcome of a rationalistic tendency that is expressed over centuries, is to produce two different accounts of the causation–meaning linkage. Weber himself would have seen both accounts as compatible. He never abandoned or revised the essential explanatory thrust of PESC when he came to republish it in 1920. What I will argue in this chapter is that, if the scope of the argument is widened, the causal arguments also change, and this has implications for the place allotted to the interpretation of meaning. I raise the stakes in comparative sociology by introducing two post-Weberian theories that demonstrate with greater clarity how expanding the causal field leads to different assessments of meaning. The first of these theories was put forward by the Canadian economic historian Harold Innis, who showed that the capabilities of political and salvation messages are determined by the technology of communication. The accessibility and diffusion of messages, and so of meaning, are dependent on technology. The second theorist is Karl Jaspers, who reconfigured the era of the world religions as the 'axial age'. Religions present a new modality of thought and a larger cradle of civilization, within which it is conceivable that more than one modernity could have emerged. This idea has been pursued by S.N. Eisenstadt, who argues for 'multiple modernities'.

Weber's argument in PESC, 1904–5, is what I will call a singularity argument. A unique 'chemical' bonding – an elective affinity – occurred between a rising middle class and a Calvinist-influenced conduct of life. Something singular happened, and the Calvinist worldview became constitutive of modernity, and there is an inescapable component of modernity that always carries the singularity of its origins. Weber's contribution rests on this assertion. Modern capitalism 'worked' in a way that no other previous capitalisms had been capable of by concentrating not on the ends of production and wealth but solely on the means. Weber's Puritans are narrow-minded. Wearing the blinkers of other-worldly salvation, their lives were organized to accumulate wealth as a confirmation and sign of their election and to deny previous notions of Christian brotherhood and ethics to fellow human beings. PESC is full of suggestions as to how this particularistic attitude entered into politics, society and science. Oliver Cromwell and the Puritan discipline of his soldiers won the English Civil War and, in marking a decisive stage in the centralization of the English state, it represented a superior sort of military violence. The Puritan soldier–saint cared little for his own life or for the lives of others – so justifying some of the more spectacular of Cromwell's brutalities. The rights of man originated not in a free-thinking Enlightenment but in the absolute conviction that no authority should intervene between God and the individual's textual and prayerful communing with the deity. Liberty, as Weber was fond of pointing out to his German contemporaries, was established through regicide, and this was inseparable from religious radicalism. Puritanism, in Weber's vivid phrase, descended like a hoar frost on Merrie England and, to this day, is inseparable from a certain gloominess, all of which can be traced back to the Puritan's almost complete devaluation of the body as a worthless and corrupt vessel. And in Weber's hands, science, while an instrument of enormous emancipation, is driven by a sober, systematic and empiricist outlook and is remorseless in its progress, so amounting to a form of disenchantment. The origins of modernity are features intrinsic to modernity, however overlaid they might have become through subsequent influences.

There is a subargument to the singular creation of modernity. Although the fortuitous nature of historical development is acknowledged by Weber, at least in his 1913 'Categories' essay and in his discussion of why particular worldviews take hold, there is a strong sense of agency in the Protestant ethic studies of 1904–5. The Puritans meant to change the world according to their religious ideas, and they were historically consequential in achieving this. Singularity, therefore, is determinative of future developments. Johannes Weiss has drawn attention to a paradox in this position.[1] Puritan doctrine and its interpretation introduced something new. Metaphysics and mankind's relation to the world had never before come up with such an imaginative permutation (redemption, grace and its attainment). This was causative in changing the development of history in an irreversible way. The movement of the Reformation had produced a spontaneous innovation that thereafter proved irreversible in the texture of human society and its mentality. This is not a determinative law at the general level of society, but a determination at the level of agency. Singularity attaches to innovation, agency, cause and meaning. Karl Popper has insisted, as a normative imperative, on the openness of history and, like Weber, that there are no laws formulable within the generality of society. Weiss points out that the (Weberian) converse of this position is that social groups can intervene decisively in human history. Human agency can be determinative in an irreversible manner. To take a contemporary example, human rights as both discourse and practice may have the capacity to transform what were/are dictatorial regimes. Human rights, as a form of human agency, would then effect and determine an irreversible change.

The notion of singularity contains another paradox. The western self-image of modernity emphasizes its universalist characteristics: law, science, politics and economics all conform to criteria that go beyond the means–end rationality. Law operates according to high-level criteria such as justice and equity; science and education are seen as the emancipation of humankind over nature as well as self-understanding; politics is seen as deliberative, democratic and a process of reconciling opposed interests; and economics as overcoming poverty and the rational allocation of resources. Weber's notoriety as a theorist of modernity is to render all these goods, defined by a sense of higher purpose, as compromised by a darker side. Justice takes second place to the administration of law and bureaucratic imperatives; likewise, politics, which also can never escape what Weber terms the pragma of power – there is a logic to the exercise of power irrespective of its inclusive and benign intentions; knowledge leads to disillusion and not to joyous emancipation; and the mechanisms of wealth creation impose a new serfdom on human personality and its autonomous expression.

Weber is (in)famous for drawing attention to these antinomies. In the singularity argument, what claims to be universalist is in fact the effectiveness of diffusion, and what is diffused may be effective because of the particularism of its origins. Modern rational capitalism originates from the deliberately blinkered conduct of life of Puritan groups. Because economic behaviour is divorced from wider questions of the ends to which economic activity should be put, it is so successful. Singular ideas and practices succeed by virtue of their extensive diffusion and not necessarily by virtue of intrinsically universal criteria. To give a contemporary example, a make of software might achieve global dominance through successful marketing and support, not because it is the best written software adjudged by universalist criteria such as design, economy, task fulfilment and generative capacity. By this argument, the singular breakthrough to modernity contains within it shortcomings traceable to the point of origination.

Modernity is a singular and, in part, vitiating event. This is not a happy place to leave the argument. If Weber has got the causation wrong or exaggerated it (as I think he did), we can vacate it; also it is not a wholly convincing argument to say that the circumstances of origination are determinative for future situations. Changes in the causal model can produce more benign outcomes.

The bias of communication

In this section, I will discuss the economic historian, Harold Innis. His work impacts upon Weber's concept of worldview and suggests that Weber was right to stress its importance, but that he remained unaware of the dimensions of its operation. Innis made no direct comment about Weber. He established his reputation with the *Fur Trade in Canada* and *The Cod Fisheries*.[2] Although these studies appeared specialist and seemingly localist in emphasis, Innis was able to show the penetrative effects of commodity trading on the development of a society. Also, the localism is misleading. The main fur trading company in Canada was the Hudson Bay Company, a capitalist concern whose headquarters were in London. The company was effectively run from London through a continuous supply of trading reports from the bases on and around Hudson Bay. And from Hudson Bay itself, there existed precarious lines of communications to the trappers of the interior. That this business was conducted as a capitalistic enterprise was taken for granted by Innis. The novel question for Innis was how did it operate, and this led him to consider not just the extensiveness of trading routes but the lines of communication themselves as an enabling precondition. Hence, the question is not one of where did capitalism come from and develop into (which, in a sense, was the German 'Fragestellung' of Marx, Rodbertus, Bücher, Sombart and Weber), but how was it enabled through the media of communication?

Harold Innis, in *Empire and Communications* (first edition, Oxford, 1950), put forward the bold hypothesis that the political systems of empires and kingdoms were conditioned by their medium of communication. Where writing is restricted to the media of clay and parchment, i.e. durable but heavy media, then an emphasis is placed on time, hierarchy and decentralization. The materials of writing themselves place a cognitive emphasis on the permanence of what is written and place physical limitations on the transmission of written material. When writing moves to the less durable materials of papyrus and paper, political systems gain an extension over space and experience a reduction in hierarchy and an increase in centralization. Writing in durable media such as stone (lithographs) and clay, such as the monuments of dynasties, seeks to emphasize the everlasting longevity of rulership. Examples of this type are Sumerian civilization c. 3000 BC and the Old Kingdom of Egypt c. 2700 BC. Papyrus is produced in restricted areas under centralized control to meet the demands of a centralized bureaucratic administration, and is limited to the smooth waters of navigation because of its fragile state. Roman rulership is the major example of a political system based on papyrus as a means of communication. Innis points out that both papyrus and parchment are accompanied by the monopolization of knowledge by rulers and priests. The political systems of the Near East and the Mediterranean world of antiquity were profoundly affected by the emergence of papyrus and the associated development of alphabets.

Innis presents a model of what Robert Bellah terms archaic kingdoms.[3] Their political capacities of rulership are determined by the availability of media of communication. The historical record is more ambiguous in classifying centralized versus decentralized rulership in terms of light versus heavy media of communication. What is important in modelling is not historical veracity but providing ways of thinking and being able to understand the limitations of rulership in eras of restricted means of communication. Weber would have designated the Innis thesis an ideal type. What he would not have appreciated, however, is that the meaningful content of messages – which for Weber is the primary datum – is itself determined by its medium. Marshall McLuhan, at one point a junior colleague of Innis at the University of Toronto, rather overemphasized the point through his aphorism, 'the medium is the message'. One modality of change in archaic kingdoms is the switch from stone and clay to papyrus. A change in technology alters the content of messages.

In late medieval Europe, to which I now turn, the major switch is from parchment to paper. A series of events – the importing of paper from China, its manufacture in Europe, the breaking of monopolies of paper production – and the parallel history of printing (the movement of small workshops from Gutenberg in 1450 across Europe, the switch from manuscript uncials to the roman, gothic and italic fonts, and the evasion of censorship) – underwrite the key developments in early modernity: vernacular languages, the breaking of religious and priestly monopolies, the formation of recognizably modern polities, the formation of self-regulating political communities – albeit only fleetingly in Scotland, Geneva, England and the Low Countries – and the ability to transmit financial information and financial assets as a basis for the formation of markets. Paper, quickly followed by the introduction of printing, allowed a massive leap in extension over a number of fields: political administration, economic markets, religious and humanistic sensibility and learning – both literature and science.

This suggests that explanations of modernity should be sought in emergent universalisms taking the place of static particularisms. As Tenbruck emphasized, world religions for Weber represent a cognitive leap forward in the movement to more universalizing worldviews. What Innis brings to the debate, however, is an argument rooted in the materiality of knowledge transmission. Obviously, he has to acknowledge, like Comte and Weber, the crucial move from magic to religions of the world based on sacred revelation. In Weber's view, magic has no inherent logic because it is based on things or objects: stars, rivers, stones, patterns, mysteries and their divination. For Innis, with the advent of writing, 'man is provided with transpersonal memory'. 'Men were given an artificially extended and verifiable memory of objects and events not present to sight and recollection.'[4]

It is instructive to reassemble Weber's PESC along the lines of Innis' argument, not least because it provides a way of seeing how Weber assembled his own argument. In what follows, my own argumentation is schematic. I use Innis' hypothesis as a heuristic in order to probe the threads of Weber's own arguments in PESC.

Weber's periodization can be construed as follows:

1   medieval monasticism as orders of a world-escaping asceticism;
2   Calvinism and the Puritan sects where the monkish attitude is released into the world as inner-worldly asceticism.

In the next section, I develop a number of points through the expedient of inserting Innis' hypothesis into the above periodization. Accordingly, the two periods become:

1   Monasticism, most notably Benedictine monasticism, is a form of asceticism whose most important accomplishment is the production of

hand-written manuscripts. These writings are devoted to a particular conception of time. Just as the pyramids stood for the conceit that the dynasts live forever, so the copying of the religious texts becomes a way of asserting that the word of God is eternal. Enormous amounts of intellectual, human and economic capital are poured into copying the sacred texts in a variety of fairly complex manuscript styles. The earliest existing Bibles are the wealth equivalents of medieval cathedrals – the Codex Argenteus (in Carolina Redivina in Uppsala) and the Codex Amiatinus, which was produced in Jarrow in Northumbria. The latter took the skins of over 1500 calves and required numerous copyists – strong men pushing the quill across the vellum for six hours a day and dependent on the intellectual resources of the 'armarium' and 'scriptorium'. It was Cassiodorus in his *Institutiones divinarum lectionum* who created, in AD 531 in his monastic foundation at Vivarium, a scheme of study for monks and provided an account of the methods and techniques of transcription. Innis notes that Cassiodorus completed the work of St Benedict 'by making the writing of books and the preservation of authors a sacred duty and an act of piety'.[5] It was as a result of these developments that the Codex Amiatinus emerged from Jarrow around AD 700.

While it is quite correct to attribute to this monastic labour the transmission of the Bible, the early church fathers and classical authors of Greece and Rome, indeed the preservation of literacy and the alphabet itself, seen as a *medium*, the monastic manuscript was highly restricted. Manuscript Bibles were the monuments of the 'Dark Ages' and, in this sense, they were meant to be revered rather than read. Transmission was confined to the perpetual task of copying; also, what was copied and what was read were subject to tight control and censorship. Hand-written script encourages conservatism as well as conservation. Extension over space – the potentiality within a rationalized alphabet – was limited by the huge resource that went into writing and the sheer weight of parchment (the Codex Amiatinus weighs over 70 lbs, consists of 1030 folios, is ten inches thick and measures 14 by 20 inches). These manuscripts were monuments of the word and, in this respect, they memorialized sacred revelation over time – for all time. The monastic escape from the world signified not only a break with the rest of the world spatially but an entirely different conception of time. While the secular world was defined by its (worthless) transience, the monastic world was based on the illusion that time, through the memorialization of the word, would be eternal.

With the transfer of Abbot Alcuin from York to Aachen in AD 781, Charlemagne became the first medieval ruler to realize the potentiality of the vector of space. The Carolingian miniscule (rationalized at Corbie in Northumbria) and parchment became, as capitularies, the medium of political administration in Europe's first medieval empire. Patrimonialism is not solely defined by dependency relationships within the 'Herrschaftsverband', but also through its media of communication. Writing comes out of the cloister, but only as the new medium that gives extension to political rulership. Within the cloister and the cathedral, the latent power of extension within a reasonably rationalized form of writing remains deliberately confined. Political time is temporality and marked by contingency. Monastic time, other than the daily round, never moves.

2   Weber prefaces his account of the Puritan movement with the path-breaking role of Luther in triggering the Reformation. For Innis, a crucial episode was Erasmus' version of the Greek Testament in 1516, printed by the Basle printer John Froben. Erasmus' desire was that the scriptures be translated into every language, 'that the husbandman should say them to himself as he follows the plough, that the weaver should hum them to the tune of his shuttle, that the traveller should beguile with them the weariness of his journey'.[6] Innis quotes approvingly Mark Pattison's remark that this 'contributed more to the liberation of the human mind from the thraldom of the clergy than all the uproar and rage of Luther's many pamphlets'.[7] Innis would place the stress on the emergence of printed Bibles and pamphlets. What is significant about Luther's 95 theses pinned to the church door at Wittenberg in 1517 is that they were quickly printed and widely distributed. Like the Internet, the new medium of paper and printing for a while evaded censorship and made information available to a new audience.

The move from asceticism in the monastery and the cathedral cloister to an asceticism pursued in the world, by the Puritans, is the move from a parchment-based scripture to a paper-based press. Both remain sacred, but the medium, let us say, enables the message. Parchment does not travel, it is not meant to, it stays within the monastic house. The Tyndale Bible (1525) belongs to a new medium: paper, print, vernacular language. It is one of the first 'handy' Bibles, in its octavo format literally fitting into the palm of a man's hand. It marked the breaking of a large number of monopolies: paper production, the control of printing presses, the monopoly of the Church and monasteries over the sacred scriptures and the breaking of Latin and Greek 'codes' through translation into vernacular languages. The Tyndale Bible is contemporary with the Luther Bible of 1522, the Czech Bible of 1488, the Dutch Bible of 1526, the French Bible of 1530, the Swedish Bible of 1541, the Finnish New Testament of 1548 and the Danish Bible of 1550.

The pietistic attitude of the Puritan to the text only becomes possible when the text itself is placed in a transmittable medium. Bibles, prayer books, sermons, etc. become permanently accessible to a newly literate society. These few books are learnt by heart, are the constant companion of religious groups and form the bases of the fanaticism of the conventicles. To know your Bible, in one's vernacular language, makes possible literacy and defines its limits. Everything is to be found within the book – morality, practical guidance, faith obviously, but also politics and economics or house-holding. The Bible took popular culture from orality to literacy. The Bible was the iPod of its day, thumbed and pored over by its enthusiastic users. It is of course a complex history with countless setbacks lasting over more than two hundred years. But its basis was paper, the printing press and written vernacular languages.

Of the new literacy generated by the printed English Bible, Adam Nicolson has recently written: 'This increasingly word-orientated section of the population was the seed-bed in which the highly intellectual, questioning and quizzing form of religion we know as Puritanism has its beginnings. A puritan ate and drank the word of God. That word was his world.'[8] And of the King James Bible, he writes: 'If you think of the King James Bible as the greatest creation of the seventeenth century, a culture drenched in the word rather than the image, it is easy to see it as England's equivalent of the great baroque cathedral it never built, an enormous and magnificent verbal artifice, its huge structures embracing all four million Englishmen, its orderliness and richness a kind of national shrine built only of words.'[9] Panegyric aside, the established medium of print becomes the cognitive and material basis for the differentiation process of the increasing separation of Church, state, moral-ity and learning that enables the development of modernity in Europe.

Obviously the 'rewrite' I have suggested above – that monastic asceticism be regarded in terms of the vector of time, that the new Puritan sensibility be thought of as an extension over space – gives us a different book from PESC. Weber does not seem to have given serious attention to the medium of transmission. He more or less takes the extreme textuality of ascetic Prot-estantism as a given without comment. In his treatment of Methodism, We-ber establishes the centrality of a revived Puritanism for the new industrial working classes. But it only takes a slight nudge to move his whole treatment of the role of revivalist religion into a movement of mass literacy. Method-ism was not only methodical with its rotas of preaching, but also positively industrial in its attitude to printing the sacred texts, their dissemination and the insistence on literacy. If the word is to be made known to the unlettered working class, literacy as well as preaching is essential. And Weber's whole argument in Chapter 4 on Calvinism and the Puritan sects is to demonstrate the intensity of belief translated into practical ethics. Overall, he weights his argument towards the psychology of belief: the factors that intensified and sustained belief as a continuous practice. But if we reweight the argument, it is the profound literacy and textuality of the Puritan divines that might be considered the medium of instruction. Jean Calvin's huge influence can be seen in the translation of the Bible into French by his kinsman Pierre Robert Olivétan, and the near simultaneous publication of his own *Institution de la religion chrétienne* (1540) in both Latin and French; Latin to influence the traditional authorities of Church, state and schoolmen, French to ap-peal to the new mass constituency. Likewise, as Weber himself reprises his arguments at the start of Chapter 5, practical ethics take their literal cues from Richard Baxter's *Christian Directory* (for English Puritans), Spener's *Theologische Bedenken* (German Pietists) and Barclay's *Apology* for Baptists (PESC, p. 156). Gangolf Hübinger has pointed out to me that Weber may well have been reluctant to explore the world of print because it was taken up by Karl Lamprecht, whose work he detested, as a research theme.

The materiality of the medium of communication ensures that ideas cannot be treated as free-floating suppositions loosely connected to the materiality of power and interests. It was this critique that Weber struggled with, continuously and angrily, as his answers to the critiques of Rachfahl, Fischer and Sombart demonstrate. Weber vehemently protested that his interpretation was not a one-sided idealist account that challenged the equally one-sided materialist–marxist account for the rise of western capitalism. But, until he came up with a satisfactory methodological way of treating ideas sociologically, which the neo-Kantian perspective of 1904 did not offer, then his thesis was always a legitimate object of attack from the materialist viewpoint. The weaknesses were not rectified until the 'Einleitung' essay of 1914, which advanced the concept of ideal interests as the equivalent of material interests. By this device, Weber ensured that ideas were no longer philosophical and theological notions, but objects of competition and power and so embedded within social structure.[10] With Innis, we encounter the materiality of the media themselves, an approach completely different from Weber's solution.

Innis himself did not deal directly with the question of how modernity originated but, clearly, he would have reserved a large role for the new medium of paper, press and vernacular that gave a hitherto immense extension to politics, religion, economics, learning, literature and science. Once the extension of paper and print is seeded into these separate fields, then an internal dynamic can proceed within each field. In those civilizations which either never develop writing as a medium extendable to the majority of a society's population or suppress and censor paper and press, then this would effectively bar the development of anything recognizable as modernity. 'Limited supplies of satisfactory writing material in India strengthened the monopoly of the oral tradition held by the Brahmans . . .', 'The bias of paper as a medium was evident in China with its bureaucratic administration developed in relation to the demands of space.' But, given the complexity of Chinese characters, printing was easily controlled as a government monopoly (p. 139). 'In areas dominated by Mohammedanism', Innis notes 'abhorrence of the image delayed the introduction of printing' (p. 165).[11]

In Innis' discussion of the bias of communication in early modernity – as the emergence of the printing press and paper as the new extendable medium – there is also a concern with the *content* of these writings. This content can be characterized as humanistic: primarily Erasmus' intent that Everyman should be able to read and learn the scriptures in their own language and that this would form the basis of a new pedagogy free of the scholasticism of the medieval schoolmen, but also embracing the claim that reason and nature were not incompatible; that induction and experiment were the new mode of science replacing the Aristotelian worldview; that philosophy would proceed by the example of Descartes – his *Meditations*, a book to be read from beginning to end without the countless and repetitive recourse to holy writ and scholastics; the philosophical anthropology of Montaigne that discussed the human, quotidian condition in a language accessible to 'l'homme moyen sensuel'; that political community could be thought about in an increasingly secular and rational manner as in Machiavelli, Pufendorf and Althusius.

This last paragraph raises issues of content and meaning. It is part of the standard history of humanism as contributory to the development of key features of western civilization and modernity. Science, education, philosophy, everyday life and its understanding, and politics belong to the print revolution and the emergence of a literate and humanistic sensibility. The ability to communicate, and to break the monopoly of writing, is causative for a decisive stage in European history. Although the stern rigours of Puritanism and the reactionary features of the counter-Reformation would slow and alter the humanist breakthrough, the decisive development lay in the vast increase in communicative capacity.

Innis does not address the matter of Puritan conduct of life on economic behaviour and, for Weber, the decisive changes in the economies of northwest Europe. Trevor-Roper has, however, put forward an argument that accommodates the economic side of the question. Like Innis, he places emphasis on the expansion of humanist knowledge, and he argues that this outlook characterized the economically sophisticated merchants of southern Europe and leading Italian cities.[12] In the counter-Reformation, the Papacy insisted on strict doctrinal purity and was intolerant of humanism. As a result, there was a middle class migration northwards to the more tolerant societies of Holland and England, which were also Protestant. The economic migrants adopted Calvinism as their religion, but practised it in a tolerant undogmatic way. It was Erasmian Christian humanism that determined their conduct of life, and their leading economic role derived from the advances in banking, finance, industry and trade that marked out some of the Italian and south German cities. This is not the place to rehearse and argue the details of the argument – not an easy one: how Calvinist were certain Calvinists?

What Innis' approach reveals is that worldviews require not just carriers in a sociological sense of social groups, but that the cognitive aspects of worldviews require a technology for their dissemination and that the interaction between medium and message creates the revolutionary effect. Weber would not have denied the historical facts concerning the breaking of the monopoly of writing. It was a given in his argument but, as such, neutral in its implication. It would also be open to him to retort that Puritan ideas displaced Erasmian ideas, and the former were the ultimate beneficiaries of the print revolution. The point to note from this is that an alteration in the causal origins and mechanisms results in different meanings being highlighted whose historical significance carries a different message.

Multiple modernities

Karl Jaspers, a younger colleague and friend of Weber's in Heidelberg, introduced the concept of the axial age in his book *The Origin and Goal of History*, first published in 1949. This offered a schematic overview of the development of civilizations throughout history and prehistory – from the origins of humankind to its future in one global world. As a philosopher, writing for a lay audience, his intention was to indicate that humankind belonged together from its earliest origins to its future purpose. He was pleading for common human consciousness in the light of the known past and, as such, he can be considered an early proponent of the global age. Jaspers sketched out four levels of civilization: (1) prehistory; (2) the ancient high civilizations of Egypt, Mesopotamia, the Indus and Hwang-ho; (3) the axial age in the east and west and China and India; and (4) the scientific and technological age in Europe, North America and Russia.

The axial age is when

> for all countries ('Völker') a common framework of historical self-understanding has arisen. This axis in world history would appear to have occurred around 500 years before Christ . . . it is here there occurs the deepest break in history. It was here that the human being with whom we live today originated. This period is to be termed, in brief, the 'axial age'. The extraordinary came together concentrated into a period of time. It was the time Confucius and Lao-Tse lived and all the directions of Chinese philosophy began and Mozi, Zhuangzi, Lie-Tsi and countless others worked; in India the Upanishads originated, Buddha lived, and, as in China, all the philosophical possibilities from scepticism, to materialism to the sophists and to nihilism were developed; in Iran Zoroaster taught the challenging worldview of the struggle between good and evil; in Palestine the prophets appeared from Elijah to Isaiah and Jeremiah and Deutero-Isaiah; Greece produced Homer, the philosophers – Parmenides, Heraclitus, Plato, the tragedians, Thucydides, and Archimedes. Everything that these names indicate arose in these few centuries almost simultaneously in China, India and the Occident without any awareness of each other.[13]

It is in this period that, for the first time, the human being becomes aware of human existence itself and the limits of human existence. There occurs the first consciousness of what the world is capable of and the powerlessness of the individual, and of emancipation and salvation. This consciousness implies reflection, that thinking can be directed to thinking itself; also that spiritual ('geistige') conflict begins with the attempt to persuade others through communication of ideas, reasons, experiences. This intellectual conflict and the breaking up of the previously unconsidered viewpoints and customs into opposing camps brought intellectual chaos. Out of this chaos were created the fundamental categories of thought, and in which we still think. These were the basis of the world religions. 'In every sense a step was taken into the universal.' The axial replaced the mythical age. The prophets and philosophers began a fight 'against the mythical from the side of rationality and of rationally explained experience (of Logos and against Mythos); further, a fight for the transcendence of one god against demons . . . and a fight against false figures of gods driven by ethical indignation.'[14] Jaspers writes that this change in human existence can be termed one of intellectualization/spiritualization ('Vergeistigung'). Human beings can ask questions they never asked before. It is the age of the philosophers, by which Jaspers means the wandering thinker in China, ascetics in India, philosophers in ancient Greece, prophets in Israel. What they have in common, despite substantive differences, is the ability to think within themselves and place human existence with its mental, corporal and instinctual attributes in opposition to the world. This gives rise to the discourses and practices of ataraxia, meditation, the consciousness of Atman, or Nirvana, harmony with Tao, or in submission to the will of God. The axial age is the (first) time that revelations can be announced ('Offenbarwerden'), which later become the ideas of reason ('Vernunft') and individuality ('Persönlichkeit'). Because there is a consciousness of the human being's position in the world – that there is a gulf rather than an unreflexive oneness between the individual and nature – the idea of the individual as a person appears.

This is obviously broad-brush philosophy attuned to the large question of what has defined our sense of common humanity. It can hardly be said to be an advance on the academic study of religion at the beginning of the twentieth century, which insisted on not intellectualizing other cultures, and which had great difficulty in separating out just what distinguished magic, cult and religion and the nature of their dynamics. Although Max Weber might have been flattered that Jaspers made such productive use of his work on world religions, he would surely have queried the divide between, essentially, the philosophical and the prephilosophical as an era-defining category. But then Weber had not experienced the shattering impact of science in the service of war and the dropping of nuclear bombs on Hiroshima and Nagasaki. Jaspers, quite rightly, was a worried man, and his book is an assertion of the common origin and destiny of humankind – a sentiment not in the foreground of Weber's thought. The validity of Jaspers' thesis still requires assent by those not in the German philosophical tradition – by scholars in China, India, Persia and so on. Modern 'Offenbarwerden' will be both declaration and dialogue.

These very pertinent issues aside, Jaspers makes an observation that escaped Weber, who was preoccupied by the differences between world religions even though he perfectly understood the move from magic to revelation. Each of the world religions, for Weber, has a directional potentiality – the switchman image. This potentiality itself is what Jaspers grasps. A new dynamic is introduced into world history by the philosophical attitude itself, and this is more important to understand than the actual developmental paths influenced by the world religions. The implication of Jaspers' thesis is that modernity is not to be tied down to a specific working out of the claims of redemption and action in the world, as occurred in the Puritan revolution, but the impulse to modernity is part of a wider axis in world history where the tensions between human existence in the world and the superempirical or transcendental framing of that existence lead to new ambitions. How the challenges of thinking about and, in part, resolving these tensions would be specific to the different world religions and their societal context – a matter that Jaspers did not enter into. But for Jaspers, all the world religions and their civilizations are in their different ways harbingers of modernity.

S.N. Eisenstadt and others have drawn the conclusion from this that modernity is not singular to the Puritan revolution in north-west Europe, but should be thought of as multiple. Eisenstadt states his thesis thus:

> The conception of Multiple Modernities entails the view that although obviously the first modernity developed in the West, in Europe, and that this modernity was presented by its bearers as the 'natural' modernity and was for long periods of time often conceived in this way also by many groups in other societies, yet in fact from the very beginning of the modern era there developed throughout the world, with the expansion of modernity, distinct patterns of modernization and of converging indus- tries- the European or Western pattern need not be repeated elsewhere, especially as these later modernities were no longer 'first' modernities and developed already in periods and situations in which European and later Western modernities were already fully established and acquired a hegemonic status in the new, modern, international systems.[15]

One implication of the Jaspers' thesis is that modernity could have origi- nated in China or India, or in an Islamic country. The classical historian Arnoldo Momigliano articulates this far wider set of possibilities. He dates the axial age to between 600 and 300 BC (not 800 to 200, which was Jaspers' dating) and writes,

> It has become a commonplace, after Karl Jaspers's *Vom Ursprung und Ziel der Geschichte* – the first original book on history to appear in post- war Germany in 1949 – to speak of the *Achsenzeit*, of the axial age, which includes the China of Confucius and Lao-Tse, the India of Bud- dha, the Iran of Zoroaster, the Palestine of the Prophets and the Greece of the philosopher, the tragedians and the historians. There is a very real element of truth in this formulation. All these civilizations display literacy, complex political organization combining central government and local authorities, elaborate town-planning, advanced metal technol- ogy and the practice of international diplomacy. In all these civilizations there is a profound tension between political powers and intellectual

movements. Everywhere one notices attempts to introduce greater purity, greater justice, greater perfection and a more universal explanation of things. New models, either mystically or prophetically or rationally apprehended, are propounded as a criticism of, and alternative to, the prevailing models. We are in the age of criticism.[16]

In Eisenstadt's extensive writings, this is an inference that is never ruled out and, certainly, in the construction of other non-western modernities, different philosophical heritages are drawn upon. With Weber, they are ruled out by his methodological approach. In his studies of China or India, or Islam, he always makes statements along the lines that capitalism, markets, finance, trade, law and technology existed in these civilizations. But the switchman intervenes in conjunction with the particular dynamics of interests, so that inevitably no rational capitalistic modernity could emerge. Confucianism was so adjusted to the world that it regarded with distaste any transcendental idea (which was the basis of the Christian transformation of the social world according to an ethical vision of what a god decreed). Hinduism had a superempirical vision, but its conduct of life led in the direction of contemplation and the lessening of the pain between earthly life and a life beyond, i.e. in the direction of apathy. The era of world religions for Weber offers the possibility of complex outcomes, but only one of these produces modernity – which happens for a series of identifiable reasons to occur in the west. Hence, the commonality of world religions as offering sophisticated accounts of humankind's relation to the universe, and being able to conceptualize such a thing, is the basis of difference in their actual developmental paths. Accordingly, modernity is singular to the west. In the Protestant ethic studies of 1905, Weber draws this singularity in narrow terms – Calvinism and the Puritan sects. It could not have happened elsewhere and, if it did, we would not be calling it modernity; rather The Way, The Umman or The Garden, perhaps.

The issue for Eisenstadt is that modernity is realized in a number of institutional, ideological and individual–state relationship formats. Modern twentieth-century societies exhibited a great variety: western European societies differ from British society, just as American society is different from Japanese. And Russia and the eastern bloc offered an alternative solution to modernity, and so on. Modernity, in this reading, is an inherently divergent phenomenon not a convergent one, as some argued in the 1950s – that modernization across the world would occur as a replication of the institutions, structures and values of the United States.

Tracking the developmental paths of diverging modernities is a major academic industry in comparative historical sociology, all registering various allegiance to Max Weber's writings. The multiple versus singular question still arises here, however. If one traces the various divergent developmental strands back in time, do they have a common origin, root or theme? Is there a singularity that originates this complex called modernity, and then unfurls outwards in different trajectories? Or is modernity a multiple birth phenomenon?

I take the Eisenstadt school to be saying the latter (and I take Weber to be saying the former). Eisenstadt is a modernization theorist, not the Parsonian AGIL convergent model, but a differentiation model that produces divergence in its formation. Speaking of developments in societies after 1945, Eisenstadt writes: 'While a general trend toward structural differentiation developed across a wide range of institutions in most of these societies – in family life, economic and political structures, urbanization, modern education, mass communication, and individualistic orientations . . . this gives rise to multiple institutional and ideological patterns.'[17] The same manner of argument would seem to apply to early modernity. In a chapter with obvious homage to Weber. 'The Sectarian Origins of Modernity', Eisenstadt outlines the start of modernity as an institutionalization of value positions. Those value positions belonged in the sphere of religion and were marked by conflict as to how a transcendental vision, such as redemption, was to be realized in the world.

> . . . the implementation of such visions constituted an inherent part of their institutionalization in the Axial civilizations. Historically such process of institutionalization of transcendental visions was never a simple peaceful one, it was usually connected with a continuous struggle and competition between many groups and between their respective visions. Because of this multiplicity of visions, no single one could be taken as given or complete. Once the conception of a basic tension between the transcendental and the mundane order was institutionalized in a society, or at least within its center, it became itself very problematic. Thus the very process of such institutionalization generated the possibility of different emphases, directions and interpretations of the transcendental visions.[18]

Institutionalization is a conflictual process of resolution – in his words, it 'crystallizes' the tensions in an institutional outcome. Without the crystallization, the axial age would remain in a state of chaos. Institutionalization operates across a number a dimensions. There is a political–religious struggle as to how transcendental visions are to be realized in the world. For example, the foundation of Buddhism was reliant on the huge support of King Ashoka, Christianity to the conversion of the Roman Emperor Constantine. Within the realm of doctrine and philosophy, revelation is tempered to an extent by reason, the latter providing the capacity of reflexivity, of being able to consider critically what in a religious sense is beyond question. Transcendental visions raise profound questions of how an ethical or godly order will be created in the mundane world. Christian theorists referred to this as realizing the Kingdom of God on earth (or, in Troeltsch's terms, reconciling sacred law with profane law). Various 'social contracts' seek to regulate the mundane life and its tendency to anarchy and selfishness with the vision of what a godly order should be like.

'The cultural program of modernity entailed a very distinct shift in the conception of human agency of its autonomy, and of its place in the flow of time'. Again, this is resolved through institutionalization. The English historian R.H. Tawney saw the developments in English society from the fifteenth to the eighteenth centuries as one of the Church, supported by the crown, moving away from the insistence that the community was the 'summum bonum' to one in which the individual, as an economic agent in his own right, could pursue his own ends.[19] The acquisition of wealth could become legitimate activity in a way, as the medieval church said, 'is not pleasing to God'. Agency – the idea that men can make their own fortune, or even that they might make their own history – is a new awareness that becomes internalized into political and economic arrangements. How agency, reason, revelation and transcendence are institutionalized is country specific. Liah Greenfeld's *Nationalism: Five Roads to Modernity* demonstrates this extensively by itemizing the differential experiences of England, France, Russia, Germany and the United States. For her, how national communities are formed and constituted in early modernity (not the nineteenth century as the title might seem to imply) is the crucial ground on which the tensions of the axial age are resolved.

Enough has been outlined about the multiple modernities position to show that the origination process throws up diversity. It is an institutional differentiation process that 'crystallizes' values that are intrinsically not resolvable in themselves. This I do not think can be claimed as Max Weberian, at least not directly. Values do not crystallize in institutional formats for Weber. They can become routinized through institutional carriers. Values here, while no longer vibrant and pristine, still belong to individuals and groups. Weber's nominalism has it that institutions do not speak for the individual, although they may well influence the individual's outlook. Crystallization takes actually held values of individuals and renders them second-order phenomena at the level of institutions. This is a separation that Weber never undertakes. His separation is between value spheres and their inevitable existential conflicts for people, such as Cromwell, who have two masters (God and politics); and his resolution is through conduct of life as a practice of life and so always an existential choice.

Of course, this does not mean that Weber is right and Eisenstadt wrong. It is far more agreeable to follow Eisenstadt because a condition of modernity in its inception is the capacity of agency, of controlling one's own destiny and the directionality of society. In politics, this reached a new high point in the English revolution of the seventeenth century, of self in the Renaissance, of society in the ideas of the Enlightenment. Eisenstadt is also quite explicit that modernity has a prodigious capacity for going wrong and for violence. This is a very long chapter, which I will not relate. But agency and renewal are linked together in Eisenstadt's account. Societies have the capacity to reform themselves politically and socially and to escape their episodes of blood-letting.

Weber regarded agency and reflexivity (to use Eisenstadt's terms) less benignly. European societies did not choose to be modern. Instead, they chose and struggled to be Puritan or some other religious denomination. English Puritans had a life conduct constructed to maintain piety, not to give birth to money-making machines. Weber's vision of reform, or routinization of values, or control, and of violence, and of ethical dehumanization is far darker. Modernity arose through the honouring of an absent god, and rationalism was an unstoppable and unceasing effort of religious intellectuals to introduce consistency and order into irrational metaphysical revelation and what were taken by intellectuals to be its assumptions. Reflexivity was not a term used by Weber and, although intellectuals are involved in reflective activity, this has an internal dynamic all of its own ('Eigengesetzlichkeit') that would exclude 'second-order reflexivity'.

A highly relevant part of the debate over modernity is its relation to a globalizing world. Eisenstadt and others have quite rightly given this due attention: 'one of the most important implications of the term "multiple modernities" is that modernity and Westernization are not identical; Western patterns of modernity are not the only "authentic" modernities, though they enjoy historical precedence and continue to be a basic reference point for others.' The history of modernity, for Eisenstadt,

> is a story of continual constitution and reconstitution of a multiplicity of cultural programs. These ongoing reconstructions of multiple institutional and ideological patterns are carried forward by specific social actors in close connection with social, political, and intellectual activists, and also by social movements pursuing different programs of modernity, holding very different views on what makes societies modern.[20]

During the twentieth century, this has produced nation states differing through their cultural and ethnic traditions, fascism and communism, as well as new nationalist movements in the Third World. What makes these different regimes modern is their reference to the forces that had created the original modernity. In a global world, there is an attempt to appropriate modernity by societies on their own terms, 'to appropriate the new international global scene and the modernity for themselves for their traditions of "civilizations" – as they were continually promulgated and reconstructed under the impact of their continual encounter with the West'.[21] Modernity for Eisenstadt is the ability of leading groups to confer agency on societal development, and this is no longer seen as a western monopoly.

In the case of India, Eisenstadt quotes Myron Weiner:

> The classical conceptions of the state and the political order were closely linked to basic concepts around which society was organized – notions

concerning equality and hierarchy, rights and duties, the individual's place in the community and the relationship between the community and authority. The introduction of European institutions and political concepts notwithstanding, India continues to retain a social order that is very different from the one upon which European political institutions were built. Moreover, many of the beliefs that underlie this social order remain intact. The result is not that Indian political institutions do not or cannot work, as some of its critics suggest, but that they work differently . . .[22]

The introduction of modern institutions of government, civil service, democracy and political parties has reflected the immense linguistic, ethnic and social stratification of the country. Governments have tended to be grand coalitions representative of religious and linguistic groups, cultural autonomy has been upheld – as opposed to the homogenizing imperative in western national states – and minority rights are guaranteed. The working through of a modern political system downwards through the mass of the people has been an intricate, gradual and pragmatic process involving the charismatic–ascetic movement of Gandhi in asserting the rights of the peasant.

This is just a snapshot, but enough to demonstrate the point that the multiple modernities concept allows that modernity itself is malleable and open to different political, cultural and religious influences. Modernity, for Eisenstadt, is practically the same as modernization. The differentiated capacity within separate institutional spheres that incorporate the crystallization of tensions within axial civilization is what makes modernity possible in the first place. In this argument, there is no singularity and no originary modernity. In the singularity argument, the actual creation of modernity is a fortuitous coming together of circumstances, driven by strong values and commitments within a dynamic of interests. Modernity as a singularity is like a great number of eschatological movements – blindly driving forwards to a superempirical goal, but more a prisoner of circumstances, even self-created ones, than controlling one's destiny.

Once modernity is seeded, then institutional patterns of law, governance, economic activity, science and education do start to perform in the way described by modernization theorists. But whether modernization can be extrapolated backwards to explain the singular event itself has to be queried. How values and interest positions are crystallized out of what Jaspers termed the 'chaos' of the axial age presents a problem of how order (modernization patterns) emerges from chaos. Robert Bellah writes of axial 'breakthroughs', '. . . there is no clear indication of the causal relation of these changes to the emergence of strikingly new cultural–religious formations'.[23] Modernization theory places the emphasis on the variety of outcomes and the complexity of process. Weber remained preoccupied with the causal question: why here in the west and not elsewhere? It is not implausible to see his work as an attempt to answer this question without ever being able to achieve closure of it.

Does this argument between singularity and multiple modernities matter? Clearly, by the seventeenth and eighteenth centuries in Europe and North America, patterns of modernization can be discerned and, although subject to wide-ranging academic debate as to the exact shape, the general movement of law, economy, government, society and culture is unmistakable. Weber is not terribly helpful here in his writings, in that having gone into the origins of the event – capitalist modernity and a rationalistic culture – he displayed no great interest in tracking its subsequent history. Likewise, in his brief remarks on how capitalist modernity would spread internationally, he simply notes that China in 1910 was well on the way to embracing capitalism, and that, in India, the caste system would disappear under the impact of nationalism.[24] What we want to know from Weber is whether he thought that capitalism in China was simply going to replicate, say, nineteenth-century British capitalism, and whether – as he does seem to imply – a modern movement such as nationalism would have a levelling effect on India's heterogeneous social structure.

'Prefatory Remarks' to the 'Collected Essays in the Sociology of Religion'

The ideas of singularity are most pronounced in PESC 1904–5, not least because, of all his religious studies, it has the closest historical focus. But the same insistence on how distinctive Puritanism was, and its impact upon occidental development, can be found in the well-known comparison between Confucianism and Puritanism. This was the last chapter of his 'Religion of China', which as we know was revised for publication in his 'Collected Essays on the Sociology of Religion'. The whole programme of the study of the economic ethics of the world religions was undertaken to discover the uniqueness of Christianity (including its Judaic heritage) on western development. His comparative studies cannot be criticized for a falsely construed image of 'the Orient' as an idealized other – in the way, for example, Edward Said has shown how a literary image of the Orient has been created by western writers and artists. Weber charts the differences at the level of religion, social structure and politics. He may have made scholarly mistakes and been dependent on unreliable sources, as he himself admitted. But his comparative studies establish the internal and external reasons for the separateness of the world religions and the effects on their corresponding societies.

When it came to the publication of his 'Collected Essays on the Sociology of Religion' in 1920, Weber was faced with the task of writing a preface that would link the original Protestant ethic studies of 1904 and 1905 with his studies of the economic ethics of the world religions. The same causal model is offered up for both the world religions and the Protestant ethic studies. Religious ideas as well as magic impact upon the practical conduct of life, and this has consequences for economic life and for prevailing social structures. The Protestant ethic exemplifies the positive causal factors; the other world religions flag up the 'spiritual obstacles' to the development of rational economic conduct (pp. 26–7). The world religions are only studied from the viewpoint of how they differ from the situation in the Occident. This enables the unique causal factors of the Occident to be better understood in terms of their distinctiveness. Weber uses a series of words here: 'eigentumlich', 'Eigenarten' and just plain 'eigen'. Parsons translates these as peculiar or peculiarities. My preference is for 'distinctive' or 'distinctiveness'. But the overall sense of what Weber is trying to capture is that the development of the Occident is something 'sui generis' to a whole culture – it was unique to itself.

The 'Prefatory Remarks' (termed 'Author's Introduction' by Talcott Parsons) introduce a change in tone and a change of argument. His preface alters the terms of comparison from why and how the Occident is different, to its being different 'tout court'. Throughout his studies, he had been creating platforms on which to analyse difference: Calvinism against Lutheranism, magic against religion, Confucianism against Islam, the western city against the city in patrimonial regimes. Each comparison could throw up possible causal factors that had meaningful consequences. Lutheranism was accommodating to the world, Calvinism was not – it was inherently radical in all its dealings with the world. Magic is rational and this-worldly, religion alters the worldview and leads to behaviour orientated to obtaining salvation goods. The western city produced the social stratum of the burghers ('Bürger'), who achieved a degree of economic and jurisdictional autonomy and self-rule, whereas the Islamic merchant was subordinate to the patrimonial ruler. In saying that the west was different in its entirety, Weber was giving up a platform on which to base his comparison.

The 'Prefatory Remarks' stretches the historical timespan of the Occident, almost as if it had no beginning. Western culture or civilization is generalized over its whole extent, and it has no clearly defined starting point. Perhaps its starting point lay in Abrahamic religion 600 BC, perhaps earlier in archaic kingdoms. Throughout his writings, Weber was keen to emphasize key episodes and developments, which mark points of divergence and change: the Greeks on the plain of Palatea, St Peter in Antioch, the role of Hebrew prophets in the face of Babylonian invasion. In the 'Prefatory Remarks', Weber generalizes occidental 'Kultur' to one characteristic, rationalism.

Weber opens his 'Prefatory Remarks' by listing the various ways in which the Occident differs from other civilizations: it has science based on empirical knowledge and experimentation; its law, historiography, painting, music and architecture have a uniquely rational character; its universities and academies pursue rational and systematic science and train specialist personnel. The Occident is unique in producing the trained, specialist official, in government, business and the professions. Its politics is based on rational, written constitutions, rationally ordained law and an administration bound to rational rules and laws. Its capitalism is unique, not for its pursuit of gain, which is universal, but 'forever *renewed* profit by means of continuous, rational, capitalistic enterprise'. This continuous dynamic capitalism is based on profit calculations made possible by budgets and distinguishing profit and loss over a fixed time period in terms of capital invested. 'Only the Occident has developed capitalism both to a quantitative extent . . . in types, forms, and directions which have never existed before'. Only the Occident has developed 'the rationalistic organization of (formally) free labour', and this has been made possible by the separation of the household from the business (unlike the classical 'oikos' and the manorial household). Both bourgeoisie and proletariat are unique, because nowhere else existed 'rational organization of free labour under regular discipline'.

At this point in his preface, Weber puts the question of origins: 'We must hence ask, from *what* parts of that structure [social structure of Occident] was it [modern capitalism] derived?' His answer is the rational structures of law and administration. But he has already listed these, and they cannot claim any special originating status. Having built up his list, Weber rephrases the question: 'Why did not scientific, the artistic, the political, or the economic development there [China and India] enter upon that path of rationalization which is peculiar ('eigen') to the Occident?' (p. 25).

His answer states, 'For in all the above cases it is a question of the specific and peculiar "rationalism" of Western culture' – 'einen spezifisch gearteten "Rationalismus" der okzidentalen Kultur' (pp. 25–6).

Weber has the opportunity at this point to distinguish the culture of the Occident in terms of the philosophical validity of rationalism. It would seem to be a strong term, implying the systematic exercise of reason and intellect in relation to a world whose empirical status (epistemologically) is acknowledged. Distinctiveness could then become superiority according to criteria of validity. Ancient India developed numbers but had no systematic mathematics, China had technology but, because of magic, no grasp of the potential of science, and it was only in Greece that there developed an awareness of how concepts conferred a critical grasp of the world and man's place in it. Weber makes all these points and numerous similar ones, in his various texts, but he insists on placing rationalism in quotation marks to indicate that western rationalism should not claim any special validity.

Spelling out validity criteria would have given Weber a platform from which he could declare the distinctiveness of western rationalism. Instead, he does the opposite. He argues that all civilizations display rationalistic tendencies. Mysticism may be rationalized by its practitioners, for example. There can be rationalizations of the 'specifically irrational, just as much as there are rationalizations of economic life, or technique, of scientific research, of military training, of law and administration' (p. 26). Weber uses the concept of rationalism extensively in his writings. In his 'Introduction' to the 'Economic Ethics of the World Religions', he outlines several (interrelated) usages of the concept:

1   The increasing theoretical mastery of reality by means of increasingly precise and abstract concepts. Systematic thinkers undertake this work on (religious) worldviews.
2   The methodical attainment of a defined and given practical end by means of ever more precise calculation of the necessary means.
3   Methodical in the sense of a planned routine for achieving some end. Weber gives the example of Buddhist prayer machines – a sequence is established and has to be followed.[25]

The ends to which these rationalisms are put are not in themselves rational. Buddhist salvation goals have led to a 'rationalist' method. Puritan ideas of predestination have received intense systematization. Confucian ethics are the closest thing to the 'rationalist' ethics of utilitarianism, in that both have clear rules of what to do and what not to do. Confucianism seeks to achieve perfection and a utilitarian happiness. Neither of these ends is validated by the rationalist system itself.

The process of applying rationalism to the conduct of life, Weber's primary interest, is termed rationalization. Each of the world religions achieves high levels of rationalization, and so the determination of life conduct. There is, then, no priority given to western forms of rationalism, which is characterized by the means–end calculativity of point 2 above. Returning to 'Prefatory Remarks', Weber notes of the various areas of life,

> . . . each one of these areas may be 'rationalized' according to very different ultimate viewpoints and directions, and what is 'rational' from one point of view may well be 'irrational' from another. Hence rationalizations of the most varied character have existed in various areas of life ('Lebensgebieten') and in all areas of culture ('Kulturkreise'). To characterize their cultural–historical differences it is necessary to know what spheres are rationalized and in what direction. This then depends first of all on recognizing the particular character ('Eigenart') of occidental rationalism – and within this of modern occidental rationalism – and of explaining how it came into existence ('in ihrer Enstehung zu erklären').[26]

The last phrase in this quote indicates that the distinctiveness of western rationalism is to be sought in terms of origins. Parsons, in his translation, emphasizes this: 'to explain genetically the special peculiarity of the Occident' (p. 26). This points to a singularity argument – that there is some genetic origin in western history that seeded its peculiar (means–end) rationalism. But this is countermanded by the position that Weber had arrived at in 1920 through his extensive comparative studies. It was the whole of western history that displayed rationalism, and it becomes very difficult and extremely implausible to trace this back to one originating event. Rationalism can be dated back to the Jewish prophets of the exilic period of Israel, but this could hardly be held to account for Attic rationalism in the second century BC or for the rationalist features of Roman law. What Weber says is that, in the various spheres of life, within occidental history, rationalism is a commonality. It might have made more sense for Parsons to translate 'Enstehung' as 'memetically' – that there was a cultural 'gene' within the civilization able to replicate the occidental features of rationalism across history and in different areas of life. This is unfair on Parsons because 'meme' is a concept that was only invented by the evolutionary biologist Richard Dawkins in 1986 (in *The Selfish Gene*). It is an interestingly line of thought, because a meme is a cultural artefact and has no biological basis in sexual reproduction (and so in genetics). It may well be that societies and civilizations can socially generate cultural patterns that are enduring and replicable. This line of inquiry, in relation to Puritanism, has been initiated and developed in a series of essays by W.G. Runicman.[27]

But this takes us far beyond Weber. His summation of both world religions and Protestant ethic studies in 'Prefatory Remarks' is a statement that 'rationalism' as a modality of thought (abstract and methodical thought, consistency, calculability) is common to all world religions. His investigations would show that the content and substantive goals of rationalism are various, and that their realization within the different areas or spheres of life adds more empirical variability. World religions display distinct patterns of development by virtue of the ordering of their salvation beliefs and how these are carried into practical conduct. The spheres of life – politics, kinship, economics, art, etc. – will in their turn receive differential impacts from religion and, conversely, religion will be impacted upon by the particular dynamics of these other spheres. Comparative history is a matter of what Weber terms a 'combination of circumstances' – it is a matter of contingency. Western rationalism is contingent upon a set of circumstances, and there is no adequate or valid theory that could deliver an explanation of that set of circumstances. Hence, all that is left ultimately in comparison is the comprehension of difference.

> A child of modern European civilization will necessarily and rightly treat problems of universal history in terms of this question: [to] what combination of circumstances may the fact be attributed that in western civilization and only in it, cultural phenomena have appeared, which – nevertheless as we like to think at least – lie in a line of development having *universal* significance and value?[28]

This is the opening paragraph in full to the 'Prefatory Remarks'. Weber's answer to the question he poses so dramatically is that western rationalism is contingent on its own history and can claim no universal validity. Westerners, especially with the global expansion of the western model of rational capitalism at the start of the twenty-first century, tend to assume the validity and superiority of many aspects of their civilization. It is a historicist statement writ large, an amplification of Herder.

It is not a rhetorical question. It is the opening question to three volumes of essays in the sociology of religion. The studies in the world religions outline the directionality and contents of rationalization processes. All the world religions have an equivalence, what separates them is the content of their salvation messages, the cognitive framework of worldviews and the contingent directionality of rationalization processes. Schluchter has captured the equivalences and differences in the world religions with respect to their rationalist tendencies (Figure 7.1).[29]

Weber wrote of this as his 'contribution . . . to the typology and sociology of rationalism' (EW, p. 216). All the world religions are arranged on the bottom row, including their variant forms. In the first row, the big divide is between rationalist systems that affirm or are adjusted to the world (such as Confucianism) and those rationalist systems that confront religious values to those of worldly values. And, in the second row, the major divide is between salvation religions that turn away from the world and those that live in the world. Buddhist contemplation and (western) monastic asceticism lead to a compartmentalization of religion separate from the world. Puritanism separates itself from the other Abrahamic legacies by, uniquely, embracing asceticism *within* the world. Puritanism distinguishes itself by the enormous tension that it generates by superimposing transcendental demands upon its believers while they live and work in the world – hence the example of Bunyan. This schema also usefully places Puritanism within the religions of the Near East. This allows the judgement that modern capitalism was a result of a late variant. Puritanism is a singularity, but one that comes out of a much longer tradition of religious rationalisms.

This, as Weber insists, is a typology. He has heuristically constructed tendencies within world religions that rarely appear with such consistency. But *because* the feature of religious rationalism is their striving for consistency and the attainment of salvation goals through methodical means, the clarity of the typology is in part justified in historical reality. What cannot be included in the diagram is the historical and contingent impact of all the other spheres of life and their various economic, political, artistic and kinship values. For example, Islam follows one trajectory when carried within a feudalistic warrior stratum and an entirely different one as an urban religion with mystical tendencies. Confucianism and a polity that looks territorially inwards led to a sort of equilibrium and stasis within the Chinese Empire. But had an outward-looking trading or political class become influential, then some of the principles of Confucianism might have undergone change or challenge. The contingency of politics in relation to Protestantism is extremely well documented. Had the Habsburg emperor, Phillip II of Spain, crushed the Protestant opposition in the Low Countries, Puritanism may never have made its historical rendezvous with the rising middle classes.

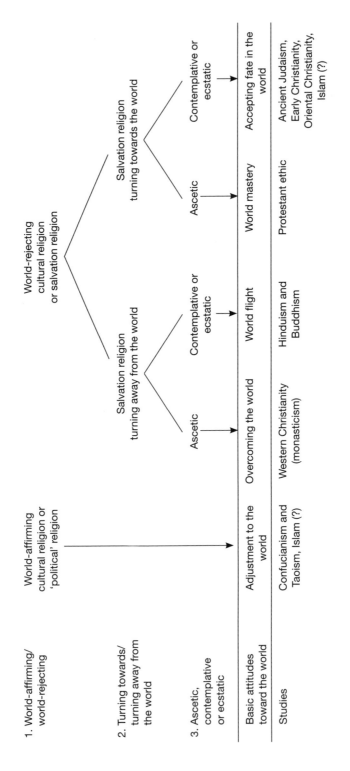

Figure 7.1 Classification of cultural religions.

Religious rationalism, and a different modernity, would have travelled on a different and less agonizingly individualistic path.

This brings us back to the fortuitous nature of modernity. History favoured a particular form of rationalism that turned out to be highly adaptive and consequential. It did not possess intrinsic validity. This perhaps is the sense of peculiarity or distinctiveness of the Occident that Weber is always worrying away at. Modernity's triumph over other civilizations is its peculiarity. Weber is quite comfortable analysing, and digressing on, the two millennia of Confucianism, and he is explicit in his admiration of the religiosity of Indian intellectuals.

> It stands out by virtue of its consistency as well as by its extraordinary metaphysical achievement: It unites virtuoso-like self-redemption by man's own effort with universal accessibility of salvation, the strictest rejection of the world with organic social ethics, and contemplation as the paramount path to salvation with an inner-worldly vocational ethic.
>
> (FMW, p. 359)

Religion and its relation to the social and economic order in India achieved an impressive stability over three millennia.

Modernity acculturated in Puritanism, in contrast, has a disturbing dynamic. Religion's enduring function was to create meaning by placing the human being in a wider cosmology. Puritanism, by the peculiarity of its path to salvation and life conduct, led to secularization and the destruction of cosmology. Science and rationality, which in the western enlightenment tradition is cause enough for validity, for Weber remains the source of disenchantment and perhaps the last step out of Edenic paradise. In civilizational comparison, there is nothing self-evident about reason, the rights of man, and a science able to validate itself through criteria of proof and evidence. While these give rise to what Weber suggests is the illusion of universality (not to say the actual empirical diffusion of this universality), it remained the fortuitous gift of individuals striving for salvation.

8   Power, legitimacy and democracy

Power is a subject that is inextricably linked to the work of Max Weber – in a double sense. Not only was he a theorist of power, but he also provided some of the most acute analyses of the political situation of his day. I will summarize very briefly his contemporary situation and his commentary on it. I will then present his academic analysis of power in the two versions provided, in the earlier version and final version of *Economy and Society*, respectively, and relate them to some recent treatments of power in political sociology. I examine his analysis of democracy and 'leadership democracy' in particular, which I argue should be looked at anew in the light of recent tendencies within British and American democracy.

Weber's political background

Weber's own family belonged to the political and cultural elite of Wilhelmine Germany and played a part in the supporting the Kaiserreich, which was founded by Chancellor Bismarck in 1871 and disintegrated dramatically at the end of 1918 with the cessation of the First World War. Weber's working life belonged to the same timespan of the Kaiserreich, he remained closely involved in the politics of the period, and he was an influential and cogent analyst of the regimes many tensions and contradictions. The origins of those difficulties can be traced through Weber's family history, and what emerges are some of the main components for the formation of the modern nation-state. As we now know, to our cost, the harmonious coming together of these components tends to be the exception rather than the rule.

His grandfather, Georg Friedrich Fallenstein (his mother's father), was a volunteer at the age of 23 in the 'War of Liberation' in 1813 against Napoleonic rule. He joined the Lützow corps, which was not a regular army unit but a band of comrades in arms who took great pride in their German heritage, creating romantic ballads in the course of their campaign. In military terms these volunteer units were insignificant, measured against the regular armies that were deployed by many states to counter Napoleon. But in the formation of the idea of the German people, the episode became hugely

significant. Of it, James Sheehan writes, 'The *Volk's* role in its own liberation was, at best, a minor one. Napoleon was defeated by regular armies,
not patriotic poets and quaintly attired gymnasts. Eventually, however, the
apostles of nationalism were able to create a historical memory of liberation which projected their own enthusiasms onto the nation.'[1] Fallenstein
went on to be a middle ranking Prussian official, who was held back in any
preferment by his obvious enthusiasm for all things German.[2] His superiors'
loyalty lay with the Prussian monarchy and they were distrustful of patriotic
fervour advancing, as it did, the cultural unification of the German people as
a political force in its own right.

Fallenstein retired to Heidelberg, built a grand villa on the banks of the
Neckar (in which Max and Marianne Weber were eventually to live) and
supported the celebration of German language, literature and folk traditions
– for example the work of the brothers Grimm. At his Heidelberg home,
Fallenstein took in Gervinus, one of the mostly widely read and most liberal
historians of his day. As a professor at Göttingen, Gervinus had been exiled
for refusing an oath of allegiance to the Prince Regent, who had suppressed
the existing constitutional rights in the state of Hanover. Gervinus took his
case to the supreme court of the German Confederation. He lost the case
but became the champion of constitutional rights among the liberal middle
class. Their political hour came in 1848 when Europe was convulsed by
revolutions of peasants and workers, from Spain to Russia. Gervinus was a
leading force in the National Assembly in Frankfurt, a collection of reformers and radicals that sought to put in place the first constitutional system for
the peoples of central Europe. The reformers, given their opportunity by
the widespread protests, deliberated too long and were split along too many
cleavages: the politics of language and ethnicity versus the claims to self-determination, and the politics of constitutionalism for the privileged middle
class versus the (then) radical demands of the democrats for a republic and
parliamentary rule.[3]

Fallenstein may be thought of as the ethnically defined cultural component, Gervinus as the liberal constitutionalist component. The option of
a democratic republic was resisted by Fallenstein and, initially, Gervinus.
Instead of looking to a newly enfranchised people as the basis of political
power, the liberals sought to conjoin their constitution to an existing dynastic state, which would retain the continuity of monarchy and the attributes
of state power – an army, fiscal system, judiciary and policing. The aspiration
of the liberals was to transfer legitimacy from dynastic autocracy to constitutional liberalism that would, in addition, recognize the basic rights of all
the people. After much wrangling in the National Assembly the leadership
of the German Nation was offered to the King of Prussia. This decision in
itself represented a betrayal of two elements in the National Assembly: those
elements who wanted self-government and democracy without monarchical
state rule from above, and the multifarious elements (Poles, Hungarians,
Ruthenes, Slovaks, Italians etc.) who wanted self-determination outwith a

German nation. These facts tend to be overlooked in face of the historic disappointment caused by the response from the Prussian king who rudely refused the offer of becoming the head of the new nation.[4]

Over the second half of the nineteenth century Prussia achieved hegemony over the separate thirty-nine German territories, which were agreed upon in 1817 at the Congress of Vienna after the defeat of Napoleon. But in 1848 the geo-politics of central Europe did not automatically favour Prussia. Bismarck was the supreme strategist, who as Minister-President of the Prussian kingdom achieved this in the 1860s. He manipulated the balance of political forces both within the state and between states. He regarded the Austrian Empire as the main threat to Prussia. Liberal as well as democratic protest was widespread across Austria in 1848. It was eventually suppressed by the Austrian authorities, just as the outbreaks of democratic radicalism in Frankfurt were suppressed by Prussian troops. Bismarck perceived that liberalism, vocalized in Frankfurt, and German unity under Austrian leadership could combine to sideline Prussia. Accordingly, in 1866 Bismarck engineered a successful war against Austria, very much against the sentiment of liberal, middle class opinion in Prussia. And in 1870 he provoked France into a war, where Prussia was again successful. This placed German territorial fortunes beyond the interference of foreign powers (Russia, Austria, France and England).

The war against France was welcomed with popular enthusiasm in Germany. Bismarck devised a constitution of his own making and the Kaiserreich (or second German Empire) was founded in 1871. The German states, excluding Austria, were incorporated into the Empire under Prussia's leadership. Nominally the monarchic constitution offered federalism to the incoming territories and universal male franchise to the people. In reality, neither people nor previously independent territories had any executive power. The historian Geoffrey Barraclough summed up the situation: 'In Bismarck's system, nationalism, long the concomitant of liberalism, was deliberately fostered as an antidote to liberal and radical demands; he offered the German people unity, but at the expense of the radical reform which alone made unity worth while.'[5] But in the attainment of German unity under Prussian rulership, Bismarck had unleashed a populist nationalism that by the 1890s had become anti-Semitic and anti-foreigner, fostered a trust in militarism, and created powers for monarch and aristocracy beyond the reach of parliamentary accountability. Although he had introduced male suffrage for elections of political parties to the Reichstag, that body had no real parliamentary powers to appoint ministers and administrations or budgetary oversight. Real power lay with the Prussian aristocracy and their 'Landtag' which had an outrageously unfair electoral system favouring the rich. And above both 'Reichstag' and 'Landtag' was the unaccountable power and influence of the Emperor. The liberals had got a constitution and German unity but the system 'was, in fact, a veiled form of monarchical absolutism vested in the King of Prussia.'[6] Weber learnt at first hand from his family what compromises and choices were involved in the construction of the German Empire.

Weber's uncle, Hermann Baumgarten, acted as a secretary to Gervinus in Heidelberg in the early 1850s. Gervinus deplored the reactionary turn in Prussian policy after the fervour of the events of 1848 had cooled, and he regretted the offer made by the National Assembly to the King of Prussia. In 1853 he wrote publicly that the political future belonged not to the middle classes but to the fourth estate of workers and peasants. For this he was charged with treason and Fallenstein, Hermann Baugarten and other friends had to organize his defence.

Following Bismarck's military successes in the 1860s, Baumgarten broke with Gervinus. In 1866 he wrote a self-critique of German liberalism, which he held was preoccupied with freedom, ideals and constitutionalism. 'Politics is action, it must always want something and achieve something; liberalism's problem is its ability to adapt its demands to reality, it must seek... to become capable of government'. State power and the 'real relations' of power had to be grasped. This was the new liberalism – and the 'unity through freedom' of the 'old liberals' was an 'obvious chimera'.[7] If Germany was to be united, then it would have to accept the leadership of Prussia. This was the new 'realpolitik', a phrase invented by Ludwig von Rochau, a journalist friend of Baumgarten's.

Weber's own father was a member of the National Liberal Party, which had despite a split given its guarded support to Bismarck. He held a number of important governmental posts in Berlin in budgetary committees and in the administration of Berlin itself. The young Weber learnt that Bismarck could govern with the support of the National Liberals and he could govern without their support. The Chancellor was not subject to parliamentary political parties, as in the English case, but only to the confidence of the Emperor. What he learnt from Hermann Baumgarten was his uncle's subsequent extreme disillusion with Bismarck's rule, which he thought had not lived up to the ideals of a Protestant German state.

Baumgarten accused Bismarck of 'Caesarism'. Bismarck had introduced universal male suffrage with the belief, it is said, that the masses would be conservative and patriotic. Bismarck would rule with popular approval. This approval was not forthcoming and Bismarck was forced to govern by manipulating and overriding an often hostile Reichstag, which sought to exercise its legislative powers. Baumgarten himself disapproved of universal suffrage, preferring a graduated suffrage – empowering the middle class prior to the entry of the working people.

This brings us to Weber's own politics. He was a bourgeois liberal, which in his case meant that he took the supreme political value to be the power of the state, and that middle class liberals should displace the incumbent Prussian aristocracy as the political class. Like his father's generation, he had no way of achieving this against the deeply entrenched power of the Prussian aristocracy. His political writings reflect his seething resentment at the lack of bourgeois leadership and they are marked by an angry but forensic skill in analysing the real interests that underlay political rhetoric. Only later in life (around 1910) did Weber seriously consider the reform of the Prussian 'Landtag' and making its powers subordinate to the Reichstag.[8] His politics also reflected his views as an economist. Germany should be a world power, taking its part in competition with the other great powers in the search for economic opportunities (trade, emigration, colonies). To this end he supported the re-arming of the German navy and he contributed a journalistic article supporting Tirpitz's Naval Bill of 1898.[9] He realized this aggressive stance could lead to war, but argued that announcing Germany's imperial claims would deter other nations from frustrating its ambitions.[10] Weber's 'nationalism' was therefore based on the power of the German state in relation to other nations, his liberalism was a belief in an expanding capitalism at national and international levels as the new competitive reality, and his political reforms were directed at making the government more vital and more responsive to the interests of the nation. He accepted that trade unions and working class political parties were inevitable under modern capitalist industrialization and he was a vigorous reformer for their right to participate in the political and economic life of the country.

When war broke out in 1914, he supported the German patriotic cause and joined up as a reserve officer. His wartime and postwar political articles for leading German newspapers are some of the best things he wrote. In the light of the sacrifices of the troops, he demanded a proper parliamentary and fair electoral system. Under pressure, and in a minority, he criticised the Kaiser and High Command. He immediately recognized the foolhardiness of unrestricted U-boat warfare by the German marine – because it would bring America into the war, as it did. After the war he helped to found the German Democratic Party within the political framework of the Weimar Republic – whose constitution he had influenced through his writings and political reputation.

Weber's participation, however much on the sidelines, in world historical events has made him a controversial figure. His name is linked with the idea of 'realpolitik'. Weber argued that Germany could not shirk its power responsibilities on the world stage. He rejected the Christian message of pacifism, which a small peace movement in Germany had been advocating. No politician at the national or international level could ignore what Weber termed the pragma of power. To act weakly, to 'turn the other cheek', was a dangerous illusion that ignores the rules of the game, and puts one's own constituents or country at risk (EW, pp. 261–2). The countering Enlightenment position was formulated by Immanuel Kant. '*Nature* herself' whether by fate or providence should produce 'concord among men, even against their will and by means of their very discord.'[11] Kant argued against secret treaties activated by states in time of war and against territorial acquisition. He argued for the reduction of standing armies, the raising of national debt for foreign policy objectives, and for the observance of the laws of war.

Weber is also controversial for his advocacy of leadership within democracy. His justification for strong leaders was in part based on his view that bureaucratic growth within the state, government and political parties would stifle the voice of the true political leader, who would articulate national values and formulate his own goals in the face of the levelling effects of modern politics. The political leader was, however, accountable to parliament and subject to constitutional laws. The mature political leader has to combine conviction, the awareness of the consequences of political actions, and an ability and judgement to cope with the normal business of politics.[12] Unfortunately, this normative list of criteria has often been cruelly abbreviated by twentieth century politicians – conviction without responsibility, and gesture over the substance of politics. Weber's case has also been diminished by the democratic election of the leaders Hitler and Mussolini, who suppressed democracy, put in train genocide and unleashed the most violent war in the history of the world. This has led to and re-asserted the view that democracies are made safer through the reduction in the powers of political leaders. The case for benign strong leaders, like Franklin Roosevelt and General de Gaulle and Willi Brandt, can, of course, be made also.

Weber, therefore, was a political commentator and activist in his own right, in addition to his academic writings on the topics of power, interests, rulership and politics. His acute sense of power and the political enters into the academic writings. He was an academic who lived through a momentous period of German history and he rarely stopped observing, debating and commentating on the political situation of his day. Weber was a scholar, but not the dry as dust variety. It is quite hard to single out his real passion – politics or scholarship. Ernst Troeltsch, it will be recalled, observed of Max Weber that he had two minds in one head. One was political, always cynically and cleverly reducing the utterances and actions of politicians to their underlying self-interest; the other mind pleaded for an absolute sense of justice and fairness – this other mind belonged in the western humanist tradition.[13]

This places Weber in a unique position: as a kind of modern Machiavelli who could impartially analyse the practice of power and was not repulsed by its choices and outcomes. The power and prestige of the nation was a noble cause for Weber, imparting dignity, culture and worth to human existence. This, he recognized, was true of all leading nations and, in addition, they were compelled to struggle for power and prestige in the international arena – hence the politics of nations could not escape a diabolical element.[14] Political leaders had to make decisions that were guided by what Weber termed an ethic of responsibility – weighing up and thinking through the consequences of their actions. They were also accountable to the values of the nation, its culture, and the prestige of the state. The leader's political values here depended on firm convictions that may, ultimately, not be compatible with the more rational ethic of responsibility (EW, pp. 261–8). Weber belonged in the long western tradition of the secular enlightenment of politics, but one sceptical of any self-evident natural law. The irrationalities of power could not be squared with philosophies that took the end of the politics of living together to be happiness.[15]

The dimensions of power

I now turn to his academic writings in the various versions of *Economy and Society*. 'Domination ('Herrschaft') in the quite general sense of power, i.e., of the possibility of imposing one's own will upon the behavior of other persons, can emerge in the most diverse forms' (ES, p. 942). Power is the ability to impose your will on others, even if they resist. Weber's definition follows most people's understanding of power. 'Domination in the most general sense is one of the most important elements of social action' (ES, p. 941). It is to be found everywhere: 'a position ordinarily designated as "dominating" can emerge from the social relations in a drawing room as well as in the market, from the rostrum of a lecture-hall as well as from the command post of a regiment, from an erotic or charitable relationship as well as from scholarly discussion or athletics.' The ubiquity of power, that it is to be found in all possible social relationships, creates difficulties for a sociology of power. 'Such a broad definition would, however, render the term "domination" scientifically useless' (ES, p. 943).

The earlier drafts of *Economy and Society*, read as a whole, produce three sociological dimensions of power: economic power, social power and political power. His sociology of rulership ('Herrschaftssoziologie') analyses the last dimension in depth and breadth. The rationale and structure of *Economy and Society* does not pursue a general theory of power, because it is the relation of the various orders of society in relation to the *economy* that is its focus. Rulership stands alongside economic activity as one of the enduring and salient features of all societies. In the modern economy, the operation of power and control in both the economic enterprise and politics resembles each other. The basic social relationship is rationally ordered according to fixed rules with operations carried out by trained officials and personnel. For most of human history, the economy has never achieved such self-direction, but remains embedded within the prevailing structures of kinship and kingship. Weber's sociology of rulership analyses the major types of rulership and shows their controlling and shaping effects on economic activity.

This should not obscure the point that the major elements of a more general theory of power are in place in these writings. Weber recognizes the centrality of economic power.

> A comprehensive classification of all forms, conditions, and concrete contents of 'domination' in that widest sense is impossible here. We will only call to mind that, in addition to numerous other possible types there are two diametrically contrasting types of domination, viz., domination by virtue of a constellation of interests (in particular: by virtue

of a position of monopoly), and domination by virtue of authority, i.e., power to command and duty to obey.

(ES, p. 943)

The exclusive possession of an economic resource places its holder in a position of domination over all those who need that resource. If a water supply is controlled unrestrictedly by one owner, or if the provision of computer software was controlled by one supplier, then this places huge economic power in the hands of those owners. In finance, Weber notes, any large central bank through its monopolistic position can control capital markets.

Weber uses the phrase 'domination by virtue of a constellation of interests'. By this, he means that the attributes of power in the economic sphere are qualitatively different from rulership itself. Weber gives the example of a powerful bank which owns the debt of another company. It can exercise its interest over that company through economic devices, for example by varying or threatening to vary the terms of its loan. Or, the relationship of power could be altered by bringing the company director(s) into the authority structure of the bank itself. Those directors would then be subject to the commands of the bank itself. This latter situation belongs to the structure of rulership within an organization and, hence, belongs to the sociology of rulership, not the 'constellation of interests'. It is the specific quality of the power relationship that is Weber's concern.

The sociology of economic power is further analysed in his writings on class and status groups. Weber defines class in terms of two variables: the ownership of property and the possession of skills that can be sold. This provides a simple but widely applicable stratification of very many societies. Slave-owners, patriarchal owners of landed estates, capitalists who own companies and stock are positively privileged, in terms of class, by virtue of property. Underneath and economically subordinated are the slaves, the peasants and serfs and the wage-earners. Possession or non-possession of skills provides a more complex picture of stratification, in that skills are often more graduated through a society. In today's societies, the economic division of labour produces a myriad of gradations in terms of types of skills in particular areas: semi-skilled, unskilled and professional skills. These gradations are not fixed, but change according to the development and dynamic of the economy, as certain skills are made redundant while new ones appear. In a medieval economy, skill differences were institutionalized through guild regulations as well as by status ascription; if one was born a peasant, one almost always remained a peasant on the lord's estate.

Status distinctions represent the third dimension of power, social power. In European medieval societies, a person belonged to a fixed status group within a clear hierarchy of social power. The feudal lord was at the top of the hierarchy, his knights in an inferior status (but only to him), with dependent peasants completely subservient. In the medieval towns, a different status order had been established, especially in those towns that had achieved jurisdictional autonomy from feudal lords, which they could have achieved by buying the privilege of autonomous rule within the city walls or by fighting the feudal lord for those rights. This then produced the status hierarchy of guild master, journeyman and apprentice. Closed status hierarchies border on becoming caste societies, in which no movement whatsoever occurs between status groups. Marriage across status boundaries is not permitted, and status distinctions are maintained through strict rituals of a religious nature. Status boundaries are policed by extraordinarily powerful measures such as pollution, magical rites and totemic symbols.

> In contrast with the 'class situation', which is determined by purely economic factors, we shall use the term 'status situation' to refer to all those typical components of people's destinies which are determined by a specific social evaluation of 'status' whether positive or negative, when that evaluation is based on some common characteristic shared by many people.
>
> (EW, p. 187)

Social power involves a struggle for social esteem. Social groups such as medieval merchants or religious priests, e.g. Brahmans, can develop into occupational status groups. Some special qualification can also be claimed through hereditary descent, or an office or profession can be appropriated through political power.

As can be expected, Weber immediately acknowledged that the dimensions of economic power interact with social power. In European medieval society, status distinctions defined economic opportunities. In today's capitalistic societies, class distinctions are becoming almost completely dominant over status distinctions, and this can be seen in the inability of professional groups to defend their special skills in the face of those who control economic and financial power. This is referred to as the 'marketization' of society. Status distinctions can also be used to buttress economic class position and, conversely, economic power may be consolidated into status distinctions. Weber covers many pages of text discussing and illustrating the interactions that occur in different periods of history and in different societies between rulership, economic power (class) and social power (status).

The overall conclusion is that all societies are engaged in a perpetual struggle for the distribution of power along these three dimensions. In addition, power registers in most forms of social relationship – for example between lovers – beyond the major dimensions picked out for treatment by Weber. An international footballer has obvious economic power through selling his skill. That economic power can be translated into status by those footballers who become celebrities, eventually becoming independent of those footballing skills. But, in theory, the celebrity footballer is subject to the complete rule of the football manager who might choose to praise or humiliate the player in whatever way he wishes. Each of the three dimensions of power

comes into a single case. The three dimensions are ideal typical ways of modelling power that, in its multidimensionality, would be extremely difficult to
analyse in the concrete case.

In these last paragraphs, I have recapitulated the introduction provided
for Part 2 of *The Essential Weber*. Reading Gianfranco Poggi's thoughtful
and informed book *Forms of Power*, I realize I should have made clear that
this exposition is not the standard account of Weber's theory of power.
Poggi asks: 'if we seek to differentiate forms of social power by referring
to the different "bases" of it, how many forms should we come up with?'[16]
He quotes Weber: 'Classes, status groups and parties are phenomena of the
distribution of power within a collectivity'.[17] This formula, for Poggi, produces a 'basic trinity of social power forms (again: normative/ideological;
economic; political) . . .'.[18] Classes are the form of economic power, status
groups of normative/ideological power, and parties the form of political parties. Poggi rightly observes that this tripartite division has been followed
by the sociologist and philosopher, Ernest Gellner, and the Italian political
theorist, Norbert Bobbio. Michael Mann's massive account of *The Sources
of Social Power* makes a similar tripartite classification, but adds in a further
dimension, military power.

Taking a closer look at Mann, he outlines 'the four sources and organization of power'. These are: (1) ideological power, where a claim to meaning is
monopolized by a social group, or moral norms are monopolized; likewise,
the ritualistic and aesthetic constructions of meaning can be monopolized.
Hence, those who control rite, morals and religion are termed, by Mann, as
exercising ideological power. (2) 'Economic power derives from the satisfaction of subsistence needs through the social organization of the extraction,
transformation, distribution, and consumption of the objects of nature.'
Mann echoes here the definitions of social economics provided by Weber
and Sombart, other than that these writers include the motivational bases of
behaviour – which in Mann are included but await his further analysis. He
continues: 'A grouping formed around these tasks is called a class . . . which
is therefore purely an economic concept.' (3) Military power 'derives from
the necessity of organized physical defence and its usefulness for aggression'.
(4) 'Political power . . . derives from the usefulness of centralized, institutionalized, territorialized regulation of many aspects of social relations'.[19]
Mann uses these definitions to provide a historical sociology of power as far-
ranging as Weber's comparative studies. Each of the four forms is an ideal
type, which enables the conceptual clarification of human history that would
otherwise appear to be hopelessly complicated. But in an empirical case,
these four types would come together, through their specific organizational
forms, to provide 'the dominant power structure of a given area'.

Poggi is quite explicit in acknowledging Weber, and Mann is more reluctant in this regard, but the similarities to Weber are fairly obvious. In my
exposition, I argue that Weber outlines three dimensions of power, but these
do not map to subsequent accounts, as suggested by Poggi and Mann. Social

power is not the overall outcome of the three or four dimensions of power, it is simply one (important) dimension in the multiplicity of relationships of power. Social power for Weber is the negative and positive distribution of prestige in status groups. The Brahman's lifestyle is an expression of his social power over lesser lifestyles. The category of prestige is couched in meaning, but is not of itself normative or ideological. It is a practice, a lifestyle, an embodiment of conduct and habitus; it is visible and forms a basis of social measurement.

This is not the same as ideological and normative power as Poggi would have it. Mann's placing it as his first form is a departure from Weber's writings. Weber's *Sociology of Religion* is the closest text to what Mann summarizes under ideological power. Priests, magicians, cultic mystagogues propagandize – Weber's term – their various beliefs and practices within social groups, and world religions represent successful propaganda on a mass scale. Weber would have had no problem with the concept 'ideological' (which in his day had a fairly narrow Marxist usage). *But* religion is not for Weber a dimension of power. There is a sense that religion exercises power within people's minds and behaviour, and Weber had the option of including it in his threefold division of power in the text 'Class, Status Group and Party'. But he did not do this. Instead, the power of religion is rendered by Weber as an 'ideal interest' and, in the architecture of his work, ideal interests are counterpoised to 'material interests'. Power belongs to the realm of material interests, and social prestige, economic class and political power are all forms of material interests. As the Outline Plan of 1914 shows, the (unfinished) chapter on religion would be separate from the chapters on power. The dynamics of ideal interests has an autonomy ('Eigengesetzlichkeit') different from the spheres of the social, economic and political order. They are not equivalent as factors in a multicausal scenario, which is how Mann conceives of the development of human societies. This brings us back to Weber's recalcitrance in treating religion as just another factor. It is a separate element, and the best that can be achieved is determination through the idea of elective affinity. Much turns on this insistence because, for Weber, historical outcomes cannot be deduced from the various input factors. The *combination* of ideal and material factors introduces a new and unpredictable historical element.

Nevertheless, both Poggi's and Mann's analysis of power forces an interesting dialogue with Weber's writings on the subject; specifically, how Weber arranged his chapters or sections in the various versions of *Economy and Society*. Both Mann and Poggi assume that the whole point of the analysis of power is to explain the allocation of resources in society. Resources, argues Poggi, can be allocated by custom, by exchange and by command.[20] Normative, economic and political power control these resources. I am not certain that this is the thrust of *Economy and Society*. In the final version of that work, Weber would have seemed to have placed the chapter 'The Basic Concepts of Economic Activity' at the core (see Chapter 9). This was then followed by the chapter on 'The Types of Rulership' and then 'Classes and Status Groups'. At that point, he unfortunately died. But he would have expected, surely, to have drawn down and revised the early drafts on religion, law and social groups. Stratification (in 'Classes and Status Groups') would be but one field of determination and co-determination in relation to the economy. Stratification, therefore, cannot be privileged as *the* explanandum, as the thing to be explained. Social economics was more than resource allocation – it was the principal types of economic activity or 'economizing' through history as conceived by Weber in terms of motivations for economic goals and organizational forms. Stratification would obviously impact upon this, but economic classes did not belong to the core analysis.

Mann provides his reader with a schematic diagram (Figure 8.1) of how he interlinks the goal-directed behaviour of human beings; how this flows through the 'boxes' of the four types of power and results in a power structure which itself contributes to the evolution of further societal development.

What might an equivalent diagram look like, were Weber to have supplied one for *Economy and Society*? In the central circle would be economizing activities and their types. Around this, in a series of overlapping circles, would be the types of law, types of rulership, face-to-face types of community and wider communities, types of religious groups and types of social stratification. The 'Basic Sociological Concepts' (Chapter 1) are intrinsic to all the other special sociologies. Chapter 1 appears to stand apart from the succeeding chapters, but it has to be read as an accompanying presence to those other chapters. Therefore, diagramatically, it has to be 'fed into' the cluster of other sociologies, for which it provides a terminological grounding (Figure 8.2).

Mann's schema demonstrates a clear linearity of motives being translated into the resources and organization of power and resulting in the evolution of societies. Weber, as we have seen, continuously rehearses and reprises themes of narrative and developmental history, but never commits himself to

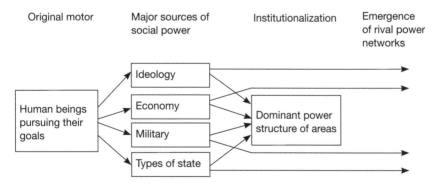

Figure 8.1 Mann's four sources and organization of power.

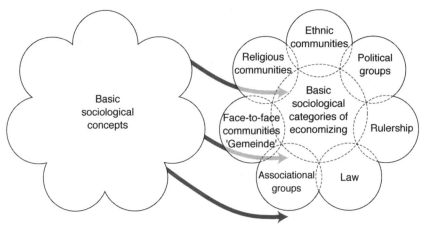

Figure 8.2 Simulation of the final version of *Economy and Society*.

any sort of evolutionary account of societal change. Instead, *Economy and Society*, most especially in its final version, pulls back away from historical development in favour of interactions between spheres of activity that are conceptualized as types of social relationships.

Figure 8.2 is hypothetical, although I would argue a reasonable surmise of Weber's final version. Discerning the overall plan of *Economy and Society* is a contentious and scholarly issue. What also has to be held in mind is Weber's readiness to execute such a programme. A sphere, such as power and rulership, is treated as a major theme in its own right. Then, it is related extensively to types of economic activity. And then, the economic bases of rulership are discussed. This procedure would then be repeated through all the special sociologies – law, religion and all the subsidiary circles of Figure 8.2. Each time Weber makes one of these manoeuvres, his mind always carries with it a ready supply of examples and empirical materials. The illustrative material is allowed to dominate the exposition, but Weber will then switch the theme and line of analysis.

Keeping this discussion in mind – admittedly, given Weber's ambitions and capabilities, not an easy task – I examine Weber's 'Herrschaftssoziologie' in the two versions that he wrote for *Economy and Society*. The older version is Chapters 10–15, and the final version is Chapter 3 of *Economy and Society*, edited by Roth and Wittich.

What follows greatly benefits from Edith Hanke's editing of Weber's 'Herrschaftssoziologie' in MWG I/22-4. Her introductions and footnotes clarify many issues.

Weber's political sociology

'Herrschaftssoziologie' was a special sociology, like those of law and of religion, and was designed to feed into *Economy and Society*. But it was also a subject especially close to Weber's heart. As a national-economist, he had to deal with issues of law, government and power structures, but it was not until 1909 that Weber started to develop his own political sociology. One impetus for this was discussions with Georg Jellinek on the setting up of a German–American Institute to be supported by the Carnegie Foundation. Weber recommended that it should research the legal, political, economic and the general cultural dispositions ('allgemeine Kulturverhältnisse') and how these determined modern nations and international relations. Other topics for study included: the internal structures of states; the role that military, bureaucratic and feudal or industrial, commercial and other bourgeois strata have on the political culture ('politische Geist') of the state; the political division of powers and the practical role of public law and administrative machinery; how all these contribute to the formation of the political culture ('öffentliche Meinung') of a country and determine its relation to other countries. 'Therefore the direct analysis of the international legal and political relations must go hand in hand with the internationally comparative analysis of the legal, political, economic and cultural structure of individual countries and states.'[21] This initiative never came to fruition and, as Hanke notes, it would have undertaken much empirical work for his ensuing contribution to *Economy and Society*.

Power, state, administration were all part of any national-economist's vocabulary, especially Weber's with his comparative abilities that, up to the point of the *Grundriss der Sozialökonomik*, had culminated in 'Agrarverhältnisse im Altertum'. The switch to a more specialized political sociology is marked by the gradual introduction of the concept of 'Herrschaft'. There is a long-running issue as to how 'Herrschaft' should be translated into English. Semantics are determined by problematics in this dispute. Talcott Parsons used the term 'authority'. In his sociology of societies and social systems, he emphasized the coordination functions of authority. Modern societies not only command, they organize and execute complex policies. For Parsons, the essence of power was not the relationship of the command of superior over subordinate, so that one person gained and one lost in the transaction – the so-called 'zero-sum' account of power. What was more important was the capacity to organize and administer, the advantages of which flowed to all members of a society.

In America, C. W. Mills embraced a conflict model of society, most notably in his book *The Power Elite* (1956). This rehearsed a tradition first articulated in modern times by Gaetano Mosca, the Italian political scientist who noted how a small organized group will always dominate a larger disorganized group. Mills brought this insight up to date, noting that US cities were controlled by small interlocking elites of administrators, political representatives and economic leaders. He also expanded on President Dwight D. Eisenhower's warning, in 1955, that democratic power in the United States was falling into the hands of the military–industrial complex. In Germany in 1959, Wolfgang J. Mommsen brought out his controversial *Max Weber und die deutsche Politik*, which argued that Weber was less a constitutional liberal (which had been the accepted picture) than a 'realpolitiker' who favoured the interests of the German state in the competitive international arena over the values of democracy, which had to take second place.[22] Following on from these influences, domination became the preferred translation of 'Herrschaft' – because it brought out the conflictual, realist side of power. And this flowed back into the problematic, with theorists such as Anthony Giddens favouring the realist view of power, in his *Nation-State and Violence* (1981).

These tensions are all expressed in the Roth and Wittich edition of *Economy and Society*. This is an amalgam of translators and translations. Parsons used 'authority', Guenther Roth uses 'domination' (in the 'Herrschaftssoziologie') and Benjamin Nelson expressed a preference for 'rule' and 'rulership'. My preference, which I should declare at this point, is for 'rule' and 'rulership'. (In the quotations below, I have not changed the translators' choice of words, although the translations in *The Essential Weber* do reflect my preferences.)

Hanke's discussion of the aetiology of 'Herrschaft' in Weber's usage is relevant here. There was clearly a 'realist' school for the analysis of power. I have already mentioned Weber's own tutelage under Hermann Baumgarten. In addition, Weber had read in Italian the first volume of Mosca's *Elementi di scienza politica*, which appeared in 1896 (although not the second volume, which appeared in 1923). Weber's close friend and academic colleague (until they fell out over German politics during the First World War), Roberto Michels, also used Mosca's ideas to argue that the revolutionary aspirations of socialism could never be achieved because of the constraints of organization. Similarly, a *Grundriss* author, Friedrich von Wieser, argued a revisionist line that mass movements have to accept the inevitability that power can only be wielded by small organized groups. This provenance points towards a realist conception and elites.

Simmel was also an influence. He published two chapters – 'The Sociology of Super- and Subordination' and 'Towards a Philosophy of Power ('Herrschaft') in his 1908 book, *Soziologie*. Within the general theme of the tension between freedom and authority and individuality and compulsion, Simmel probed the social–psychological issues of why free individuals allow themselves to be subject to authority and power. As Hanke notes, this is the psychologically equivalent question to Locke and Hobbes' formulation of the acceptance of a social contract between the ruler and the ruled.

This psychological aspect is directly reflected in Weber's definition of 'Herrschaft', that is

the situation in which the manifested will (*command*) of the *ruler* or rulers is meant to influence the conduct of one or more others (*the ruled*) and actually does influence it in such a way that their conduct to a socially relevant degree occurs as if the ruled had made the content of the command the maxim of their conduct for its very own sake. Looked upon from the other end, this situation will be called *obedience*.

(ES, p. 946)

Hanke makes the very pertinent point that this formulation is close to Kant's categorical moral imperative. Morality is internalized by the individual, and moral imperatives are followed for their own sake (and not for some other instrumental purpose). This does not mean that Weber had adopted the German Lutheran idea of obedience or, for that matter, Heinrich Mann's obsequious notion of 'the subject' ('Untertan'). The phrase 'as if' is crucial in Weber's definition. Commands are obeyed – obviously a feature of power – but 'as if' the command is accepted legitimately as an obligation on the behalf of the ruled.

Explaining why someone should so accept a command in this way is finely balanced between psychology and sociology. There is a large field of psychology that deals with hierarchical dispositions in human beings, and the very word 'domination' signals the wide variety of forms of dominance and abjection between human beings. Weber did indeed recognize this psychological side, for example in erotic relationships but, as a political sociology, the issue for him is the acceptance of legitimacy in a particular power structure ('Gebilde'). This brings the balance down firmly on the side of sociology, or – more exactly – interpretative sociology. Hanke argues convincingly that the essay 'Some Categories of Interpretative Sociology' not only expounds Weber's distinctive emphasis on meanings and types of social action, but that 'Herrschaft' is used as a major example of the new method.

> For its ['Herrschaft'] sociological analysis depends decisively on the varying possible subjectively meaningful bases of that *legitimacy* consensus that determines in fundamentally significant fashion the specific character of domination wherever naked fear of directly threatening power does not condition the submissiveness.
>
> (Cat, p. 177)

The idea of consensus is a direct extension of Weber's concept of agreement through consensus ('Einverständnis') – a fundamental concept of action that Weber elaborates in the 'Categories' essay (Cat, pp. 166–8). Likewise, 'Verband', another sociological category, is crucial for the analysis of close-knit power groups.

Legitimacy represents the validity claims of rule in the minds of the ruled. The whole of Weber's 'Herrschaftssoziologie' follows according to this formulation.

> The 'validity' of a power of command may be expressed, first, in a system of consciously made *rational* rules (which may be either agreed

upon or imposed from above), which meet with obedience as generally binding norms whenever such obedience is claimed by him whom the rule designates . . . Obedience is thus given to the norms rather than to the person.

The validity of a power of command can also rest, however, upon *personal authority*.

Such personal authority can, in turn, be founded upon the sacredness of *tradition*, i.e., of that which is customary and has always been so and prescribes obedience to some particular person.

Or, personal authority can have its source in the very opposite, viz., the surrender to the extraordinary, the belief in *charisma*, i.e. actual revelation or grace resting in such a person as a savior, a prophet, a hero.

The 'pure' types of domination correspond to these three possible types of legitimation. The forms of domination occurring in historical reality constitute combinations, mixtures, adaptations, or modifications of these 'pure' types.

(ES, p. 954)

It should also be said that the type of legitimacy is interdependent with the structure of rulership. Weber organizes his chapters (in the old version of *Economy and Society*) in the following sequence: 'Bureaucracy'; 'Patriarchalism and Patrimonialism'; 'Feudalism, Ständestaat and Patrimonialism'; 'Charisma and its Transformation'. Bureaucracy not only proceeds on grounds of rule-bound behaviour, but this is also the precondition of its elaborate rational, centralizing and hierarchical apparatus. Traditional legitimacy, as exemplified in the manorial household or 'oikos', is a far looser 'organization' where, while there might be status distinctions between members of the household, they are all ultimately dependent on the lord/ruler. Charismatic structures are not organized, they simply represent the 'following' of the charismatic ruler. Traditional rulership has limitations placed on its apparatus formation; power structures based on charisma are inherently unstable. Michael Mann places great emphasis on the extensibility of power structures in their political and military forms. This is not ignored by Weber, but he brings his analysis back to the ideal typical principle of legitimacy.

Hanke's scholarly research has provided the best approximation that we have of the dating of the various chapters of the 'Herrschaftssoziologie'. Chapter 15 in *Economy and Society*, 'Political and Hierocratic Domination', is one of the earliest compositions. It lacks the social action types and, hence, is not a beneficiary of Weber's interpretative sociology. It does not have any cross-references to other sections of *Economy and Society*. It stands in close relationship to the 'Agrarverhältnisse', and its excursus on sacerdotal power and the economy indicates that it is a direct reworking of the Protestant ethic studies. The chapter on patrimonialism also lacks the use of 'Herrschafts-verhältnis' as a concept, and Weber's treatment emphasizes the structure and apparatus of power and its constraints. The chapters on bureaucracy and charisma do display the interpretative categories of legitimacy, but there is some evidence that Weber inserted this into the draft at a later date (c. 1913). This is especially apparent in the chapter on bureaucracy, which tends to read as an analysis of structure rather than social action.

'The City' was not completed and is certainly a very early composition. The first editors of *Wirtschaft und Gesellschaft*, Marianne Weber and Melchior Palyi, had difficulties integrating it into the volume. Two major topics, which were trailed in the 1914 Outline – 'The Development of the Modern State' and 'Modern Political Parties' – never received a proper exposition.

Hence, the circles of political groups and rulership in Figure 8.2 are themselves incomplete. Weber revised his political sociology ('Herrschaftssoziologie') in 1919–20 – as Chapter 3 of 'Part 1' of *Economy and Society*. Weber achieved a highly disciplined encyclopaedic format as well as providing a cross-analysis with the economy. The analysis flows directly from the definitions of power and legitimacy. The historical illustration and developmental digressions are severely pruned, and all civilizational arenas are treated equally. Wilhelm Hennis has observed that the 'Herrschaftssoziologie' would be extremely hard work if we possessed it in only this final version.[23] Hanke recommends the public lecture 'Politics as a Vocation' as the most complete summation of Weber's sociology of rulership: the sociological conceptualization of the state, the types of rulership and their corresponding forms of administration in their mature formulation.[24]

Weber's conceptualization of democracy

A frequently asked question of Weber's three types of legitimacy is why there is no separate category for democratic legitimacy. Stefan Breuer, in an essay entitled 'The Four Pure Types of Democracy. A Proposal for Systematization', has provided the most resolute response. He argues that the ideal types of legitimacy are a value-free conceptualization. They do not involve criteria of normative desirability or undesirability. In a normative sense of justice, probably most people, if they were offered the choice, would prefer to live in a democracy. The answer to this Rawlsian hypothetical question is quite unsurprising – who would elect, if they did not know what position they might be born into, for a tyranny or traditional rulership or a charismatic rulership (although some might prefer the last for its excitements)? To demand normative criteria for the analysis of rulership entirely misses the thrust of Weber's political sociology. Legitimacy is a way of analysing the nature of obedience, organization and the inequality of power. In universal–historical terms, Weber offers three main, not to say gargantuan, ideal types. To demand normative criteria is to ask Weber to become a political philosopher who should frame his argument in terms of legitimation criteria. Legitimation criteria provide validity. When Weber uses the term validity, he usually places it in quotation marks to indicate that no normative judgement is being made. The traditional ruler would argue that he provided a sense of continuity and security for his subjects. The charismatic ruler would point to his grace, his protection against all enemies and the belief in the extraordinary. Legal–rational rulership offers the assurance that everything that happens accords with legally enacted procedures – safe even though rather predictable.

These are all value judgements, and the political philosophy of legitimation is dedicated to arguing the normative superiority or inferiority of the various principles of rulership. Weber, instead, is interested in the empirical grounds on which those subject to commands should carry them out, even against their resistance and reluctance, because they accept the legitimacy of the command. Very many people in societies operating under legal–rational rulership might not wish to obey the commands or instructions of their employer, their tax office or parking fines, but they do so because they accept the underlying legitimacy of the command structure. In individual cases, they can and often do refuse to do what is asked, but this does not alter the salience of Weber's ideal type of legal–rational rulership/authority. (I have expanded here on Breuer's insistence on value-free conceptualization.)

Breuer's second point is that Weber did have a concept of democratic legitimacy – indeed, there are a number of subtypes, all of which expressed the principle of rule from below. In Chapter 3 of *Economy and Society*, Weber devotes a section (7) to 'The Transformation of Charisma in a Democratic Direction'. In successor stages of a charismatic leadership, the 'following' can come to elect their next leader. This marks a shift 'to the belief that the group has a right to enact, recognize, or appeal laws, according it its own free will, both in general and for an individual case' (ES, p. 267).

A second subtype is rule by notables (Chapter 3, Section 20), whose principal feature is that the notable is economically qualified to provide the administration of rule from his own resources. Selecting this person can involve democratic procedures. 'In the American township the tendency has been to favor actual rotation on grounds of natural rights. As opposed to this, the immediate democracy of the Swiss Cantons has been characterized by recurrence of the same names . . .' (ES, p. 291). As Weber indicates, there are limitations to this route to democracy. 'Both immediate democracy and government by notables are technically inadequate, on the one hand in organizations beyond a certain limit of size, constituting more than a few thousand full-fledged members, or on the other hand, where functions are involved which require technical training or continuity of policy' (ES, p. 291). Weber notes that the permanent technical officials appointed to assist the notable tend to control 'actual power', while the nominal leaders 'remain essentially dilettantes'.

The third subtype is discussed in the representative forms of rulership (Chapter 3, Section 9). 'The primary fact underlying representation is that the action of certain members of an organization, the "representatives", is considered binding on the others or accepted by them as legitimate and obligatory' (ES, p. 292). A patriarchal ruler can choose to appoint a representative in his stead; feudal nobles can form an estate and represent their appropriated rights and privileges as independent from the feudal or patrimonial king; a representative can be instructed and given a mandate – Weber notes, in the context of the period 1917–19, that this was a feature of revolutionary soviets and was used as a substitute for mass democracy and its organization. Finally, Weber comes to 'free representation' and parliamentary rule. Weber devotes a page to this. As this subtype conforms to the normatively most accepted form of rule, parliamentary democracy, a close examination of this page of text is required.

The free representative is not mandated by a community but makes his own decisions.

> He is obligated only to express his own genuine convictions, and not to promote the interests of those who have elected him . . . the representative, by virtue of his election, exercises authority over the electors and is not merely their agent. The most prominent example of this type is the modern parliamentary representation. It shares with legal authority the general tendency to impersonality, the obligation to conform to abstract norms, political or ethical.
>
> This feature is most pronounced in the case of the parliaments, the representative bodies of the modern political organizations.
>
> (ES, pp. 293–4)

Reading this passage is rather like trying to find somebody famous in *Who's Who?* At last, in a very large book, there the person is, just as we might have been beginning to doubt his or her inclusion. Likewise with democracy. Nevertheless, Weber has included one of the most preferred types of representative rule in modern history, even though, in the sweep of universal history, it does appear as a subtype. Clearly, the treatment is ideal typical, the intensified contrast turning on the instructed mandate and the freely deciding agent. The most important point to grasp is that parliamentary rule is an example of legal–rational legitimacy. It is subsumed under that type. Also, it has normative principles, which Weber treats in a value-free manner. These norms are abstract and therefore confer an impersonality upon parliamentary rulership. The sorts of abstract norms that Weber would have had in mind are the rights of man or the commitment to happiness (to think of the United States).

Breuer's systematic comment on Weber's treatment of democracy draws a contrast between those forms of direct democracy that possess no apparatus (in a Swiss commune or soviet, or in the charismatic following) and those forms that exist through structures (parliamentary representation and plebiscitary democracy). Weber's analysis of power in these two situations is that democracy may be genuine in the small face-to-face groupings, but it cannot acquire extension of its powers as it lacks the organizational means.

Or, where it does possess an administrative bureaucracy, the organizational machine becomes more powerful than the voice and convictions of the politicians themselves.

Breuer correctly identifies the critical thrust of Weber's political sociology. Obviously, it is not a celebration of democracy or a justification of its philosophical validity. This strikes the reader quite forcibly today when the process of democracy can make a strong case for universal validity, both in terms of diffusion and in terms of reasoned arguments. Instead, Weber treats democracy just like any other rulership: it has legitimacy grounds, it is organized on certain principles, it has various structural limits and contradictions. So, while we might wish to complain that Weber's coverage of democracy could have been more expansive and not have been placed in the subtype classification, there is still something to be learnt from its critical intent.

Leadership democracy

Because democracy has now spread and is spreading so extensively around the world – it is not just a European-bound invention – we need to attend to Weber's critical remarks, whose applicability may be all the more pertinent. In many democracies, a gap is opening up between the face and the content of those rulerships. 'The Transformation of Charisma in a Democratic Direction' is a perverse way of alighting upon the presence of democracy – it is hardly the normal route to democracy – but the section is worth pursuing. Weber says that leaders who are dependent on the vote of their predecessor's following are a transitional case of plebiscitary leadership. 'Both the Napoleons are classical examples, in spite of the fact that legitimation by plebiscite took place only after they seized power by force. The second Napoleon also resorted to the plebiscite after a severe loss of prestige' (ES, p. 267).

Both the Napoleons acquired power in very unstable situations. The first Napoleon emerged from a period of vicious revolutionary in-fighting in the new French republic and consolidated his power through military means as a general. A plebiscite, a ballot of the whole of the French people, confirmed him as Emperor. The second Bonaparte did the same with the added threat of the deposed monarchy claiming to be the 'Legitimists'. Hanke notes that these debates and events were still very current when Weber was writing.[25] The critical thrust of this argument is to point out that a democratic procedure is used to legitimize what is little more than an opportunist grab for power.

This leads Weber to put forward plebiscitary democracy as 'the most important type of *Führer-Demokratie*', i.e. leadership democracy (ES, p. 268). Contemporary democracies have generally built up thick structures or dense interweavings of democratic culture, democratic accountability, democratic media (i.e. not censored), representative and party structures, intermediate groupings of civil society, overlapping constituencies (local, regional, national, federal) and different voting systems and so on. In these respects, they are far more robust than some of the pseudodemocracies of the nineteenth century. But very many contemporary democracies approximate to or are tending towards a form of leader democracy. In certain countries, the power of Presidents and Prime Ministers has grown, and grown in such a way that the organization of rulership structures and legitimacy is coming to be moulded around the leader. This does not amount to a leadership principle, which would be antithetical to democratic norms. But, in Weber's always dispassionate analysis of rulership, it is the task of the political sociologist to analyse power – its distribution, its hierarchies, its organization, its choice of meanings and emotions. Democratic rulership, even direct democracy, involves the exercise of power, the construction of hierarchy and the building of organizational structures. Democracy is just another form of rulership and is not immune to conflict and hierarchy.

Using his long historical perspective, Weber supplies a chastening list of measures through which the democratic leader has consolidated power. In 'Führer-Demokratie', the leader hides behind a legitimacy 'that is formally derived from the will of the governed. The leader (demagogue) rules by virtue of the devotion and trust which his political followers have in him personally. In the first instance his power extends only over those recruited to his following, but if they can hand over the government to him he controls the whole polity' (ES, p. 268). This happened in the ancient classical world, in the medieval towns and in Reformation Switzerland. 'In modern states the best examples are the dictatorship of Cromwell, and the leaders of the French Revolution and of the First and Second Empire.'

Weber's analysis of demagoguery is a good example of his value-free approach.

As a political commentator in his day writing for the public, Weber expressed judgements, many of which condemned the demagogue. On the other hand, in academic mode, he makes a cool and considered assessment of the role and function of demagoguery in democracy. Democracy in Athens would not have emerged had it not been for the demagoguery of its first democratic politicians.

> The charismatic politician – the 'demagogue' – is the product of the western city states. In the city state of Jerusalem he appeared in religious garb as the prophet; the Athenian constitution after the innovations of Pericles and Ephialtes was tailored to the existence of the charismatic politician, without whom the state machine would have had no prospect of functioning.
>
> (EW, p. 140)

Weber emphasizes that his comments should be understood in a value-free sense – 'the demagogic gifts of Cleon [a tyrant] are in sociological terms just as good "charisma" as the qualities of a Napoleon, Jesus or Pericles'.

And in his public lecture, 'Politics as a Vocation', he reminds his audience of the unavoidability of demagoguery.

> Since the time of the constitutional state, and definitely since democracy has been established, the 'demagogue' has been the typical political leader in the Occident. The distasteful flavor of the word must not make us forget that not Cleon but Pericles was the first to bear the name of demagogue. In contrast to the offices of ancient democracy that were filled by lot, Pericles led the sovereign *Ecclesia* of the demos of Athens as a supreme strategist holding the only elective office or without holding any office at all. Modern demagoguery also makes use of oratory, even to a tremendous extent, if one considers the election speeches a modern candidate has to deliver. But the use of the printed word is more enduring. The political publicist, and above all the journalist, is nowadays the most important representative of the demagogic species.
>
> (FMW, p. 96)

'Periclean democracy, too, which according to the intent of its creator was the domination of the *demagogos* by means of the spirit and the tongue, received its characteristic charismatic trait by virtue of the election of one of the *strategoi*, the other being determined by lot, if Eduard Meyer's hypothesis is correct' (ES, pp. 1126–7). Needless to say, Weber was fully informed about Athenian political history. The 'strategie' was a military command of nine people, eight of them elected by lots cast by clan groups. For the first time, the people of Athens were given the opportunity of voting for the ninth member. Pericles' rhetorical gifts swung the vote his way. Hence, in one of those historical first instances much loved by Weber, both the art of speaking and the first emergence of democracy were tied together. It is probably also from Greece that Weber learns his cool dispassion. Ancient democracy was a winner-take-all scenario. Losers were killed, ostracized or exiled. Ancient democracy, as Weber reminds the reader in *The City*, was intimately connected to war. Under democracy, war was chronic. 'Almost every victorious battle was followed by the mass slaughter of the prisoners, and almost every conquest of a city ended with the killing or enslavement of the entire population' (ES, p. 1362).

Modern constitutional democracy also cannot exist without the demagogue. Bismarck was one, and Weber disapproved of the use to which he put his gifts (ES, p. 1452). The British Prime Minister, Lloyd George, is obliquely referred to as a plebiscitary leader. He would not have achieved the premiership had it been decided by 'the confidence of the parliament and its parties'. Instead, as a war leader, he received the support of the masses and the army in the field. Weber could well have added that Lloyd George's ability to reach beyond the parliament and his (Liberal) political party was based on his oracular artistry. He knew how to speak to the people – the issues they cared about, and in a language that captured their imagination and attention.

Furthermore, Lloyd George was supported by Lord Northcliffe's *Daily Mail* – the first mass newspaper to become an effective tool for propaganda. The same points can be made in relation to Winston Churchill, who followed the career route Weber saw as typical of the modern politician: From being a journalist to adoption by a political party and then through demagogic talents, the construction of a party beyond rapport with the electorate – also supported by leading newspapers. This was a typical route for the leader in a democracy ('Führer-Demokratie'). 'Democratization and demagogy belong together . . .' (ES, p. 1450).

In 'Führer-Demokratie', the arts of demagoguery can extend to the manipulation of the emotions of voters and to the use of spectacle.

> It is characteristic of the *Führer-Demokratie* that there should in general be a highly emotional type of devotion to and trust in the leader. This accounts for a tendency to favor the type of individual who is most spectacular, who promises the most, or who employs the most effective propaganda measures in the competition for leadership. This is a natural basis for the utopian component which is found in all revolutions. It also dictates the limitations on the level of rationality which, in the modern world, this type of administration can attain. Even in America it has not *always* come up to expectations.
>
> (ES, p. 269)

Weber's comment on America is that the pattern of leadership in the American political system tends to produce leaders who articulate not the normative criteria of democracy (whose values flow from the American Revolution of 1776 and the founding of the Constitution) but psychological values of trust. Examples of this would be American populism where leaders have presented themselves as having the same 'folksy' values as lower strata of the population.

Weber noted that, in America, the appointment of officials may follow charismatic not legal–rational principles. Civil servants and administrators in Germany and Great Britain would accord to Weber's ideal type of rational–legal bureaucracy. They would be trained officials who gained their posts through competitive examinations whose criteria would be formally rational. Candidates are selected according to administrative competence – for example the ability to work with complex documents – and not because they possessed a sympathetic attitude to citizens or sections of them. But, using America as an illustration, Weber writes:

> Once the elective principle has been applied to the chief by a reinterpretation of charisma, it may be extended to the administrative staff. Elective officials whose legitimacy is derived from the confidence of the ruled and who are therefore subject to recall, are typical of certain democracies, for instance, the United States. They are not 'bureaucratic'

types. Because they have an independent source of legitimacy, they are not strongly integrated into a hierarchical order.

(ES, p. 267)

If these two statements are taken together, Weber would seem to be suggesting that America has the capability of becoming a plebiscitary leadership democracy with its administrative officials chosen on charismatic criteria. Emotional and demagogic appeals to the electorate are possible, and these stand outside modern legal–rational legitimacy. In fact, Weber is not being as 'tough' on America as the above passages suggest. He deeply admired the American political system for its vitality, its openness, its fluidity, and he held it up as an example to his German compatriots of the primacy of politics over bureaucratic administration. The major critical thrust of Weber's political sociology is directed against the soullessness of bureaucracy. It was a machine, impersonal, formally rational, 'sine ira et studio' (an aloof impartiality). He joined his brother Alfred in 1909 in an attack on the Prussian bureaucratized state, where the administrative class had displaced democratic politics and where the bureaucracy was seen as a deadening and suffocating force in society. Alfred Weber referred to Germans as being in love with the 'metaphysics of bureaucracy'.[26] America, in refreshing contrast, cut its civil service down to size, making it directly electable. Hence, the usual interpretation of Weber's political sociology is that he saw and analysed the danger of legal–rational bureaucracies stifling the life blood of politics. And it is for these reasons that Weber is associated with the call for strong parliamentary leaders who can override the power of bureaucracy in the civil service and in their own political parties.[27] Rather in the same way as today George Ritzer predicts the 'McDonaldization' of the world, so Weber bemoaned the bureaucratization of the world – not only politics, but also trade unions, companies, voluntary associations, the churches and so endlessly on. (And, of course, all these are rationalization processes that seem to possess an inherent and unstoppable dynamic in which rational procedure and instrumentalism become the sorcerer's apprentice – enabling yet controlling.)

The peculiarity of Weber's treatment of democracy is that he does not start from the normative grounds of legitimation and its presumed superiority over other political systems. That, one suspects, would be to accept democracy's credentials at face value and impede the political sociology of power, interest and bureaucratization. Weber places democratic rule within the ideal type of charismatic rulership, and this gives the analysis a critical awareness of tendencies not immediately associated with democracy. In the case of America, populism, recall and elected officials introduce a vigour into the political system (whose merits have subsequently been much debated over the twentieth century). In the case of the British political system, Weber pointed out the dangers of 'Caesarism', that the British prime minister can, without adequate safeguards in the constitutional system, assume semi-dictatorial powers.

Parliament's function, writes Weber, is to protect the people against the supreme ambitions of the leader, who might have what Weber terms 'Caesarist' ambitions. It safeguards the continuity of leaders and oversees their power position. It preserves civil rights and serves as a proving ground for 'wooing the confidence of the masses'. It steps in to peacefully eliminate the leader when he [or she] has lost the confidence of the masses (ES, p. 1452). Weber then notes: 'However, since the great political decisions, even and especially in a democracy, are unavoidably made by few men, mass democracy has bought its successes since Pericles' times with major concessions to the Caesarist principle of selecting leaders' (ES, p. 1452). Weber's overall judgement of the tendencies towards caesarism and demagoguery are conditional upon the system concerned. He is scathing about demagoguery without parliament – addressing the masses in the street. Strong leaders and weak parliaments (the Bismarck case) also attracted his condemnation. Britain and the United States would seem to have enough democracy in depth for these tendencies to be held in check.

Political scientists have recently been drawn to the cases of the prime ministers Margaret Thatcher and Tony Blair, because of – in Weberian terms – their 'Führer-Demokratie' tendencies. While they have emerged as parliamentary leaders through their respective political parties, they have also – not least through their rhetorical skills – appealed to the mass of the electorate over the head of their parties. Both have been dependent on the support of the most powerful sections of the mass media, who have been happy to amplify attacks on political opponents within both their parties and the parties of opposition. Weber took the locus of political power to lie in the British Cabinet, which he observed has no constitutional underpinning or check. It exists within the political framework of parliament and its oversight. This is not out of line with the concern of political scientists today. Their concern is the movement of the locus of power to the leader and his or her private office, and the relegation of members of parliament to a passive rather than an active role in parliamentary debate.[28]

From these examples, it makes more sense today to examine the potentiality of a transition from and within constitutional and parliamentary democracies to plebiscitary and Caesarist features as described by Weber. The transition from charisma to plebiscitary democracy, as expounded by Weber, is not very often exemplified historically, 'pace' Pericles. It is the universal–historical constants of power that matter. As Kari Palonen has shown, the exercise of power through persuasion leads to the analysis of rhetorical discourse – whatever the normative pretensions of the rulership.[29]

There is a further step in these arguments on power and democracy. Power does not belong to the dimension of politics and rulership alone. What happens when the dimensions of status and class are brought into the analysis? Power is a distributional process within society, working within the channels of politics, economics and status. This not only has allocation outcomes, it also determines the structuring of outcomes, as Poggi quite rightly stresses.[30]

If class comes to determine status, as it does increasingly in the twenty-first century world (for reasons yet to be adequately explained), then two dimensions of power are aligned. The sphere of politics and rulership has its own dynamic, but what happens when its operation becomes dependent on the financial backing of the wealthy? A contemporary Weberian would be asking these questions, which revisit the debates between C. W. Mills' analysis of the power elites and the thick and resistant structures of pluralist democracy and stratification.

9 Sociological categories and
the types of economic activity
A final account

The 'logic' of the final version of *Economy and Society* has now been established. Developmental histories take second place to universal–historical themes. Ideal types are built on meanings and social relationships, and they tend towards being classificatory devices. Arguably, this is a tension. An ideal type cannot be a culturally heuristic explanatory instrument as well as a method of classifying different types of societies and their structures ('Gebilde'). When the ideal type was first presented in PESC in 1904, it referred to a 'historical individual', and was highly specific in what it referred to and intensified in terms of meaning. At the level of universal–historical comparison, this 'historical individualism' is given up in favour of interrelated typologies. But, nevertheless, meaning remains crucial to the method.

The last chapter examined Michael Mann's ideal typical analysis of the sources of social power. This was a modelling device that allowed the analysis and comparison of a huge range of empirical cases, which in their specificity offered complexity and combinations of ideal types. Weber developed the ideal type to perform just this sort of exercise. But, in Weber's political sociology, the classification turns on meaning. Power is ubiquitous in all societies and in a large range of situations. The value-related question is: what aspects of power is the researcher interested in investigating? With Weber, it is the legitimacy bases of rulerships with structures, hierarchies and apparatus following on from the identification of the typifying meanings that structure the social relationships of power.

By following the Outline Plan of 1914, we can form a good idea of what special sociologies should have been in the final version of *Economy and Society*: the 'gemeinschaftlich' communities, the sociologies of religion, the market, law and rulership and the state, and stratification of class and status groups. We know from the revised first four chapters of *Economy and Society* how he handled 'Herrschaft' (Chapter 3) and 'Classes and Status Groups' (Chapter 4). It is possible to speculate how he would have amended the special sociologies of law and religion. His basic task here was to make these fit within the cross-referring structure of *Economy and Society* as a contribution to the encyclopaedic *Grundriss der Sozialökonomik*. He had to stop treating them as subjects in their own right. Law in its first (and only) version was his own area of expertise by training, and his draft generated an enormous complexity of classification, definitions, examples and historical digressions. We still await the 'definitive' version of this draft in the Max Weber Gesamtausgabe, which it is hoped will provide the 'correct' sequencing of the chapters as well as his thinking behind his legalistic conceptualization. The sociology of religion, we have established, was a problem case, in that no ready classification on universal–historical terms was available, and evolutionary accounts, while attractive for explaining an inner logic of development, created all sorts of problems of fitting to a recalcitrant reality. As Robert Bellah notes, nothing is forgotten: rites, magic and religion are still to be found in all areas of modern societies.[1]

In the final version of *Economy and Society*, he had to relegate his grand question: why did modernity originate in the west? In part, this had gravitated into the question: what is so specific and unique to the west? A Millsian logic of causation simply could not be made to work. The comparative studies of the world religions might have suggested the method of difference would produce the decisive causal factor that was present in the west but absent elsewhere. But comparison, as in its nature, tends to confirm difference, period. The 'Prefatory Remarks' to the 'Collected Essays in the Sociology of Religion' came up with a summating answer to the question of difference. It was western rationalism. But this was diffuse across occidental history and societies and had none of the clarity of Puritan ascetic conduct that could be identified as *the* crucial causal factor. In conducting his world religion studies, and not forgetting all the studies he planned to carry out, Puritan asceticism turned out to be one episode in a longer and wider tradition of religious rationalism. And, finally, Weber was quite happy to concede that all the world religions had rationalization processes whose 'rationalist' motors drove them in directions simply different from that of western religion; he refused to accord any superiority to the validity claims of western rationalism over other cultures.

One issue that still reverberated was the issue that Bücher was supposed to have addressed and dealt with. Could the dynamic of historical development be dealt with legitimately (in social science terms) through a stage theory? To this was added the question of moving out of 'primitivism' – how did societies attain a developmental path that would pull them out of the circle of face-to-face 'gemeinschaftlich' relationships into what Jaspers would call 'the axial age'? This question underlay the whole German approach to national-economy. In 1919–20, Weber was again lecturing as a national-economist, at the University in Munich, and he was still lead editor of the *Grundriss der Sozialökonomik*. More still had to be said about social economics.

Bearing these issues in mind, in this chapter, I will examine what are probably the least understood parts of Weber's oeuvre. These are Chapters 1 and 2 of *Economy and Society*: 'Basic Sociological Concepts' and 'Basic Sociological Categories of Economising ('Wirtschaftens')'. (The Talcott Parsons' translation of Chapter 2 is 'Sociological Categories of Economic Action'. I have preferred the more literal translation.)

Economy and Society, Chapter I: Basic Sociological Concepts

I have given a fairly extensive exposition of Chapter 1 in *The Essential Weber* (EW, pp. 296–308), not least because it is a summation of his writings. It is often taken out of the context of *Economy and Society*. It has been published as a stand-alone book, and is frequently seen as a kind of fundamental statement of how sociology should proceed. This is not unconnected with the theory of social action, which has remained one of the central debates in the discipline. Weber was seen, by different camps, to assert the primacy of meaning, of individual action and of social relationships, in place of the reifications of market, state, mode of production, class as living entities and social system. He was seen as anti-market (as a reification), anti-social system, anti-positivism. All these assertions were valid but, somehow, Chapter 1 taken in isolation produced a rather bland version of sociology. Where were the determining structures that govern people's lives? Where were the issues of power, of economic inequality and culture couched in meaningful terms current to contemporary issues? Not so many authors use Weber's theory of social action, tying it to issues of power, market and the structuring of social groups.[2] Rex and Moore's *Race, Community and Conflict* is a good example of how to approach Weber's 'Basic Sociological Concepts'. In this study of a West Midlands town in the 1960s, the housing market was analysed in terms of stratification of ownership and renting, and the 'gemeinschaftliche' attitudes were interpreted in terms of ethnic groups and attitudes. Social action theory was used to probe issues of market power, social prestige and prejudice, and the working of local politics and local government.[3] A more recent example in the same vein, but with different conclusions, is Dench, Gavron and Young's study, *The New East End*. The study investigates housing markets and their (limited) opportunities for the communities of London's East End, the values that underpin the face-to-face communal relationships of family and neighbourhood – and the dispersion of those communities by individualistic values, how ethnicity affects the sense of different communities, and the changing political prioritization of welfare needs by local government.[4]

Rex and Moore's study uses an explicitly Weberian framework, the Dench, Gavron and Young study does not. But in both studies, the investigators operate with a conceptual language not dissimilar to the 'Basic Sociological Concepts'. This is unsurprising because what Weber outlines in that chapter is a set of universal categories that are relevant to any investigation of social reality. The survey and interviewing methods, which inform *The New East End*, reach the same language by a different route. What makes both studies important, within the sphere of inner city living, is their ability to relate the experience of key social relationships of neighbourhood, family and settlement to the wider structures of society – economic markets, stratification and demographic movements.

It would clearly be artificial to separate the concepts of social action from those wider structures or, as Weber would put it, the social 'Gebilde' with the German word's more mutable emphasis. But, when we turn to the final version of *Economy and Society*, there is an impression of isolation, and so of artificiality, of the theory of social action. Weber himself knew that his 'casuistry', which is how he referred to 'Basic Sociological Concepts' and which was also delivered as a lecture course at Munich, was driving his students away in droves.[5]

The chapter can only be rescued from its seeming abstractness – an irony as the whole position is to argue for the understanding and explanation of actual behaviour. Above all, the chapter has to be related to the ensemble of *Economy and Society*. Just to repeat the remarks made in the previous chapter with reference to Figure 8.2 (p. 232), Chapter 1 sits apart from all the other chapters (both those that were written and those intended) as a key. Small groups, household economizing, market economies, political groups, rulerships, structures of law, ethnic communities and so on – these should relate to the compendium of basic sociological concepts. The basic concepts underwrite the analysis of the substantive sociologies. Weber had undertaken this process once already with the 'Categories' essay of 1913, whose conceptualization occurs more or less across the range of the first drafts of his writings in the period 1911–14. The 'Categories' essay, however, was too difficult and too abstruse. Nobody understood what he was trying to achieve.[6] Chapter 1 represents a very careful and very clear reworking of his concepts – to make them accessible and applicable. These then become 'basic' to the rest of the exposition of *Economy and Society*. But the rest of that exposition was never completed, adding to the sense of limbo of Chapter 1. This perceived difficulty can only be got around by referring back to the Outline Plan of 1914, which presents the full range of substantive sociologies as originally conceived by Weber (see above, p. 157).

Chapter 2, on economizing, should probably be assumed to be the centre of gravity of the final version of *Economy and Society*. In the first drafts (1910–14), the smallish chapter on economic groups was dwarfed by the special sociologies. The new version would rectify that problem, but Weber only got as far as Chapter 4 (and this chapter itself, as its notation form suggests, might not have been the final version). Hence, Chapter 2 predominates, but itself remains somewhat stranded in the absence of the completion of the whole project. It is reasonable to place the major stress on Chapter 2, as national-economy and then social economics were his constant concern from his lecturing in the 1890s, through his editorship of the *Archiv*, the studies on the economic ethics of the world religions and, finally, the *Grundriss der Sozialökonomik*.

Chapter 2 along with the other chapters, both completed and intended, therefore has to be read through the explanatory exposition of Chapter 1. Weber's revision of Chapter 1 reflects a clarification and maturing of his views on the central issues of understanding, meaning, causality, explanation, the proper subject matter of the social sciences and the exposition of concepts central to the special sociologies. It reprises, in a compressed form, the debates on meaning and causation that arose in the context of PESC 1904 and the essay on 'Objectivity'. Weber's conclusions, in clarified form, are relevant and applicable to universal–historical investigations, but they do not constitute a 'general sociology'. 'Sociology, a word used in quite diverse ways, is to mean here: a science which seeks interpretative understanding of social action, and thereby will causally explain its course and effects.' Weber is interested only in behaviour that is meaningful to the social actor. Behavioural psychology or evolutionary psychology would be excluded by Weber, in the first instance, because its subject matter deliberately excludes behaviour governed by meanings (in favour of behaviour governed by revealed preferences – outcomes independent of intention, or evolutionary traits in the human brain). Behaviour becomes *social* action 'where the meaning intended by actor or actors is related to the behaviour of others, and conduct so oriented' (EW, p. 312).

'*Correct* causal *interpretation* of a concrete action requires its apparent course and motive to be *accurately* recognized and meaningfully *understood* in context' (EW, p. 319). Motive, action and context of meaning involve the operation of 'Verstehen', in the way I outlined in Chapter 4, and followed in the footsteps of Dilthey (even though Weber renounced his tutelage). In line with German hermeneutics, the establishment of understanding enables the grasping of the truth of what was intended. This is an empirical matter because it involves the investigations of the expression of motives (in a document, in a cultural artefact, in observed behaviour). Weber, in his opening footnote to Chapter 1, distances himself from the subjective method of Simmel that appealed through empathy to a common medium of the soul or psyche. This was interpretation with no means of ascertaining truth. Because the observed, or the artefact, has an objective concretization, a courtroom method of imputation after the event can be used to establish correct motive. In sciences of culture (rather than the actual courtroom), imputation is enabled by the construction of ideal types. Is an action a pure type of rage (affect), or tradition, or of purposeful rationality? Having constructed the ideal type, to what extent does social action in empirical reality diverge from the pure type? Causation involves the understanding of motive and meaning and its empirical elucidation in concrete cases that the imputed motive did in fact result in specific outcomes and consequences.

Although social action is always denominated in and by the individual person – all other entities are abstract and not real, i.e. state, law, market, society – the individual exists in social contexts invariably made up of various groups. The sociologist is interested in individuals insofar as their actions are similar, and interpretative sociology is interested in meaningfully similar behaviour. It rains and many individuals on the street put up their umbrellas in a non-meaningful reaction to rain. A football crowd collectively leap to their feet to applaud (or condemn) a brilliant goal – this is meaningful behaviour in common to a group of people.

Individuals orientate their action and behaviour to laws and customs. Laws and customs form part of their context of meaning and cannot be ignored (or else would have to consciously be rejected, i.e. ignoring or breaking the law). Individuals relate, therefore, not to other isolated individuals, but to what a group or a law or a convention means in the minds of individuals. Again, something like *the* law may be regarded by jurists as having an objective reality with normative obligations but, for Weber, the law as a living entity cannot be presupposed. Its consciousness in the minds of individuals can be presupposed. 'Pace' Durkheim, social facts are not social things ('choses'), but they can exert obligation on the individual. Weber articulates this as the orientation of the individual to law or particular laws. So, a whole 'order' may be regarded by individuals as legitimate by virtue of tradition, or emotional appeal, or values or, lastly, legality. The legality of law does not exist by virtue of its enactment as legal (positive law) but because it is either agreed to or imposed. Each of the reasons for accepting the legitimacy of an order relates to the creation of meaning (by Weber in the ideal type) and the imputation of motives to social actors (EW, pp. 337–9. The 'Categories' essay also discussed this more extensively, but with less clarity.) The typology of legitimacy of an order, Weber then signals, will form the basis for the special sociologies of law and rulership.

The seesaw point in the developmental histories of so many societies – the central problem in economic history within German national-economy – is handled through the concepts of the forming of community ('Vergemein-schaftung') and the forming of associative relationships ('Vergesellschaftung'). The former turns on feelings of mutuality and smaller scale, local interactions, the latter on association through rational motives or the pursuit of interest (which Weber appears to assume is self-evidently rational). In the sociology of religion, we saw how Tiele and other scholars saw this breaking out beyond the bounds of communal face-to-face groups as being achieved through religion, just as, in economic history, Sombart thought of it as the acquisitive drive or, in the work of Bellah or Innis, the rise of ar-chaic kingdoms.[7] Sociology assists the historian in ascertaining cause-specific explanations by being able to note the fundamental changes in social action. Weber does note (EW, pp. 344–5) that associative relationships turn around struggle and competition in a way not true of the mutuality of communal relationships.

The first reference to Chapter 2 occurs here – to markets. It gives an indication of Weber's approach to social economics.

> Participation in a 'market' (see ch. II of *Economy and Society*) is structured differently. A market creates associational relationships (princi-

pally one of 'competition') between prospective exchanging parties, for in each case these agents have to orient their behaviour towards each other. But associational activity only develops from this if some of the participants seek to improve their competitive situation, or reach agreement on ways to regulate and stabilize transactions. (The market and the commercial economy based upon it is incidentally the most important type of mutual influence of action through sheer self-interest, characteristic of modern economic organization.)

(EW, pp. 345–6)

'Market behaviour' is a term that is now frequently heard. An entity is assumed – the market – and people orient their behaviour towards it. With Weber, the assumption in the first instance still has to be justified. A market presumes an attitude of conflict, pursuit of self-interest and benefit to participants; only then can a 'market' be understood to exist. 'Market behaviour', like marginal utility, can then be analysed by economic theory.

Paragraph 10 of 'Basic Sociological Concepts' defines open and closed social relationships. A market is an open economic relationship, and a guild is at times open and expanding its numbers and, at other times, restrictive. Weber also refers to the English 'closed shop', which restricted entrance to certain occupations. Neo-liberal reforms in Britain in the 1980s forced many of these closed shops to move to open market labour access. Again, this demonstrates that 'market behaviour' is a construct of specific types of social relationships that are either reached through agreement or imposed from outside.

Section 12 takes up the definition of a 'Verband'. 'A social relationship that is either closed to outsiders or restricts their admission according to set rules will be called a group body ('Verband'). 'Verband' is quite difficult to translate. Normally, one would use 'organization'. But that implies that the group has a degree of openness, whereas 'Verband' has the sense of a small band of people who act together as a controlling group within a range of organizations. Within government, an opposition party, a university, a church, a company, a warrior band, a criminal network, there is a 'Verband' who control the wider organization. The translator Dr Yano suggested 'corps' as in army corps to try to get this sense. Weber retains something of the legal theorist and historian, Otto von Gierke's, usage. The 'Verband' is like an 'individuum', it is a 'leiblich–geistige Lebenseinheit' – 'a bodily–spiritual entity'.[8] It is a central concept for the analysis of power and relates directly to the discussions in the previous chapter,[9] as do the concepts of power ('Macht') and rulership ('Herrschaft') in Section 16. A 'Verband' can be hierocratic – order is guaranteed by psychic coercion in a religious context. There is no application of hierocracy in the final version of *Economy and Society*, although it is discussed in a brilliant historical digression in an earlier version (ES, pp. 1158–204). Weber's own imposed intellectual division of labour is between preparatory, not to say bland, conceptualization and brilliant sketches of developmental history on a comparative basis. A close reading of Chapter 1 should register the full range of applications that Weber intended for his compendium of terms (although this cannot be undertaken here).

Economy and Society, Chapter II: The Basic Sociological Categories of Economising

This opens with a rather deprecatory admission.

> What follows is not intended in any sense to be 'economic theory'. Rather, it consists only in an attempt to define certain concepts which are frequently used and to analyze certain of the simplest sociological relationships in the economic sphere. As in the first chapter, the procedure here has been determined entirely by considerations of convenience.
>
> (ES, p. 63)

This tends to imply that Weber is going to duck the big question about the origins and emergence of modern capitalism, just as in Chapter 1 the whole question of moving out of 'primitivism' was made into one of appropriate terminology. What we are offered in subject matter does not differ greatly from his 1898 lectures in national-economy. All the topics in Book One of the lecture course (see above, pp. 23–27) are repeated in Chapter 2 of *Economy and Society*, although the latter expands its treatment of the technical and the social division of labour and, post 1917, registers the economic arrangements of communism. Although Weber says he is not offering economic theory, the chapter does provide an opportunity to show how he finally dealt with the opposition of the 'two economic schools' – marginalist and historicist. In addition, the chapter should be read according to the schema in Figure 8.2 (p. 232). The special sociologies of groups, law, religion and rulership cannot be separated from the economy, just as economic relationships cannot be divorced from those special sociologies. Weber is supplying in Chapter 2 a complex piece of cross-referencing for universal–historical comparative studies.

The opening definition is standard national-economy put into the language of social action theory.

> Action will be said to be 'economically oriented' so far as, according to its intended meaning, it is concerned with the satisfaction of a desire for utility ('Nutzleistungen'). 'Economising' ('Wirtschaften') is a peaceful use of the actor's control over resources, which is rationally oriented, and so deliberately planned, to economic ends. An 'economy' is an autocephalous, and 'economic enterprise' an organized system of continuous economic action.
>
> (ES, p. 63)

What has to be brought out is the *meaning* that all economic processes and objects have for human action in terms of ends, means, obstacles and by-products. Returning to the scene of his anti-psychologism, Weber notes that, while valuation of goods is subjective, the explanation is not to be found within a psychologism of utility; rather, explanation is given through meaning underlying economic action. Satisfaction of consumption does not constitute a sufficient explanation. There has to be a desire for certain needs and, as in his 1898 lecture course, Weber goes on to discuss how desires are sociologically given. Economic action is a conscious orientation to achieving or choosing between certain ends. These ends are valued for certain reasons by economic actors. They also have to think about the means for their achievement, but activity solely oriented to means without thinking about ends is relegated to the category of 'the technical' (ES, pp. 65–6).

It is difficult to expound the intricacies of Weber's analysis without this chapter becoming a textbook treatment itself. Weber proceeds in the steps of the Austrian school and places their analysis within a framework of social action. The Austrian school formulated economic analysis in terms of the motivations of economic 'units' ('Einheiten') in their mutual relation to each other. This was ready-made, so to speak, for Weber's absorption of their analysis into his own theory of social action, which had the same 'individualizing' methodology. Austrian utility theory, however, tempted theorists to produce an underlying psychology of utility, which Weber regarded as futile and pointless. Why someone values an extra five sheep to be exchanged against one cow can quite simply be referred to the value of one farming enterprise and the structure of its household economy, for example, against another. The values placed on objects represent desire which, in its turn, is formed by a person's social environment. The theory of marginal utility, provided by Menger, gives a rationalist explanation of the exchange. In Section 3, entitled 'Modes of Economic Exchange', Weber points out that economic orientation may be traditional or may be goal-oriented rationality. In the latter, the exchange of sheep against cows will follow according to marginal utility as a form of calculation; in the former, it is set by custom.

In Section 4, Weber discusses the rational allocation of goods and services in terms of present and future uses following Menger's own analysis of the individual using marginal utility. (Menger provided an important strand of investment theory by thinking of the choice between present consumption and investment for future consumption in terms of a choice of marginal utility – foregoing 'x' units of consumption for 'y' future units.) In the process of exchange, agreements are reached between parties – this is 'Vergesellschaftung', one of Weber's basic sociological concepts.

Section 5 produces a flurry of sociological terms applied to the economy.

> According to its relation to the economic system, an economically oriented organization may be: (a) an 'economically active organization' (*wirtschaftender Verband*) if the primary non-economic organized action

oriented to its order includes economic action; (b) an 'economic organization' (*Wirtschaftsverband*) if its organized action, as governed by
the order, is *primarily* autocephalous economic action of a given kind;
(c) an 'economically regulative organization' (*wirtschaftsregulierender
Verband*) if the autocephalous economic activity of the member is directly oriented to the order governing the group; that is, if economic
action is heteronomous in that respect; (d) an 'organization enforcing
a formal order' (*Ordnungsverband*) if its order merely guarantees, by
means of formal rules, the autocephalous and autonomous economic
activities of its members and the corresponding economic advantages
thus acquired.

(ES, p. 74)

This is difficult to understand, and it is hard to grasp its significance; it
also stands as an indication of why Chapter 2 does not count as the most
read piece of Weberiana. (d) is a free market order with little interference or
regulation by the state; (b) is when a body, such as a medieval gild, regulates
economic activity. (b) is simply an economic enterprise from the smallest
workshop to the largest international company, and (a) is a non-economic
institution such as a church or a state that manages its own financial affairs.
When this analysis is rendered as a 2 by 2 matrix, it forms the basis of a
theory of regulation. Medieval gilds and modern companies or corporations
are primarily economic organizations. The Church is primarily a religious
organization, but does act in an important secondary capacity as an owner
of extensive real estate (Figure 9.1).

Weber adds that, even in economically independent enterprises with light
regulations, principles of law and taxation will have a considerable effect
upon the enterprise, and he cross-references to his sociology of law.

Section 6 offers a sociology of money, drawing on the monetary theory
of Knapp and von Mises. Weber outlines two axes: means of payment and
means of exchange. In a modern market economy, both are automatically
thought of in terms of money. But in economic history, exchanges occur

		Regulation	
		High	Low
Type of economic organization	Primary	Medieval gild	Company in free market environment
	Secondary	Church lands	Voluntary organization

Figure 9.1 Types of economic regulation.

without money through the use of ornaments, clothing or other useful objects. Whether through money or other means, value has to be guaranteed by law or conventions that confer their validity ('Geltung'). Money itself is subdivided by Weber into free available coinage (through a national mint), limited money and regulated money, both of the last two operating under restrictions of the issuing body. The means of exchange and the means of payment rarely coincide in 'primitive conditions', whereas the modern state is dependent on both coinciding – effective taxation assumes a monetized economy. The argument can be used today where financial instruments, exclusive to financial traders, represent innovative means of payment that have repercussions for exchange in the modern economy. As economic activity is always time related – decisions are made in the present with regard to future outcomes, e.g. consumption versus investment – the nature of the economy would change if the means of payment no longer coincided with the means of exchange (Figure 9.2).

A similar sort of analysis can be carried out for Section 8 'The Market', in which Weber introduces the two axes of regulation of markets and the extension of marketability of goods and a further subdivision of rational and non-rational regulation (ES, p. 83).

Section 9 'Formal and Substantive Rationality of Economic Action' produces a complex set of options. One axis is formal rationality, which Weber defines as quantitative calculation or accounting. Calculation in terms of money (the other option is in kind) is closely tied to accounting, which is designed to allow a periodical comparison of expenditure and revenue. Substantive economic rationality is the meeting of the needs of groups of persons where economic action is oriented to certain specific values that are treated as ultimate, 'whether they be ethical, political, utilitarian, hedonistic, feudal, egalitarian or whatever'. Economic activity could therefore be orientated to feudal and knightly ostentation, i.e. governed by a lifestyle, or it could be governed by wartime economic criteria of austerity and armaments. Today, in Organization for Economic Co-operation and Development (OECD) countries, economic competence is judged in terms of formal procedures

		Medium of exchange	
		Chartal	Non-chartal
Means of payment	Fully circulating	Monetary economy	Tokens e.g. shells in simple economy
	Restricted circulation	Private coinage	Futures and options in commodities

Figure 9.2 Economic sociology of money.

(fiscal prudence, open markets, commercial law, accountancy methods). These criteria approximate to what Weber means by formal rationality. In substantive terms, they are seen to deliver wealth and hedonism, but these substantive goals are subsidiary to the means of attainment. Weber's analysis of modernity is borne out in that means are elevated over ends. But this is a fine judgement. The motivational bases of the modern economy would probably not be sustained without a commitment to consumerist hedonism, which, as a substantive goal, strongly influences the nature of capitalist production. Also, other substantive goals remain a focus of oppositional groups and social movements. The fight against poverty is an egalitarian goal, just as environmental sustainability is an ethical goal, both of which are substantively rational. They could only be forced through by political means. This would then permit economic policy to introduce rational economic measures for the attainment of those substantive goals. Weber, as an academic, would have remained value free in such debates, not least because the interaction between formal and substantive rationality is complex, and the adoption of substantive goals would undoubtedly have unintended and unwanted consequences. Amartya Sen's work on famine relief, which is substantively rational in moral criteria, demonstrates that certain features of the market – its ability to process information quickly, i.e. the needs of starving people – favour formal rationality.[10]

In Section 11 'The Concept and Types of Profit-making. The Role of Capital', Weber distinguishes the interests of consumers from those of profitability of the entrepreneur. There is a distribution of power between consumer and owner. Economic theory treats each decision as governed by marginal utility. Weber, however, holds that the accounting calculations of profit-making enterprises differ fundamentally from those of consumers' utility. This inserts an opposition of interests in their respective economic activities. Furthermore, the entrepreneur will try to 'direct' and to 'awaken' the wants of the consumer, i.e. the capitalist, given the opportunities, will manipulate the consumer. The market is a '*battle of man with man*' (ES, p. 93; Weber's emphasis). 'Profitability is indeed *formally* a rational category, but for that very reason it is indifferent with respect to *substantive* postulate unless these can make themselves felt in the market in the form of sufficient purchasing power' (ES, p. 94). A contemporary example of the latter would be 'fair trade' products in supermarkets.

Ownership and property tends to be taken as axiomatic in market economies. In Section 11, Weber refers the reader back to his definition of property in Chapter 1. The relevant section there concerns closed relationships. 'Appropriated advantages will be called "rights"'. 'Appropriated rights which are enjoyed by individuals through inheritance or by hereditary groups, whether communal or associative, will be called the "property" of the individual or of groups in question; and, insofar as they are alienable, "free" property' (ES, p. 44). It is helpful here to think of the appropriation of communally held rights in the Soviet Union and People's Republic of China – first, by the respective Communist Parties and, then, by individuals. Such, in an accelerated case (compared with England), is the process of creating property. Considerable legal effort is now being expended in making those property rights alienable, i.e. they can be bought and sold. The Russian oil giant Yukos is doing this (in 2006) through the expedient of bringing the company on to the market through the London Stock Exchange, although this would not necessarily exclude Russian citizens legally disputing the right to do this. At a later point, Weber points out that the firm, like any technological product, has first to be 'invented' (ES, p. 200; Weber's quotation marks).

It becomes increasingly apparent in the course of the long Chapter 2 how Weber inserts a sociology underneath economic theory and its treatment of markets and other related phenomena; also that Weber's social economics still has direct relevance today to uncover the sociological foundations of processes that would otherwise be glossed over as normal market behaviour. The trend to formal economic rationality, as Weber noted, gathers pace with the move to a market economy and its extension.

> The organization of economic activity on the basis of a market economy presupposes the appropriation of the material sources of utility on the one hand, and market freedom on the other. The effectiveness of market freedom increases with the degree to which these sources of utility, particularly the means of transport and production, are appropriated.
>
> (ES, p. 112)

On capital accounting, Weber writes, 'it will be shown that the most varied sorts of external and subjective barriers account for the fact that capital accounting has arisen as a basic form of economic calculation only in the Occident' (ES, p. 92). These two quotes indicate a developmental trend: only in the west is there the rationalism of markets, accounting and formal rationality. Chapter 2 is repeating the overwhelming trend to rationalism in the west, summarized in 'Prefatory Remarks'. Yet, the predominant impression of Chapter 2 is a neutrality towards history in favour of universal–historical analysis (often of a conceptual matrix character or conceptual algorithm, as in the above figures, rather than 'mere' classificatory typologies). How, it may be wondered, will Weber deal with his pronounced 'historicist' phase of the PESC?

A number of passages cast light on the question. In Section 11, Weber insists on a conceptual distinction between private wealth and capital, and the household unit and the profit-making enterprise. Wealth and profit making may seem to be identical but are, in fact, driven by different motivations and meanings. The enterprise is oriented to maintaining and improving profitability and its market position. It will ensure this through accurate budgeting. The holder of wealth will orientate his behaviour to security of wealth and its increase: 'the purchase of securities on the part of a private investor who wishes to consume the proceeds is not a "*capital*-investment", but a "*wealth*-investment" (ES, pp. 98–9). This is of course no surprise today when wealth holders are able to destroy enterprises for their capital assets. What is surprising is that Weber applies this to the economy in the ancient world and the dispute over the 'oikos', ignited by Rodbertus, and resolved, to an extent, by Bücher. Without these distinctions, says Weber, 'it is impossible to understand the economic development of the ancient world and the limitations on the development of capitalism of those times. (The well-known articles of Rodbertus are in spite of their errors and incompleteness, still important in this context, but should be supplemented by the excellent discussion of Karl Bücher.)' (ES, p. 99).

Unpacking this comment a little: Weber argues that antiquity had capitalism and wealthy owners, but they did not have profit making on a rational basis capable of reckoning the return of investment and expenditures over a fixed time period. The ancient world had capitalism (as well as the 'oikos', 'pace' Rodbertus) but, without rational profit making, it lacked any continuous dynamic growth. This is a more sophisticated version of his comments in 1909 in the 'Agrarverhältnisse im Altertum'. But, unlike his 1909 article, Weber has a marked disinclination to involve himself in developmental history and its controversies.

A similar comment occurs in Section 15, 'Types of Economic Division of Labor'. Weber makes the still valuable analytical separation of the technical division of labour (organizing production), the social division of labour (how autonomous firms exist in a given social structure and its system of social stratification) and the economic division of labour (how the organization of production relates to budgetary administration and profit-making enterprise). Schmoller had advanced a theory of economic development that identified a series of stages: domestic economy, village economy, seigneurial and princely patrimonial household economy, town economy, territorial economy and national-economy. Weber rejected this stage theory because its descriptors did not pick up the underlying division of labour. Karl Bücher reworked the stage theory according to a more theoretical account of the division of labour (in *Die Enstehung der Volkswirtschaft* – see above, p. 127). In Chapter 2, Weber endorses Bücher against Schmoller – to an extent. Then in a long passage explains why his chapter did not relate to history.

> It should be emphatically stated that the present discussion is concerned only with a brief summary of the *sociological* aspects of these phenomena, so far as they are relevant to its context. The *economic* aspect is included only insofar as it is expressed in what are formally sociological categories. The presentation would be economic in the *substantive* sense only if the price and market conditions, which so far have been dealt with only on the theoretical level, were brought in. But these substantive aspects of the general problem could be worked into such a summary introduction only in the form of terse theses, which would involve some very dubious distortions.
>
> (ES, p. 115)

What Weber finds dubious is the use of economic theory in economic history.

'To take an example: It might be argued that for the development of medieval, corporately regulated, but "free" labor the decisive period should be seen in the "dark" ages from the tenth to the twelfth century, and in particular in the situation during that period of the skilled (peasant, mining and artisan) labour force whose production activity was oriented to the revenue chances of the feudal lords . . .' (ES, p. 115). Feudal lords fought to secure these revenue sources through their control over manpower, creating a spurt forward in the economy. Weber declares his disinterest in applying theory to history in this way, fearing it could be erroneous. (It is interesting to note that one of the major theories, now canvassed, for this economic spurt is climate warming.)

At a later point in the chapter – the section on the 'Social Division of Labour' – Weber returns to Rodbertus and Bücher as well as his own work on agrarian conditions east of the Elbe. Each of these subjects was strongly tied to historical and developmental change; Rodbertus because of his 'oikos' theory, Bücher an amended stage theory, and Weber's own study that showed the dynamism of capitalistic labour relations in place of traditional ones. The historical dimensions are all 'flattened' to fit within a systematic exposition of types of the social division of labour. The 'oikos' represented 'autarky of want satisfaction through the utilization of the services of household members or of dependent labor . . .' (ES, p. 124). The agricultural estate 'of the German East with a labour force holding small plots of estate land on a service tenure and entirely oriented to the order of the estate (*Instleute*)' is equated with the enterprise and division of labour of the 'putting out' system (ES, p. 125). And Bücher is mentioned in connection with household enterprises and casual labour. Weber's comparisons here work *across* history, not with history as a developmental sequence.

He gives another example, provocatively, from sixteenth-century Europe. 'The decisive period for the development of capitalism could be claimed to be the great chronic price revolution of the sixteenth century.' The economic theory, Weber notes, argues that rising prices stimulated agrarian economic activity – in England, as capitalistic enterprise, and East of the Elbe, through forced labour. Also, according to theory, industrial prices fell relative to agricultural prices, triggering changes in the organization of enterprises to improve competitiveness. Of these theories, Weber opines, 'In order to verify *theoretical* reasoning about the *substantive* economic conditions of the development of economic structure, theses such as these and similar ones would have to be utilized.' One such 'similar theory' could of course be Weber's own Protestant ethic thesis. Weber makes it abundantly clear that he has no interest in becoming engaged in such manoeuvres. 'These and numerous other equally controversial theories, even so far as they could be proved not to be wholly erroneous, cannot be incorporated in the present scheme which is intentionally limited to sociological *concepts*.' Weber is being severe, and it should not be overlooked that, had he chosen, he could have put up his own theory against the erroneous theory of price inflation, which after all is how knowledge progresses. But no.

> In renouncing any attempt of this sort, however, the following exposition in this chapter explicitly repudiates any claim to concrete 'explanation' and restricts itself to working out a sociological typology. The same is true of the previous discussion in that it consciously omitted to develop a theory of money and price determination. This must be strongly emphasized. For only the facts of the economic situation provide the flesh and blood for a genuine explanation of also that process of development relevant for sociological theory. What can be done here is only to supply a scaffolding adequate to provide the analysis with relatively unambiguous and definite concepts.
>
> It is obvious not only that no attempt is made here to do justice to the historical aspect of economic development, but also that the typology of the genetic sequence of possible forms is neglected. The present aim is only to develop a schematic system of classification.
>
> (ES, p. 116)

This statement is reinforced towards the end of the chapter in Section 39 where Weber discusses the impact of intellectual disciplines that have incorporated ethical and religious values and convictions. These 'have tended to limit the development of an autonomous capitalistic system of the modern type to certain areas.' He continues,

> In an historical analysis, we can only point out certain circumstances which exert negative influences on the relevant thought processes – that is, influences which impede or even obstruct them – or such which exert a positive, favoring influence. It is not, however, possible to prove a strictly inevitable causal relationship in such cases, any more than it is possible in any other case of strictly individual events.
>
> (ES, p. 200)

I have made clear from the start of this book that we should be wary of trying to draw connections and unities and trajectories when they might well not exist. But the above statements so trumpet Weber disinterest with history in its development and genetic sequence that they deserve some comment. Clearly, this is not the Weber of 1904–5, who sought to develop heuristically honed cultural concepts in order to explain a causal process of a crucial juncture in European history. That may well have been a too adventurous undertaking, but one nonetheless undertaken by an extremely well-informed lecturer in national economics. And Weber always defended the Protestant thesis to the hilt against his critics.

The move into the respective projects c. 1910 of 'Economy and Society' and the 'Economic Ethics of the World Religions' cannot be described as the abandonment of the Protestant ethic thesis – although as noted below (pp. 122–3), Weber did fail to follow up on detailed studies of the Reformation. Rather, the two projects represent a dilution of the thesis and its highly culturally attuned methodology. Puritanism becomes but one episode in the long history of occidental rationalism, and the comparative studies into the religious influence of economic ethics reveal not causative factors but simply the difference between ways of life and cultures. The final version of *Economy and Society* is forced to withdraw from the developmental thrusts that characterized the special sociologies of law, rulership and religion. Typologies, while built around orientation in respect to meaning, are offered as a practical step to further detailed research. The typologies in the final version are universal–historical and 'renounce' any claim to stages, development and genetic history.

Chapter 2 is infrequently studied and has remained something of a puzzle. Its purpose, I think, is pretty clear – it was to be the key text of *Economy and Society* as it fitted into the *Grundriss der Sozialökonomik*. This is not a very satisfying thing to say, because the final version of the whole book was never completed, so it is extremely hard to gain a sense of how it fitted into the overall scheme. But it does repay study, it is still very relevant, and Weber's discipline of social economics needs to be relaunched. It is a highly considered and dense piece of writing. We may ask whether Weber himself considered he had gone out on a limb with the Protestant ethic thesis. The consensus of scholarly opinion is that it is a very hard thesis to sustain, not least, as I have shown in Chapter 4, because of its (impossible) methodological demands. Weber, like a good professional sportsman, never showed or admitted weakness. His footnotes addressing his critics in the revised 1920 PESC are pugilistic. But in crafting Chapter 2, Weber was demonstrating that he not only understood economics but, above all, capitalism. Further research to settle the issues more decisively would, for Weber, require a firm sociological underpinning.

Coda: is there a Weber paradigm?

In early 1920, Weber broke off from writing his 'Basic Concepts of Sociology' to read the 240 pages of Volume 1 of Robert Liefmann's *The Principles of Modern Economic Theory*.[11] Liefmann had been pressing Weber for his views of the book, which included a critique of sociology and a presentation of Weber's own standpoint. Weber replied to Liefmann on 9 March with a long letter. Weber pointed out that he was now also a sociologist under the terms of his contract. As a sociologist, he is making an end of the bad enterprise with collective concepts, 'for sociology is individualistic'.

> The state, for example, is a place where one finds prospects of certain types of action, the action of definite people. 'Subjective' means that action is oriented to definite ideas ('Vorstellungen'). The 'objective' for us

observers is the chances that with this orientation to ideas the action will ensue. So, if certain actions did not ensue, there would not be a state.

Weber raises this clarification as a correction to Liefmann's treatment of utility and prices in economic theory. Subjective value, writes Weber, in an economic transaction is what one party reckons or estimates a particular commodity is worth to him. The actual price paid for a commodity is an objective, historical fact.

Liefmann had written of Weber that he says that the knowledge value of theory is 'small'.[12] Weber protested.

> Where did I say that? Theory creates ideal types and for me this function is simply indispensable. That sociology and economic history *never* re-place theory is one of my basic convictions. What interests me (accord-ing to your page 17) is more the 'special' situation ('Zusammenhang')? *Yes*, if one is asking the question: *why only* in the Occident has rational (profit-making) capitalism originated, and one can call that a 'special' situation! There have to be people who investigate this question. In this, only highly paradoxical complexes are important. The modern economy presupposes not only the rational state, in the sense of its calculable functions, but also rational technology (science) and a defined form of rational life-conduct. Why didn't modern capitalism originate in China? It had many thousand years for that! For centuries they have had ex-change, paper money for 1100 years, coinage for 2600 years.[13]

These passages are part of a point-by-point rebuttal and discussion of Liefmann's book, and so are contextually specific. It is also worth noting that Liefmann appears to misunderstand the fundamentals of Weber's approach. One inference to be drawn from the exchange between Liefmann and Weber is that it is difficult to be conclusive about Weber. When he wrote the let-ter – with its summating insights as to his approach – he was in another of his expansionary periods of work. He was completing the final version of *Economy and Society* – at speed – and he had revised his collected essays in the sociology of religion. He might have continued with his advertised plans to expand his studies on the world religions. But he might not have. Bavaria and Munich had experienced revolution, rule by soviets and counter-revolu-tionary violence – all before his own eyes. In Russia, the revolution of 1917 had held. Weber could have returned to his studies of Russia and expanded his political sociology of revolution, and of the limits of direct democracy. The conclusion to be drawn from this book is that Weber was unpredictable in the direction of his writings. His was not a neatly built academic career and reputation.

Nevertheless, certain constants can be drawn throughout the variation in his studies. Methodology is the foremost. Weber does give the impression that he had solved the methodological problems in national-economy and its related disciplines to his satisfaction. There is a consistency from his essay on 'Objectivity' in the social sciences (1904) through to 'Basic Sociological Concepts in 1920. His position presumes that academic knowledge in the social sciences is precarious and provisional in a way that is less so for the natural sciences, which are able to uncover more enduring regularities and produce law-like statements. His epistemology, i.e. his assumptions about social scientific knowledge, held that there was an unbridgeable gulf between investigator and the ever-changing flux of social reality. Moreover, the investigator was himself, or herself, part of the ongoing flux of reality. Academic knowledge does not stand apart from the world, fixed somehow in time while an objective study of social reality is conducted. What distinguishes academic knowledge is the motivation of the social scientist to choose a topic or research problem for study, because it has knowledge value ('wissenwert'). These values could be intrinsic to a discipline as a community of researchers, which is how Rickert thought about this issue. Or the individual researcher might be motivated by a wider pool of ideas, including that of his or her own creativity, which at its extreme reaches the artistic licence of a Nietzsche. The connection between investigator and the social/cultural/historical situation studied is transmitted through the medium of values and meanings. It was Dilthey who pointed out that this was not only the distinguishing feature of the human sciences that separated it from the natural sciences, it was also its major advantage and not a limitation. Human beings can understand other human beings through a process of interpretation of meaning. The medium through which this interpretation of meaning operates was and remains an issue of controversy. Simmel and others inclined to the view that there existed some kind of psychological meta-soul, into which we could also somehow dip and intuit the motivation of other people, now and across time. Dilthey, to his credit, pointed out that the interpretation of meaning is worked out, more arduously and with claims to correctness and truth, through the techniques of textual hermeneutics. Weber assumes that the interpretation of meaning is possible and is achieved through the Diltheyan route of empathy and re-experience. He asserts this, rather than justifying it in his methodology. He secures the reliability of interpretation through the procedure of casual attribution of motivation, which, as a retrospective and empirical exercise, ascertains the hypothetical nature of understanding motives and meanings.

The ideal type functions as the equivalent of experimental design in the natural sciences. The methods of both are quite easy to outline. In an experiment, the investigator matches two situations with the exception of one key factor. In the ideal type, an interpreted meaning is intensified in order to provide conceptual clarity. In both situations, the complexity and sheer messiness of the world in its immediate state have to be manipulated to discern underlying causal mechanisms. Pure affect, pure instrumental rationality, pure tradition are ways of heuristically manipulating what is being studied to reach an empirical assessment of how each meaning should be weighed – how ideas are actuated in social reality. The ideal type in *Weber's* hands is, however, more than a method. Just as an academic psychologist will point out that it is not the experimental method *per se* but the cleverness of the design that is the real contribution to knowledge, so with the imaginative and theoretical power of Weber's own ideal types. Weber's comments to Liefmann slot in here. Ideal types stand for theory and are 'indispensable'. Weber's own ideal type of ascetic life conduct and its effects on economic behaviour have become part of the canon of sociological ideas as well as entering public consciousness, just as charisma has. To some small degree, the world is seen through Weber's ideas, testifying to the power and creativity of the ideal type.

'That sociology and economic history never replace theory is one of my basic convictions.' Weber's position on methodology and ideal type, which are generic to the social and cultural sciences, are in my view paradigmatic; his views on sociology less so. In Thomas Kuhn's concept of paradigm, it was not simply a new unifying theory and research programme, but the accommodating capacity of a theory to researchers on institutional, normative and social grounds. Weber's thinking about sociology is not broadly accommodating. He always turned his back on a general sociology, disputing its claims to a totalizing, or organicist, or positivist, or evolutionary view of the world. He had a disinclination to build in the features that the later twentieth century has thought indispensable. He preferred to conceptualize the sociological field exclusively in terms of social relationships of particular kinds. He did not develop an explicit theory of institutions, he had no notion of role and he rejected a formal theory of system differentiation. Above all, he was never tempted to construct a frame or social system within which the actions of the individual were to be integrated. This sets him apart from prominent sociologists such as Talcott Parsons or Pierre Bourdieu, whose whole oeuvre is a continuing attempt to reconcile action at the level of the individual and group with the structures or systems of society. For Weber, this would be akin to trying to square a circle. The same point can be made with respect to sociologists such as James Coleman and George Ritzer, who would unify the micro with the macro. For Weber, there is only one level – sociology is 'individualistic' – as he wrote to Liefmann. This I do not think should be read that sociology is atomistic; rather, as a statement against any form of reification. Of all the major sociologists, Weber had the lowest tolerance threshold to reification. Structures, classes, regimes, orders, value spheres all feature, unavoidably, in Weber's sociology, but not as sociological objects or things. Law, noted Weber, exists as a living entity insofar as the state enacts law, and lawyers and courts process it. But sociologically, what counts is the idea or meaning of law in the mind and actions of the individual. The operation of 'structures' (Weber's 'Gebilde') is denominated in the motives, meaning, thinking and actions of individuals. Hence, the purpose of sociology is to depict the basic sociological relationships.

In one sense, this is dismaying for sociology because it is permanently reduced to an underlabouring role: to theory on one side and to verification on the other, which is carried out by historians and economic history. But underlabouring does not capture Weber's fashioning of sociology, which for him, in the form of a theory of social action, underwrites any study in the social sciences, to the extent that meaning is constitutive of people's actions. Hence, sociology also turns out to be indispensable even though it does have to restrict its ambitions.

Dismay, however, on the part of sociologists can be countered by the place of theory. The whole thrust of the Weberian enterprise is theoretical. Ideal types are heuristic nets cast into the flux of social reality. They create a rapport at the level of meaning; they are interventions into social reality. Theory is generated by economists, political scientists, academic theologians ('Religionswissenschaft'), the study of law, ethnography and anthropology. Referring back to Figure 8.2 (p. 232), these other disciplines can be envisaged as substantive sociologies. Today, we would say that Weber demands an interdisciplinary science of society, with the basic sociological concepts underwriting the enterprise. A pure sociology, therefore, is somewhat ineffectual by itself. To ask the important questions about power, interests, want satisfaction, culture, religion, the nature of the human animal requires the presence of substantive sociologies committed to the large issues and questions of the day.

Future tasks and debates

In the Introduction to this book, I stated that the revaluation of Weber's work would involve a critical engagement with some of his central questions. In one part, this demands a critical scholarship in relation to his writings, and this has taken up the majority of this book. But another part necessitates emerging from the scholarly cave and engaging with contemporary issues and debates. There are a number of central questions that are relevant to both Weber's day and ours and, in this sense, they may be described as classic. A critical scholarship should be making the full complexity of his writing accessible to contemporary debates, and it should also challenge interpretations that patronize, reconstruct or fail to acknowledge both the complexity and the multiple directions of the writings. I list four central questions for further debate.

1   Social economics. Weber's whole academic life existed within the intellectual framework of national-economy. He was one of the very few proponents in Germany of the Austrian marginalist revolution in economics, yet clearly he remained committed to the historical, cultural and social analysis of economic activity. The marginalist heuristic exercise, the fiction of pure rationality, entered into his formulation of the ideal type. His sociology developed in parallel with his immense project to found a social economics. But very little of that latter project

remains, and the critical question is whether we should be making more use of that buried legacy. It is a little strange that Weber can be honoured as a sociologist but more or less forgotten as an economist. Richard Swedberg has made important contributions in this department, but are we yet able to characterize social economics and state what value it still has in relation to the dominant paradigm of neo-classical economic theory – a huge and powerful edifice that Weber would have termed economic rationalism.[14]

Part of this task involves a critical scrutiny of the account provided of social economics and of Weber in general by Joseph Schumpeter in his *History of Economic Analysis*. Schumpeter was part of the stable of authors who composed the project of social economics. His contribution to the *Grundriss der Sozialökonomik* – first published in German in 1912, translated as *Economic Doctrine and Method* and published after his death in 1954 – makes a more measured assessment of the potential of Weber's approach than that provided in his later *History of Economic Analysis*.[15] No mention is made by Schumpeter of Weber's familiarity with the economic writings of Carl Menger, Bohm-Bäwerk and von Wieser. Much of this is perhaps bound up with the disastrous situation of economic life and economic policy in central Europe after 1918 and the sense that marginalist economics was to be developed in the Anglo-Saxon world. Nevertheless, the question remains whether our remembrance of Weber's social economics is adequate.

2   Weber's central position on hermeneutics (a term he did not use) connects meaning with causal attribution. Weber can be criticized for not engaging in an explicit acknowledgement and critique of Dilthey. Weber used his method of 'Verstehen', but wanted to remain distant from any hint of psychologism and of 'Lebensphilosophie'. This is a disservice to nineteenth-century hermeneutics, whose function and technique was to establish textual truth. The great bifurcation between analytical philosophy and the positivism of the Vienna circle, on the one side, and phenomenological and interpretive philosophies on the other side – which gets under way in the 1920s – might have developed differently had hermeneutics not been seen as reductive, relativist and unreliable. Weber's method of 'Verstehen' in practice resisted any such bifurcation. The interpretation of meaning is an attribution of a cause or reason for acting, whose consequences are empirically ascertainable. The debate remains. It is still controversial to assume that a reason for acting can be considered as a cause of acting. Also the interpretation of meaning as a reason or motivation for acting requires the application of ordinary language philosophy, as for example in Donald Davidson's essays.

3   Philosophy of history. Weber was against this in its guises of Hegelian idealism, Marxist historical materialism, and evolutionism in its Comtean or Frazerian forms. Weber held that the empiricism of historical

'nacheinander', the cause and effect of concrete events, was a necessary discipline and source of verification. But his historical sociology was founded in strong theory construction. His developmental history on a comparative basis revolved around the coming together of certain material and ideal interests. The causal model that underlay this coming together was the theory of 'elective affinity'. Culture bonds with material and political interests to produce determinative outcomes in the course of civilizational history. I cannot see that Weber ever progressed beyond this conception, which was introduced as an explanatory metaphor in PESC in 1904–5. Chemical bonding – and elective affinity is its nineteenth century equivalent – is, as we now know, an immensely strong force. Just how one can explicate the mechanisms of elective affinity within historical sociology is an issue that remains unresolved, indeed barely even addressed seriously. For Weber, it is handled as cultural ideas determining life conduct in interaction with material interests. The alternatives are the programme developed by W.G. Runciman of selectionism in history, in which the initiation of cultural ideas and interests becomes subsidiary to their uptake within the temporally subsequent social environment. Or the most popular alternative is the historical sociology of multifactorialism, discussed in relation to Michael Mann's work on power. Multifactorial causation and selectionism can claim lineages to Max Weber but, along with elective affinities, they are each separate and different programmes.

4   Singularity of modernity. The benign position on the origins and nature of modernity is to argue that its constitution includes a reflexive capacity in politics, science, technology and culture to steer the direction of societal development in a desired direction; also that the modernity, which originated in the west, is in fact adaptable by other cultures and civilizations to their own values. This is the multiple modernities position as developed by S.N. Eisenstadt and colleagues. It owes more to Karl Jaspers than it does to Max Weber who, I would argue, saw modernity as the singular accomplishment of western rationalism. At root, it is a pessimistic vision. Western science was rooted in the reflexive innovation that concepts, resulting from rational thought, could be intervened between the human beings and their immediate experience of the world. As such, it was the intellectual successor to cultural religions, which had already made metaphysical interventions of various sorts. In that sense, science represented progress but also disenchantment. Once the tree of knowledge is bitten into, the magic garden of existence becomes subject, inescapably, to rational discourse. Puritanism was uniquely inimical to magic, rite and superstition, and jolts, as a minor but historic episode, a civilizational configuration into an irreversible direction. To an extent, Weber might even have underplayed the role of what the Toronto school would term the 'symbolic technologies' at work in this process, which accelerate social relationships away from the 'Gemeinschaft' of face-

to-face relationships to the associative patterns of relationships made possible through modern communication.

Weber writes that mechanism supervenes over meaning:

> This order is now bound to the technical and economic conditions of machine production which to-day determine the lives of all the individuals who are born into this mechanism, not only those directly concerned with economic acquisition, with irreversible force. Perhaps it will so determine them until the last ton of fossil fuel is burnt.
>
> (PESC, p. 181)[16]

This has an even more ominous ring to it some hundred years after it was written. In another hundred years, it is most probable that the last ton of fossil fuel will have been burnt. In the singularity argument, this is an irreversible process of rationalization driven by the inner logic of occidental rationalism; and if modernity is singular, there is no other, alternative modernity. By its nature, modernity is concerned with the perfection of means rather than the deeper reflection on the ends of humankind.

Notes

Introduction

1 Nelson, B., 'Max Weber's "Author's Introduction" (1920): A Master Clue to his Main Aims', *Sociological Inquiry*, 44, 4, 1974, pp. 269–78.
2 Nelson, p. 275.
3 Colliot-Thélène, C., *La Sociologie de Max Weber*, Paris: La Découverte, 2006, p. 6.
4 See his *The Rise of Western Rationalism. Max Weber's Developmental History*, Roth, G. (transl.), Berkeley, CA: University of California Press, 1981 and *Rationalism, Religion and Domination. A Weberian Perspective*, Solomon, N. (transl.), Berkeley, CA: University of California Press, 1988.
5 Scaff, L., 'Weber before Weberian sociology', in *Reading Weber*, Tribe, K. (ed), London: Routledge, 1989, pp. 15–41.
6 See Roth, G., *Max Webers deutsch–englische Familiengeschichte 1800–1950*, Tübingen: Mohr Siebeck, 2001; Radkau, J., *Max Weber. Die Leidenschaft des Denkens*, Munich: Hanser, 2005; Whimster, S., (ed.), *Max Weber and the Culture of Anarchy*, Basingstoke: Macmillan, 1999.
7 See the collection *Max Weber zum Gedächtnis*, König, R., and Winckelmann, J. (eds), Cologne: Westdeutscher Verlag, 1963.
8 Graf, F.W., 'Ernst Troeltsch's Evaluation of Max and Alfred Weber. Introduction and Translation of a Letter by Ernst Troeltsch to Heinrich Dietzel', *Max Weber Studies*, 4.1, 2004, p. 105.
9 Lepsius, M.R., 'Münchens Beziehungen zu Max Weber und zur Pflege seines Werks', *Das Faszinosum Max Webers. Die Geschichte seiner Geltung*, Borchardt, K. and Ay, K.-L. (eds), Constance: UVK, 2006, p. 23.
10 *Zur Geschichte der Handelsgesellschaften im Mittelalter. Nach südeuropäischen Quellen* (Stuttgart: Ferdinand Enke, 1889) has been recently translated and edited by Lutz Kaelber, as *The History of Commercial Partnerships in the Middle Ages* (Lanham, Mary: Rowman & Littlefield, 2003).
11 In April, 1919 Weber became 'Professor für Gesellschaftslehre, Wirtschaftsgeschichte und Nationalökonomie'. See Lepsius, *Faszinosum*, p. 19 and p. 259 below.
12 Strauss, L., *Natural Right and History*, Chicago, IL: Chicago University Press, 1953, pp. 35–80.

1 Weber before Weberian sociology, revisited

1 First published 'Weber before Weberian Sociology', *British Journal of Sociology*,

35, 1984, pp. 190–215; reprinted in *Reading Weber*, Tribe, K. (ed.), London: Routledge, 1989, pp. 15–41.

2 Scaff, L., in *Reading Weber*, p. 16.

3 Turner, B.S., *For Weber. Essays in the Sociology of Fate*, London: Routledge, 1984, p. 354.

4 Turner, p. 353.

5 Dawe, A., 'The Two Sociologies', *British Journal of Sociology*, 21, 2, 1970, pp. 207–8.

6 Giddens, A., *Central Problems in Social Theory: Action, Structure and Contradiction in Social Analysis*, Berkeley, CA: University of California Press, 1979; *Modernity and Self Identity*, Oxford: Polity, 1991.

7 Colliot-Thélène, C., *La Sociologie de Max Weber*, Paris: La Découverte, 2006, p. 5.

8 Schroeder, R., *Max Weber and the Sociology of Culture*, London: Sage, 1992, p. 9. The reference to Kalberg, S. is 'Weber, Max (1864–1920)' in *The Social Science Encyclopaedia*, Kuper, A., and Kuper J. (eds), London: Routledge, 1985. Stephen Kalberg's integration of social action types with macrohistorical process was further developed in his *Max Weber's Historical-Sociology*, Chicago, IL: Chicago University Press, 1994.

9 Scaff, L., in *Reading Weber*, p. 16.

10 In 1871, a number of German kingdoms, principalities and small states were consolidated under Prussian leadership into a unitary state. The King of Prussia became its Emperor, and an electoral franchise and parliamentary system were introduced. The German (Second) Empire ceased to exist in November 1918. The period 1892–1918 is also often termed Wilhelmine Germany after the name of its emperor, Kaiser Wilhelm II.

11 Webb, S.B., 'Agricultural Protection in Wilhelmian Germany: Forging an Empire with Pork and Rye', reprinted in *The Economic Development of Germany since 1870*, Fischer, W., (ed.), Lyme: Edward Elgar, 1997, pp. 400–18. See also the recently discovered article by Max Weber, 'Germany – Agriculture and Forestry', reprinted in *Max Weber Studies*, 6.2, 2006, pp. 207–18.

12 This was a long established tradition in the autocratic Prussian state. See Rosenberg, H., *Bureaucracy, Aristocracy and Autocracy. The Prussian Experience, 1660–1815*, Cambridge, MA: Harvard University Press, 1958.

13 Riesebrodt, M., 'Einleitung' to Max Weber's *Die Lage der Landarbeiter im ostelbischen Deutschland, 1892*, in MWG, I/3, pp. 1–33.

14 Mommsen, W.J., and Aldenhoff, R., 'Einleitung' to *Landarbeiterfrage, Nationalstaat und Volkswirtschaftspolitik. Schriften und Reden 1892–1899*, MWG I/4, pp. 16–20.

15 From the point of view of research design, the *Verein*'s questionnaire favoured an inductive methodology. The study was not designed to test specific propositions, such as for instance the relationships between wages and migration. Data were gathered and conclusions were drawn afterwards.

16 Those who left the land were mostly unmarried and young, although curiously no explicit demographic questions were included in the main questionnaire.

17 Weber, M., *Die Verhältnisse der Landarbeiter im ostelbischen Deutschland*, Leipzig: Duncker & Humblot, 1892, p. 4.

18 *Die Verhältnisse der Landarbeiter*, p. 5. The emphases are Weber's.

19 'Employment regime' is a little strong as a translation but does pick up the element of national-economy in his thinking. The alternative translation is work organization, which is somewhat misleading.

20 Weber, M., 'Entwickelungstendenzen in der Lage der ostelbischen Landarbeiter', *Gesammelte Aufsätze zur Sozial- und Wirtschaftsgeschichte*, Marianne Weber (ed.), Tübingen: Mohr Siebeck, 1988, p. 474.

21 *Die Verhältnisse der Landarbeiter*, p. 16.
22 *Die Verhältnisse der Landarbeiter*, p. 701.
23 *Die Verhältnisse der Landarbeiter*, p. 795–6.
24 For a more detailed analysis of Weber's argument, see Agevall, O., 'Science, Values, and the Empirical Argument in Max Weber's Inaugural Address', *Max Weber Studies*, 4, 2, 2004, pp. 157–77.
25 *Die Verhältnisse der Landarbeiter*, p. 797.
26 Mommsen, W.J., *Max Weber and German Politics, 1890–1920*, Steinberg, M. (transl.), Chicago, IL: University of Chicago Press, 1984, pp. 35–59.
27 Weber, M., *Die römische Agrargeschichte in ihrer Bedeutung für das Staats- und Privatrecht*, Stuttgart: Ferdinand Enke, 1891. This has now appeared in the Max Weber Gesamtausgabe, edited by Jürgen Deininger, MWG I/2.
28 MWG I/2, p. 160.
29 MWG I/2, p. 216.
30 Mommsen, W.J., 'From Agrarian Capitalism to the "Spirit" of Modern Capitalism: Max Weber's Approaches to the Protestant Ethic', *Max Weber Studies*, 5, 2, 2005, pp.185–6.
31 Mommsen, pp. 186–7.
32 Kaelber, L., 'Introduction. Max Weber's Dissertation in the Context of his Early Career and Life', *The History of Commercial Partnerships in the Middle Ages*, Lanham, MD: Rowman & Littlefield, 2003. See also Kaelber, L., 'Max Weber on Usury and Medieval Capitalism: From *The History of Commercial Partnerships* to *The Protestant Ethic*', *Max Weber Studies*, 4, 1, 2004, pp. 51–75.
33 Borchardt, K., 'Max Weber's Writings on the Bourse: Puzzling Out a Forgotten Corpus', *Max Weber Studies*, 2, 2, 2002, p. 153.
34 Weber, M., quoted in Borchardt, p. 160, n. 53.
35 Quoted in Borchardt, 154.
36 Bruhns, H., 'Max Weber's "Basic Concepts" in the Context of his Studies in Economic History', *Max Weber Studies, Beiheft 1*, 2006, pp. 61–8.
37 Weber, M., *Grundriss zu den Vorlesungen über Allgemeine ("theoretische") Nationalökonomie (1898)*, Tübingen: J.C.B. Mohr (Paul Siebeck), 1990.
38 Weber commissioned Schumpeter to write this book as part of the encyclopaedia *Grundriss der Sozialökonomik*. It appeared as *Epochen der Dogmen- und Methodengeschichte*, Tübingen, J.C.B. Mohr (Paul Siebeck), 1912. It was published in English translation by George Allen & Unwin in 1954.
39 Subsection 7 of Section 2 of Weber's lecture outline is paraphrased below. It contains an exposition of value taken from the theory of marginal utility.
    7 Economic value ('Wertschätzung') in the isolated economy.
    7.1 The 'laws of value' ('Wertgesetze').
      Goods whose value is given through exchange and price. This is the normal quality of economic goods. Neither the urgency of need nor the scarcity of a good determines the price level. The specific economic good being exchanged by economic actors ('Einzelwirtschaften') is valued according to a subjective component plus motive. Cannot see this in the complexity of today's economy, so abstract theory constructs an isolated economy with no exchange, like a primitive household in the past or a communist society in the future. Economic subject meets perceived economic needs and their subjective urgency through economic decision on consumption and means of production (as above). Economic subject proceeds like a modern businessman in calculating the whole situation of supply and need. Theoretically, this operates (1) from simplified assumption of an isolated economy with given, fixed needs in a fixed period of employment of labour and material needs of production that are also fixed; (2) through assumption that the supply of goods can be increased in relation to consumption

and production means available to the household. Economic subject makes an estimate of value of the particular goods, as presumed above (1 and 2).

What is the motive that determines the level of value of a unit ('Einheit') of the absolute limited supply of consumption good 'x'? Supply of 'x' will be expended on most (subjectively) pressing needs and, at a certain point, will be forced to stop expenditure; the shorter the supply, the more pressing psychic need, the more plentiful, the less pressing. Satiation of least pressing need is dependent on an unrestricted supply of units of 'x'. This is the marginal utility of the unit of 'x'. Restriction in the supply of units of 'x' places the satiation of psychic need ('Bedürfnisregung') in question – the economic subject knows he is dependent on unrestricted supply. The consciousness of dependence is the source of value, and the intensity of dependence corresponds to marginal utility. So, declining marginal utility (increasing supply), and rising marginal utility with declining supply.

So case (1) is a law of marginal utility, the estimation of value in a monopoly situation (limited goods in isolated economy) according to measure of rank ordering of needs economically to their expected ('erzielenden') 'marginal utility'.

Case (2) is like (1) except a consumption good 'y' is reproducible (and not limited). There is a decline in the marginal utility of 'y' with the more complete satisfaction of needs, which 'y' serves, and 'costs'. In buying in 'y', the marginal utility of other goods rises. Supply of 'y' could increase costs of 'z' so long as the marginal utility of 'y' does not drop below that of 'z'.

The value of increasable goods ('cost goods') follows the specific formulation of 'law of costs' under (1) conditions of labour and capital under given technical conditions, (2) rank ordering of needs to lowest marginal utility possible. State of need and costs (not costs of labour but economic material goods) are the components of value estimation of cost goods.

40 Bohm-Bäwerk, E., *Karl Marx and the Close of His System*, McDonald, A. (transl.), London: T. Fisher Unwin, 1898. Reprinted in *Karl Marx and the Close of His System*, New York: Augustus M. Kelley, 1949.

41 In his inaugural lecture in Freiburg in 1895, Weber went out of his way to demonstrate that all economic policy judgements have to be referred in the last instance to the interests of the state. In this sense, he was not 'value free', a scientific norm that he insisted upon. In his lecture course, however, Weber was quite prepared to outline views and theories that he personally would not support. Weber thought it was wrong to reveal to students what one's own personal viewpoint was. Quite how he squared that with his inaugural lecture remains a mystery – unless the lecture was only open to academic staff.

42 Quoted by Mommsen, p. 194. The quote itself comes from Weber's own lecture notes, which will be published shortly in MWG III/1.

43 Mommsen, p. 194.

2 Capitalism in contemporary debates

1 Lehmann, H., 'Friends and Foes. The Formation and Consolidation of the *Protestant Ethic* Thesis', in *The Protestant Ethic Turns 100. Essays on the Centenary of the Weber Thesis*, Swatos, W.H., Jr, and Kaelber, L. (eds), Boulder, CO: Paradigm Publishers, 2005, pp. 1–22.

2 Lehmann, p. 3.

3 This letter, Brentano's reply, has yet to be found.

4 Lehmann, p. 4.

5 Lehmann, p. 4.

6 Quoted by Lehmann, p. 5.

7 'Geleitwort der Herausgeber', *Archiv für Sozialwissenschaft und Sozialpolitik* (Neue Folge), I, 1904, pp. I–VII.

8 Quoted by Lindenlaub, D., *Richtungskämpfe im Verein für Sozialpolitik. Part 2: Wissenchaft und Sozialpolitik vornehmlich von Beginn des "Neuen Kurses" bis zum Ausbruch des ersten Weltkrieges (1890–1914)*, Wiesbaden: Franz Steiner, 1967, p. 276.

9 Naumann, F., 'Das Suchen nach dem Wesen des Kapitalismus I', *Die Hilfe*, 17, 37, September 1911.

10 Lindenlaub, p. 280. Friedrich Naumann is cited in Lindenlaub, p. 281. These are averaged judgements, by Naumann and followed by Lindenlaub, for a group of national-economists. Weber, however, should be judged as below the average with respect to the Marxist problematic. As we have seen, Weber had already accepted the economics of marginalism and, it should be noted, Weber had an ability to hold on to not necessarily compatible positions.

11 Sombart, W., *Der moderne Kapitalismus*, Berlin, Duncker & Humblot, I, 1902.

12 Sombart's progressive views of 1902 drift away to romantic anti-modernity, and his downgrading of racial characteristics in 1902 falls prey to ethnic characterizations of capitalism.

13 See the article by Lehmann, 'Friends and Foes'; also Lenger, F., *Werner Sombart. 1863–1941. Eine Biographie*, Munich: Beck, 1994.

14 *mK*, p. 51.

15 Talcott Parsons' influential essay '"Capitalism" in recent German literature: Sombart and Weber' (1928–9, reprinted in *Talcott Parsons. The Early Essays*, Camic, C. (ed.), Chicago, IL: University of Chicago Press, 1991, pp. 3–37) uses the second editions of *mK* (1924 onwards) and PESC (1920) and overlooks the linkages as they existed in the first editions. See also the informative essay by Lehmann, H., 'The Rise of Capitalism: Weber versus Sombart', in *Weber's Protestant Ethic. Origins, Evidence, Contexts*, Lehmann, H., and Roth G. (eds), Cambridge: Cambridge University Press, 1993.

16 *mK* I, p. 383.

17 *mK* I, p. 391.

18 Gothein, E., *Wirtschaftsgeschichte des Schwarzwaldes*, I, p. 674, Strasbourg: Trübner, 1892. Quoted by Sombart, *mK* I, p. 381, note 1. Gothein's book is generally supportive of Sombart's position in that he comes down against the institutionalist/jurisdictional analysis of historians such as Georg von Below, but it is organised very much within those problematics and lacks the primacy of economic principle that Sombart demanded.

19 For a contemporary account of Darwinian selectionism applied to the Protestant ethic thesis, see the series of articles by Runciman, W.G., 'Was Max Weber a Selectionist in Spite of Himself?', *Journal of Classical Sociology*, 1.1, 2001, pp. 13–32.

20 See PESC, p. 47 and GARS, I, Mohr Siebeck, 1920, p. 30: 'In der Überschrift dieser Studie ist der etwas anspruchsvoll klingende Begriff: "Geist des Kapitalismus" verwendet. Was soll darunter verstanden werden? . . .' The quotation marks around 'Geist' become quite intriguing at this point. If Weber is objecting to the pretentiousness of 'Geist', the quotation marks become scare quotes. But they could only become scare quotes through an implicit recognition that Sombart was the one who was pretentious. Note also the remark by Lehmann in 'The Rise of Capitalism: Weber versus Sombart': 'In my view, we should not be misled by the fact that Weber mentioned Sombart only two or three times in the first version of his essay, that is, in 1904 and 1905, and that those places were quite insignificant' (p. 198).

21   *mK* I, p. 193.
22   *mK* I, pp, 396–7.
23   Not to say flamboyance. In 1530, Anton Fugger, when entertaining the Emperor Charles V, lit a cinnamon fire using an imperial i.o.u. Simmel observes that the Fuggers came to grief because their banking empire operated internationally at a time (sixteenth century) of restricted money economy. Lending money to the Emperor in Madrid did not extend his credit in Holland where it was needed. *Die Philosophie des Geldes*, Leipzig: Duncker & Humblot, 1900, p. 139.
24   PESC, p. 64; GARS, I, p. 49.
25   PESC, p. 75; GARS, I, p. 60. Weber entered a long footnote in 1920 attacking Sombart's position. PESC, note 29, pp. 202–3; GARS, I, pp. 56–9.
26   Friedrich Lenger needs to be credited with the insight that Sombart, Simmel and Weber can be usefully tied to together on the subject of 'Geist'. See his *Werner Sombart 1863–1941. Eine Biographie*, pp. 121–3.
27   *Jahrbuch für Gesetzgebung, Verwaltung und Volkswirtschaft*, vol. 13, no. 4, 1889, pp. 1251–64; now best archived through the Heptagon CD, Berlin, 2001: *Georg Simmel. Das Werk*.
28   See 'Introduction to the Translation', p. 37, note 3, in *The Philosophy of Money*, Frisby, D., and Bottomore, T. (eds/transl.), London: Routledge & Kegan Paul, 1978.
29   Weber, Marianne, *Max Weber. A Biography*, Zohn, H. (transl.), New Brunswick, NJ: Transaction Books, 1988, p. 253.
30   See Sombart, *mK*, I, p. 383: 'Damit aber war die Zeit erfüllt, daß sich jener merkwürdige psychologische Prozeß in den Menschen abermals vollzog, dessen Verlauf uns neuerdings mit gewohnter Meisterschaft Georg Simmel geschildert hat: die Erhebung des absoluten Mittels – des Geldes – zum höchsten Zweck.' Parsons provides an excellent summary of Sombart on money, not realizing it is taken from Simmel: 'All the qualitative differences of the most diverse economic goods are reduced to a single common denominator, money. This quantitative measure gives a means of comparison of diverse goods on the one hand. On the other hand it gives an objective purpose for all economic activity, which is primarily the making of profit in terms of money, and only indirectly the securing of the goods for which money can be exchanged. Thus a wedge is driven between the "natural" end of economic action, the satisfaction of needs, and the means to that satisfaction.' *Early Essays*, p. 8. Sombart, in applying Simmel's theory to the period of the end of the Middle Ages, left himself short of historical evidence; this is reflected in the criticisms of the historians, from which the Sombart thesis never really recovered.
   Weber, PESC, p. 52; GARS, I, p. 34, note 1: 'The concept of the spirit of capitalism is here used in this specific sense [Franklin not Fugger], it is the spirit of capitalism.' Weber footnotes this sentence as follows: 'This is the basis of our difference from Sombart in stating the problem.' 'For Sombart's view see op. cit. [*mK*] pp. 357, 380, etc. His reasoning here connects with the brilliant analysis given in Simmel's *Philosophie des Geldes* (final chapter).'
31   This is difficult to reference because it takes us to the heart of Simmel's analysis. But: 'The projection of mere relations into particular objects is one of the great accomplishments of the mind; when the mind is embodied in objects, these become a vehicle for the mind and endow it with a livelier and more comprehensive activity. The ability to construct such symbolic objects attains its greatest triumph in money' (Simmel, G., *Philosophy of Money*, 1978, p. 129). 'All the implications of money for other parts of the cultural process result from its essential function of providing the most concise possible expression and the most intense representation of the economic value of thing.' . . . 'This process might be called the growing spiritualization ('Vergeistigung') of money, since it is the

essence of mental activity to bring unity out of diversity' (*Philosophy of Money*, p. 198; 1900 German edition, p. 175).

32 'Über einige Kategorien der verstehenden Soziologie', *Logos. Internationale Zeitschrift für Philosophie der Kultur*, 4, 3, 1913, pp. 253–94; reprinted in GAWL, p. 427; translated as 'Some Categories of Interpretive Sociology', Graber, E.E. (transl.), *The Sociological Quarterly*, 22, 1981, pp. 151–80. In footnote 1, Weber references Simmel's *Probleme der Geschichtsphilosophie*. At the end of the footnote, he indicates he wishes to separate subjectively meant meaning more sharply from the objectively valid. This same point is repeated in the 're-write' of 'Soziologische Grundbegriffe' of 1921 (GAWL, p. 541), but this time Simmel's *Philosophie des Geldes* is explicitly mentioned, as is his *Soziologie*.

33 This corresponds to the distinction drawn by Martin Hollis, in a different idiom, between plastic man and autonomous man. See Hollis, M., *Models of Man. Philosophical Thoughts on Social Action*, Cambridge: Cambridge University Press, 1977, pp. 1–21.

34 This is quite a remarkable statement for it offers a unification of the human and natural sciences. The natural sciences take as foundational the assertion of causality – the influence of one event on a subsequent event – and that of energy. The English translation does not quite capture the significance of the original statement. 'Der Kompetenzstreit zwischen Kausalität und Teleologie innerhalb unseres Handelns schlichtet sich also so: indem der Erfolg, seinem Inhalte nach, in der Form psychischer Wirksamkeit da ist, bevor er sich in die der objektiven Sichtbarkeit kleidet, wird der Strenge der Kausalverbindung nicht der geringste Abbruch getan; denn für diese kommen die Inhalte nur, wenn sie Energien geworden sind, in Betracht, und insofern sind Ursache und Erfolg durchaus geschieden, während die Identität, die die ideellen Inhalte beider zeigen, wiederum mit der realen Verursachung überhaupt nichts zu tun hat' (Simmel, G., *Philosophy of Money*, 1978, p. 205; Heptagon CD, Berlin, 2001, p. 198).

35 It is possible for advanced paper currencies to operate in complex but premodern societies, such as the Tang dynasty, c. AD 1000.

36 Nipperdey, T., 'Max Weber, Protestantism and the Debate around 1900', in *Weber's Protestant Ethic*, p. 73.

37 Simmel, *Philosophy of Money*, p. 56.

38 It is as well to note that, in the first edition, Simmel qualified what he meant by historical materialism: 'it might be more exact to call this historical sensualism'.

39 Simmel, *Philosophy of Money*, p. 54.

40 Simmel, *Philosophy of Money*, p. 56.

41 Riesebrodt, M., in *The Protestant Ethic Turns 100*, p. 33.

42 Riesebrodt, M., in *The Protestant Ethic Turns 100*, p. 35.

3 The Protestant Ethic and the 'Spirit' of Capitalism

1 There is neither an exact translation equivalence between 'Kultur' and civilization nor between 'Kultur' and culture.

2 Winckelmann, J. (ed.), *Die protestantische Ethik*, Gütersloh, Gütersloher Verlagshaus Mohn, 5th edn, 1979.

3 'Studies' in the plural because, in 1906, Weber wrote a second (and shorter) essay on the Protestant sects and modern capitalism, reflecting his experience of contemporary religion in North America.

4 Green, R.G., *Protestantism and Capitalism. The Weber Thesis and its Critics*, Lexington, MA: D.C. Heath, 1959.

5 *Max Weber and the Spirit of Capitalism – 100 Years On*, special edition of *Max Weber Studies*, 5.2 and 6.1, 2005–6; *Das Faszinosum Max Webers*, Ay, K.-L.

(ed.), Constance: UVK, 2006; Swatos, W.H. Jr and Kaelber, L. (eds), *The Protestant Ethic Turns 100. Essays on the Centenary of the Weber Thesis*, Boulder, CO: Paradigm Publishers, 2005.

6   To be edited by Peter Ghosh.
7   Hedstrom, P., and Swedberg, R. (eds), *Social Mechanisms: An Analytical Approach to Social Theory*, New York: Cambridge University Press, 1998.
8   The translator, Talcott Parsons, makes a half-hearted cross-reference to Weber's 'Wissenschaftslehre' at this point.
9   To gauge this, consider the complexity and scholarship involved in a recent 'generalist' history – see MacCulloch, D., *Reformation. Europe's House Divided. 1490–1700*, London: Penguin, 2003.
10 Weber, M., *Roscher and Knies. The Logical Problem of Historical Economics*, Oakes, G. (ed./transl.), New York: Free Press, 1975.
11 Weber, Marianne, *Max Weber. A Biography*, Zohn, H. (transl.), New Brunswick, NJ: Transaction Books, 1988, p. 310.
12 See Baumgarten, E., *Werk und Person*, Tübingen: J.C.B. Mohr (Paul Siebeck), 1964. See also Baehr, P., *The Protestant Ethic and the 'Spirit' of Capitalism and Other Writings*, Baehr, P., and Wells, G.(eds/transl.), London: Penguin, 2002, p. 12.
13 Baehr, P., and Wells, G. (eds/transl.), *The Protestant Ethic and the 'Spirit' of Capitalism and Other Writings*, London: Penguin, 2002, p. 28.
14 Liebersohn, H., 'Weber's Historical Concept of National Identity', in *Weber's Protestant Ethic. Origins, Evidence, Contexts*, Lehmann, H., and Roth, G. (eds), Cambridge: Cambridge University Press, 1993, p. 125.
15 Ghosh, P., 'Max Weber's Idea of "Puritanism": a Case Study in the Empirical Construction of the Protestant Ethic', *History of European Ideas*, 29, 2003, pp. 183–221.
16 Dowden, E., *Puritan and Anglican. Studies in Literature*, London: Kegan Paul, Trench, Trübner, 1900, p. 235.
17 Dowden, *Puritan and Anglican*, p. 235.
18 Dowden, *Puritan and Anglican*, p. 232.
19 Dowden, *Puritan and Anglican*, p. 248.
20 PESC, p. 129.
21 PESC, p. 119.
22 See Dilthey's analysis of Luther's hymns.
23 Davies, N., 'Gesang' in Davies, N. (ed.), *Europe. A History*, Oxford: Oxford University Press, 1996, p. 486.
24 *The Protestant Ethic and the 'Spirit' of Capitalism and Other Writings*, pp. 35–6.
25 MacCulloch, p. 378.
26 MacKinnon, M.H., 'The Longevity of the Thesis. A Critique of the Critics', in Lehmann and Roth, *Weber's Protestant Ethic*.
27 See Geyerz, K. von, 'Biographical Evidence on Predestination, Covenant, and Special Covenant' in Lehmann and Roth, *Weber's Protestant Ethic*; Kaelber, L., 'Rational Capitalism, Traditionalism and Adventure Capitalism. New Research on the Weber Thesis', in Swatos and Kaelber, *The Protestant Ethic Turns 100*, pp. 157–61.
28 Westminster Confessions: 'Those who truly believe in the Lord Jesus, who honestly love him and try to walk in good conscience before him, may in this life be assured with certainty that they are in a state of grace.' Quoted by MacKinnon in Lehmann and Roth, *Weber's Protestant Ethic*, p. 220.
29 Zaret in Lehmann and Roth, *Weber's Protestant Ethic*, p. 249.
30 An important area of research, see Kaelber, L., in Swatos and Kaelber, *The Protestant Ethic Turns 100*, pp. 154–6.

31 Zaret, D., 'The Use and Abuse of Textual Data' in Lehmann and Roth, *Weber's Protestant Ethic*, p. 247.
32 In the German, Weber does not use the subjunctive tense, which indicates indirect speech.
33 I have changed the Parsons' translation from 'coal' to 'fuel', and 'iron cage' to 'casing as hard as steel'.
34 Nielson, D.A., '*The Protestant Ethic and the 'Spirit' of Capitalism* as Grand Narrative: Max Weber's Philosophy of History', in Swatos and Kaelber, *The Protestant Ethic Turns 100*, p. 75.
35 Weber himself treats the 'isolated economic man' ('Wirtschaftsmenschen') as a Robinson Crusoe figure (p. 176). It is merely an aside in his argument, but indicates that Weber was well aware of the way in which a form of rationalism came to give birth to this construction. This is further underlined by referring in his lectures on national-economy, in which he had grasped the scientific (as opposed to novelistic) fiction of 'economic man'.
36 *Max Weber. Das Werk*, Müller, T. and Pentzel, A. (eds), Berlin: Heptagon Reader, 2002. Many of these are lost by Parsons who may well have been affronted by Weber's tendency to vitalism. Or he may well have interpreted the work from the side of the sober Protestant rather than the sensuous individual. The art of translation is the art of interpretation, going as deep as the fundamental attitudes of the translator himself or herself. See the recent research by Lawrence Scaff on the Parsons translation, 'The Creation of the Sacred Text', MWS 5.2/6.1, 2005–6, p. 205–28.
37 Lepsius, R.M., 'Mina Tobler and Max Weber: Passion Confined', *Max Weber Studies*, 4.1, pp. 9–21. There is a Goethean flourish in Tobler's statement. From his retreat in Dornburg in 1828, Goethe wrote, 'the rational world can be considered as a great, immortal individual which ceaselessly produces that which is necessary and thereby comes to control the accidental'. Quoted by Dilthey, W., *Introduction to the Human Sciences*, Makreel, R.A., and Rodi, F. (eds), Princeton, NJ: Princeton University Press, 1989, p. 103.
38 Lepsius, p.19.

4 'Wissenschaftslehre'

1 J.G. Fichte presented his ideas on 'Wissenschaftslehre' at the University of Jena during the 1790s and reformulated them on his move to the University of Berlin in 1800. The Weber–Fichte link cannot be entered into here, even though there is more to be said on the subject. Fichte is conventionally seen as an arch-proponent of philosophical idealism, a post-Kantian who switched German philosophy in the direction Hegel developed further. In this account, there is nothing Fichtean about Weber. The young philosophy don at Heidelberg, Emil Lask, wrote on Fichte, and we know that Weber was in conversation with Lask around 1900. At the same time, Marianne Weber wrote a dissertation on Fichte and Marx, with both Lask and Max Weber acting in the role of supervisors. There is a sense in which Fichte was talismanic for the Heidelberg circle. In the preface of his book on Fichte, Lask makes clear that he is indifferent to Fichte's own philosophical system but is drawn to the individuality and irrationality problematic, which is revealed by a historical treatment of Fichte's philosophy; see his *Fichtes Idealismus und die Geschichte*, Tübingen: Mohr (Paul Siebeck), 1902, p. vi.
2 Turner, S.P., 'Defining a Discipline: Sociology and its Philosophical Problems, from its Classics to 1945', *Handbook of the Philosophy of Science*, Vol. 15: *Philosophy of Anthropology and Sociology*, Turner, S., and Risjord, M. (eds), Amsterdam: Elsevier; Eliaeson, S., *Max Weber's Methodologies*, Cambridge: Polity Press, 2002.
3 Harrington, A., *Hermeneutic Dialogue and Social Science: A Critique of Gad-*

amer and Habermas, London, Sage, 2001. Friedman, M., *A Parting of the Ways: Carnap, Cassirer, and Heidegger*, Chicago, IL: Open Court Publishing Company, 2000. Turner, S. 'The Continued Relevance of Weber's Philosophy of Science', *Max Weber Studies*, 7.1, forthcoming 2007.

4 See the glossaries in Hodges, H.A., *Wilhelm Dilthey. An Introduction*, London: Kegan Paul, Trench and Trubner, 1944, pp. 157–60; and *Wilhelm Dilthey, Selected Works*, Vol. 1, Makreel R.A., and Rodi, F. (eds), Princeton, NJ: Princeton University Press, 1989, pp. 503–9.

5 See "Max Weber on the Road to Prague", transcribed and translated by Messer, E., *Max Weber Studies*, 3.2., 2003, pp. 223–6.

6 'Introduction' to *W. Dilthey. Selected Writings*, Rickman, H.P. (ed.), Cambridge: Cambridge University Press, 1976, p. 12.

7 Dilthey, W., *Introduction to the Human Sciences*, Makreel R.A., and Rodi, F. (eds), Princeton, NJ: Princeton University Press, 1989, p. 56.

8 Dilthey, *Introduction to the Human Sciences*, pp. 57 and 96.

9 Dilthey, *Introduction to the Human Sciences*, p. 57.

10 Dilthey, *Introduction to the Human Sciences*, p. 58.

11 Weber takes this line of thought furthest in his research on the industrial psychology of workers – see 'Zur Psychophysik der industrielle Arbeit (1908–09)', in Weber, M., *Gesammelte Aufsätze zur Soziologie und Sozialpolitik*, Tübingen: J.C.B. Mohr (Paul Siebeck), 1988, pp. 61–255.

12 It is worth noting the similarity of Simmel's definition of desire to that of Dilthey's definition of will. On Simmel, see above, pp. 42–3.

13 Weber, M., 'Logic of the Cultural Sciences', Weber, M., *The Methodology of the Social Sciences*, Shils, E.A., and Finch, H.A. (eds/transl.), New York: Free Press, 1949, p. 124.

14 Dilthey, *Introduction to the Human Sciences*, p. 78.

15 Dilthey, *Introduction to the Human Sciences*, p. 92. In the sciences of biology and zoology in Germany, there had been a tendency – actually stemming from Goethe – for life to be defined by an essence, a 'vital' life force that was part of nature. This naturalism was carried over only too enthusiastically into the human and cultural subjects, and allowed the contemporaneous formulation of nation and race on biological lines, leading eventually to social Darwinism and eugenics. See Whimster, S., 'Liberal Eugenics and the Vitalist Life Sciences: Incongruities in the German Human Sciences in the 19th Century', *History of the Human Sciences*, 8, 1, 1995, pp. 107–14. It is entirely to Dilthey's credit that he saw what a mistaken approach this was.

16 Dilthey, *Introduction to the Human Sciences*, p. 84.

17 Dilthey, *Introduction to the Human Sciences*, p. 154.

18 Popper, K., *The Open Society and its Enemies*, Princeton, NJ: Princeton University Press, 1950, and *The Poverty of Historicism*, London: Routledge and Kegan Paul, 1957. What lacks from Popper's criticism is a distinctive way forward for the human sciences, other than a reflection of the correct protocol of the natural sciences.

19 Dilthey, *Introduction to the Human Sciences*, p. 158.

20 Dilthey, *Introduction to the Human Sciences*, p. 95.

21 Dilthey, *Introduction to the Human Sciences*, p. 112.

22 Dilthey, *Introduction to the Human Sciences*, p. 109.

23 Dilthey, *Introduction to the Human Sciences*, p. 120.

24 Dilthey, *Introduction to the Human Sciences*, p. 95.

25 Dilthey, *Introduction to the Human Sciences*, p. 95.

26 In a letter to his mother (24 January 1886), Weber relates Frensdorff's uncanny ability to make the student doubt what he at first thought was certain.

27 See Evans, R.J., *In Defence of History*, London: Granta, 1997.

28 *Wilhelm Dilthey. Selected Writings*, Rickman, H.P. (ed./transl.), Cambridge: Cambridge University Press, 1976, p. 247.

29 *Wilhelm Dilthey. Selected Writings*, pp. 248–9.

30 *Wilhelm Dilthey. Selected Writings*, p. 249. Emphases are Dilthey's.

31 *Wilhelm Dilthey. Selected Writings*, p. 256.

32 *Wilhelm Dilthey. Selected Writings*, p. 254.

33 See Graf, W.F., 'Friendship between Experts: Notes on Weber and Troeltsch', in *Max Weber and his Contemporaries*, Mommsen, W.J., and Osterhammel, J. (eds), London: Allen & Unwin, 1987; and Whimster, S. 'R.H. Tawney, Ernst Troeltsch and Max Weber on Puritanism and Capitalism', *Max Weber Studies*, 5.2, 2005, pp. 297–316.

34 *Wilhelm Dilthey. Selected Writings*, pp. 255–7.

35 *Wilhelm Dilthey. Selected Writings*, p. 257.

36 See Weber's footnote in his first reply to Rachfahl, where he quotes the Puritans' dictum: 'We must obey God rather than men' – a sentiment that was lacking in the Lutheran formation of German political culture; *The Protestant Ethic Debate*, Chalcraft, D., and Harrington, A. (eds), Liverpool: Liverpool University Press, p. 83.

37 Modern hermeneutics would insist on a greater separation of explication and the different phases of understanding. See Mueller-Vollmer, K., *The Hermeneutics Reader*, Oxford: Blackwell, pp. 12 and 45.

38 *Wilhelm Dilthey. Selected Writings*, pp. 257–9.

39 Dilthey, *Introduction to the Human Sciences*, p. 50.

40 For the full exposition of the categories of life, see *Wilhelm Dilthey. Selected Writings*, pp. 231–45.

41 Dilthey, *Introduction to the Human Sciences*, p. 51.

42 See the introduction by his editors, Makreel and Rodi, pp. 3–43.

43 Smith, Woodruff, D. *Politics and the Sciences of Culture in Germany, 1840–1920*, Oxford: Oxford University Press, 1991.

44 Marianne Weber, p. 260. See the argument in Hans Henrik Bruun that, even by 1903, Weber was sceptical of the metaphysical implications of Rickert's value selection position – 'Weber on Rickert: From Value Relation to Ideal Type', *Max Weber Studies*, 1.2, 2001, pp. 138–60. Rickert himself acknowledged that Weber's own paths led him away from a Rickertian philosophy of values and retained only a pragmatic use of his 'logic'. For Rickert's (almost tearful) assessment of Weber's relation to his writings, see the Preface to the 3rd and 4th editions of Rickert, H., *The Limits of Concept Formation in the Natural Sciences*, Cambridge: Cambridge University Press, 1986, pp. 8–11.

45 Quoted in Bruun, H.H., *Science, Values and Politics in Max Weber's Methodology*, Copenhagen: Munksgaard, 1972, p.85.

46 Weber, M., *Roscher and Knies. The Logical Problem of Historical Economics*, New York: Free Press, 1975, pp. 55–73.

47 Bruun, H.H., *Science*, p. 89.

48 An example of this might be Michael Thompson's *Theory of Rubbish*, Oxford: Oxford University Press, 1979.

49 Bruun, H.H., *Science*, pp. 91–2.

50 This procedure also carries with it a danger of imposing current public values on to the past, what Skinner terms retrospective interpretation. In large part, historians contemporary to Weber were guilty of this on a massive scale. The search for the state in the medieval period, in German nineteenth-century historiography, predetermined what was studied and, in part, how it was studied. See Whimster, S., 'Patrimonialism: Its meaning for nineteenth century German historians with special reference to Max Weber's adoption and use of the term in his *Herrschaftssoziologie*', Doctoral dissertation, London: University of London, 1976; and Schorn-Schütte, L., *Karl Lamprecht. Kulturgeschichtsschreibung*

zwischen Wissenschaft und Politik, Göttingen: Vandenhoeck & Ruprecht, 1984. In contrast, Dilthey's treatment of the processes of communal and associational life are entirely open-ended, and his analysis is explicitly concerned with avoiding premature conceptual closure (see above).

51 Rickert, H., *The Limits of Concept Formation in the Natural Sciences*, Cambridge: Cambridge University Press, 1986 (translation based on 4th edn, 1921), p. 145. This is a strange title, as its thrust is the possibility and conditions of concept formation in the historical sciences. It perhaps acknowledges a book that Dilthey explicitly addresses: du Bois-Reymond, E., *Über der Grenzen der Naturerkennens*, Leipzig: Veit, 1872; see Dilthey, *Introduction to the Human Sciences*, p. 61, note 10.

52 Rickert, p. 146.

53 Oakes, G., *Weber and Rickert*, Cambridge, MA: MIT Press, p. 69.

54 Rickert, p. 141. I have changed 'goods' to 'things' in the translation.

55 It is no less strange, however, than the work of modern logicians, such as Quine, who face the same problem – how do our descriptions of reality stand in relation to reality? A technical language is used by 'logicians' in the theory of knowledge, and this probably sounds strange to social scientists.

56 Rickert, p. 159, note 29.

57 *Wilhelm Dilthey. Selected Writings*, pp. 258–9.

58 Rossi, P., 'Weber, Dilthey und Husserls Logische Untersuchungen', in Wagner, G., and Zipprian, H., (eds), *Max Webers Wissenschaftslehre*, Frankfurt a.M.: Suhrkamp, 1994, pp. 199–223.

59 Huff, T.E., *Max Weber and the Methodology of the Social Sciences*, New Brunswick, NJ: Transaction Books, 1984, p. 50.

60 Weber, M., 'Marginal Utility Theory and the Fundamental Law of Psychophysics', Scheider, L. (transl.), *Social Science Quarterly*, 56, 1975, pp. 21–36.

61 Quoted in Huff, T.E., *Max Weber and the Methodology of the Social Sciences*, p. 61.

62 Simmel, G., *The Problems of the Philosophy of History*, Oakes, G. (ed./transl.), New York: Free Press, 1997, p. 94.

63 Huff, T.E., *Max Weber and the Methodology of the Social Sciences*, pp. 72–4. See also the recent article by Turner, S. 'The Continued Relevance of Weber's Philosophy of Science', *Max Weber Studies*, 7.1, forthcoming 2007.

64 Die Herausgeber, 'Geleitwort', *Archiv für Sozialwissenschaft und Sozialpolitik*, XIX, 1, 1904, pp. I–VII.

65 There is not, however, a direct correspondence between Kant's triad and Weber's elaboration of value spheres. See Harrington, A., 'Value spheres and validity', *Max Weber Studies*, 1.1, 2000, pp. 84–103.

66 See Rickert, H. 'Vom System der Werte', *Logos*, 4, 1913, pp. 295–327.

67 Habermas, J., *Knowledge and Human Interests*, London: Heinemann, 1972. Habermas' position assumes, 'contra' Dilthey, the opposition of science and hermeneutics. For Habermas, the latter rests on the transcendental possibilities of intersubjectivity. Dilthey, in contrast, wanted to create a science of mental life but one made possible by a human science based on hermeneutics.

68 Bruun, H.H., *Science*, p. 79.

69 It is unclear whether Weber is saying that the world out there is irrational or that mankind is placed in an irrational stance because it has no secure basis for overcoming the divide. The first position is not strictly logical for, if you cannot know the nature of reality, how can one say it is an irrational chaos. Bruun has discussed this issue in relation to Dieter Henrich's Kantian and perceptual attitude to reality and Tenbruck's ontological assumption of the irrationality of the world – *Science*, pp. 140–4.

70 'The Vocation of Science', EW, pp. 283–7.

71 We have seen this with Dilthey, but it is a position firmly asserted by Spinoza, whose influence over German thought at the time was considerable.
72 EW, pp. 359–404.
73 Weber, M., *The Methodology of the Social Sciences*, Shils, E.A., and Finch, H.A. (eds/transl.), New York: Free Press, 1949.
74 Hollis, M., 'Two Models', in *Models of Man, Philosophical Thoughts on Social Action*, Cambridge: Cambridge University Press, 1977.
75 Durkheim said this in *Suicide*, and Weber in 'The Logic of the Cultural Sciences', *The Methodology of the Social Sciences*, pp. 126–8.
76 In a Weberian world of infinite complexity, there would be little sense in pursuing a long counterfactual train of thought, as if a historical event, such as the Russian Revolution, had not happened. Weber is concerned with actual events and their attribution back to causes.
77 See Turner, S.P., and Factor, R.A., *Max Weber. Lawyer as Social Thinker*, London: Routledge, 1994. Wagner, G. and Zipprian, H. 'The Problem of Reference in Max Weber's Theory of Causal Explanation', *Human Studies*, 9, 1986, pp. 21–42.
78 Strauss, A., and Corbin, J., *Basics of Qualitative Research. Grounded Theory Procedures and Techniques*, Newbury Park, CA: Sage, 1990. On sensitizing concepts, see Atkinson, P., and Hammersley, M., *Ethnography. Principles in Practice*, London: Routledge, 1995.

5 The reluctant sociologist

1 Lehmann, H. 'Weber's Use of Scholarly Praise and Scholarly Criticism in *The Protestant Ethic and the 'Spirit' of Capitalism'*, *Max Weber Studies*, 5.2, 2005, pp. 233–4.
2 Quoted in *The Protestant Ethic Debate, Max Weber's Replies to his Critics, 1907–1910*, Chalcraft, D.J., and Harrington, A. (eds), Harrington, A., and Shields, M. (transl.), Liverpool: Liverpool University Press, 2001, p. 27.
3 *The Protestant Ethic and the 'Spirit' of Capitalism and Other Writings*, Baehr, P., and Wells, G. (eds/transl.), London: Penguin, 2002, p. 26.
4 *The Protestant Ethic and the 'Spirit' of Capitalism and Other Writings*, pp. 264–5.
5 Troeltsch, E., *Protestantism and Progress. A Historical Study of the Relation of Protestantism to the Modern World*, Montgomery, W. (transl.), London: William & Norgate, 1912.
6 Kippenberg, H., 'Einleitung' to *Wirtschaft und Gesellschaft. Religiöse Gemeinschaften*, MWG I/22-2, Tübingen: Mohr Siebeck, 2001, pp. 7–8.
7 PE Debate, p. 118.
8 PE Debate, p. 131.
9 Reference to Georg Siebeck.
10 Peter Ghosh argues that capitalism 'was the central element in Weber's conception of modernity' in the period from 1890 to around 1907–8. Thereafter 'capitalism was replaced as a central focus by rationality and rationalization. As a result Weber's central conceptual reading of modernity would now be routed through bureaucracy and not capitalism, though he always supposed that the two were closely linked.' Ghosh, P., 'Not the *Protestant Ethic*? Max Weber at St Louis', *History of European Ideas*, 31, 2005, p. 382.
11 *Briefe*, MWG II/5, 26 December 1907, p. 426.
12 Quoted in 'Introduction' by Roth, G., in Weber, M., *Economy and Society*, New York: Bedminster Press, 1968, p. lxiv.
13 M.I. Finley, letter to F. Hinchelheim, 17 November 1947, quoted in Nafissi, M., *Ancient Athens and Modern Ideology. Value, Theory and Evidence in Historical*

Sciences. Max Weber, Karl Polanyi and Moses Finley, London: Institute of Classical Studies, 2005, p. 213.

14 The English translation rather garbles its title and subheadings. *The Agrarian Sociology of Ancient Civilizations*, Franks, R.I. (transl.), London: New Left Books, 1976.

15 Roth, Introduction, p. xlv.

16 See Deininger, J., MWG I/6, p. 139.

17 Weber opens the section on Mesopotamia with this paragraph: 'Cuneiform scholars have astonishing achievements to their credit, but nevertheless the sources – including the Code of Hammurabi – have not yet been made available for interpretation by non-specialists, The scholar who has not mastered the field and must depend on translated texts cannot therefore reach definite conclusions regarding the Mesopotamia economy. Furthermore it is precisely the texts most important for legal and social history which often elude interpretation (AS, p. 83).

18 Colognesi, L.C., *Max Weber und die Wirtschaft der Antike*, Göttingen: Vandenhoeck und Ruprecht, 2004. Bruhns, H., 'Max Weber's "Basic Concepts" in the Context of his Studies in Economic History', *Max Weber Studies*, Beiheft 1, 2006, pp. 33–69. Deininger, J, 'Einleitung', *Zur Sozial- und Wirtschaftsgeschichte des Altertums. Schriften 1896–1909*, MWG I/6, 2006. Nafissi, M., *Ancient Athens and Modern Ideology. Value Theory and Evidence in Historical Sciences. Max Weber, Karl Polanyi and Moses Finley*, London: Institute of Classical Studies, 2005.

19 Bücher, C., *Industrial Evolution*, (trans S. Morley Wickett), London: George Bell, 1901, pp. 83–149.

20 Nafissi, p. 44.

21 Quoted in Nafissi, pp. 45–7.

22 Quoted in Nafissi, p. 37.

23 See Chapter 8.

24 Sombart, W., 'Der kapitalistische Unternehmer', *Archiv für Sozialwissenschaft und Sozialpolitik*, XXIX, 1909, pp. 689–758.

25 See EW, pp. 35–54.

26 See Nippel, W., 'Einleitung' to *Die Stadt*, MWG, I, 22-5, 1999, pp. 12–13.

27 Mommsen, W.J., 'Max Weber's "Grand Sociology": The Origins and Composition of *Wirtschaft und Gesellschaft. Soziologie*', *History and Theory*, 39, 2000, p. 366.

28 Orihara, H., 'From "A Torso with a Wrong Head" to "Five Disjointed Body-Parts without a Head": A Critique of the Editorial Policy for *Max Weber Gesamtausgabe* I/22', *Max Weber Studies*, 3.2, 2003, pp. 133–68. Baier, H., Lepsius, M.R, Mommsen, W.J., and Schluchter, W., 'Overview of the Text of *Economy and Society* by the Editors of Gesamtausgabe', Harrington, A. (transl.), *Max Weber Studies*, 1.1, 2000, pp. 104–14.

29 *Grundriss der Sozialökonomik*, I. Abteilung, *Wirtschaft und Wirtschaftswissenschaft*, brought to press by Bücher, K., Schumpeter, J., and Freiherrn von Wieser, Fr., Tübingen: J.C.B. Mohr (Paul Siebeck), 1914, p. vii.

30 The outline of materials for the '*Handbuch der politischen Ökonomie*', which comes from the Siebeck archive, is reprinted in *Briefe*, MWG, II/6, pp. 766–74.

31 The editorial report on this text in the Max Weber Gesamtausgabe reckons it to have been written in 1910, MWG, I, 22-1, p. 108.

32 *Briefe*, MWG, II/8, pp. 449–50.

33 Weber, Marianne, *Ehefrau und Mutter in der Rechtsentwicklung. Eine Einführung*, Tübingen: Mohr, 1907. On the reciprocal influences of Max and Marianne Weber, see Lichtblau, K., 'Die Bedeutung von "Ehefrau und Mutter in der Rechtsentwicklung" für das Werk Max Webers', in *Marianne Weber. Beiträge zu*

Werk und Person, Meurer, B. (ed.), Tübingen: Mohr Siebeck, 2004, pp. 208–9; and Editorial Report to 'Hausverband, Sippe und Nachbarschaft', MWG, I/22-1, pp. 282–90. Roth had already noted the link in 1968, see his Introduction, ES, p. lxvii.

34 Weber, Marianne, *Max Weber. A Biography*, Zohn, H. (transl.), New Brunswick, NJ: Transaction Books, 1988, p. 420.

35 Scaff, L.A., *Fleeing the Iron Cage. Culture, Politics, and Modernity in the Thought of Max Weber*, Berkeley, CA: University of California Press, 1989, p. 141.

36 Scaff, p. 142.

37 Scaff, p. 141.

38 See Whimster, S., 'The Secular Ethic and the Culture of Modernism', in *Max Weber, Rationality and Modernity*, Whimster, S., and Lash, S. (eds), London: Allen & Unwin, 1987, pp. 278–80.

39 Quoted in Käsler, D., *Max Weber. An Introduction to his Life and Work*, Cambridge: Polity, 1988, p. 188.

40 Quoted in Käsler, p. 190.

41 Quoted in Scaff, pp. 143–4. Letter to Roberto Michels, 9 November 1912.

42 For a translation of the MWG views, see 'Overview of *Economy and Society* by the Editors', p. 104–14.

43 Orihara, pp. 133–68.

44 'Some Categories of Interpretive Sociology, Graber, E.E. (transl.), *Sociological Quarterly*, 22.2, 1981, p. 179.

6 *The Sociology of Religion*

1 *Briefe*, MWG, II/8, pp. 449–50.

2 Schmidt-Glintzer, MWG I/19, p. 31–4.

3 Quoted by Schmidt-Glintzer, MWG I/19, p. 40.

4 Reproduced in MWG, I/19, pp. 28–9.

5 Quoted by Schmidt-Glintzer, MWG I/19, p. 40.

6 The American translations were scattered over different books. The situation is discussed in Whimster, S., 'Translator's Note on Weber's Introduction to the Economic Ethics of the World Religions, *Max Weber Studies*, 3.1, 2002, pp. 74–98.

7 A theme given recent prominence by Shlomo Eisenstadt.

8 Schluchter, W., *Rationalism, Religion and Domination. A Weberian Perspective*, Berkeley, CA: University of California Press, 1989, pp. 411–61.

9 Discussion of pre-animism, magic and religion in SocRel (pp. 3–10) are to be found in the 'Introduction' (to the Economic Ethics of the World Religions) (EW, pp. 66–9); likewise exemplary prophecy (SocRel, p. 24) in the 'Introduction' (EW, pp. 73–4), theodicy (SocRel, pp. 138–140) in 'Introduction (EW, pp. 62–4), carriers of religion (SocRel, pp. 80–94) in 'Introduction' (EW, pp. 57–8 and 71–2), and virtuosi (SocRel, p. 163) in 'Introduction' (EW, pp. 76–7). Chapters 13 and 14 of the *Sociology of Religion* correspond to the main argument and its divisions of the 'Intermediate Reflections' (EW, pp. 215–44).

10 Kippenberg, H., 'Einleitung' to *Religiöse Gemeinschaften*, MWG, I/22-2, p. 4.

11 *The Social Science Encyclopaedia*, Kuper, A., and Kuper, J. (eds), London: Routledge, 1985, p. 871.

12 *The Social Science Encyclopaedia*, p. 698.

13 Wellhausen, J., *Prolegomena zur Geschichte Israels*, Berlin: Georg Reimer, 1883. See Kippenberg, MWG I/22-2, p. 41.

14 See *Essential Weber*, pp. 35–54.

15 Kippenberg, MWG I/22-2, p. 31.

16 Siebeck, H., *Lehrbuch der Religionsphilosophie*, Freiburg: Mohr Siebeck, 1893.

17 Evans-Pritchard, E.E., *Theories of Primitive Religion*, Oxford: Oxford University Press, 1965, Ch. 2.
18 Macrae, D.G., *Max Weber*, London: Fontana, 1974, pp. 80–1.
19 Marett, R.R., *The Threshold of Religion*, London: Methuen, 1909. See the discussion in Kippenberg, MWG, I/22-2, p. 47.
20 Windelband, W., 'Das Heilige', in *Präludien, Aufsätze und Reden zur Einleitung in die Philosophie*, Tübingen: Mohr Siebeck, 1907.
21 Cat, p. 154.
22 Tracing Husserl in Weber is not an easy task, but Weber had read his *Logische Untersuchungen*. In the context of Hugo Münsterberg's psychological approach to understanding, Weber wrote, 'See also Husserl, *Logical Investigations*, Appendix to Volume II, p. 703. He *contests* the view that inner experience possesses a specific "certainty" and a higher "ontological status".' Weber, M., *Roscher and Knies, The Logical Problems of Historical* Economics, Oakes, G. (transl.), New York: Free Press, 1975, p. 261.
23 Gerth and Mills translated, presumably wittingly in the case of Hans Gerth, 'Heilsgüter' as 'cultural values' – more homage to Rickert than confronting Weber.
24 Yair, G. and Soyer, M., 'The Golem myth in German thought', *Max Weber Studies*, 6.2, 2006, pp. 231–55.
25 Weber's quotes; it was Dilthey's term.
26 See Jenkins, R., 'Disenchantment, Enchantment and Re-Enchantment: Max Weber at the Millennium', *Max Weber Studies*, 1.1, 2000, pp. 11–32.
27 EW, pp. 220–41.
28 EW, pp. 263 and 266.
29 EW, pp. 274 and 277.
30 See the discussion in Zubaida, S., 'Weber and the Islamic City', *Max Weber Studies*, 6.1, 2006, pp. 111–18.
31 See the discussion in EW, pp. 17–18.
32 Quoted in Rickman, H.P., *Wilhelm Dilthey. Selected Writings*, Cambridge: Cambridge University Press, 1976, p. 44.
33 Runciman, W.G., 'Was Max Weber a Selectionist in Spite of Himself?', *Journal of Classical Sociology*, 1.1, 2001, pp. 13–32; 'Not Elective but Selective Affinities', *Journal of Classical Sociology*, 5.2, 2005, pp. 175–87; and 'Puritan American Capitalists and Evolutionary Game Theory', *Max Weber Studies*, 5.2, 2005, pp. 281–96.
34 Runciman, W.G., 'Not Elective but Selective Affinities', pp. 180–3.
35 Lepsius, M.R., 'Eigenart und Potenzial des Weber-Paradigmas' in *Das Weber-Paradigma*, Albert, G., Bienfait, A., Sigmund, S., Wendt, C. (eds), Tübingen: Mohr Siebeck, 2003, pp. 32–41.

7 Going beyond Weber

1 Weiss, J., 'On the Irreversibility of Western Rationalization and Max Weber's Alleged Fatalism', in *Max Weber, Rationality and Modernity*, Whimster, S., and Lash, S. (eds), London: Allen & Unwin, 1987, pp. 154–63.
2 Innis, H.A., *The Fur Trade of Canada*, Toronto: Oxford University Press, 1927; *The Cod Fisheries: the History of an International-economy*, New Haven, CT: Yale University Press, 1940.
3 Bellah, R.N., 'What is Axial about the Axial Age?', *Archives Européennes de Sociologie*, 46, 1, 2005, pp. 69–89.
4 Innis, H.A., *Empire and Communications*, Toronto: Toronto University Press, 2nd rev. edn, 1972, p. 10.
5 Innis, *Empire and Communication*, p. 118.

6 Quoted in Fisher, H.A.L., *A History of Europe*, London: Edward Arnold, 1936, p. 490.

7 Innis, *Empire and Communication*, p. 144.

8 Nicolson, A., *Power and Glory. Jacobean England and the Making of the King James Bible*, London: HarperCollins, 2003, p. 122–3.

9 Nicolson, p. 70.

10 I have sought to explain this in 'Translator's Note on Weber's "Introduction to the Economic Ethics of the World Religions"', *Max Weber Studies*, 3/1, 2002, pp. 74–98.

11 Innis, *Empire and Communications*, pp. 139 and 165.

12 Trevor-Roper, H.R., *Religion, The Reformation and Social Change and other Essays*, London: Macmillan, 1967, pp. 1–45.

13 Jaspers, K., *Vom Ursprung und Ziel der Geschichte*, Frankfurt: Fischer, 1955, p. 14.

14 Jaspers, p. 15.

15 Eisenstadt, S.N., *Comparative Civilizations and Multiple Modernities*, vol. 2, Leiden: Brill, 2003, p. 575.

16 Quoted in Bellah, p. 72.

17 Eisenstadt, p. 535–6.

18 Eisenstadt, p. 643.

19 Tawney, R.H., *Religion and the Rise of Capitalism. A Historical Study*, London: John Murray, 1926. See also Whimster, S., 'R.H. Tawney, Ernst Troeltsch, and Max Weber on Puritanism and Capitalism', *Max Weber Studies*, 5.2, 2005, pp. 297–316.

20 Eisenstadt, p. 536.

21 Eisenstadt, p. 517.

22 Quoted in Eisenstadt, p. 811.

23 Bellah, pp. 170–1.

24 *The Religion of China. Confucianism and Taoism*, Gerth, H.H. (ed./transl.) New York: Free Press, 1951; *The Religion of India. The Sociology of Hinduism and Buddhism*, Gerth, H.H., Martindale, D. (eds/transl.), New York: Free Press, 1958.

25 See FMW, pp. 293–4.

26 'Prefatory Remarks', p. 26 – translation modified.

27 Runciman, W.G., 'Was Max Weber a Selectionist in Spite of Himself?', *Journal of Classical Sociology*, 1.1, 2001, pp. 13–32; 'Not Elective but Selective Affinities', *Journal of Classical Sociology*, 5.2, 2005, pp. 175–87; and 'Puritan American Capitalists and Evolutionary Game Theory', *Max Weber Studies*, 5.2, 2005, pp. 281–96.

28 See the discussion in Scaff, L., 'The Creation of the Sacred Text. Talcott Parsons translates: *The Protestant Ethic and the Spirit of Capitalism*', *Max Weber Studies*, 5.2, p. 220. The quote used is taken from the manuscript version of Parsons' translation of PESC.

29 Schluchter, W., 'Weber's Sociology of Rationalism and Religious Rejections of the World', in *Max Weber, Rationality and Modernity*, Whimster, S., and Lash, S.(eds), London: Allen & Unwin, 1987, p. 112.

8 Power, legitimacy and democracy

1 Sheehan, J.J. *German History. 1770–1886*, Oxford: Oxford University Press, 1989, pp. 385–6.

2 See Roth, G., *Max Webers deutsch-englische Familiengeschichte 1820–1950 mit Briefen und Dokumenten*, Tübingen: Mohr Siebeck, 2001, p. 210.

3 For a fuller exploration of the discourses being articulated in Frankfurt, see

Vick, B., *Defining Germany: The 1848 Frankfurt Parliament and National Identity*, Cambridge, MA, Harvard University Press, 2002.

4 See Barraclough, G., *The Origins of Modern Germany*, Oxford: Blackwell, 1946, p. 415; Namier, L. 1848. *The Revolution of the Intellectuals*, Oxford: Oxford University Press, pp. 24–33.

5 Barraclough, p. 418.

6 Barraclough, p. 424.

7 Baumgarten, H., *Hermann Baumgarten: Der deutsche Liberalismus. Eine Selbstkritik*, Birke, A.M. (ed.), Frankfurt: Ullstein, pp. 14–15.

8 Mommsen, W.J., *Max Weber and German Politics 1890–1920*, Chicago: Chicago University Press, 1984, pp. 148-53.

9 Roth, G., 'Max Weber's Articles on German Agriculture and Industry in the Encyclopedia Americana (1906/7) and their Political Context', *Max Weber Studies*, 6.2., 2006, pp. 185–8; on Germany as a world power, see Roth, *Max Webers deutsch-englische Familiengeschichte*, pp. 25–57.

10 See Wolfgang Mommsen's assessment of this position in his *Max Weber and German Politics*, pp. 64–7

11 Caygill, H., *A Kant Dictionary*, Oxford: Blackwell, 1995, p. 314.

12 See his lecture 'Politics as a Vocation', in EW, p. 269.

13 Graf, F.W., 'Ernst Troeltsch's Evaluation of Max and Alfred Weber: Introduction and Translation of Letter by Ernst Troeltsch to Heinrich Dietzel', *Max Weber Studies*, 4.1, 2001, pp. 101–8.

14 This viewpoint is most strongly presented in Weber's inaugural lecture at Freiburg in 1895: 'The national state and economic policy', *Reading Weber*, Tribe, K. (ed.), London: Routledge, 1989, pp. 188–209.

15 As Wolfgang Mommsen points out he shared something of Baumgarten's pessimism as well as Burckhardt's view of politics. See Mommsen, *Max Weber and German Politics*, pp. 47–8.

16 Poggi, G., *Forms of Power*, Cambridge: Polity, 2001, p. 16.

17 EW, p. 182.

18 Poggi, p. 19.

19 Mann, M., *The Sources of Social Power*, Vol. 1, Cambridge, Cambridge University Press, 1986, pp. 22–30.

20 Poggi, p. 18.

21 Hanke, E., 'Einleitung', *Wirtschaft und Gesellschaft. Die Wirtschaft und die gesellschaftlichen Ordnungen und Mächte. Nachlass*, MWG, I, 22–4, *Herrschaft*, Hanke, E. (ed.) with Kroll, T., Tübingen: J.C.B. Mohr (Paul Siebeck), 2005, p. 51.

22 David Beetham provided a more balanced analysis of power and the role of parliament in Weber's writings. See his *Max Weber and the Theory of Modern Politics*, Cambridge, Polity Press, 1985.

23 Hennis, W., *Max Weber und Thukydides. Nachträge zur Biographie des Werks*, Tübingen: Mohr Siebeck, 2003, p. 163.

24 Hanke, MWG, I/22-4, pp. 90–1.

25 Hanke, MWG, I/ 22-4, pp. 45–6.

26 Hanke, MWG, I/ 22-4, p. 53.

27 See Mommsen, W.J., *The Age of Bureaucracy. Perspectives on the Political Sociology of Max Weber*, Oxford: Blackwell, 1974.

28 On these themes, see Beetham, D., *Democracy under Blair. A Democratic Audit of the United Kingdom*, London: Politico, 2002, also his discussion in *Max Weber and Theory of Modern Politics*, p. 115; Hennessy, P., *Rulers and Servants of the State. The Blair Style of Government, 1977–2004*, London: Office for Public Management, 2004.

29 Palonen, K., *Politics, Rhetoric and Conceptual History*, Jyväskulä: Julkaisuja Pub-

lications, 1994; also *Das 'Webersche Moment'. Zur Kontingenz des Politischen*, Wiesbaden: Westdeutsche Verlag, 1998.

30 Poggi, pp. 15–28.

9 Sociological categories and the types of economic activity

1 Bellah, R.N., 'What is Axial about the Axial Age?' *Archives Européennes de Sociologie*, 46, 1, 2005, pp. 69–89.

2 In the United States, the most accomplished practitioner of a Weberian approach was Reinhard Bendix in a series of substantive studies. For an exemplary instance, see his *Work and Authority in Industry. Ideologies of Management in the Course of Industrialization*, Berkeley, CA: University of California Press, 1974.

3 Rex, J., and Moore, R., *Race, Community and Conflict: A Study of Sparkbrook*, Oxford: Oxford University Press, 1967.

4 Dench, G., Gavron, K., and Young, M., *The New East End. Kinship, Race and Conflict*, London: Profile Books, 2006.

5 See Roth, G., ES, p. xciv.

6 Weber wrote to Hermann Kantorowicz in December 1913. The latter had complained of being unable to understand his 'Some Categories of Interpretative Sociology'. Weber replied how 'miserably he must have formulated' the essay. 'It is an attempt to eliminate all "organicist", Stammlerian superempirical "valid" (= the normatively valid) and to understand the "sociological theory of the state" ("Staatslehre") as a theory of the purely empirical typical human action – in my view the only *way* – and the individual *categories* are questions of practicality ('Zweckmäßigkeitsfragen')' (MWG, II/8, pp. 442–3). Whether Kantorowicz was enlightened by this reply is not known.

7 On archaic kingship, see Bellah.

8 Hanke, E., MWG, I/22-4, p. 21.

9 A 'Verband' and associative behaviour should probably not be taken to belong to the same sort of social relationships. Much of modern organizational life is instrumentally rational, but it is instructive to think of its controlling body as operating according to the rules of a clique or gang bound by norms of face-to-face camaraderie.

10 Sen, A., *Poverty and Famines. An Essay on Entitlement and Deprivation*, Oxford: Clarendon, 1981.

11 Liefmann, R., *Grundsätze der Volkswirtschaftlehre*, Stuttgart: Deutsche Verlags-Anstalt, Vol. 1, 1917, Vol. 2, 1919.

12 Liefmann, Vol. 1, p. 15: 'Max Weber, among others, in his essay "The objectivity of knowledge in social science and social policy" in the *Archiv für Sozialwissenschaft und Sozialpolitik*, Vol. 19, 1904, p. 59ff, puts forward the proposition that the knowledge value ('Erkenntniswert') of economic theory is small.'

13 'Doch nun zum Einzeln. (Seite 15) Ich soll behaupten der Erkenntniswert der Theorie sei "gering". Wo wäre das geschehen? Die Theorie schafft Idealtypen und diese Leistung ist gerade bei mir die unentbehrlichste. Dass Soziologie und Wirtschaftsgeschichte Theorie *nie* ersetzen ist eine meiner Grundüberzeugungen. Mich interessieren (nach Ihnen Seite 17) mehr die "spezielle" Zusammenhänge? *Ja*, wenn man die Frage: *Warum nur* im Okzident rationaler (Rentabilitäts-) Kapitalismus entstanden ist, einen "speziellen" Zusammenhang nennt! Es muss doch auch Leute geben, die dieser Frage nachgehen. Hierfür sind nun einmal höchst paradoxe Zusammenhänge massgebend gewesen. Moderne Wirtschaft setzt sich nur den rationalen d.h. in seinen Funktionen berechenbaren kalkulierbaren Staat, sondern rationale Technik (Wissenschaft) und eine bestimmte Art rationaler Lebensführung voraus. Warum wäre sonst der moderne Kapitalismus nich in China entstanden? Er hatter viele Jahrhtausende Zeit dazu! Getauscht

worden ist dort seit Jahrtausenden, Papiergeld gab es vor 1100 Jahren, Münzen vor 2600 Jahren. Dass ich irgendwo bestritten hätte, dass man Tauschvorgänge *anders* als aus den Erwägungen der *Einzelnen* bestimmen könne, ist mir unbewusst (Seite 37).' *Geheimes Staatsarchiv Preußischer Kulturbesitz*, Rep. 92, Weber, Nr. 30, Bd. 8, Aufnahme 78.

14   Swedberg, R., *Max Weber and the Idea of Economic Sociology*, Princeton, NJ: Princeton University Press, 1998.

15   Compare p. 172 of Schumpeter, J., *Economic Doctrine and Method*, London: George Allen and Unwin, 1954, with pp. 818–19 of Schumpeter, J., *History of Economic Analysis*, Oxford: Oxford University Press, 1954. See Swedberg, pp. 158–62.

16   Talcott Parsons made a crucial translation slip here, rendering 'Brennstoff' as 'coal' rather than 'fossil fuel'.

Index